Polish-Jewish Literature in the Interwar Years

Judaic Traditions in Literature, Music, and Art
Ken Frieden *and* Harold Bloom, *Series Editors*

Other titles in Judaic Traditions in Literature, Music, and Art

Contemporary Jewish American Writers and the Multicultural Dilemma: The Return of the Exiled
Andrew Furman

The Dybbuk and the Yiddish Imagination: A Haunted Reader
Joachim Neugroschel, trans. & ed.

Enlarging America: The Cultural Work of Jewish Literary Scholars, 1930–1990
Susanne Klingenstein

Facing the Fires: Conversations with A. B. Yehoshua
Bernard Horn

Hurban: Responses to Catastrophe in Hebrew Literature
Alan Mintz

The Image of the Shtetl
Dan Miron

Jews in the American Academy, 1900–1940: The Dynamics of Intellectual Assimilation
Susanne Klingenstein

The New Country: Stories from the Yiddish about Life in America
Henry Goodman, trans. & ed.

Nineteen to the Dozen: Monologues and Bits and Bobs of Other Things
Sholem Aleichem; Ted Gorelick, trans.; Ken Frieden, ed.

Old Jewish Folk Music: The Collections and Writings of Moshe Beregovski
Mark Slobin, trans. & ed.

A Room of His Own: In Search of the Feminine in the Novels of Saul Bellow
Gloria Cronin

Songs from Bialik: Selected Poems of Hayim Nahman Bialik
Atar Hadari, trans.

The Stories of David Bergelson: Yiddish Short Fiction from Russia
Golda Werman, trans. & ed.

A Traveler Disguised: The Rise of Modern Yiddish Fiction in the Nineteenth Century
Dan Miron

Vagabond Stars: A World of Yiddish Theater
Nahma Sandrow

Polish-Jewish Literature in the Interwar Years

Eugenia Prokop-Janiec

Translated from the Polish by Abe Shenitzer

Syracuse University Press

First Edition 2003
03 04 05 06 07 08 6 5 4 3 2 1

Financial support for the publication of this work was given by the Komitet Badań Naukowych (Committee for Scholarly Research).

The paper used in this publication meets the minimum requirements of American National Standard for Information Sciences—Permanence of Paper for Printed Library Materials, ANSI Z39.48–1984.∞™

Library of Congress Cataloging-in-Publication Data

Prokop-Janiec, Eugenia.
[Miedzywojenna literatura polsko-zydowska jako zjawisko kulturowe i artystyczne. English]
Polish-Jewish literature in the interwar years / Eugenia Prokop-Janiec ; translated from the Polish by Abe Shenitzer.
p. cm.—(Judaic traditions in literature, music, and art)
Includes bibliographical references and index.
ISBN 0-8156-2984-2 (alk. paper)
1. Polish literature—Jewish authors—History and criticism. 2. Polish literature—20th century—History and criticism. 3. Poland—Intellectual life—1918-1945. I. Title. II. Series.
PG7035.J48P7613 2003
891.8'5098924'09042—dc21 2002044583

Manufactured in the United States of America

For my parents

Eugenia Prokop-Janiec teaches modern Polish literature at the Jagiellonian University in Cracow. She is the editor of the anthology *Polish-Jewish Poetry in the Interwar Years.*

Abe Shenitzer is professor emeritus in the department of mathematics and statistics of York University, Toronto, Canada.

Contents

Illustrations

Acknowledgments

This book was written between 1983 and 1989 at the Institute for Polish Philology of the Jagiellonian University as a doctoral dissertation under the supervision of Prof. dr. hab. Henryk Markiewicz. The author takes this occasion to express her deep gratitude to her teacher during her years of apprenticeship, a teacher and a benevolent and faithful companion of his students on their chosen roads. I also want to offer my sincere thanks to the reviewers of my dissertation: Prof. dr. hab. Irena Maciejewska, Prof. dr. hab. Jan Błoński, and Prof. Chone Shmeruk of the Hebrew University in Jerusalem, whose works on the trilingual culture of Polish Jews in the interwar period were for me an important source of intellectual stimulation. Last but not least, I wish to thank the following friends in Israel, the United States, and Canada for help with collecting materials and for useful advice: Alicja Hertz, Magdalena Opalska, Ruth Shenfeld, Nathan Gross, Richard Loew, and Mike Steinlauf. My nearest know best that without their presence in my life this book could not have been written.

Eugenia Prokop-Janiec

Translator's Note

Names are spelled as in the Polish original, except that writers are referred to by their published names, with their actual names, where different, enclosed in brackets—or in parentheses if noted by author—at first instance, and again enclosed in brackets in the selected bibliography. I also would like to take this opportunity to acknowledge the editorial assistance of the author, the late Sarah Shenitzer, Jeffrey H. Lockridge, and Hardy Grant.

Introduction

In the only serious and substantial attempt made so far to investigate the role of Jews in Polish culture, Aleksander Hertz mentions interwar poets (that is poets in the period between the two World Wars) who "wrote in Polish but identified with the Jews."[1] He says that they "used Jewish themes but constituted a distinct group of whom the general Polish public knew little."[2] This reference, other references in the works of Michał Borwicz[3] and Artur Sandauer,[4] and the essays of Władysław Panas[5] are, so far as I know, the only postwar traces in Polish memory that bear on the interwar literary activity of the then expanding Polish-Jewish cultural borderland. I mention works published in Poland; in Israel this memory continues to live.[6] But no serious critical synthetic analyses of this phenomenon have appeared, even in Israel.

Matters were different during the interwar period. Then, this literary activity seemed important and interesting enough for Kazimierz Czachowski and Ignacy Fik, authors of the first pre-1939 synthesis of the literature of Reborn Poland, to pay it considerable attention.[7] Chaim Löw, author of the fair-sized study *Smok w słowiczym gnieździe: Żydzi w poezji Odrodzonej Polski* (Dragon in a nightingale's nest: Jews in the poetry of Reborn Poland)[8] discussed Polish-Jewish poets in a separate chapter "Poeci polsko-żydowscy" (Polish-Jewish poets). It is this now almost forgotten area of literature that I propose to investigate.

Like all phenomena belonging to a cultural borderland, Polish-Jewish literature does not lend itself readily to a precise, orderly overview. Those who attempt such an overview face the additional difficulty that the phenomenon to be analyzed existed for just two decades and was suddenly destroyed when full of the promise of life. Listening to the voice of Polish-Jewish literature silenced in midword, one may find it difficult to hear the barely audible tones that would have resounded later and would have shed new and crucial light on its character. Without these tones, descriptions and interpretations must be poorer than they should be.

It is true that history influences the changes, turns, and reorientations that occur in literature. But there are hardly any situations in Polish literature in which this influence has been equally disastrous, situations that resemble the one [I] propose to deal with: each day brings closer the extinction of this group of writers and of the readers for whom they wrote.

The literary material involved is complicated and our perspective on it is unavoidably distorted. These obstacles hinder clear descriptions, precise definitions, and neat interpretations. But the task of describing, defining, and interpreting must be undertaken.

The most urgent and difficult part of the task is to determine the area to be referred to as "Polish-Jewish literature." I think that the best approach is the historical reconstruction of the literary sensibility of the period. I rely on materials from the most important institution of the Polish-Jewish borderland, namely, the Jewish press in Polish, already inventoried and described in a preliminary manner.[9] My basic sources are the dailies *Chwila* (Moment; Lvov 1919–39), *Nowy Dziennik* (New daily; Cracow 1918–39), *Nasz Przegląd (Our review; Warsaw 1923–39),* Nowy Głos (New voice; Warsaw 1937–38); the weeklies *Opinia* (Opinion; Warsaw 1933–35), *Nasza Opinia* (Our opinion; Lvov 1935–39), *Lektura* (Reading matter; Warsaw 1934), *Ster* (Rudder; Warsaw 1937–38); and the monthlies *Nowe Życie* (New life; Warsaw 1924), and *Miesięcznik Żydowski* (Jewish monthly; Warsaw 1930–35). I intend neither to define Polish-Jewish literature nor to draw its precise boundaries. Instead, I will try to reconstruct how the concept of Polish-Jewish literature functioned in the interwar period and what were its content and scope. After locating and describing the historical content of the concept, I will use it as a tool for the ordering of phenomena. Viewed as a literary phenomenon, Polish-Jewish literature is unique in the sense that no such form of artistic activity existed in Poland either before or after the interwar period. My proposed research approach fully respects this uniqueness.

There is another, and weighty, reason to respect the self-awareness of this epoch. We are moving in regions whose boundaries cannot be determined by purely literary [or] purely artistic criteria. We must also be guided by factors that can be described in a very general sense as sociological. Above all, we must take into consideration the complex of phenomena bound up with the emergence of the modern Jewish national consciousness, and especially questions of national and cultural identification of the relevant writers. It is obvious that these are extremely complicated and delicate issues. The only approach that is intellectually and morally proper is one that respects the self-identification of the writers. But this approach is not free from complications. Obviously, it would be simplest to base one's work on autobiographical documents, as Clara Pomeranz-Carmely does in *Das Identitätsproblem jüdischer Autoren im deutschen Sprachraum: Von der*

Jahrhundertwende bis zu Hitler (The identity problem of Jewish authors in the German language area: From the turn of the century to the time of Hitler; 1981). In our case, however, biographical documents are very few and incomplete. In some cases we know nothing whatever about the authors apart from their works. But reliance on works alone is not entirely unobjectionable. Madeline Levine, who tried to distinguish "two very different literatures just after the war and later, namely, Polish-Polish and Polish-Jewish literature,"[10] has this to say in her essay "Polish Literature and the Holocaust":

> I regard as Jewish writers those who so identify themselves. They usually devote themselves to Jewish topics, and especially to the topic of the Holocaust. The question of this definition is a delicate one, for it is improper to use racial categories to "unmask" Polish writers of Jewish descent. But the consequence of classifying as Jewish only those authors who want to be regarded as such is to arrive unavoidably at the false conclusion that all Jewish writers are primarily interested in Jewish themes.[11]

I think that by designating as my most essential research source the Polish-Jewish press, a press of a decidedly national-Jewish orientation that addressed itself primarily to Jewish readers, I avoid quite a few of the difficulties identified by Levine.

I [also] think that the need to consider sociological factors determines the general research perspective: Polish-Jewish literature must be viewed as a sociological as well as a literary phenomenon. This point is crucial. If we view Polish-Jewish literature from an exclusively artistic perspective and ignore the sociocultural conditions that gave rise to it, then it loses its expressiveness and importance and is reduced to a literary curiosity dug up "in the rubbish heap of literary print"[12] by a researcher fascinated by its strangeness.

While the sociohistorical perspective alone is obviously insufficient, it is necessary and irreplaceable in the initial phase of research. This is so because it makes possible the delineation of the boundaries of the area to be described and subjected to literary analysis. And it is only the combination of the sociohistorical and artistic perspectives that can bring us closer to grasping the phenomenon of Polish-Jewish literature.

Abbreviations

The following abbreviations are used for poetry or prose collections cited in chapters 4 through 6 and in the notes to chapter 5.

AiJ H. Adler [pen name Neszer], *Ariela i Jubal* (Ariela and Jubal), Warsaw, 1931
Czd R. Feldszuh [pen name Ben Szem], *Czerwone dusze* (Red souls), Warsaw, 1932
Ep S. Pomer, *Elegie podolskie* (Podolian elegies), Warsaw, 1931
Fl A. Madler, *Falista linia* (Wavy line), Warsaw, 1932
Hin K. Dresdner, *Heine i nieznajoma* (Heine and the stranger), Lvov, 1928
I M. Schlanger, *Idę . . .* (I walk . . .), Cracow, 1936
Ktś R. Brandstaetter, *Królestwo trzeciej świątyni* (Kingdom of the third temple), Warsaw, 1934
Mch A. Eker, *Melodia chwili* (Melody of the moment), Lvov, 1937
Ncs A. Eker, *Na cienkiej strunie* (On a thin string), Lvov, 1937
Np R. Feldszuh [pen name Ben Szem], *Noce palestyńskie* (Palestinian nights), Warsaw, 1928
Odz A. Eker, *Ojców dzieje* (History of the fathers), Warsaw, 1931
Otco H. A. Fenster, *O tym, co opuszczam* (About the things I leave), Warsaw, 1932
P J. Appenszlak, *Piętra* (Stories), Warsaw, 1933
Pch B. Mayer [pen name Arieh], *Pieśni chaluca* (Songs of a *halutz*), Stanisławów, 1934
Pdd M. Szymel, *Powrót do domu* (The return home), Warsaw, 1931
Ph J. Lewittes, *Posthumus (Posthumous),* Warsaw, 1930
Sp M. Szymel, *Skrzypce przedmieścia* (Violin of the suburbs), Warsaw, 1932
T B. Zimmermann, *Tirsa,* Warsaw, 1930
Wcł K. Rosenfeld, *W ciszy łez* (In the silence of tears), Cracow, [ca. 1920]
Wl M. Szymel, *Wieczór liryczny* (Lyrical evening), Warsaw, 1935

PART ONE

The Literature of the Cultural Borderland

1

The Jewish Aspect

Polish-Jewish Literature: The Term and the Concept

The terms "Polish-Jewish literature" and "Polish-Jewish writers" appeared for the first time in the weekly *Izraelita* (The Israelite) in 1901. In an article titled "Nasz dorobek literacki" (Our literary assets), Adolf Jakub Cohn proposed "organizing a special society for Polish-Jewish literature; extending some form of recognition to Polish-Jewish writers."[1] This was a repeat of Cohn's appeal of 1862 to create "a society for the cultivation of Polish-Israelite literature."[2] In both cases the proposer had in mind the creation of a "special [literary] division, to be cultivated primarily by Jews, that would focus on the life of the Jews, on their learning and religion," a "literature about Jews to be cared for by Jews."[3]

The response to these appeals was poor. In 1901—that is, close to forty years after his first appeal—Cohn deplored the "unparalleled poverty" of Jewish literature in Polish. In concluding his pessimistic evaluation, Cohn urged a broad discussion of the issue of a society for Polish-Jewish literature. But this appeal also fell on deaf ears.

It is important to note the shift from "Israelite" to "Jew" and "Jewish" in Cohn's appeals. In the nineteenth century, assimilating Jews and Polish proponents of Jewish assimilation tended to use the positively regarded term "Israelite" to replace the term "Jew," with its pejorative emotional coloration.[4] By the beginning of the twentieth century, the connotations of the two terms had changed; from the 1880s "Israelite" was used less frequently and "Jew" was "rehabilitated" and used as a neutral or positive term.[5]

We do not know exactly how the terms introduced by Cohn were received, but it is a safe guess that their reception was tepid, one indication being the apparent rebirth of the term "Polish-Jewish literature" in the interwar period. It now appeared as one of a group of related terms such as "Polish-Jewish poetry and prose," "Polish-Jewish (or Jewish-Polish) poets and writers," "Polish-Jewish press," and "Polish-Jewish theater." There is no doubt that these terms were inspired to a significant extent by German terminological influences between the wars and before.[6] In the early 1920s, the term "Polish-Jewish writer" referred to all writers who wrote in Polish and were of Jewish origin and not—as Cohn wanted it—to those who wrote "about specifically Jewish matters."[7] In 1924, M. B. (probably Maksymilian Bienenstock) complained in the monthly *Nowe Życie* (New life), edited by Majer Bałaban [Meyer Balaban]: "We have very few Polish-Jewish poets, and the ones we have are usually in deadly fear of Jewish themes lest they—God forbid—betray or recall their Jewish origins."[8] In the early 1930s, the term "Polish-Jewish writer" became more popular and its sense, while definitely different from Cohn's, bore some resemblance to it. As Roman Brandstaetter wrote,

> at this moment, when the fast plow of the *halutz** cuts the ridge of Palestinian soil and the wind again rustles in the lush vineyards, here, among us, on the silver Vistula, a kind of Polish-Jewish writer is slowly evolving who is unassimilated nationally and culturally, who sings in the Polish tongue his Hebrew yearning for the land of his fathers and completely expresses in his works . . . the specific Jewish soul. . . . We bow in humble homage before the great poetic achievements of the Polish writers . . . but form today a distinct group of poets reared in the shadow of high Jewish culture; we are clearly aware that we are, in the full sense of the word, the first national Jewish writers who create in Polish.[9]

Maurycy Szymel spoke of "a number of Polish-Jewish writers who showed a deep interest in Jewry in their literary activity."[10] Clearly, both authors called a writer who wrote in Polish a "Polish-Jewish writer" only if he openly manifested his Jewish identity and his connection with Jewish culture and favored the ideals of national revival and Zionism. This position, the position of a Jewish writer who wrote in Polish, was opposed to the position of a writer of Jewish origin who identified with Polish culture.

The new meaning of the concept of a Polish-Jewish writer was clearly linked with the idea of Jewish art and culture in Polish that began to emerge in the late 1920s. The birth of this idea was preceded by analyses, in the early 1920s, of Jewish "songs of exile" and of Jewish "foreign song,"[11] that is, of literary works produced by assimilated Jews. The first of the stormy discussions of Polish-Jewish art took place in 1929 and was related to the activities of Andrzej [Arn-

*In Hebrew, a Jewish pioneer in Palestine, or a Jewish pioneer getting ready to go to Palestine. [Trans.]

stein] Marek. Between 1925 and 1929, Marek staged Yiddish dramas in Polish and referred to these productions as "Polish-Jewish theater." He intended these plays—An-ski's *Dybbuk,* Asz's *Bóg Zemsty* (God of Revenge), Lejwik's *Golem,* Gordin's *Mirele Efros* and *Bóg, człowiek i diabeł* (God, man, and the devil)—for Poles as well as for Polish-speaking Jews; in fact, he may have intended them primarily for the latter.[12]

The terms "Polish-Jewish poetry" and "Polish-Jewish prose," which appeared in the early 1930s, were clearly tied to the notion of Jewish art in Polish. In a review of Maurycy Szymel's first small volume of poems, we read of

> splendid, purest Polish-Jewish poetry. . . . creations that are Jewish not only because of the spirit that enriches them. The authors sing their Jewishness with pride. They are poets who regard the poor, simple, believing Jew as a brother. They do not desert the ghetto, in which the Jewish masses are locked up, to serve foreign cultures. They do not want to stay in the ghetto. They want to begin a new, regenerated life together with their people. We hear this in the sonorous, refined Polish language. This poetry enriches the culture of two nations, it intercedes for two societies, it serves the Polish-Jewish cause.[13]

Thus Polish-Jewish poetry was Jewish poetry in Polish, and it included Polish poems with Jewish themes whose authors identified themselves with Jewry and were connected with Jewish culture. Polish-Jewish works were distinguished by their themes and the national and cultural identification of their authors.

In summary, between the wars the term "Polish-Jewish literature"—Jewish literature in Polish—denoted works that satisfied two criteria: (1) they were written in Polish and dealt with Jewish themes (thematic criterion); and (2) the authors defined themselves as Jews and manifested their connection with Jewish culture (biographical and cultural criterion).

In the period between the wars, Polish-Jewish literature was viewed as a new form of Jewish cultural activity typical for that time. Before this period writers did not declare their Jewish identity, seldom dealt with topics taken from Jewish life, and had a negative or indifferent attitude toward Jewish culture. The only recognized forerunners of Polish-Jewish writers were Alfred Nossig, Zygmunt Bromberg-Bytkowski, and Jakub Appenszlak (who published before 1918). These were "the only national Jews" at a time when the "*meches* epidemic" [*meches* is a Jewish convert to Christianity—Trans.] raged in Polish literature.[14]

It can be argued that the concept and term "Polish-Jewish literature" were shaped not only by German terminological models but also by such popular Polish literary terms as "Polish-Latin literature," "Jewish romance," and "Jewish novel and short story." The use of these terms must be clarified.

The term "Polish-Latin literature" was applied to works written in Latin by Poles or by foreigners connected with Poland and Polish culture. This concept could be the basis for inclusion in the national literature of works in a nonnational tongue.[15] The terms "Jewish romance," "Jewish novel," and "Jewish short story" were applied in the nineteenth century to all Polish works dealing with Jewish themes. "Jewish romance" was used as a generic name by Julian Ursyn Niemcewicz, who made it part of the title of his novel *Lejbe i Sióra czyli Listy dwóch kochanków* (Lejbe and Sióra or Letters of two lovers; 1821). (His likely predecessor was Anna Mostowska, author of *Lewita z Efraim* [The Levite from Efraim], subtitled *Powieść izraelska* [An Israelite novel; 1809].) The terms "Jewish novel" and "Jewish short story" appeared in literary criticism not later than the last decade of the nineteenth century, became popular at the beginning of the twentieth century, and were used in the interwar period in historical-literary works.[16] In her dissertation *Powieści i nowele żydowskie Elizy Orzeszkowej* (Jewish novels and short stories of Eliza Orzeszkowa; 1937) Irena Butkiewiczówna said of the terms in the title: "These novels are called Jewish novels because of the problems they deal with and the milieu they discuss."[17]

The categories of "Jewish" novel and short story derived from the thematic criterion, [which] played an essential role in shaping the concept of Polish-Jewish literature. This is so because their topics isolated Polish-Jewish works from the totality of works in Polish. As noted earlier, the choice of topic depended on an author's relation to his Jewishness and to Jewish culture. Hence the importance of an author's cultural orientation and worldview. Attempts to restrict the thematic criterion were rare. Some of these attempts were due to Brandstaetter, who claimed that he "did not make a writer's Jewishness dependent on the Jewish topics he worked out."[18] Basically, a writer's biography was important to the extent it was reflected in his works. The prime manifestation of the Jewishness of authors and their works was their "choice of topics, [their] favoring of Jewish topics."[19]

But the tendency to diminish the thematic criterion in favor of the biographical must under no circumstances be taken lightly. Indeed, between the wars, the concept of Polish-Jewish literature had a narrow range, marked by the importance of the union of the thematic criterion and the criterion of national and cultural self-identification.

The year 1933 was an important turning point in the history of the concept of Polish-Jewish literature, which became the subject of a polemic waged in the Polish-Jewish press, primarily the Warsaw weekly *Opinia,* the Cracow daily *Nowy*

Dziennik, and the Tarnów weekly *Tygodnik Żydowski.* This polemic, which [I] will discuss later, established the concept of Polish-Jewish literature and gave currency to the distinction between Polish-Jewish writers, that is, writers who wrote in Polish but identified themselves with Jewry, and Polish writers of Jewish extraction who identified themselves with matters Polish. After 1933, the label "Polish-Jewish" for poetry, prose, and literature, and for poets and writers, entered the language of literary criticism in the Polish-Jewish press, and phrases such as "Jewish poetry sung in Polish"[20] and "Jewish writers who pray in the holy Polish tongue"[21] became extremely popular. Such terms could be found not only in *Opinia,* the weekly of Polish-Jewish poets, and in its continuation, *Nasza Opinia,* but also in *Chwila, Nowy Dziennik, Nasz Przegląd, Nowy Głos, Ster,* and *Miesięcznik Żydowski.*

Polish-Jewish Literary Circles in the Interwar Period

New concepts arose to reflect new cultural phenomena: the concept of Jewish writing in Polish, which came up in the interwar period, was an attempt to diagnose the literary status quo. In the article "Żydzi w literaturze polskiej" (Jews in Polish literature), written in 1933, Stefan Pomer described the issue as follows:

> Here live and create multitudes of writers . . . who, while making their contributions to the treasury of Polish culture, while enriching and developing it, remain conscious Jews shaping Jewish themes in their works and raising ideas and problems that pervade Jewry. This seemingly imperceptible and abnormal phenomenon is actually robust and normal, and springs not only from numerous social and political sources, but, above all, from the very structure and spirit of the Jewish nation.[22]

The combination of Jewish national consciousness and literary creativity in Polish described by Pomer seems indeed strikingly original when considered against the background of the previous Jewish literary output in Polish. Indeed, from the time when they entered Polish literature in significant numbers, that is, from the middle of the nineteenth century, Jewish writers quickly abandoned Jewish themes;[23] this is true even of writers such as Julian Klaczko, Henryk Merzbach, and Aleksander Kraushar who made their debuts with "Poezje syońskie" (Poems of Zion).

The project (mentioned earlier) of creating a "society for the propagation of Polish-Israelite literature" failed to materialize. This project was sketched in the early 1860s by Adolf Jakub Cohn, a journalist writing for *Izraelita,* in the introduction to *Zbawca* (The savior; 1862), his translation of the German novel. Citing German models, Cohn appealed to Jewish writers to "create images of the family and social life of our people, its many customs, superstitions, and biases." Thus Jewish writers were asked to present Jewish life and traditions, subject to the provision that this was to be done "with full truth, with complete honesty."[24] The aim of such works was to bring the Jewish world closer to the Poles and to promote in this way Polish-Jewish understanding.

A dozen or so years later, in 1878, Zygmunt Librowicz continued in a sense Cohn's idea, urging Jewish writers to use the novel as the medium for a faithful and honest depiction of the Jewish world, a world hitherto presented in Polish literature in a tendentious and stereotyped manner. He too noted that "Jewish writers in Germany . . . created a novelistic section of Jewish literature devoted exclusively to the relations of Jewish life and to its characterization"[25] and deplored the fact that "In our country, apart from a few little tales, no Jew has so far traced a large-scale image of Jewish life."[26]

Preceded by translations and adaptations from the German (for example, *Jom Kipur czyli Dzień Odpustny: Romans przełożony z niemieckiego przez H. L.* [Yom Kippur or Indulgence Day: A novel translated from the German by H. L.], 1840 (the translator was probably Henryk Liebkind); Jakub Tugenhold's *Mirmo czyli Tułacz pokutujący* [Mirmo or The expiating exile], 1851, an adaptation, by [Liebkind's] brother, of the German novel *Der Denunziant* [The informer]; and [Cohn's] translation, *Zbawca,* 1862, mentioned earlier), and initially few in number, such images of Jewish life began to appear. Their authors were Jakub Tugenhold, Józef Goldszmit, Malwina Meyerson [Meyersonowa], Michał Wołowski, Wilhelm Feldman, Henryk Nussbaum, Aniela Korngut (pen name A. Kallas), Czesława Endelman-Rosenblatt [Endelmanowa-Rosenblattowa] (pen name Czesław Halicz), Michał Mutermilch, Andrzej Marek, Leon Wiesenberg, and Marceli Sachs. While rare in the 1850s, 1860s, and 1870s, such works began to turn up with greater frequency at the turn of the century. They appeared not only in book form but also—indeed, primarily—as numerous press publications by writers, now mostly forgotten, who wrote primarily for Jewish newspapers in Polish, such as *Izraelita* and *Ojczyzna* (Fatherland), because they were proponents of Enlightenment ideals and favored assimilation and Polonization. Their works might have been, as urged by Cohn and Librowicz, depictions of Jewish life by competent and inside observers, but in fact their image of that life was tendentious rather than objective. They presented the Jewish world from the perspective of the *maskil* [follower of the Haskalah (Hebrew for "enlightenment"), a progressive and assimilationist cultural movement of the eighteenth and nineteenth centuries among central and eastern European Jews—Trans.]. They criticized backwardness and propagated progress and education. They called for modernization of traditional Jewish culture and for joining the life of Europe. They did point out, however, the social and psychological difficulties encountered by assimilating individuals.

The beginning of the twentieth century was marked by an awakening of Jewish national consciousness. There began to appear a Jewish press in Polish with a completely new ideological orientation. *Rocznik Żydowski* (1901–06), *Moriah* (1903–14, 1917–19), and *Żydowski Almanach* (The Jewish almanac) also published original literary works that paralleled their ideological profile, works that accepted the idea of a national Jewish renaissance and the renaissance of Jewish culture. (Assimilationist publications that resented the new phenomenon were highly critical of the new Jewish literature in Polish and of its Zionist leanings. The poetic experiments published in *Żydowski Almanach* provoked the following response in *Izraelita:* "Let us close the yearly book of Zionist wisdom, let us pass over in silence the pseudo-poetry scattered throughout this volume that outrages the demands of style, rhythm, and rhyme.")[27]

Zionism, and especially cultural Zionism, provided ideological support for this new tendency. Martin Buber, the creator of the concept of cultural Zionism, regarded Zionism not as a political movement but as "an approach to living, to bringing up a new generation . . . an aspiration to inner liberation and perfection, a cultural and moral renewal of national strengths."[28] These ideas were readily accepted by the Jewish intelligentsia, which became ever more convinced that "not everything one observes in Europe is really spiritual Europe. . . , that one must aspire to a synthesis of Europe and ancient Judaism."[29] Zionism had a cultural aspect in yet another, more general, sense: the heir as well as opponent of assimilation, it is sometimes interpreted as one of the roads to modernization of traditional Jewish culture, as a manifestation of its secularization and Europeanization.[30]

Already at the beginning of the century, the "return to Jewishness" by members of the intelligentsia, a process inspired by Zionism, became a literary topic in works such as the play *Salomea Blumstein* (1902) by Jakub Lewkowicz, which presented the conflict between the nationally unaware and the nationally aware as a collision between totally assimilated parents, who try at all costs to erase all traces of their Jewish origin, and their children, who are new, proud Jews.

The interwar period witnessed the rapid growth of Jewish newspapers in Polish that espoused the new orientation. The well-known Zionist activist Leon Reich wrote that these papers "found prepared ground in the work of the last two decades."[31] This flourishing of national Jewish newspapers, which was one of the most characteristic phenomena of Jewish culture in the interwar period, was an expression of essential transformations: from the end of the nineteenth century, the assimilationist ideology began to irreversibly lose its influence and the modern Jewish national consciousness began to take shape.[32] This was a process of European scope: from the turn of the century, Jewish circles underwent an increasingly radical ideological diversification that was reflected in the literatures of many [different] language areas.[33] At the beginning of the twentieth-century, Adolf Stand explained the reasons for this phenomenon as follows: "We are at the sources of Zionism. . . . It comes into being when Jewish youth in the dispersion sees no way out of the labyrinth called the Jewish question. For these youth, a return to the ghetto was a cultural impossibility. To rush for the open gates of European culture meant to perish—and such a step was anyway blocked by Aryan society."[34]

The idea of a national renaissance was due to people who, to quote Stand, were "too Europeanized to be satisfied with the ghetto and too Jewish to ape Europe."[35]

Speaking of the Jewish press in Polish in the period between the wars, Chone Shmeruk said that "when it comes to ideology, it invariably supported Zionism and, with the government in mind, stated the Jewish position in all spheres pertaining to Jewish life in Poland in a firm and uncompromising manner."[36] I think, however, that the profile of the press must not be interpreted too narrowly by restricting it to the ideological plane. Indeed, I am certain that what is needed here is a broader sociocultural perspective; a pro-Zionist position was often a declaration of national identity rather than a purely political option. The role of national demonstrations by Jewish circles during the interwar period cannot be overestimated. The best proof of this is that during the 1931 census Jews demonstratively stated that their mother tongue was Hebrew.

Students of the Polish-Jewish press stress that it was largely ideologically independent. True, Artur Sandauer, who at one time had close ties to this press, did not hesitate to call *Chwila, Nowy Dziennik,* and *Nasz Przegląd* "salon-Zionist" [*salonowosyjonistyczne*] publications.[37] But as Michael C. Steinlauf explains, "on the whole, the Jewish press had a far more pronounced ideological bias than the Polish-Jewish press. Thus during the period between the wars even *Haint* (Today) and *Der Moment* (The moment), founded as politically independent, came close to various Zionist factions and occasionally established formal ties with them. In distinction to this, the Zionism of *Nasz Przegląd* was "non-party" and thus independent; it was a tendency rather than a fixed ideology."[38]

It seems that the term "national-Jewish press," popular in the period between the wars, conveys well this state of affairs. The liberal course of this press was at least partly connected with the cultural profile of its prospective readers.

Thus Majer Bałaban characterized the subscribers of *Miesięcznik Żydowski,* one of the most valuable and ambitious Polish-Jewish periodicals, in these words: "[I]t is to inform the Jewish intelligentsia about current problems from a certain historical perspective. . . . The monthly was assigned the apologetic task of properly informing the Polish-Christian intelligentsia about issues of our life of which it usually knew nothing."[39]

There were many such interpretations of the function of the Jewish press. Wilhelm Berkelhammer wrote about *Miesięcznik Żydowski:*

> It pointed out on countless occasions that the numerically insignificant German Jewry creates a splendid national Jewish literature and press in German, whereas in Poland, apart from Polish-Jewish dailies in Warsaw, Cracow, and Lvov, we create nothing, or next to nothing. Clearly, this is not a competition vis-à-vis the printed Hebrew and Jewish word, which is obviously the core and base of Jewish creation in this area as well, but a question of a literature and press for Jewish classes which are limited to just the language of the country, as well as for non-Jewish society with which we must maintain a constant and comprehensive contact.[40]

The weekly *Opinia* described its aims and tasks in a programmatic article as follows: "*Opinia* is a Jewish weekly that will be published in Polish. In this way, we want to put before Polish society, with which we coexist in the same land, a mirror in which it can see an honest picture of the Jewish community; we want to create an organ that will be the voice of honest and genuine Jewish opinion."[41]

The newspapers in question—the dailies *Chwila* (Lvov 1919–39), *Nowy Dziennik* (Cracow 1918–39), *Nasz Przegląd* (Warsaw 1923–39), *Nowy Głos* (Warsaw 1937–38); the weeklies *Opinia* (Warsaw 1933–35), *Nasza Opinia* (Lvov 1935–39), *Ster* (Warsaw 1937–38)—played a key role in the evolution of Polish-Jewish literary circles. This press, primarily the dailies, was the most significant institution of Polish-Jewish culture, and thus the support of Polish-Jewish writing throughout the interwar years, 1918–28 being the period of closest contact between the two. Beginning in 1928, literature began to go beyond the pages of the newspapers; it began to "emancipate itself" and to be accepted as an independent, autonomous phenomenon. The transition from the twenties to the thirties was a clear turning point in the dynamics of Polish-Jewish literary life. Here it is significant to compare the number of small volumes of Polish-Jewish poetry before and after 1928. Before 1928: Jakub Appenszlak, *Mowie polskiej* (For the Polish language; 1915), Karol Rosenfeld, *W ciszy łez: Poezje golusu* (In the silence of tears: Poems of the Diaspora; ca. 1920), Lucjan Krasucki, *Wiersze wybrane* (Selected poems; 1923). After 1928: Karol Dresdner, *Heine i nieznajoma* (Heine and the stranger; 1928), Jakub Lewittes, *Posthumus* (Posthumous; 1930), Maurycy Szymel, *Powrót do domu* (The return home; 1931), *Skrzypce przedmieścia* (Violin of the suburbs; 1932), *Wieczór lyriczny* (Lyrical evening; 1935), Stefan Pomer, *Elegie podolskie* (Podolian elegies; 1931), Hersz Awrohem Fenster, *O tym co opuszczam* (About the things I forsake; 1932), Syda Richter, *Wiry* (Eddies; 1932), Roman Brandstaetter, *Królestwo trzeciej świątyni* (The kingdom of the third temple; 1933), *Jerozolima światła i mroku* (Jerusalem of light and dusk; 1935), Daniel Ihr, *Pożegnanie młodości* (Farewell to youth; 1934), Bronisław Mayer ([pen name] Arieh), *Pieśni chaluca* (Songs of the *halutz*; 1934), Anda Eker [Ekerówna], *Na cienkiej strunie* (On a thin string; 1935), *Melodia chwili* (Melody of the moment; 1937), Maurycy Schlanger, *Idę* (I go; 1936), Minka Silberman, *W cieniu życia* (In the shadow of life; 1936), Irma [Irena] Kanfer, *Dwa akordy* (Two chords; 1936), *W mleczną drogę* (Into the milky way; 1937), Fryderyk Bertisch, *Kwiaty na ugorze* (Flowers on the fallow; 1939).

The differences in the dynamics of literary life in the first and second decades of the interwar period undoubtedly influenced the perception of Polish-Jewish literature. While it is true that in 1924 Wilhelm Berkelhammer hailed Zygmunt Bromberg-Bytkowski's translation of the *Song of Songs* as "the first splendid Jewish book in Polish" and the augury of "the birth of a Polish-Jewish book market,"[42] the first Polish-Jewish novels and small collections of poems met with a rather tepid reception from Jewish cultural opinion. The reviewers of the novels *Jehoszua* (Joshua; 1928) by Józef Hartblaj and *Tirsa* (1930) by Bernard Zimmermann, of the stories *Noce palestyńskie* (Palestinian nights; 1928) by Rubin [Reuwen] Feldszuh [pen name Ben Szem], of the small volume *Heine i nieznajoma* (Heine and the stranger; 1928) by Karol Dresdner, did not yet speak of Jewish literature in Polish. Rather, they emphasized the unusual topics treated in these Polish language works and the distinctive positions of the authors. Some voices even spoke of the incongruity of the Polish language and Zionist ideas.[43] The initial lack of interest was partly due to the newness of the phenomenon and partly—without a shadow of a doubt—to the artistic shortcomings of these works. It must be admitted that Polish-Jewish literature was for the most part artistically mediocre and at times even linguistically awkward. In his 1928 evaluation of Polish-Jewish literature of the 1920s, Samuel Hirszhorn wrote that "we now have a new type of Polish writers—national Jews writing in Polish. Their primary duty is to acquaint the Polish public with the national movement through fiction, just as others are doing through chronicles and the press. In this area we are still waiting for major talents."[44]

When such talents appeared in the early thirties, in the small volumes of

Maurycy Szymel, Stefan Pomer, Roman Brandstaetter, and Daniel Ihr, the new phenomenon began to attract ever greater attention. The birth of the idea of Polish-Jewish literature in the interwar period was the natural consequence of the size and artistic rank of this phenomenon. For it was only in the early thirties that the quantity and artistic quality of Polish-Jewish publications justified the claim that "there are now in Poland Jewish writers . . . who are not ashamed of Zion and the Jordan, of their historical past and customs; writers who love both Zion and the Wawel,* both the Vistula and the Jordan; writers who sing the land they live in and the joys, the pain, and the sorrows of their nation. There are quite a few of them and there will be more and more."[45]

The quickening of the early thirties was clearly related to the generational "changing of the guard." A new generation of writers born between 1900 and 1914 entered Polish-Jewish literature. Their predecessors, born in the 1880s and 1890s, and active primarily in the youth-oriented Zionist press after 1900, were for the most part not true writers but rather journalists who occasionally wrote prose works or poetry. There were no outstanding and original talents among them. Their generation concentrated its literary ambition on a large-scale action to popularize Jewish literature through Polish translations. They were served by the publishing house Safrus (from the Hebrew *sifrut,* literature), established in 1924, which launched the *Biblioteka Pisarzy Żydowskich* (Library of Jewish writers). Samuel Wołkowicz, the editor of the *Biblioteka,* regarded it as a significant editorial enterprise. An announcement issued in 1924 stated:

> The publishing house Safrus, whose aim is to introduce large groups of readers to masterpieces of Jewish and Hebrew literature, is embarking on the publication of *Biblioteka Pisarzy Żydowskich.* The *Biblioteka* will publish translations of the greatest Jewish writers. In addition to the publication of fictional works, Safrus is preparing a number of works in Jewish science and history. The volumes of the *Biblioteka* will appear in 2-to 3-week intervals, will number 200–250 pages of larger format, will be printed on fine paper, and will be decorated by the most eminent Jewish artists.[46]

The *Biblioteka* enterprise was not trouble-free. There were many breaks in publication. But it managed to get together a sizable number of older translators. Its participants included Paulina and Jakub Appenszlak, Mojżesz Kanfer, Samuel Hirszhorn, and Saul Wagman.[47]

*A complex of monumental buildings on the Wawel Hill in Cracow. It includes the royal palace and a cathedral with the graves of Polish kings. Wawel was the seat of the Polish kings for some 500 years. [Trans.]

From the literary standpoint, the first generation of editors and journalists of the interwar Polish-Jewish press—to be referred to as the "Young Poland" generation—differed radically from the younger generation in their aesthetic preferences, their choice of artistic patrons (Stanisław Przybyszewski contributed to the debut of Karol Rosenfeld, and Władysław Orkan [Franciszek Smreczyński] evaluated the first literary attempts of Jakub Lewittes), and their artistic conventions. They had definite links with the new interwar literary trends, and it was they—for example, Maurycy Szymel, Stefan Pomer, Karol Dresdner, Daniel Ihr, and Anda Eker—who shaped the tone of Polish-Jewish literature. They wrote its manifestos, created programs, and organized artistic groups.

The Young Poland generation consisted of people whose strong initial assimilationist tendencies evolved toward a Zionist worldview. This was undoubtedly the reason for their extreme sensitivity to the squaring of assimilationist accounts. Bienenstock, Berkelhammer, Kanfer, Hescheles, and Hirszhorn devoted many penetrating, affecting, and beautiful—yes, beautiful—texts to these ideas.[48] They frequently recalled the atmosphere of their youth, the milieu of their ideological maturation, and the influence of Young Poland trends. They described such specific items as the Tarnów Literary Society, named after Adam Mickiewicz, that enjoyed the cooperation of Tadeusz Pini, Zygmunt Bromberg-Bytkowski, and . . . Karol Radek [Sobelson],[49] and the reading of Wilhelm Feldman's *Krytyka* (Criticism) and Stanisław Przybyszewski's *Życie* (Life) in . . . Buczacz. The following quotation from Mojżesz Kanfer adds a personal touch to these remarks:

> Jewish intellectuals owe very, very much to [Feldman's] *Krytyka.* Each issue was for us a revelation. Only those who lived through those years of the shaping of our intelligentsia in godforsaken corners of Galicia can appreciate the educational value of criticism. It is safe to say that Jewish members of the intelligentsia had greater respect and reverence for Żeromski, Wyspiański, Kasprowicz, Przybyszewski, and Miciński than a typical member of the Polish intelligentsia.[50]

The inspiring role of the national press emphasized earlier is apparent in the evolution of Polish-Jewish literary circles. The reason for this becomes clear if we keep in mind that the key centers of Polish-Jewish literary life were also the key publication centers of Polish-Jewish dailies distinguished by high editorial standards. These dailies were stable and continued to appear until the outbreak of the war. They were published in Lvov, Cracow, and Warsaw.

The Galician centers in Lvov and Cracow had an unquestioned superiority in the 1920s, a superiority that diminished somewhat in the 1930s due to the migration of the best provincial writers to the capital. It is perhaps more appropriate to speak not of literary circles of various cities but of literary rings associated with particular dailies. It is understandable that people from Lvov were in the majority in the literary ring around *Chwila,* people from Cracow in the ring around *Nowy Dziennik,* and people from Warsaw in the ring around *Nasz Przegląd.* On the other hand, it was common practice to publish materials not just in the "mother" newspapers. Thus Cracow writers published in Stanisławów, Stanisławów writers in Lvov, and Lvov writers in Warsaw. The Lvov *Nasza Opinia* published special regional—Lvov, Stanisławów, and Cracow—issues.[51] It was also common practice to publish the same material in different regional papers. Literary and critical items were published from time to time, in fact quite regularly, by [Jewish] Palestinian pioneers.

All this shows that, local differences notwithstanding, Polish-Jewish literary life was marked by a strong integrating tendency, a tendency that favored the creation of a relatively uniform grouping whose institutional foundation was the Polish-Jewish press. But these strong ties between [literary] centers must not obscure the fact that the history and the literary achievements of particular literary rings were clearly individualized.

As already noted, the earliest rings were the Galician ones centered around *Chwila* and *Nowy Dziennik,* respectively. Their history proves that the immediate predecessors of interwar Polish-Jewish literature were the casual, and even amateurish, Zionist materials in Polish from the beginning of the twentieth century. Many authors—such as Anzelm Lutwak, Henryk Salz, Samuel Hirszhorn, and Szymon Wolf—who actively cooperated with the Zionist press before 1918, published their works in *Chwila,* which managed to form the most dynamic literary center and thus determined the character of Polish-Jewish literary life in the 1920s.

During the first five years of the existence of *Chwila,* its "Dział literacko-naukowy" (Literary and scientific section), edited from 1920 by Henryk Hescheles and renamed a year later "Dodatek literacko-naukowy" (Literary and scientific supplement), boasted few outstanding literary contributors. The supplement was for the most part made up of literary and critical essays and of translations. The writers involved were Maksymilian Bienenstock, Henryk Hescheles (who sometimes used the pen name Henryk Trejtwart), Ozjasz Tillemann, Szymon Lustig, Wilhelm Berkelhammer, Mojżesz Kanfer, Ignacy Schipper, Jehudith Malz, Franciszka Bienenstock, Samuel Hirszhorn, Maksymilian Koren [Kornreich], and Dow Sztock (who later became the eminent Israeli historian Dow Sadan). Wilhelm Fallek and Benedykt Rosenzweig joined *Chwila* in 1922, and Jeremiasz Frenkel in 1923.

The first poets to publish in *Chwila* (Lutwak, Salz, and Wolf), and the authors, such as Abraham Ehrlich, Jerzy Reitman, Rudolf Taubenschlag, and Zofia Cukierowa who published in *Chwila* in the early 1920s, were clearly lyrical poets and writers from an older generation. In 1924, Artur Lauterbach's poems brought a certain quickening and the promise of a "changing of the guard." Lauterbach was also to become a productive translator. In the same year, *Chwila* began to publish "Obrazki palestyńskie" (Palestinian images) by Rubin Feldszuh ([pen name] Ben Szem) and articles by Emil Igel and Albert Wepper (pen name Alwe); 1925 marked the debut of Izaak Deutscher [pen name Krakowski] as a critic.

The end of 1925 was a turning point in the history of the literary ring around *Chwila*. In mid-December there appeared the first issue of *Chwilka* (Little moment), a supplement for children and youth. It featured work by the then twenty-year-old Maurycy Szymel, who published poems, dramatic fragments, and stories (signed "Maurycy Sch.," "Sch.," "M. Sch.," and "Maurycy Schimel") and soon became one of the pillars of the supplement. He was joined by Juliusz Wit [Witkower], Karol Dresdner, Minka Silberman, and Riwka [Regina] Gurfein in 1926, by Anda Eker and Samuel Druck in 1927, and by Stefan Pomer in 1928. That was the beginning of the Lvov Polish-Jewish young literary circle. Some of its members were virtually children—youngsters of 13 or 14, whose work appeared in columns such as "Z prac naszych czytelników" (From the works of our readers) and "Pierwiosnki poetyckie" (Poetic primroses). These young writers enjoyed the support of no less a personage than Janusz Korczak [Henryk Goldszmit].[52]

After 1926, the literary circle of *Chwila* was joined by the translators Estera Tresówna, Miriam Wolman-Sieraczkowa, Leona Weinstock, Jack Frühling, Anatol Mühlstein, and Fryderyka Eichel, and by the critics Fryderyk Aszkenazy, Edward Aldstaetter, Dina Karlowa, Ben Hillel, and Henryk Adler. Yet another writer to join *Chwila* was Pesach Stark, known later as Julian Stryjkowski. Years later he described his Zionist youth in the autobiographical work *Wielki strach* (The great fear), as follows: "[Artur] wrote Hebrew poems and was certain that they would be published in the future. He acquired a taste for old and new culture and translated into Polish Isaiah, Brenner, the psalms, and Awigdor Hameiri. The translations appeared in the Zionist *Chwila*."[53] In the thirties the following people began to write for *Chwila:* the poets Lola Szereszewska, Lola Engelmanówna, Leon Szajewicz, Bronisław Mayer (Arieh), and Stanisław Lec; the critics Artur Sandauer, Chaim Löw, Juliusz Feldhorn, Debora Vogel, Rachela Auerbach, Jehuda Warszawiak, Pinchas Kon, Leon Gutman, and Gabriel Talpir;

and the translators Samuel Ripp, Hersz Buchman, Giza Fraenklowa, Arnold Spaet, Salomon Dykman, and Paulina Sandauerowa.

The consolidation of the literary ring of *Chwila* took place in the 1920s. By 1929, Polish-Jewish poetry was part and parcel of the newspaper and its group of literary contributors was well defined. The regular contributors were the poets Anda Eker, Karol Dresdner, Maurycy Szymel, Stefan Pomer, Daniel Ihr, Minka Silberman, Horacy Safrin, Hersz Awrohem Fenster, Artur Lauterbach, Rafael Friedmann, Juliusz Wit, Roman Brandstaetter, and the critics Izydor Berman [pen names Adam or Iber Niedźwiecki], Ozjasz Tillemann, Mojżesz Kanfer, Benedykt Rosenzweig, Henryk Hescheles, Benzion Zangen, and Hermann Sternbach.

The work of Lvov writers appeared in newspapers other than *Chwila*—specifically, in the Cracow *Nowy Dziennik* after 1925, in *Nasz Przegląd* in the 1930s, and later in *Opinia.* Around 1929, there emerged from the literary ring of *Chwila* a group of poets distinguished by a definite Galician regional tone. Due to the outstanding and original talents of its members, this group came to occupy a leading position in Polish-Jewish literature. It was not without pride that Maurycy Szymel wrote in 1933: "The strongest group of Polish-Jewish poets from Lvov had a decisive influence on the evolution of Polish-Jewish poetry."[54] In the same year, he recalled the emergence of this group in the following words:

> The Lvov *Chwila* played, and continues to play, a crucial role in the evolution of our work. Almost the whole galaxy of Polish-Jewish poets collects around this newspaper. One must emphasize the most lively and affectionate interest toward the young adepts of poetry on the part of Henryk Hescheles, a subtle connoisseur and lover of the lyrical art. It was in *Chwila* that Karol Dresdner and Artur Lauterbach took their first steps. *Chwila* opened its pages to Stefan Pomer and Daniel Ihr. The writer of these words owes this serious paper a great deal. Thus *Chwila* was our nurse. *Chwila* opened its pages not just to poets. A host of splendid Polish-Jewish critics of the younger generation, headed by Dr. Berman, took its first literary steps in *Chwila.*[55]

To judge by the available materials, the lyric poets of *Chwila* formed a situational poetic group: their primary objective was to find a place in the literary marketplace.[56] One cannot overestimate the inspirational role of the newspaper in the rise of this group. It not only published the works of its members, but also organized evenings of poetry readings by its authors. To judge from press reports, these evenings enjoyed considerable popularity. Of one such evening in

Anda Eker and Maurycy Szymel in Lvov. *Chwila: Dodatek Ilustrowany* 1934, no. 47, p. 4.

the fall of 1929, Artur Lauterbach wrote that "The recitations of works of three young Lvov poets, Daniel Ihr, Stefan Pomer, and Maurycy Szymel, took place in a packed auditorium. . . , the huge audience left the Technological Institute with a feeling of profound satisfaction."[57] Sometimes critics connected with *Chwila,* such as Izydor Berman, Artur Lauterbach, and editor-in-chief Henryk Hescheles, accompanied the authors.[58] For the most part, the readings took place at the Technological Institute on Bourlard Street; less frequently, they were given in the Teatr "Rozmaitości" ("Variety" Theater).[59] The poems were recited by actors, most frequently by Teodora Kipeniówna and Józef Rittel. The recitations were sometimes enhanced by musical accompaniment. As a rule, Szymel's poems enjoyed a very warm reception. Then Szymel began to appear by himself and soon became famous, in and beyond Lvov, as an excellent reciter of his poems. Sometimes Anda Eker also appeared by herself. In a description of a reading by Szymel in Lvov in the winter of 1934 Izydor Berman praised his declaiming talent and said that "Szymel has a supple, superbly controlled, voice that lends itself to various modulations. He captivated his audience, led it, enthralled it, and, when he lowered his voice, they listened with rapt attention, conquered and seduced."[60]

The joint public poetry readings undoubtedly consolidated the group around *Chwila* and shaped its collective image in the minds of the listeners. The readings continued even after Szymel and Pomer "emigrated" to Warsaw in 1930. Usually Szymel, Pomer, and Ihr appeared together. They were frequently joined by Anda Eker and less frequently by Karol Dresdner. It seems that these five were linked by strong bonds of poetic friendship, one of whose manifestations was that they dedicated poems to one another or wrote them jointly.[61]

The poets of *Chwila* did not limit themselves to Polish-speaking Jewish circles. They also took part in the undertakings of the Kasyno (Casino) and of the Koło Literacko-Artystyczne (Literary and Artistic circle),[62] which made a significant contribution to Lvov cultural life in the thirties. They often participated in discussions of the cultural life of the city.[63] It is safe to say that the group was regarded as one of the major elements of Lvov's artistic life. To quote a recollection by Jan Śpiewak:

> In addition to poets grouped around *Sygnały* (Signals) and poets publishing in *Słowo Polskie* (Polish word) and *Kurier Poranny* (Morning courier) there were poets who published volumes of poetry without publishing in dailies. Here belong Karol Dresdner, author of *Heine i nieznajoma,* Stefan Pomer, author of *Elegie podolskie,* Daniel Ihr, Maurycy Szymel, a highly gifted poet and author of a number of volumes of poetry, Anda Eker, Rafał Friedmann, Józef Nacht Prutkowski, and Leonard Hanin.[64]

From the group around *Chwila* came also lyric poets who, in 1931, formed in Stanisławów a group—or as they put it an association [*zrzeszenie*]—called "Wzlot" (Upward Flight). This group consisted of poets, literary critics, and journalists who wrote in Polish and in Yiddish. It also included sculptors. In October 1932, the group published the only issue of its own literary monthly *Wzlot* and in 1933 a collective volume *Wieczór i myśli* (Evening and thoughts).[65] Unfortunately, all the information I have about these items is secondhand; neither has been preserved in the Polish, Israeli, or American archives I know of. This is a great loss because this group was a visible symbol of a new interpretation of Jewish literature as a polyglot literature, one of whose languages was Polish.

The anniversary publication of the Stanisłwów *Słowo* (Word)[66] tells us something of the circumstances of the birth of Wzlot. The initiative was due to four poets: Minka Silberman, Bronisław Mayer, Leon Schopenfeld, and Leon Streit.

They were soon joined by Syda Richter, Fryderyk Bertisch, Hanka Brandmark, Adolf Bloch, Eliasz Leon Tabak, Gizela Gold, and Natan Füllenbaum. The painters Dawid Elber, Bronisław Rubinstein, and Dora Zuckerkandel cooperated with the writers. Wzlot was housed in the premises of the local Revisionist-Zionist organization Betar, and the public that attended the initial evenings organized by the authors were young people belonging to Jewish youth organizations.[67] In 1936, Minka Silberman deplored the slow decline of the once buoyant Jewish artistic milieu (*hakhsharas* [Hebrew for "pioneer training"—Trans.] and *aliyas* [Hebrew for "emigration to Palestine"—Trans.], the drive to independence, tore people away from us. . . . The group was getting smaller and smaller. Some ended up in Palestine and some in Lvov. Just a handful remained here");[68] but at that very time Wzlot became active again. This was the result of its acquiring a platform of its own—the literary column of the local *Słowo* edited by Natan Füllenbaum. In his humorous "Pean o poezji stanisławowskiej" (Paean about Stanisławów poetry) of 1938 Horacy Safrin, who was loosely connected with the group, mentioned as its members Silberman, Richter, Brandmark, Bertisch, and Füllenbaum.[69] Information dating from the same year refers to the group's cooperation with the Yiddish paper *Shtegn* (Paths; edited by Maks Tabak) and the poets of *Chwila* who remained in Lvov.[70] In other words, Wzlot remained active in the late 1930s.

Like the Lvov *Chwila,* so, too, the Cracow *Nowy Dziennik* was a "fortress" of Polish-Jewish literature. Most of the authors who published in Cracow just before the 1920s had previously written for the Zionist press. They were Karol Rosenfeld, Samuel Hirszhorn, Zygmunt Foebus Finkelstein, Jakub Appenszlak, and Anzelm Lutwak.[71] Even Wilhelm Berkelhammer, editor-in-chief of *Nowy Dziennik,* had debuted as a poet in one of the Galician Zionist almanacs.[72] In the early twenties the most active lyric poets of *Nowy Dziennik* were Rudolf Taubenschlag and Karol Rosenfeld, members of the older generation. Franciszka Bienenstock, Maksymilian Koren, and Szymon Wolf were active as translators. Wilhelm Fallek, Ozjasz Tillemann, Jeremiasz Frenkel, Maksymilian Bienenstock, Mojżesz Kanfer (pen names Moassi, -assi), and Juliusz Feldhorn were critics. Beginning in 1924, the works of members of a new generation of writers began to appear in ever increasing numbers. Among those collaborating with *Nowy Dziennik* were Chaim Löw [later name Przemski], Benedykt Rosenzweig, Zygmunt Korn, Samuel Ripp, Lew Haym, Artur Lauterbach, and Izaak Deutscher. Years later, Mieczysław Jastrun was to say of Deutscher's poems that they were "far better than those that appeared in the Cracow papers. They were hymns influenced by the 'Hymns' of Kasprowicz but somehow inwardly stronger, closer to the psalms of David."[73]

In 1925, "Literatura i Sztuka" (Literature and art), a literary section edited by Mojżesz Kanfer that later became a literary supplement, made its debut. In 1926, it published the first works of Karol Dresdner, Juliusz Wit, Edward Dorthaymer, Marek Korn, and Rubin Feldszuh, and in 1927, the first works of Roman Brandstaetter, Wanda Kragen, Aleksander Łęczycki, Meir Korzennik, and Zygmunt Schenker.

When *Dzienniczek* (Little daily), the counterpart of *Chwilka* (Little moment), came into being in 1928, Lvov writers began to publish in Cracow. The first to do so were Szymel, Eker, Safrin (in 1928), Pomer, Ihr, and Silberman (in 1929). Hersz Awrohem Fenster joined them later. The writers who published in *Nowy Dziennik* increased in number from year to year: Jakub Lewittes, Beniamin Schlager, Hersz Weber, Riwka Gurfein, Jan Rauchwerger, Ludwig Machauf (pen name Ludwik Maschoff), Maurycy Schlanger, Henryk Luft, Juliusz Grot, Adam Madler, Perec Nowomiast, Irma Kanfer, Salomon Dykman, Hanka Brandmark, Maria Hochberżanka, Cwi Wohlmut, Jehuda Warszawiak, Szlomo Erlik, Mosze Waldman, Henryk Pfeffer, Melech Lusternik, Maria Dick, Ryszard Apte, Izydor Berman, Maksymilian Boruchowicz, Artur Sandauer, Henryk Vogler, and Jan Kleinberg. No literary group like the *Chwila* group emerged from the Cracow milieu. Although Bradstaetter and Wit jointly presented authors' evenings,[74] one certainly cannot say that they formed a poetic partnership. On the other hand, there was a circle of talented critics connected with *Nowy Dziennik:* Chaim Löw, Juliusz Feldhorn, Maksymilian Boruchowicz, Hersz [Henryk] Weber, Wanda Kragen, Henryk Vogler, and Artur Sandauer.[75]

Until the early thirties, Warsaw had no Polish-Jewish artistic milieu as active as those of Galicia. The ring that centered around *Nasz Przegląd* was dominated by members of the older generation whose initiative had brought it into being.[76] The people who published in it were Samuel Hirszhorn, Jakub Appenszlak (pen name Pierrot), Saul Wagman, Paulina Appenszlak [Appenszlakowa], Henryk Hescheles (pen name Henryk Trejtwart), Mojżesz Kanfer, Maksymilian Koren, and Z[ygmunt] F. Finkelstein. Its first poets were Celina Meerson-Becker [Meersonówna], Eleazar Merchentraum, Zygmunt Mer (1923), Paulina Appenszlakowa (1924), Artur Lauterbach (1925), Sabina Raciążkówna (1926), Mieczysław Braun [Braunstein] (1927), Sulamita Szapiro, Ewa Wittenberżanka, Ignacy Melodysta, and Lena Sölm (1930). The newspaper had no literary supplement and no permanent literary column. "Felieton Literacki *Naszego Przeglądu*" (Literary column of *Nasz Przegląd*) did appear in the twenties but only sporadically and for a short time (1926–27). Its publication was largely in the hands of Izaak Deutscher, who "emigrated" at that time from Cracow to the capital.

The situation changed radically when Szymel and Pomer, who settled in Warsaw in 1930, joined the paper. In the early thirties, *Nasz Przegląd* began to carry works by Roman Brandstaetter, Karol Dresdner, Władysław Szlengel and, somewhat later, by Salomon Dykman, Leon Baumberg, Stefan Lebenbaum, Dawid Wolsztejn, and Józef Lipski. Just before the war, Jerzy Kamil Weintraub and Włodzimierz Słobodnik joined the paper. Other writers who published in the paper in the thirties were Mikołaj Wadyas, Róża Muszkattblit, Henryk Nowogródzki, Jakub Bleiberg, Artur Prędski [Adolf Pfeffer], Leon Gutman, Leo Finkelstein, Maksymilian Boruchowicz, Jehuda Warszawiak, Michał Weinzieher, Miriam Wolman-Sieraczkowa, Wilhelm Fallek, Izrael Trief, Melech Lusternik, Szlomo Reiss, Sz[muel] L[ejb] Schneiderman, Artur Mandel, and Irma Kanfer. Janusz Korczak, who worked for *Nasz Przegląd* beginning in the twenties, edited the famous [daily] *Mały Przegląd* (Little review). Unlike *Chwilka* (Little moment) and *Dzienniczek,* it published exclusively materials by young readers. The literary profile of the daily changed in 1936. A permanent literary column was introduced, and valuable and interesting critical articles by Jerzy Bros, Tadeusz Heller, and Barbara Lewit [Lewitówna] began to appear.

The vicissitudes of the literary ring of *Nasz Przegląd* reflect a significant phenomenon. In the early thirties there took place a "regrouping of forces" that changed to a large extent the geography of Polish-Jewish literary life. The capital attracted poets from the provinces, as it had in the twenties (recall Izaak Deutscher's migration to Warsaw), except that now the phenomenon had a generational aspect. Once in Warsaw, the young—Szymel, Pomer, Brandstaetter—joined the sociocultural weeklies.

An important tendency in the history of the Polish-Jewish press in the thirties consisted in attempts to create a stable journal literature. The most important of the journals that came into being at that time (they are usually described as "political, social, and literary journals") was the weekly *Opinia* (1933–35), later *Nasza Opinia* (1935–39), which quickly became the most important journal of Polish-Jewish literary life. Roman Brandstaetter, who managed its literary section, attracted to it a considerable number of talented writers and critics such as Szymel, Pomer, Ihr, Dresdner, Eker, Dorthaymer, Dykman, Madler, Berman, and Bleiberg. Clearly, *Opinia* was a publication of the younger generation of writers, [although,] from time to time, it printed contributions by older writers, such as Rosenfeld and Marek. The journal had obvious pedagogical ambitions and ran a kind of literary school for the very young by publishing "Próbki literackie naszych czytelników" (Literary samples from our readers) and a permanent column called "Świat młodych" (World of the young).[77]

Undoubtedly, the literary editor of *Opinia* [Brandstaetter] wanted to make the weekly a journal of Polish-Jewish poets that would have an inspiring effect on the whole Polish-Jewish literary milieu. An essential and indisputable achievement in this area was the debate it initiated in 1933, the most heated and serious debate [to take place] within Polish-Jewish literary circles on the conditions, character, values, and perspectives of their own creative activity.

Another—short-lived and failed—attempt at consolidation of the Polish-Jewish literary milieu was the grouping of writers, both young and old, around the literary weekly *Lektura* (Reading matter; 1934), edited by the Appenszlaks. In addition to the editors, its contributors included Szymel, Pomer, Berman, Marek, Hirszhorn and L[eo] Finkelstein. The group of writers for the newspaper *My sami* (We ourselves; Warsaw 1935–36), headed by Rubin Feldszuh, had similar ambitions. They planned to publish an almanac of the prose writings of the group and they organized literary competitions for their readers (1936, issue 7).

When *Opinia* ceased publication in Warsaw in 1935, its work was continued by the weekly *Nasza Opinia,* which attracted older writers such as Anzelm Lutwak, Samuel Hirszhorn, Ozjasz Tillemann, Mojżesz Kanfer, Wilhelm Fallek, Herman Sternbach, and even assimilationists such as Leo Belmont [Leopold Blumental]. In addition to Szymel, Pomer, Brandstaetter, Ihr, and Eker, its contributors included Mieczysław Braun, Jakub Lewittes, Natan Füllenbaum, Fryderyk Bertisch, Horacy Safrin, Hersh Awrohem Fenster, Minka Silberman, Perec Nowomiast, Ignacy Buchstab, Mieczysław Dengel, Juliusz Wit, Leonard Hanin, Józef Nacht [later name Prutkowski], and Leon Pasternak. It published critical pieces by Izydor Berman, Chaim Löw, Wanda Kragen, Deborah Vogel, Bruno Schulz, Artur Sandauer, Benzion Zangen, Maksymilian Boruchowicz [later name Michał Borwich], Marek Fritzhand, Leon Baumberg, Benedykt Rosenzweig, Maria Dickówna, and Eliasz Leon Tabak, and the work of translators such as Arnold Spaet, Salomon Dykman, Henryk Luft, and Cwi Wolmuth. Since it was ideologically close to *Sygnały,** it opened its columns to Tadeusz Hollender, Franciszek Gil, and Antoni Gronowicz, as well as to Stanisław Vincenz, and Tadeusz Zaderecki. On the other hand, the weekly maintained close contacts with the Lvov Jewish Artistic and Literary Society [Żydowskie Towarzystwo Artystyczno-Literackie], at whose premises evening poetry readings were given by Leon Pasternak and Józef Nacht.[78]

The year 1935 was a turning point in the history of *Opinia-Nasza Opinia* as well as in Polish-Jewish literary life. The years of greatness of *Opinia*—1933–35—were also in Polish-Jewish circles the period of the most intense

*A socio-cultural journal published in Lvov in the years 1933–34 and 1936–39. Its orientation was liberal-democratic. [Trans.]

search for artistic identity and of the formation of a literary consciousness. After 1935, this activity declined somewhat and took on new forms. The ablest of the young authors of the crisis of the early thirties announced new books, but published hardly any. In 1936, Szymel published a small collection in Yiddish, *Mir iz umetik* (I am sad), and in 1938, in serialized form, the novel *Gdzie jesteś Ewo* (Where are you, Eve) in the paper *Nowy Głos.* He also did a considerable amount of translating, and from time to time published poems. Hersz Awrohem Fenster also published Yiddish poetry, *Di levone geit unter* (The moon sets; 1938). Brandstaetter concentrated on anti-anti-Semitic journalism ("Zmowa eunuchów" [A conspiracy of eunuchs; 1936]. Anda Eker died.

The press again became the mainstay of literature. The Polish-Jewish dailies and journals that came into being in the late thirties attracted various constellations of authors earlier associated with *Chwila, Nowy Dziennik, Nasz Przegląd, Opinia,* and *Nasza Opinia.* Szymel, Brandstaetter, Pomer, Dresdner, Safrin, Berman, Szereszewska, Prędski, S[tanisław] T. Lec, and J[erzy] K[amil] Weintraub collaborated with *Nowy Głos* (Warsaw 1937–38). Szymel, Pomer, Brandstaetter, Braun, Szereszewska, Dorthaymer, L. Gajzler, R[ubin] Feldszuh, S[tefan] Rumelt, J[akub] Bleiberg, Ch[aim] Löw, L[eon] Baumberg, B[arbara] Lewit, and S[alomon] Dykman wrote for *Ster* (Warsaw 1937–38). Emil Tenenbaum and Maurycy Schlanger wrote for *Kontratak* (Counterattack; Lvov 1936–39).

The history of *Opinia-Nasza Opinia* points to yet other changes in Polish-Jewish literary life after 1935. After this turning point the Polish-Jewish press was forced to engage to an ever growing extent in the fight against anti-Semitism, and anti-anti-Semitic satire became an increasingly important current in Polish-Jewish writing. The fact that the writers for *Nasza Opinia* included young and old Polish-Jewish writers, Zionists and assimilationists, nationalist and leftist intellectuals (Jews as well as Poles) points to an integration of the internally differentiated Jewish intelligentsia induced by a clear rightist turn on the part of the national government as well as by the collaboration of the Jewish intelligentsia with Polish democratic circles.

Our sketch of the map of the Polish-Jewish literary circles is certainly incomplete. Much points to the fact that they formed not only in large centers but also in the provinces. Michał Strzemski recalls that the "*Żydowskie Kółko Literackie* (Jewish literary circle) was formed in Puławy around 1938. It publicized the substantial output of the young Jewish writers of Puławy, which included a considerable amount of poetry in both Yiddish and Polish, a few short stories, and a huge novel in the style of Thomas Mann's *Buddenbrooks* that told the story of an authentic Jewish family over the period 1830–1930."[79]

It is likely that there were people in small towns similar to Puławy who launched artistic undertakings which were not documented in special book publications or in the Polish-Jewish press.[80]

Speaking of the press. It should be stated that it was undoubtedly the most important institution of Polish-Jewish culture and the foundation of Polish-Jewish literary life. A far weaker (indeed, the weakest) institution of literary life was criticism. Its interest in Polish-Jewish literature, which was minor in the twenties, increased considerably in the next decade when there appeared critical contributions by I[zydor] Berman, O[zjasz] Tillemann, Ch[aim] Löw, W[ilhelm] Fallek, M[arek] Kanfer, M[aksymilian] Boruchowicz [later named Michał Borwicz], P[aulina] Appenszlak, and Sz[muel] L[ejb] Schneiderman. Nevertheless, Polish-Jewish authors felt that the critics' interest in their work was definitely inadequate.

Thus Szymel and Brandstaetter complained that the critics failed to support their literary endeavors. Brandstaetter went so far as to claim that "Jewish literary criticism (in Polish) is virtually nonexistent."[81] He did give some credit to Berman, Fallek, and Löw. Szymel agreed: "Only Fallek, Löw, and Berman brought themselves, now and then, to hint at our existence. I mention this to emphasize the glaring disregard on the part of Polish-Jewish critics for initiatives of Jewish poets (regardless of the language they create in), for their honest efforts and for their occasional beautiful achievements."[82]

While these complaints were somewhat exaggerated, it is true that most of the notes, descriptions, and reviews of Polish-Jewish books were by the writers themselves, and that Brandstaetter was right to complain that "we can depend on no one but ourselves, and so must support and write about one another. For close to five years only Pomer writes about Szymel, Szymel reviews Dresdner's books, and Dresdner the books of Brandstaetter."[83]

In all fairness, it must be pointed out that Polish-Jewish critics paid considerable attention to Jewish literature in Yiddish and Hebrew as well as to Polish literature and to some world literatures (mostly German, French, Russian, and American). They were especially interested in the part played by Jewish writers in the literatures of different language areas. We owe to these preferences (as well as to other causes) the intense efforts to popularize the works of Franz Kafka in interwar Poland.[84]

It seems that Polish-Jewish writers were not satisfied with the reception of their works in the Yiddish and Hebrew press. They paid considerable attention to all responses and scrupulously noted all echoes. To the best of my (unfortunately secondhand) knowledge, Polish-Jewish poetry was discussed in the Warsaw *Haint* (1931), the American *Der Tog* (The day), and the Palestine papers *Gazit*

(Hewn stones; 1935) and *Davar* (1935). Szmuel Werses, a professor at the Hebrew University in Jerusalem, has a bibliography of many Hebrew translations of Polish-Jewish poems from the thirties.[85] Most of these are by Szymel, Ihr, and Brandstaetter.

We see that the Polish-Jewish literary life that developed during the two interwar decades was rich and varied and had well-developed independent institutions that included a press, literary groups and circles in Lvov, Cracow, and Warsaw as well as in the provinces. It produced poetry, prose, literary criticism, and translations.

The Year 1933: Manifestos and Discussions

The year 1933 was one of the major turning points in Polish-Jewish literary life. It was the birth year of *Opinia,* the weekly that played an important role in the shaping of that life, as well as the year in which it launched a stormy discussion that soon spread to other papers (such as *Nowy Dziennik* and *Tygodnik Żydowski*) and played an important part in the shaping of the literary consciousness of Polish-Jewish circles. What gave this discussion special significance was that it highlighted not only artistic questions but also the complex social and artistic circumstances in which Polish-Jewish literature developed.

The polemic began with a cycle of articles published in *Opinia* by Roman Brandstaetter and titled "Sprawa poezji polsko-żydowskiej" (The issue of Polish-Jewish poetry).[86] Brandstaetter's initiative had a programmatic character. He referred to his texts as "discussion articles." In a sense, he was challenging Jewish cultural opinion. However one looked at the matter, it was beyond doubt that Brandstaetter's most important merit was to launch a public debate on the role and position of authors who wrote in Polish but thought of themselves as Jews and identified with Jewish culture. In a broader sense, the debate dealt with the problem of the cultural activity of that part of the Jewish intelligentsia which could function only in non-Jewish languages but felt responsible for Jewish culture and wanted to shape it. The reaction to Brandstaetter's initiative was proof of the importance and significance of the problem. There was a broad response in *Opinia* and the polemic became quite heated. Soon its focus shifted from poetry to culture because the question "Is Polish-Jewish poetry possible?" called for answers to such fundamental questions as ["What was] the state of the culture of Polish Jews in the third decade of the twentieth century[?"] and, more generally, ["W]hat was the right model of Jewish culture[?"]

That the discussion would take this direction could have been predicted from the outset. When explaining and justifying his program, Brandstaetter re-

Roman Brandstaetter. *Wiadomości Literackie* 1928, no. 23, p. 3. Reproduced by A. Musielak.

ferred to sociocultural processes taking place in the Jewish collectivity. He began by characterizing Jewish participation in Polish literature. First there were "literary brokers," then patrons, then writers of Jewish origin, and finally Polish-Jewish writers. Jewish participation was becoming progressively more creative and original, thus proving the emancipation of the Jews in Polish culture. This emancipation would lead to independence, and even to the separation of Jewish literature written in Polish from Polish culture. Brandstaetter regarded Polish-Jewish poetry created by authors who identified with Jewry as national Jewish poetry, and opposed the group of Polish-Jewish poets to writers of Jewish origin who declared their connection with things Polish. He granted the fundamental significance of the question of self-identification: Polish-Jewish poets were Jews who felt at home in Polish culture rather than Poles of the Mosaic persuasion. He wrote: "Thrown between two cultures, till now brought up, in most cases, on the boundary between cultural assimilation and a shallow "Sabbath Jewishness," we went through . . . a long spiritual martyrology, and finally managed to create in ourselves the notion of our proud national affiliation. It was then that we began to endow our poetry with all those values that add up to the spiritual structure of a national Jew."[87]

He attacked assimilating writers very sharply. "We are a group whose creations rehabilitate the activities of the renegade [Julian] Klaczko, whose existence negates Feldman's whole ideology, refutes it, routs it, and plows to the depths the soul of the Polish Jew."[88] It was the new model of Jewish identity that was to serve as the foundation of a new type of cultural activity.

As an expression of national consciousness, Polish-Jewish poetry must not only deal with Jewish topics but also contain and propagate the ideals of national regeneration, it "must breathe the national Jewish spirit into the Polish poetic word."[89] Thus Brandstaetter assigned to poetry the status of an engaged art, an art that was applied, propagandistic, fulfilling, as he put it, "a national service." Its function was the creation of "an atmosphere of legend and enthusiasm." In his view, it was "impossible to create a nation" without these factors. He postulated close cooperation between the poets and the Jewish National Fund: "to ignite with a poem the idea of national regeneration, to thrill with rhythm not only minds but also Jewish hearts, to light the actions of Jewish politicians and diplomats with the flame of pathos."[90] Engagement—"national," Zionist, political—had to be more than a local oddity. Anticipating the charges of his opponents, Brandstaetter referred to Western European writers such as Else Lasker-Schüler, Hugo Zuckermann, Edmond Fleg, and André Spire, all of whom espoused the Zionist cause.

The aims of Polish-Jewish literature were to be, in principle, similar to the aims of the Hebrew literature that was being created in Palestine. Its only distinctive feature was its language—Polish—a consequence of "having been thrown between two cultures." But language was also to some extent a carrier of content: "We charm our own Jewish longings into Polish speech, we melt, for the first time on Polish soil, the pain of the Jewish heart into the sound of the Czarnolesie word [that is, the word of Jan Kochanowski, the famous fifteenth-century poet from Czarnolesie—Trans.], we unite the word of Mickiewicz with the holy word of the Bible."[91] One employs "the Polish word inspired by the Hebrew spirit," but since this word is part of the Polish tradition it clearly actualizes it, as witness the references to Kochanowski and Mickiewicz. Also, according to Brandstaetter, because it used the Polish language, Polish-Jewish literature depended to some extent on institutions of Polish literary life, namely, on critics and publishers.

Thus regardless of ideological declarations, Polish-Jewish literature seemed to be a product of cultural interference. Brandstaetter regarded this interference as an obvious fact, at once a "historical necessity" and an anomaly—a stigma of the Diaspora. He predicted that having fulfilled its mission of awakening the national consciousness this literature would lose its raison d'être as a result of the coming into existence of a homogeneous Hebrew national culture of the Jews. This was the central paradox of his program: while urging the creation of Polish-Jewish literature he viewed it as a necessary evil and denied any reason for its future existence. To quote Brandstaetter: "We would rather . . . write in Hebrew and be read by Hebrew readers; but, after all, we are an emanation of our whole political-cultural situation and therefore must not be faulted or accused."[92] In the group of Polish-Jewish poets he included, beside himself, Maurycy Szymel, Karol Dresdner, and Stefan Pomer. He saw the situation of this group in the literary marketplace as exceptionally dramatic: its members were practically unnoticed by critics connected with the Polish-Jewish press, unappreciated by readers, and ignored and materially unsupported by national Jewish institutions. The fact that he attacked the critics, the readers, and Jewish organizations proves that Brandstaetter's aim was to call attention to Polish-Jewish poetry and to achieve for it appropriate recognition by the Jewish readership.

The response to Brandstaetter's manifesto combined acceptance of his appeal to develop Jewish literature in Polish with rejection (at times extremely harsh) of his view of its underlying conception, as stated in "Sprawa poezji polsko-żydowskiej." Of course, there were voices that condemned the author as well as his program. The harshest of such condemnations appeared in the Tarnów *Tygodnik Żydowski.* There, Meir Korzennik accused Brandstaetter (who, incidentally, had been his fellow student of Polish) in the same breath of "megalomania, arrogance, and irresponsible journalistic jokes."[93]

The most extensive reply was Maurycy Szymel's cycle of articles "Kij w mrowisku: W sprawie artykułów Romana Brandstaettera o poezji polsko-żydowskiej" (Stick in an anthill: Concerning Roman Brandstaetter's articles on Polish-Jewish poetry).[94] In spite of crying "Bravo, Brandstaetter!" Szymel openly referred to Brandstaetter's vision and evaluation of Polish-Jewish poetry as "completely false," and demystified it by writing "the truth about Polish-Jewish poetry." This demystification was, in fact, a distinct, opposing, and competing manifesto of Polish-Jewish literature.

Szymel granted that, without exception, all Polish-Jewish writers were "returning to the home" of Jewishness. Brandstaetter was a member of this group who stood out because of his zealotry, a zealotry associated with his recent conversion to Zionism. He even called him a "prodigal son" returning to Jewishness, and stressed that his opponent had published a few small volumes of poetry devoid of even a trace of Jewishness but replete with glowing tributes to Polishness and the Czarnolesie Muse. According to Szymel, Brandstaetter's Zionism was an ideological and esthetic utopia. He merely replaced the utopia of Polishness (Brandstaetter said about himself that before his "Zionist illumination" he "had loved Poland like Srul from Lubartów")[95] with the utopia of a "Hebrew State." His visions of a noble Hebrew culture and of Palestine—the stirring "Cedar Fatherland"—were a new embodiment of the classicist ideals of beauty to which he had paid allegiance in *Jarzma* (Yokes) and in *Droga pod górę* (The uphill road). This put in doubt the inner maturing toward Jewishness and the spiritual turning point on which Brandstaetter waxed so eloquent. His system of values remained unchanged—he just realized it in a different cultural medium.

It is difficult to determine the role played by personal dislikes in the storm that swirled around the author of "Sprawa poezji polsko-żydowskiej." One must bear in mind that he was a controversial figure in literary circles,[96] and that Adolf Nowaczyński bestowed on him the telling epithet "literarischer Brandstifter" [German for "literary fire setter"—Trans.].[97] But there is no doubt that the resistance to his attempts to win the position of leader and legislator of Polish-Jewish poetry had a certain larger dimension. What was clearly at issue was the role in the Polish-Jewish literary movement of authors who had earlier tried to win for themselves a place in Polish literature and turned, by choice (as they claimed) or out of necessity (as others claimed), to Polish-Jewish literature. It was no accident that Szymel began his reply with a short chapter about "the one who started the discussion." Undoubtedly, Brandstaetter's position as an outsider had grave consequences for his program. Though seceding from Polish literature, he was not inclined to acknowledge that Polish-Jewish literature was an independent phenomenon with definite artistic features. He insisted that "[t]he modern Jewish national poet (regardless of the language in which he writes) must be a programmatic writer in the Zionist sense of the word. . . . "[98] The literature whose creation he urged was to be tendentious and engaged. For him, the most important aspect of this literature was its ideological dimension.

By contrast, Szymel, who from the very beginning of his literary career took part in the Polish-Jewish literary movement, regarded it as a formed phenomenon of spontaneous origin. In "Prawda o poezji polsko-żydowskiej" (The truth about Polish-Jewish poetry), he described its birth in the years 1918–33: the role of the Polish-Jewish press and the formation of the group around *Chwila*. The birth of this poetry was for him a natural fact, and certainly not an anomaly. "I am a genuine son of my nation, and I express my Jewishness in one of the many tongues it uses."[99] He went so far as to claim that the rise of Polish-Jewish literature accorded with the "spirit of [Jewish] history." He praised folk culture, and emphasized the significance of the Diaspora and the role of Yiddish:

> The Jewish masses, this concrete, real nation does not express its will in Hebrew. It sings and cries, speaks and dreams in strange, for Brandstaetter, Yiddish, in

> "jargon." How can Brandstaetter, in love with classical beauty, reconcile all this within himself? How can he refrain from loving Hebrew Palestine in which all attributes of classical Jewish beauty are resuscitated? . . . The grim and splendid heroism of the Diaspora has not yet manifested itself to Brandstaetter.[100]

Szymel objected strongly to the notion of politicizing Polish-Jewish poetry, and emphatically insisted that it was independent of party movements. He went so far as to sharply rebuke Zionist exaltations: "[T]o be a good Polish-Jewish poet one must know the language and culture of the Jews. He who has written a few little poems about palms and *halutzim* does not thereby become a Polish-Jewish poet."[101] He thus favored a manifestation of Jewishness in literature that relied on a cultural tradition and not exclusively on ideology. But he too saw the situation of Polish-Jewish poets as extremely complicated and difficult: "[They were] thin literary people" struggling to publish their poems, without their own paper, and unappreciated by Polish-Jewish critics. He urged: "Our duties are self-defense and self-help. We must form a cartel of Polish-Jewish poets."[102]

We see that the source of the antagonism between Szymel and Brandstaetter was their different views on the essence of Jewish culture and on what constitutes the true Jewish heritage. They represented culturally different groups of Polish-speaking intelligentsia and their visions of Polish-Jewish literature depended on the cultural ideals and standards of these groups. Responding to Szymel's charges, Brandstaetter wrote: "Szymel is a man of the people. I come from the so-called intelligentsia. We come from social poles separated by a huge distance. Szymel's grandfather spoke and thought in Yiddish, while mine thought and wrote in Hebrew."[103] Hebrew versus Yiddish. Palestine versus the Diaspora. Biblical culture versus the culture of the shtetl. Brandstaetter stated this ideological difference in a formula: the Messiah from Jerusalem [versus] the Messiah from the Diaspora.

The biographies of the two poets are typical and, in a sense, symbolic. As mentioned, Szymel represented the intelligentsia of folk origin, bilingual and linked with the culture of the shtetl. The language spoken in his home was Yiddish. He himself also wrote in Polish. Brandstaetter was the grandson of a well-known Galician prose writer of the Haskalah and a Polonist by education. Their debate proved that the degree of acculturation was an important factor that differentiated the Jewish intelligentsia and determined its attitude and worldview. Their clash in the pages of *Opinia* over Polish-Jewish poetry proved that—all differences notwithstanding—this literature was in the interwar period a vital and essential issue for members of the Jewish intelligentsia. Both were well aware of the cultural differentiation of the milieu of Polish-Jewish writers. As Szymel put it: "Roughly speaking, we are divided into those who attach greater importance to the first part of our name and those who stress the second part of the accepted nomenclature."[104] Their respective poetic manifestos expressed the ideals of the two groups united by the idea of Jewish literature in the Polish language.

In the summer of 1933, Adam Madler published in *Opinia* an article titled "O szerszy punkt widzenia" (For a broader viewpoint). It was a third literary manifesto intended as a *complement,* rather than a reply, to Brandstaetter's "Sprawa poezji polsko-żydowskiej." Madler wrote:

> I would like to add the following to the arguments in Roman Brandstaetter's articles: 1. We are addressing Polish as well as Jewish readers. . . . We show Polish readers what genuine Jews are like. . . . 2. The subtitle of the third article . . . is "Polish-Jewish poets." It should be "Polish-Jewish writers." . . . There are few Polish-Jewish novels but many topics are taken up in them. . . . 3. Polish-Jewish writers are a kind of link between the Polish and Jewish societies. . . . [T]hose on the boundary of the two cultures who appreciate both dispel prejudices and contribute to mutual understanding. They soften friction, address people of good will. . . . [W]e gain friends in Polish society for the Palestinian idea.[105]

Thus Madler asked for a place for Polish-Jewish prose writers, described the double readership of Polish-Jewish literature, and stressed its importance beyond Jewish society.

There is no doubt that the most strongly attacked part of Brandstaetter's program was his idea of Polish-Jewish literature as a tool for propaganda and politics. It was not just Szymel and Korzennik who objected to it. In an article in *Tygodnik Żydowski* that was also titled "Sprawa poezji polsko-żydowskiej," Samuel Stendig asked with obvious disapproval: "Should your poetry and talents be at the service of propaganda in the true sense of the word?"[106] He also very much doubted the social effect of poetry in general and the social effect of Zionist poetry in Polish in particular, and claimed that prose was the best tool for literary propaganda (he cited Bernard Zimmermann's *Tirsa* as a work of great popularity and merit). To the extent to which he was inclined to grant poetry any value as a propaganda tool, he limited it exclusively to Hebrew poetry. For he agreed with Brandstaetter that the future literature and culture of the Jews would be in Hebrew.

Brandstaetter's call for the creation of political poetry was not taken up by the Polish-Jewish poets, and it was not without bitterness, disappointment, and rancor that, in 1936, he admitted the defeat of his program.[107] Shortly thereafter, Izydor Berman remembered the 1933 discussion and concluded that the reason for Brandstaetter's defeat was that "issues of poetry, or of art in general, cannot be decided from the viewpoint of some national, social, or political utility, and certainly not from a narrow utilitarian viewpoint. A work of art is above all, mainly and primarily, an aesthetic value, and its social and political relations are secondary."[108]

Thus the source of the defeat of Brandstaetter's program was its minimalism, the reduction of an artistic phenomenon to an ideological tool, the constriction of art into the narrow confines of political tendentiousness.

"Is Polish-Jewish Poetry Possible?"

Acculturation

"Is Polish-Jewish poetry possible?" asked Chaim Löw in connection with the discussion in *Opinia.* Indeed, this question was asked by all participants in the debate. A particular individual's answer depended on his evaluation of the contemporary culture of Polish Jews and on his conception of national Jewish culture. Many views collided. But it was clear to everyone that Jewish culture was experiencing fundamental transformations, and the "invasion" of Jewish life by the Polish language was one manifestation of these processes. This is how Löw described Brandstaetter's initiative:

> No one who has watched carefully, and for a long time, the participation of Jews in Polish poetry should have been surprised at the call for Polish-Jewish poetry and at its implementation as a program in the pages of *Opinia.* Anyone could notice that in the large group of Polish poets of Jewish origin a significant handful was beginning to emerge that differed fundamentally from the rest by its relation to its origin and by its dignified attitude with respect to the problems of its nation. . . . It began with sad little images of the Jewish street, with sentimental ballads about Jewish destitution and hymns about Hebrew, but then this poetry toughened, grew virile, and crystallized into a program of conscious national poetry.[109]

Löw saw manifestations of Polish-Jewish literature in the order of the changes that led to the "interpenetration of Jewish culture and the Polish language,"[110] in the order of the phases of the process of acculturation connected with the formation of a Jewish national consciousness.

This combination of feeling at home in Polish culture and identification with Jewishness became more common at the turn of the century. It was now readily conceded that assimilation was a preliminary and necessary stage in the evolution of the modern national consciousness of the Jews. Around 1900 there appeared descriptions of a third spiritual type of Polish Jew, other than the traditional Jew and the Polonized Jew: "the in-between type: the Jew brought up on the Polish past, on its art and landscape, speaking exclusively Polish, and yet having a deep emotional link with his own past, inwardly and sincerely feeling Jewishly with his soul, and united by empathy with our present and past martyrology."[111]

Beginning at the turn of the century, there was ever louder talk of the disintegration of traditional Jewish culture and the growth of Polish influences in Jewish life. In 1910 the *Żydowski Almanach* (The Jewish almanac), edited by Leon Reich, carried an essay "O kulturze żydowskiej" (On Jewish culture), whose author, Wiktor Pordes, wrote: "The resistance of a truly live Jewish culture to the societal culture—in our case Polish—that surrounds it on all sides is truly insignificant, and its arrangement is in and of itself, a verdict of destruction that is confirmed ever more bluntly by each succeeding generation . . . such is the process of cultural assimilation. It is guided by irresistible sociological laws."[112]

The author claimed that, as a result of "unconscious cultural assimilation," the world of traditional Jewry would "vanish in the sea of the foreign society—not at once, and not without resistance, but imperceptibly, unnoticeably, and yet irresistibly."[113]

Thus the problem of "being a Jew" in the changed cultural situation characteristic of the post-Haskalah period existed already at the beginning of the twentieth century. Being a Jew after the Haskalah called for self-identification under historically novel circumstances, demanded a choice of Jewishness in a new way, required building a model of Jewish identity in a culture that had ceased to be homogeneous, and was moreover becoming ever more open to European influences.

Acculturation—which is what Pordes had in mind when he spoke of "cultural assimilation"—reached its highest point in the interwar period. It is striking that, in spite of the absence of a specific Polish term, efforts were made during this period to distinguish assimilation as an ideology from assimilation as an objective social process. This was already done by Pordes, and also, for example, by Wilhelm Berkelhammer, who wrote: "What is assimilation? It is a social process that . . . appears throughout the world, in all nations, today as well as in the past. . . . It follows that, given the right conditions, assimilation is a necessary and spontaneous social process that is virtually unstoppable."[114]

The term "acculturation," introduced by cultural anthropology in the thirties, was defined as "an idea in the history of culture and cultural anthropology that designates the encounter of elements of different cultures and their synthesis into a new entity that exists in a state of unstable equilibrium of different duration."[115] It is regarded as more neutral than the category of assimilation and integration and is generally used today to describe and interpret the cultural status quo of the Jews in interwar Poland.[116]

The most obvious indication of the processes of acculturation then in progress was undoubtedly the rapid advance of linguistic Polonization. It was this advance that determined the rise and development of the Jewish press in Polish. "The tremendous development of the Jewish press in Polish shows that polonization was making rapid progress in the interwar period."[117] Polish was becoming ever more popular among members of the middle class and the proletariat, hitherto faithful to Yiddish, and so-called external bilingualism gained in these circles the status of a linguistic norm. Estimates of the actual linguistic Polonization of the Jews in the interwar period differ, and its determination today encounters many difficulties.[118] An indirect indication of the influence of the Polish language is that many Polish-Jewish writers wrote for children and fought for Jewish fairy tales written in Polish, that Polish-Jewish papers included periodicals for young readers (such as *Nasza Jutrzenka* [Our dawn; 1921–38] and *Okienko na Świat* [Little window on the world; 1937–39]), and that the daily press published supplements for its readers consisting for the most part of texts written by these readers. *Chwilka, Dzienniczek,* and Janusz Korczak's [Henryk Goldszmit's] *Mały Przegląd,* the most famous of these publications, with the telling subtitle *Pismo dzieci i młodzieży* (newspaper for children and youth), were a literary school for many Polish-Jewish writers. One often found in their pages special literary columns, and even works such as a serialized novel written by students in one of the classes of a Jewish grammar school in Lodz.[119]

The increased popularity of the Polish language among Jews was accompanied by certain literary ambitions. Thus Adam Czerniaków [Cherniakov], senator, social activist, later head of the Jewish community in the Warsaw ghetto, and Samuel Hirszhorn, noted historian, journalist, and translator, published poetry. Well-known Zionist activists such as Nachum Sokołów [Nahum Sokolow], Bernard Zimmermann, and Rubin Feldszuh published prose writings. When *Opinia* organized a literary competition for its readers in 1934, the number of participants—not only from Poland but also from Palestine and France—reached 202.[120] Literary editors frequently justified the rejection of a submission by noting its author's substandard Polish.

The career of Icchok Farberowicz, famous as Urke Nachalnik, author of the *Życiorys własny przestępcy* (Autobiography of a criminal; 1933), was a sign of the times. It was undoubtedly because of Nachalnik's popularity that Czachowski noted in his *Obraz współczesnej literatury polskiej* (Picture of modern Polish literature) the influx into modern Polish literature of Jews from low social levels, for the most part incapable of quickly acquiring the indispensable foundations of Polish literary culture."[121]

During the interwar period, the Polish language was used by Jews not only in, but also as a means of expressing and describing, daily life. Those who discussed this phenomenon in the pages of *Chwila* in the summer of 1933 regarded Polish as the second—next to Yiddish—language of the Polish Jews and, more important, a language of growing popularity. This expansion of the Polish language seemed to support the claim that Polish-Jewish literature was not only possible but, indeed, indispensable through a kind of "historical necessity." Samuel Hirszhorn asserted in 1930: "Since the process of linguistic 'Polonization' cannot be arrested, we must develop our nationality within the framework of the Polish language."[122] Adolf Rudnicki wrote in *Lato* (Summer) (1938): "the Jewish masses for the most part speak Polish, this is their everyday language, this is the language they speak to express their emotions. . . . "[123] By that time it was noted that there was an "ever denser forest of Polish-Jewish journalism, whose status was practically the same as that of the Jewish press and even privileged in comparison with the Hebrew press. . . ,"[124] and that the 'phalanx' of Polish-Jewish poets was growing by the day. Ben-Hillel deplored the fact that

> Cultural assimilation expands in such ever-widening circles and subjugates in its conquering march such large Jewish masses that the day is not far off when our Polish-Jewish poets will be promoted to the rank of "national" poets. The Jewish intellectual, who will draw his spiritual nourishment from the Polish-Jewish press, will not hesitate to look upon Polish-Jewish poetry as the only expression of the national genius, because he will neither know nor have access to its other embodiments.[125]

Clearly, Ben-Hillel was pessimistic about the future of Yiddish and, by analyzing the situation in former Galicia, attributed the gains of the Polish language to the Polish school system.[126]

The reference to the cultural situation in Galicia was not accidental. This is shown most persuasively by the geography of Polish-Jewish literary life. Its main, "senior," centers were Lvov and Cracow, and the intensification of literary life in the capital coincided with the "invasion of Warsaw" by Galician provincials. Most of the writers were born in the eastern regions of former Galicia.[127] According to the historian Ezra Mendelsohn, the political and national relations in the eastern province of the Habsburg Empire determined the significant cultural distinctness of the Galician Jews who, unlike the Jews of Congress Poland or of the Belarus-Lithuanian borderlands, were the most culturally Polonized group (due to the Polish school system), as well as the group in which Zionism scored its greatest triumphs.[128] In terms of language, The Galician Zionist press was Polish. . . . [129] [Paul] Glikson's bibliography is most instructive: during the interwar period, not a single Polish-Jewish newspaper was published in Wilno [Vilnius], the capital of Yiddish culture!

As noted earlier, the Polish-Jewish literary circles were culturally differentiated. More specifically, the degree of acculturation was different for different authors: during the interwar period, the children and grandchildren of *maskil*s as well as the children and grandchildren of inhabitants of the shtetl wrote in Polish. Hersz Awrohem Fenster and Salomon Dykman studied at the Institute for Judaic Studies [Instytut Nauk Judaistycznych] in Warsaw. Izaak Deutscher, dressed in the traditional long garment, would come running from the yeshiva to the Cracow Planty* for discussions with students. Zimmermann and Feldszuh were well-known Zionist activists. Szymel, Fenster, Silberman, and Safrin also wrote poetry in Yiddish. Löw published a textbook for the study of Hebrew for elementary schools and Hebrew short stories for children. Benedykt Rosenzweig published Hebrew texts. Polish-Jewish authors also collaborated with the Yiddish press: Szymel with *Haint* and with the literary papers *Shriftn* (Writings) and *Globus* (Globe, which also published the work of Pomer), and Fenster with *Literarishe bleter* (Literary pages), *Wochnshrift far literatur* (Weekly for literature), *Folks tzaitung* (People's newspaper), and *Arbeter tzaitung* (Workers' newspaper). Some of the Polish-Jewish journalists were bi- and even trilingual authors, connected not only with Polish but also with Hebrew and Yiddish papers. For example, it was said of Samuel Hirszhorn that he wrote simultaneously with two pens, in Polish and in Yiddish.[130] Nachum Sokołów, at one time the editor in chief of *Izraelita* and at the time an eminent Zionist activist, was trilingual.

If they used pennames, Polish-Jewish authors emphasized rather than masked their Jewishness: "Neszer," "Ben Szem," "Arieh," "Riwka z[from] Karkur." But Szymel signed his Polish poems "Maurycy" rather than "Mosze"[131] and of the spelling variants of his last name—"Schimmel," "Schimel," "Szymel"—selected the most Polish-sounding, "Szymel." Name changes, an obvious sign of acculturation, were quite common: "Wolf" to "Wil-

*A green belt, planted in the 19th century, that replaced the city walls of the old city of Cracow. [Trans.]

helm" and "Hinda" to "Anda." Polish-Jewish authors made many "gestures of Polishness," which they were reluctant to talk about publicly.

They passed over in silence a particularly characteristic one. In Polish-Jewish literary circles there were many Polonists—students, teachers, and researchers in Polish literature. Thus Dresdner, Pomer, Ihr, and, for a short time, Safrin studied with [Juliusz] Kleiner in Lvov. Boruchowicz, Löw, Brandstaetter, and Korzennik studied with [Ignacy] Chrzanowski and [Stanisław] Pigoń in Cracow. What influenced the choice of profession, especially in the case of members of the younger generation, was the quota [*numerus clausus*] provision in higher education. In 1929, *Chwila* summarized the effect of restrictive admission policies with respect to Jewish students at the Jan Kazimierz University in Lvov: there were 190 Jewish students in the humanities division where the quota provision was not adhered to, and only 13 in the medical division, where it was adhered to most scrupulously.[132] Nevertheless, it seems that academic policies were not the only factor that made Jewish students choose the study of Polish.

Daniel Ihr described his own and his fellow students' years at the university in stories, titled "Po drodze" (On the way) and published in *Chwila* in the late twenties and early thirties, whose hero was a youngster toiling over the historical grammar of the Polish language in the Jewish student house. These students later became teachers, journalists, and of course authors. For many years Löw and Juliusz Feldhorn taught Polish literature in the Hebrew grammar school in Cracow. Brandstaetter taught in Warsaw, and Deborah Vogel at the Hebrew seminary in Lvov. Wilhelm Fallek was a member of the Lodz Society of Polonists, a coorganizer of *Prace polonistyczne* (Polonistic papers, which continues to appear to this day), and a teacher of Polish at the Jewish grammar school in Lodz. It is interesting to consult their scientific and popular-scientific Polonistic papers. [I] have in mind a few of the more substantial and larger texts.[133] Their authors were interested in particular problems, such as Jewish motifs in Polish literature, the part played in Polish literature by writers of Jewish origin, and Polish-Jewish cultural societies. Thus, generally speaking, they were primarily interested in the tradition of describing the Jewish world in Polish and in the tradition of its use by Jews as a literary tool. It is characteristic that they were especially attracted by the study of romantic literature, which endowed Jewish motifs and themes with a hitherto unencountered aesthetic value and historico-philosophical dimension and, at the same time, formed the core of the Polish tradition and a kind of "mystical key" to the Polish collectivity. It is intriguing that in his *Elegje podolskie,* one of the finest collections of Polish-Jewish poetry, described as the "lyrical geography of a small Jewish town," Pomer reverted to the tradition of regional romanticism by putting at the head of his collection an epigraph from Maurycy Gosławski's poem "Podole."

In the interwar years, acculturation seldom resulted in Polonization in the national sense of the term. With increasing frequency, it was connected with the sense of Jewish identity. There are different estimates of the dimensions of this phenomenon.[134] Celia Stopnicka Heller goes so far as to claim that, [during this] period, all attempts at assimilation were assimilation "without integration,"[135] and Aleksander Hertz tells in his bitter *Wyznania starego człowieka* (Confessions of an old man) of the painful de-Polonization, at that time, of people who had felt comfortable with Polishness for generations. Be that as it may, cultural proximity to things Polish was linked in Polish-Jewish circles with a feeling of national distinctness. In this connection, the most spectacular case is perhaps once more that of Brandstaetter. The grandson of a Hebrew writer, he completed his Polonistic studies with a doctoral dissertation on Mickiewicz as a critic of Polish literature. The bard was for him one of the Polish "national saints" who was also, in a special way, close to Jewry: as an offspring of Frankists,* as a believer in [Andrej] Towiański's teachings about "Israel, the older brother," and finally as . . . a precursor of Zionism. Thus in his literary program Brandstaetter combined homage to Mickiewicz and Kochanowski with the Zionist credo and loudly proclaimed his "conversion to Jewishness."

The combination of acculturation and affirmation of Jewish values and patterns yielded a new entity, hitherto unknown in Jewish life. The existence and spread in the interwar period of the cultural borderland open to Polish as well as to Jewish influences was an obvious fact. The Polish-Jewish press and Polish-Jewish literature belonged to just this area.

The mode of encounter of elements derived from the two cultural sources can be inferred from an analysis of the cultural journalism of the Polish-Jewish press. On the one hand, it supplied a great deal of information about Hebrew and Yiddish literatures, as well as about Jewish theater, sculpture, and film. It also published quite a few translations of Mendełe, Szołem Alejchem [Rabinowicz], Perec [Peretz], Friszman, An-ski, Bialik, Czernichowski, Grynberg, Mastbojm, Segałowicz, Horończyk, Perle, Lejwik, Opatoszu, Burla, Brenner, Manger, Bomse, Asz, and the Singer brothers [Israel Joshua and Isaac Bashevis]. As is well known, the extensive and varied supply of information about cultural activities in both Jewish languages was meant to serve a particular cause: it was linked

*Members of a mystical and messianic religious movement founded in Poland in the 18th century by Jakub Frank. The term also referred to their progeny. [Trans.]

with the didactic aims of the Polish-Jewish press, with its sui generis missionary activity among the circles that were Polonized culturally as well as nationally, and with its desire to bring Jewish culture closer to Polish society. On the other hand, the periodicals in question supplied Jewish readers with information about Polish literature, theater, and film.[136] When Brandstaetter and Szymel wrote that Zionist papers succumbed to the attractions of what was happening "beyond the Rubicon,"that is, about their vulnerability to the charms of Polish culture, they exaggerated, but their exaggeration was not unfounded. Their own paper, *Opinia,* was accused of not paying a great deal of attention to Jewish literature and of engaging instead in debates with Boy[-Żeleński] and Słonimski. . . . [137]

The evaluations of the new cultural forms differed, and the discussion of Polish-Jewish literature led to collisions of views, some of which were very extreme. Some branded Polish-Jewish writers as "Jewish nationalists of Polish culture" who "simplify their task in an all too obvious manner. To avoid carrying the burden of duties that flow from the notion of nationality, they follow . . . the line of least resistance and attach the national label to a false commodity,"[138] and they rejected Brandstaetter's demand that the "Jewish National Fund . . . should finance Polish poetry plied by 3–4 talented Jews."[139] Others accepted their works as the "emanation of that part of the national intelligentsia which, while staying with its nation, has assimilated linguistically to the point where the Polish language is its everyday cultural organ for the expression of thoughts and emotions" (Löw).[140]

The cultural options of Polish-Jewish writers, a topic of primary interest in this study, were distinctive. Even when these writers claimed, as did Stefan Pomer, that they "make a contribution to the treasury of Polish culture, they enrich and develop it,"[141] they definitely regarded themselves as a distinct Jewish group in Polish literature. In his 1934 review of Leon Pomirowski's well-known book *Nowa literatura w nowej Polsce* (New literature in the new Poland), Stefan Pomer wrote:

> There is not a word in this book that refers to the group of Polish-Jewish writers. And yet a historian of literature cannot but know that such a group of writers has emerged in the last few years. Its specific regional character (in the ethnic sense) is undoubtedly an interesting phenomenon that deserves attention from every point of view. After all, the Jewish group consists of a dozen or so writers, active in prose and in poetry, who express their membership in the Jewish nation in a manner that is new and unprecedented in Polish literature.[142]

We can interpret Pomer's statement as implying that this Jewish group was a kind of regional school in the national and cultural sense, rather than in the geographic sense.

There were some (Szymel, Löw, Pomeranz) who granted the Polish-Jewish literary output dual—namely Polish-Jewish—status. But even then, one concentrated on justifying its connections with Jewish culture. The clearest statement to this effect is found in Samuel Hirszhorn's article "Kongres Penklubów a pisarze żydowscy" (Congress of PEN Clubs and Jewish writers):

> When it comes to membership in the Jewish nation, the mature part of our society dropped the language criterion a long time ago. A person who feels that he belongs to this nationality is a national Jew regardless of whether he uses Yiddish, Hebrew, or the language of his non-Jewish environment. A similar attitude should, all the more, be adopted with respect to Jewish writers, because a Jewish writer not only feels that he belongs to the Jewish nation but also gives striking expression to his national feelings in his works. This fact has already been understood in politics and in cultural-professional associations of writers and journalists, of which "workers with the pen" in our country who write not only in Yiddish and Hebrew but also in Polish, are members. . . . The Jewish PEN Club in Poland must . . . represent Jewish literature that exists here in three languages.[143]

Arguments about the Form of Jewish Culture

The discussion about the possibilities and the conditions of existence of Jewish literature in Polish was at the same time a discussion about the conditions and the possibilities of existence of Jewish *culture* in Polish. One more issue, closely related to the central ones but not expressly stated, was the role of linguistically Polonized circles as creators of Jewish culture. Indeed, the campaign in the pages of *Opinia* was a kind of settling of accounts within the Polish-speaking Jewish intelligentsia. This group was getting more numerous and internally differentiated. It regarded itself as responsible for Jewish culture and tried to work out for it a new formulation which agreed with the post-Haskalah status quo. Seen in this light, the Polish-Jewish literary manifestos were simply an indication of the new cultural situation.

The "invasion" of Polish, so much talked about, was an irrefutable fact of the growing heterogeneity of Jewish culture, which was taking in and assimilating elements of the surrounding culture. The resulting entity was generally sensed to be new, distinct, and syncretic. It was described by the term "Polish-Jewish" culture and it was the focus of an intense debate. Some argued that "unfortunately, Polish-Jewish culture gained citizenship rights by usucaption" and deplored the fact that "instead of a single uniform national culture there come into being many new fragmentary and makeshift cultures that have nothing in common with the actual national culture."[144] Others objected to this idea, which suggested that the Jews are "a loose group . . . whose culture depends on the culture of the surrounding . . . society."[145] The discussion was complicated because it obviously confused two things, namely, a description of cultural facts with their—clearly ideological—evaluation.

The key issue was whether Jewish culture could also accommodate works written in non-Jewish languages. The two extreme positions among Polish-Jewish writers were the conception of a national Jewish culture identified with the Hebrew literary output and free of traces of the Diaspora, and the conception of a multilingual culture that did include traces of the Diaspora. More generally, the two competing conceptions were those of a pure culture and an open culture.

These conceptions treated and evaluated Jewish multilingualism differently. Each embodied a distinct sociolinguistic component. The circles which supported the national movement looked upon Hebrew as an important social value of symbolic character.[146] As a national language, it was to integrate the Jewish collectivity and be a sign of its ethnic distinctness and independence.[147] Be that as it may, in point of fact, the cultural system in Hebrew was the weakest of all [such] systems in interwar Poland. As Chone Shmeruk put it:

> Hebrew literature declined because it lacked writers as well as readers. There was no local Hebrew theater. Polish Jews were unable to support a daily Hebrew press, and not a single weekly managed to publish until the outbreak of World War ll. Only 12.6% of Jewish children of school age attended elementary Hebrew schools and only 6.2% of Jewish grammar-school students attended Hebrew grammar schools. There were no Hebrew postsecondary schools. The one exception was the Institute for Judaic Studies [Instytut Nauk Judaistycznych], which dealt with a limited number of disciplines.[148]

Even so, as an ideological Zionist postulate, the conception of a uniform Hebrew culture had many supporters among linguistically Polonized Jews. Especially in Galicia there were connections between small but prestigious groups that cultivated Hebrew culture and Jewish circles for whom Polish was the language "of choice."[149] The reason for this was the sometimes subconscious dislike of Yiddish as the "stigma of the Diaspora."[150]

It is reasonable to assume that considerations of this kind were the source of Brandstaetter's "Hebrewism." In his program for Polish-Jewish poetry, he wrote: "when a homogeneous Hebrew nation in the free land of Palestine will express its thoughts in the language of our biblical forebears, then we may become a sad document of the former Diaspora. . . . Then not a few may condemn us."[151] Szymel's position was diametrically opposite to Brandstaetter's. He fought against the "linguistic chauvinism" of the Hebraists. In his view, Jewish national literature comprised works in all the languages that Jews spoke throughout their history. This divergence of views led to different evaluations of Polish-Jewish literature. Brandstaetter regarded it as an abnormal and transitional phenomenon, whereas Szymel approved of it as a new but enduring and natural, even typical, fact of Jewish life.

Most of the participants in the debate in *Opinia* and *Nowy Dziennik* shared Szymel's ideas.[152] The reason was simple. The idea of a pure culture based on orthodox Hebraism undermined the position of the part of the intelligentsia that identified with Jewry but could pursue its cultural activities only in non-Jewish languages, and so this group found the idea of a multilingual culture familiar and attractive. Small wonder that in the end it triumphed in the pages of *Opinia.* To quote one of its readers who participated in the debate: "Polish-Jewish poetry . . . does not break up our culture; it extends and completes it. Whatever . . . Jews create, regardless of the language, all that is permeated with the Jewish spirit, belongs to our great, all-embracing national culture."[153]

It can hardly be denied that multilingualism emphasizes the heterogeneity of a culture. In the case of Jewish culture, those who looked for elements that would uniformize it frequently appealed to romantic and neoromantic views of culture as objectifying the national spirit. There are many studies, dating back to the turn of the century, of the influence of neoromanticism on Jewish thought.[154] But it is useful, at this point, to quote the definition of culture that appeared in the 1910 almanac of Galician Zionists: "the internal style, . . .the internal and external distinctness of manifestations, the totality of things that endow the life of a nation with its particular, invariably characteristic, cast that reflects the bright, albeit half conscious, expression of the same national psyche."[155] It is worth noting that already in the first decade of the twentieth century the same circles were suggesting that one should separate from Polish literature works written by Jews, and, after "penetrating the essence of the literary production of this group, one should distill some special element or elements characteristic of the Jewish mind."[156]

There is no doubt that neoromantic notions widely circulating during the interwar period clearly influenced contemporary evaluations of Jewish cultural activity in the Diaspora. The psychological approach to the latter was particularly widespread. Followers of this approach considered, for example, "the foundation and background of creative Jewish individuals who wrote in languages of different nations."[157] The most common conclusion of such analyses was the assertion that "the characteristic . . . mark of Jewish writing reveals itself in the spiritual products of Jewish creative individuals regardless of the topic and background."[158]

Maurycy Szymel was one of the Polish-Jewish writers who was especially fond of resorting to these ideas.[159] He defended the idea of a multilingual culture: "We are the most authentic emanation of the Jewish spirit, of its noble thirst for conquest and imperialism. And the Jewish spirit speaks all the languages of the world."[160] He presented his position most fully in the 1935 cycle of articles "Krajobraz duszy żydowskiej w liryce polskiej" (The landscape of the Jewish soul in Polish lyrical poetry), published in *Opinia*[161] as a polemical response to Chaim Löw's disquisition *Smok w słowiczym gnieździe: Żydzi w poezji Odrodzonej Polski* (1934). In it, Löw attacked the *endek* [derived from "ND," the initials of the (anti-Semitic) National Democratic Party—Trans.] actions of stigmatizing literary works as "crypto-Jewish" and "Jewish mimicry." He poked fun at the sounding of the alarm due to—as he ironically put it—the (Jewish) dragon's invasion of the (Polish) nightingale's nest. He argued in a factual manner that the ideas that the leader of the literary "self-defense," Karol Hubert Rostworowski, ascribed to the "Jewish spirit"—pacifism, urbanism, cosmopolitanism—were simply manifestations of the postwar atmosphere, and that authors of Jewish origin did not form an "anonymous great power" of poets but joined the trend of changes in Polish lyrical poetry. He ascribed the distinctness of Jewish writers ("they can be . . . easily singled out in the great pleiad of modern Polish poets")[162] to their social position and to the Jewish complex, which they manifested in different degrees. He thus ascribed this distinctness to sociological and psychological factors.

On the other hand, Szymel described the aim of his initiative as follows: "I am very much interested in the extent and manner of the penetration of Polish poetry by the Jewish spirit and in what new elements it brings to it. . . . It means nothing to me that many . . . writers are ashamed of their Jewishness. It is a question of race, which often appears against their will."[163]

In the atmosphere of the late thirties, greatly disturbed by chauvinism and *endek* shouts, Jewish circles, which essentially approved of Löw's dissertation, responded in a decidedly negative way to the position adopted by Szymel.[164] A discussion ensued. Löw asked: "Does Szymel think that replacing 'Nordic' by 'Hebrew' changes matters radically?"[165] In a three-part study titled *O tzw. cechach narodowych w literaturze pięknej* (On so-called national characteristics in belles-lettres), Izydor Berman argued against the category of "national soul" and the thesis that art is a sphere in which so-called national characteristics are manifested. "Psychology as a scientific discipline," he wrote, "does not recognize . . . supra-individual collective characteristics of nations. And analysis of works of art makes literary nationalism an untenable position."[166]

In addition to the neoromantic quest for the "fluid of Jewishness," there were other attempts to justify the conception of a multilingual open Jewish culture. New conceptions, initially submerged by the neoromantic position, were articulated with increasing vigor. Szymel argued with Brandstaetter and wrote not only about the Jewish spirit but also about the "spirit of Jewish history." The same category appeared frequently in the writings of Stefan Pomer. Both had in mind the unprecedented situation of the Jews as a non-territorial collectivity whose home was—the dispersion. That was why, they argued, "[t]he ideal of the modern nation and state is far from the ideal of Jewry."[167]

The appeal to history as the court that decides the form of national existence and culture was of key importance for this position. Since Jewish history is in a way unique, different from the history of other nations, Jewish culture must be conceived in terms of its indigenous special categories. There were historical and philosophical justifications of its multilingual characteristic. "If there can be Jewish literature in Aramaic and German why not in Polish? This enterprise is basically correct and even supported by our national tradition." This is how Chaim Löw evaluated the manifestos of Polish-Jewish literature.[168] From a historical perspective, Jewish multilingualism was an undeniable fact and Polish was one of the many languages used by Jews to create their cultural values. From a historico-philosophical perspective, multilingualism took on a special meaning for the historical mission of the Jews. Szymel wrote:

> Narrow linguistic nationalism was always foreign to the Jewish nation. By virtue of its dispersion, it continued its apostolic mission in all languages of the world! . . . By looking at the essence of Jewishness in this way, we see the phenomenon of assimilation in a different light. He who states the eternal truths of Jewishness in Greek is not an assimilationist. But he who writes in, say, Yiddish and denies the right to existence to a Jew who expresses his Jewishness in, say, Czech, is an assimilationist.[169]

We see that, however different their justifications, [these positions] shared a single aim, which was to regard Polish as a legitimate language of Jewish culture.

The resort to historico-philosophical arguments and the appeal to the idea of the mission of the Jews among the nations point to yet another important component of the view of Jewish culture as an open culture. What was also essential was the view of multilingualism as such. To its advocates, it was a kind of gift of languages, whereas the Hebraists regarded it as the curse of confusion.[170]

Reflection upon the peculiar character of the national modus vivendi in the Diaspora, and comprehension of the contemporary post-Haskalah cultural situation of the Jews in the Diaspora, led some beyond the acceptance of multilingualism to the recognition of heterogeneity as the natural state of Jewish culture. "Jewry is the 'Ukraine of nations' because it lives in the borderland of nations" was how some put it.[171] Thus "while other nations have more or less precisely defined geographic peripheries along which they have contacts with other nations (and thus with other national cultures) . . . we Jews, dispersed throughout the world, have such an abundance of peripheries that we have nothing but peripheries, that is, we live everywhere in "borderlands," and are everywhere insignificant minorities . . . we touch on foreign cultures everywhere."[172]

It has been the lot of the Jews to be permanently in contact with other cultures. It has been the lot of those Jews who do not isolate themselves from Europe and are not isolated from it to be open to the influence of European cultures. As Herbert Strauss might say,[173] acculturation is Jewish destiny.

In 1937, Polish-Jewish literary circles defined Jewish writing in Poland as "the whole literary output in Hebrew, Yiddish, and Polish created by Jews who have not lost contact with Jewishness in the national, social, or cultural sense, and for whom the problem of Jewish culture is the foundation of their worldview and of their artistic consciousness."[174] The author of this definition of trilingual Jewish literature was Roman Brandstaetter. Notwithstanding his "Hebraic fascinations," he was, in a way, consistent in his views on literature. The axiom underlying his conception was the conviction that Jewish literature consisted of the works of all writers who identified themselves nationally and culturally with Jewishness. He invariably emphasized the free and authentic choice of Jewishness made by the artist and not the language of his work. These emphases made it possible to look at Jewish literature as writing that went beyond the boundaries of a single closed language area.

This definition of a trilingual Jewish literature shows clearly that in the post-Haskalah period, in a culture that was becoming ever more modern and heterogeneous, "being a Jew" was becoming a matter of choice and of self-definition by the individual. It is likely that this insight was an important component of the awareness of many Jewish circles during the interwar period. In 1931, Ozjasz Thon, an eminent Cracow Zionist leader, wrote in an article titled "Znamiona narodowości" (Characteristics of nationality): "national affiliation is primarily

. . . an emotional matter based on a subjective feeling that follows from free choice."[175]

The modern Jewish historian Lucy Dawidowicz captures the evolution of models of Jewish identity in the last two centuries in a distinctive formula: "Jewish identity: a matter of fate, a matter of choice."[176] For Polish-Jewish writers, the question of choice she speaks about was of fundamental importance.[177]

It seems that when Polish-Jewish writers fought for the recognition of Polish as a fully legitimate language of a multilingual Jewish culture, they were close to the kind of thinking about the culture of the Jews in Poland recently proposed by Chone Shmeruk, a historian of Jewish culture and literature.[178] Indeed, the assumptions underlying his conception of a trilingual culture of Polish Jews, a polysystem based on Hebrew, Yiddish, and Polish, coincide with the ideas of that milieu, namely, the acceptance of Polish as a language of Jewish life and the vision of a modern, post-Haskalah, culture of the Jews as an open culture.

2

The Polish Aspect

Language as a Bridge

In interwar Polish-Jewish literary circles, Polish was regarded as a language of Jewish culture. They fully realized that, within the framework of Jewish culture, Polish was a special language because it opened Jewish culture to non-Jews and formed a bridge between the Jewish and Polish cultures. This fact was not taken lightly, nor was it passed over in silence.

It was impossible not to notice that the Jewish languages [Yiddish and Hebrew] played an important role in the creation and preservation of Jewish cultural and national distinctiveness.[1] Critics of this state of affairs were even prepared to claim that these languages were the foundation of Jewish "separatism" and formed a barrier that separated the Jews from Europe. Of course, it was not only the Jewish languages that erected the "Jewish wall." This "wall" undoubtedly protected and held together the Jewish Diaspora society, but just as undoubtedly separated that society from the non-Jewish milieu and so made the Jewish world inaccessible to it. The "wall" consolidated [Jewish society] and helped it survive, but it also made it foreign to the outside world.[2] The call to Jews to adopt "national languages" was one of the most important watchwords of groups promoting emancipation and enlightenment and opposing the elimination of Jews from the cultural, political, and social life of the lands of the Diaspora. These languages were viewed as bridges to the European world. It was hoped that their adoption would give the Jews access to European thought and civilization, promote their inclusion in the life of the lands of the Diaspora, and even—this was the most optimistic prognosis—bring about their integration into European societies. Thus the bridge of language was to be the foundation of the bridge of culture and the basis for new social bonds.

The circles that supported from the end of the eighteenth century onward the linguistic Polonization of the Jews[3] regarded the Polish language as an essential factor in the integration of the Jews into Polish society. They viewed the increase, after 1850, in the number of works written in Polish by Jewish authors as an indication of the desire for such integration and as an attempt to achieve it.

As early as the beginning of the nineteenth century, the idea arose that an attempt should be made to use literary works in Polish to educate the Jewish masses. Some nineteenth-century authors who used Jewish themes found it necessary to emphasize that their works were didactical through and through and were aimed at Jewish readers. In the introduction to *Lejbe i Sióra* (Lejbe and Sióra; 1821), Julian Ursyn Niemcewicz wrote: "Every reasonable orthodox Jew who will read this small work will admit that the superstitions pointed out in it are faithfully lifted from the Talmud and from commentaries on it."[4] That Niemcewicz's contemporaries regarded such attempts as rhetorical and utopian is clear from the following description by one of them of the inadequate knowledge of Polish, typical of Jews at the beginning of the nineteenth century:

> They [the Jews] lived in their native country like newly arrived foreigners unable to read items that were sometimes of the greatest importance for them. It is easy to see that this resulted in great inconvenience and often in losses. It was extremely rare for one of them to have learned by chance to read and write Polish. Such a person was regarded as very learned and conversant with lay matters, although he was not really very different from the common people. Other orthodox Jews thought that this art is extremely difficult and virtually inaccessible.[5]

It is clear, then, that even if Niemcewicz's works contained didactic messages aimed at inhabitants of the shtetl, Hasidim, and the Jewish populace, they could not possibly reach them and have the desired enlightening effect for the simple reason that the language of these groups was Yiddish. While many Jews spoke Polish, few read it, because of a religiously motivated aversion to the Latin alphabet.[6]

This state of affairs still prevailed in the eighties, when Klemens Junosza (Szaniawski) charged journalists writing for *Izraelita* with having an unrealistic image of their readers and harboring illusions as to the enlightening effect of the newspaper on the Jewish masses.[7] Nevertheless, Junosza himself was convinced that his satirical works could have the effect of turning small-town Rothschilds or Dogpatch Jankels into citizens. . . . [8]

But most writers recognized cultural realities and—like Eliza Orzeszkowa—wrote for Polish readers and "for Israelite society in the largest cities of the country made up of educated gentlemen and scholars in the intellectually most demanding professions, and ladies whose charm, elegance, and wit often match those of the most outstanding women of other societies," and appealed to them to offer those leaving the ghetto a "sincere, prompt, brotherly hand of friendship and help."[9] This excerpt from the introduction to *Meir Ezofowicz* (1878) proves that even in the early eighties the literary public was, in the main, restricted to the Polish milieu and to the small circle of the assimilated Jewish elite. Reading Wilhelm Feldman's *Żydziak* (Jewboy), which appeared a decade later (1889), one is bound to arrive at a similar conclusion. While the author does not disclose his view of the potential reader of his novel as openly as Orzeszkowa, this view nevertheless emerges just as clearly from the book's tendentious foreword. When Niemcewicz, with the Jewish reader in mind, described the vicissitudes of the emancipated Lejbe, he was framing a positive model to be emulated by the young who found the ghetto stifling. Feldman proceeded very differently. The story he tells is a harsh indictment of those who caused the defeat of his hero, the "dreamer from the ghetto," after his flight to the longed-for outside world.

The narrative strategy of relevant nineteenth-century texts leaves no doubt as to which readers were being addressed. Their authors spoke of the Jewish world as a "cultural reality different from the [cultural] reality of the recipient,"[10] as of a foreign world. These authors commented on, explained, and presented realities in a manner that made it obvious that they assumed their readers' ignorance of that world.

There is no doubt that the poetics of the Jewish theme should be researched. It is of intrinsic interest and it can shed light on more general theoretical problems in the area of literary communication, and especially on the problem of the image of the reader and of his competence as an important factor in the construction of a text.[11]

The existence of a cultural barrier in representations of the Jewish world in Polish was a simple consequence of [an inescapable] fact: the language of the description was different from that of the described. Description [thus entailed] a kind of cultural translation: values and categories had to be coordinated, terms and concepts explained. In addition to the question of language, there was the question of the putative image of the reader. Both forced the narrator to adopt the role of a guide in an unknown realm. Malwina Meyersonowa's *Z ciasnej sfery* (From a narrow class; 1878) provides an excellent illustration of this assumed incompetence on the part of the reader. All categories of Jewish culture required in a realistic description are first named in Yiddish and immediately translated into

Polish in the main text; some of them are extensively annotated, and these annotations form a kind of subsidiary text of the novel,[12] its cultural commentary.

The fact that, until the end of the nineteenth century, few Jews [in Poland] could read Polish had serious consequences for Jewish authors writing in Polish. When they chose topics from Jewish life, they could not but be aware that they were primarily addressing Polish readers, and that for this readership such works had the quality of a Jewish self-portrait—a well-known term due to [the modern literary critic] Jan Błoński. Projects for the creation of "Polish-Israelite literature" that began to appear after 1850 contain quite a few explicit references to this "foreign" readership. The earliest initiative of this kind was mentioned previously. It was Adolf Jakub Cohn's idea of forming a "society for the cultivation of Polish-Israelite literature." Cohn's suggestion appeared in his introduction to the novel *Zbawca* (The savior), which he translated from the German. In this introduction Cohn publicized the idea of a Polish-Jewish rapprochement through literature:

> I dare claim that for a true union to take place, for the more or less explicit demarcation line to disappear, the brothers must get to know each other thoroughly, each must penetrate to the depth of the heart of the other, must overhear the beating of the other's pulse, must learn to read in the other's soul. . . .
>
> I think that the best, if not the only, way to realize our relatedness is to merge our thoughts, to unbosom ourselves before our countrymen through the medium of written works, through literature. I claim that there cannot, and will not, be mutual trust until our Christian compatriots will have acquired precise knowledge of our history in this land, until we can prove to them, by means of a detailed written image of our past and present family and social life, that even in the past, in moments of horrible suffering, we had not ceased to wish this our fatherland well, and that it was our limited range of activity and not debility or ill will that prevented us from bending every effort to the general welfare. . . . Therefore, if we truly desire unity, if we want to be of the flesh and blood of the nation, then we must enthusiastically cultivate its literary field and add our widow's mite to the great treasury of Polish life!
>
> Let us apply ourselves to the task of discovering and unearthing monuments of our past that are bound to exist throughout the lands of the Lechs [legendary ancestors of the Poles], the stage on which it was acted out. . . . [W]e shall find them if we but learn to look for them. . . . Let us create and describe images of the family and social life of our people, its customs, superstitions, and prejudices, and let us not forget its fables and stories, which sometimes depict so characteristically and strikingly the fate, the oppression, and the life of Jews in the past. Let us describe it all truthfully, faithfully, without hiding anything.[13]

Cohn's argument seems typical of the thinking of the first Jewish writers who wrote in Polish when they discussed the literature that utilized Jewish themes. Similar ideas occur in, for example, the essays of Zygmunt Librowicz, first published in *Izraelita* and then issued in book form with the title *Z wrażeń kapociarza* (From the impressions of a capote wearer; 1878). While encouraging Jews writing in Polish to depict the Jewish environment, Librowicz limited the role of such works to what may be called the "self-representational function." It was this function that was to be the basis for the social mission of such works, a mediating mission whose major role was to fight the misconceptions, biases, and stereotypes that Poles had about Jews.[14]

Given the nineteenth-century cultural realities, the self-representational function, or the clearly self-representational intention, harbored a considerable element of danger. In fact, it rendered the success of the mission of "Polish-Israelite literature" questionable. The element of danger was implicit in the advice offered to Jews and to Polish-Jewish writers by Michał Sawicki, a supporter of Polonization and the author of a small work titled *Żydzi, ich dzieje ze względu na stan obecny Polski mieszkańców wyznania mojżeszowego* (The Jews, their history in view of the present state of the inhabitants of Poland who are of the Mosaic persuasion; 1865). According to Sawicki, the adoption of Polish by the Jews would open to Poles the hitherto hermetically sealed Jewish world: "Let the Polish Jews speak Polish, let them not differ from their countrymen, and let them not provide the slightest opportunity for being regarded as a nation within a nation. For then the Jews will cease to be an unfamiliar people and will no longer prompt us to conjectures that often make us think ill of them."[15]

As for Polish-Jewish writers, Sawicki claimed that the best means of promoting understanding was Jewish literature in Polish [specifically] intended for Jewish readers, to which Poles would also have access. "If there appeared a Jewish literature in Polish, who could possibly say that the author of a work intended for Jews failed to tell the truth,"[16] argued Sawicki. What was implicit in his recommendations was that he regarded depictions of the Jewish milieu written by authors of Jewish origin and addressed to Polish readers as untrustworthy. Indeed, Polish readers would be inclined to suspect that these creations were tendentious and apologetic. It is striking and thought-provoking that the first Polish authors who came from Jewish circles—Julian Klaczko, Aleksander Kraushar, Henryk Merzbach—quickly abandoned "Zionist" poems. The attempts by Józef Goldszmit, A[dolf] J[akub] Cohn, and Malwina Meyersonowa to write prose works were continued much later by Wilhelm Feldman and Aniela Kallas [Korngut]. One of the heroes of Aniela Kallas's novel *On i oni wszyscy* (He and all of them; 1910) complained that Polish cultural opinion rejected the Jewish writer who used Jewish themes. There is a solid basis for the view that the failure of such nineteenth-century literary works was brought about by the indifferent response of the Polish literary public. The writers in question were fully aware of this. In 1901 Cohn returned to the project he had launched forty years earlier in an article titled "Nasz dorobek literacki" (Our literary assets): "He who writes about specifically Jewish matters, he who is sensitive to charges brought against Jews and tries to confute them, is likely to see himself cut off from the rest of the literary brotherhood and ignored by the reading public and is likely to find himself one morning the butt of taunts in some anti-Semitic rag."[17]

The interwar period realized, in a certain sense, the dreams of the assimilationists. Jews actually began to use the "national" language in everyday discourse.[18] But all the phenomena that accompanied the progress of linguistic Polonization negated assimilationist prognoses. The predictions about the integrating mission of European languages proved deceptive and false: emancipation, assimilation, and acculturation were not greeted by European nations with approval and goodwill. Be that as it may, after the Haskalah, the cultural situation of Jewish circles changed radically (see the previous chapter) and writing in the "national language" became extremely popular. Under the new conditions it had new, previously unknown functions. On the other hand, the old function, while weaker, did not disappear.

The most important factor shaping the new circumstances was the new public reading works by Jewish authors writing in Polish. This public differed fundamentally from the public of the time of Klaczko, Kraushar, or even Feldman. Linguistic Polonization of Jewish circles was ever more prevalent and, to judge by the existence of a Jewish daily press in Polish, in the interwar period, there existed a large Jewish public that read Polish. The fact that the readers of Szymel and Brandstaetter came largely from linguistically Polonized circles did not incline Polish-Jewish writers to give up the aim of reaching Polish readers. Rather, all signs indicate that these writers' desire to reach Polish readers was strong and conscious but its motivation was different from that of Cohn and Librowicz.

The different motivation was clearly related to the birth of the modern Jewish national consciousness. The faith in the value of what the Jewish world could offer Europe, the conviction of the equivalence of the partners in Polish-Jewish cultural contacts, the propagandistic enthusiasm that accompanied the development of the Zionist movement—all these lay behind the ambitious and serious initiatives toward a Polish-Jewish cultural rapprochement that issued from Zionist, or at least pro-Zionist, circles during the interwar period. No comparable initiatives could have come from the nineteenth-century supporters of the Haskalah or of assimilation. As a result of the growth in popularity of the idea of cultural Zionism and of the progress of Jewish national consciousness, Polish-Jewish contacts clearly acquired a new quality and were transacted in a new plane. The new version of the nineteenth-century watchword of understanding through literature and art, which was revived in the twenties by older Polish-Jewish writers, could be regarded as a sign of the times. This was no longer a call for expurgated [*ad usum Delphini*] creations, a call to create images of the Jewish world that would, in some way, assist assimilation and integration. Now it was a question of the Polish language making Jewish literature a familiar part of Polish culture. The Jewish literature in question was primarily literature in Yiddish, regarded as a reflection of Jewish life or of "the Jewish soul," a reflection worthy of inclusion in a broadly interpreted European cultural tradition.

The resulting translation activity deserves closer attention for a number of reasons. First, it preceded the flowering of Polish-Jewish literature and supplemented, or substituted for, original Polish-Jewish writing that was neither plentiful nor distinguished in the twenties. Second, the translations showed clearly that, as a result of the linguistic Polonization of the Jews, Polish-Jewish literary contacts took new, hitherto unknown, forms. That the initiative was due to the Jewish side came as no surprise to careful observers of these contacts: the conviction of the inferiority of Jewish culture, the pronounced dislike of Yiddish, the belief that Hebrew was infinitely difficult and esoteric were all deeply rooted in Polish society. In fact, before and during the interwar period the translators were exclusively Jews. (When Klemens Junosza, the apparent exception to this rule, adapted the novels of Mendełe, he made use of Russian translations.)[19] But this was the first time that Jews had undertaken a systematic publishing program.

What is rather paradoxical is that this action was to some extent influenced by the "Jewish fashion" that existed in France in the twenties. News from France quickly reached the shores of the Vistula, and translations of the works of the brothers Tharand, of Pierre Benoit, and of Jacques de Lacretelle could be read in Polish soon after their publication in France.[20] Their novels were addressed to Western readers and some of them (for example, the novels of the Tharaud brothers [Jérôme and Jean]) represented East-European Jewish life in the most fantastic and exotic colors. The Poles were informed about a world that was a step away via . . . Paris! In 1922, when discussing one of the translations from the French, Mojżesz Kanfer dreamed of Jewish literature and art "building a bridge of understanding" in a different way, namely, through direct Polish-Jewish contacts, without the mediation of Western fashions.[21]

Such contacts were to be facilitated by Biblioteka Pisarzy Żydowskich (Library of Jewish writers), advertised by the publishing house Safrus, and by Biblioteka Pisarzy i Klasyków Żydowskich (Library of Writers and Jewish Classics) of the publishing house Orient. Their creation was also explained by the need to launch a kind of "apostolic" mission in thoroughly assimilated circles, but this was certainly not the only motive. All cultural activity of Jews in Polish—Jewish culture in Polish—could promote intergroup contacts. Without being a national community, Poles and Jews were becoming a linguistic one.

The significance of this fact was appreciated in Polish-Jewish literary circles. Andrzej Marek spoke about the Polish spectator in the Polish-Jewish theater.[22] In terms of readers, Polish-Jewish literature had a double "reader address." With Polish readers in mind, Safrus was advertised as a publishing house "whose success can contribute substantially to showing the Jewish soul as it is represented in the mirror of Jewish writing, not embellished by a philo-Semitic tendency and not soiled—a much more common occurrence—by anti-Semitic expediency."[23] Some thought that literature—more precisely, a cultural rapprochement through literature—could be a first step toward a political understanding. This is why they criticized the choice of translated works published by Biblioteka Pisarzy Żydowskich as improper, as tending to dazzle with exoticism and sensationalism, and as devoid of serious intellectual aspirations.[24]

It seems that the faith in the conciliatory mission of literature that animated nineteenth-century *maskil*s, their characteristic utopia of "salvation through art," was not abandoned by Jewish circles throughout the interwar period. The publishing activity of Safrus gained the support of the very important and popular prose writer Shalom Asz (many of whose works were translated into Polish).[25] But this enterprise ran into many obstacles and, especially during the thirties, the number of new volumes grew irregularly. Nevertheless, the conviction of the mission of literature in intergroup contacts remained strong. Despite the tremendous intensification of anti-Semitic sentiments, in 1938, Zusman Segałowicz (an eminent prose writer and Yiddish poet) renewed the call for "systematic preparatory work that would make our literature more accessible to Polish society. What is needed is not knowledge of Judaism, not rabbinical and old literature, but modern literature, a mirror of our time."[26] Barbara Lewit, a journalist and translator working for *Nasz Przegląd,* maintained that "a Jewish book in Polish is synonymous with cultural rapprochement, a weapon in the fight against anti-Semitism."[27]

How much one counted on Polish readers in all translation activities undertaken at the time is attested by, say, the introduction to Samuel Hirszhorn's *Antologia poezji żydowskiej* (Anthology of Jewish poetry; 1921), and by the many advertisements, notices, and reviews that greeted the successive volumes of the Biblioteka [Pisarzy Żydowskich] published by Safrus. In one such review, Andrzej Marek wrote:

> When we meet in the common hallway, on the stairs, or at the entrance gate we look at each other like strangers.
>
> So:
>
> —Let's build glass houses!
>
> Agreed? Fine. Take a look at the interiors of our homes through the glass walls of our literature and you will see our life as it is, in the very essence of its deepest truth of which we have no reason to be ashamed. . . . In the past we did not know each other, for our literatures were for each other like two closed books.[28]

We see that Marek's interpretation extracts and emphasizes mainly the social significance of the translation enterprise. Even if the envisioned rapprochement is not—to use assimilationist phraseology—that of "sons of the same land," it is nevertheless a rapprochement of neighbors inhabiting the same land, the same street, and the same house. The most important task of Jewish literature functioning in the dress of the Polish language is to show Jewish life to Poles. Language, to use Marek's term, plays here the role of glass walls that contain and, at the same time, disclose the interior of the Jewish world, of glass walls that do away with the hitherto impermeable nature of Jewish life for Polish observers.

The desire for rapprochement and for cultural and national understanding also came to the fore in manifestos of Polish-Jewish literature. Members of Polish-Jewish literary circles had a clear appreciation of the role of the Polish language in shaping the relations between the two groups, relations developing in a changed cultural situation. By becoming a language of Jewish culture and literature, Polish no longer served the interests of integration or emancipation. Instead, it became a medium for the articulation of Jewish life in a manner as natural as that of other languages used by Jewish writers, and thus could contribute to greater understanding between the two national groups.

Polish-Jewish literature was also supposed to contribute to such understanding or rapprochement. Here an emphatic voice was that of the prose writer Adam Madler who broadened Brandstaetter's program by adding the point about the mission of Polish-Jewish literature to the Polish public. In his view, this literature could transmit to the Polish public the truth about Jewish life, its values and ideals, and explain the Zionist rationale.

Bronisław Mayer had a similar view of the task of a Jewish poet writing in Polish:

> And I continue to build, indefatigably,
> A bridge between the Diaspora Jew and the Aryan

And am the one who lights the dullness
of the unenlightened Aryans with the Palestinian sun.
("Pieśń o poecie żydowskim" [Song
about a Jewish poet])[29]

Apropos of the Polish "reader address" of Polish-Jewish works, when such a work contained translations of specialized Hebrew terms on the *halutz* movement (as was the case with Lucjan Krasucki's small volume of poems, in which they formed a small dictionary added to the volume), or translations of longer Hebrew items in the text (for example, Polish versions of many Hebrew songs in the novels of R[ubin] Feldszuh), they could be regarded as useful for Jewish as well as non-Jewish readers unfamiliar with the problems of Jewish pioneers in Palestine, or for readers without a substantial knowledge of Hebrew. But some Polish-Jewish works included explanations of the simplest cultural motifs, and these were certainly included for the benefit of Polish readers alone. Some of these explanations were also included in volumes of poetry, and their form proves conclusively that they were intended for Polish readers: elul—"the Jewish month of repentance before the new year," shofar—"a horn blown after [certain] prayers," Sambatyon—"a legendary Jewish river."[30]

During the interwar period, the slogan of a Polish-Jewish rapprochement through art had eminent Polish supporters such as Boy[-Żeleński]. Boy noted, and valued highly, the activity of Andrzej Marek's theater and saw in it substantial social values:

> He [Andrzej Marek] wants to create a kind of theater at the borderland; to get the Jewish masses into the Polish theater and to get us interested in the Jewish theater with advantages to both sides. . . . There is hardly any need to emphasize how much we should be in favor of this activity and how desirable it is. It is high time to put the question of "international" relations on a sincere and loyal basis. Possible friction in other areas notwithstanding, it is the task of literature and art to build bridges of mutual understanding.[31]

Clearly, this review of the play *Małka Szwarcenkopf* (performed in the Teatr "Nowości" ["Novelties" Theater] in 1929) contained ideas very close to the ideas of the people centered around the Biblioteka Pisarzy Żydowskich. For them, the older Polish-Jewish writers, Boy was a true and important authority not just in matters of artistic life, and Kanfer or Fallek frequently supported and propagated his views in the Polish-Jewish press. His friendly pronouncements were immediately received with joy on the Jewish side and he was frequently quoted.[32]

Boy returned on a number of occasions to the idea of the need to establish cultural relations and to the mission of art as a bridge for mutual understanding. Writing about a performance of I[cchak] L[ejb] Perec's *Nocą na starym rynku* (At night in the old market square) by the famous *Trupa Wileńska* (The Wilno troupe) he asked: "Given that we live next to one another, does it make sense to know so little about each other, to be such total strangers? We often produce trivial and poor plays from anywhere in the world and do absolutely nothing to get to know the soul of a nation we are destined to live with."[33]

Such truth about Polish-Jewish cultural relations was not very popular among Poles, who disguised their conviction of the superiority of their own heritage and their dislike of Jewish culture (especially Jewish folk culture) with charges that the latter was esoteric and inaccessible precisely because of the language barrier. That such an attitude could lead neither to cooperation nor to a rapprochement is proved by Henryk Galle's 1905 article "Żydzi w beletrystyce dzisiejszej" (Jews in modern belles lettres), which described the attitude of Poles to Jewish literature in these words: "What is hidden in this dark and universally inaccessible literature, what seeds it sows in a fertile soil we neither know nor are able to know. And no one can demand that we should learn Hebrew or the jargon [Yiddish] in order to find out."[34]

The dissonance between the positions of Galle and Boy is obvious. It must be stated with all clarity that during the interwar period Boy's pronouncement (extremely honest in its evaluation of the state of cultural contacts and of the reasons for this state) was an isolated event. Even *Wiadomości Literackie* (Literary news), Boy's main ideological ally, adopted a rather negative attitude toward Jewish culture exemplified by its dismissing a volume of short stories *Płomienie i zgliszcza* (Flames and embers), translated from the Yiddish, with the epithet "provincialism and nationalism."[35] Small wonder that, in 1929, Henryk Adler wrote with bitter irony about the hypothetical route from Jewish writers to Polish readers: "They will begin to translate Singer into all languages, including Polish (but this will happen only after Singer will have achieved popularity in China)."[36] In this connection it should be noted that, many years later, Czesław Miłosz drew a similar picture of this route when describing, in *Rodzinna Europa* (Native Europe), his own reading experience: Jewish literature created in his native Wilno reached him in the form of English translations when he was already an émigré.

It is clear that, given the catastrophic state of cultural contacts, all writing by Jews in Polish—the press, the theater, literature—could (regardless of its purposes and functions in Jewish circles) serve as an important means of positive communication with the Polish side. An additional reason for assigning this task to Polish-Jewish literature was the conviction that the image of Jewish life was oversimplified and falsely construed by "the Polish side." Literature supplied many proofs of this. A logical consequence of this conviction was the postulate that the basic mission of Polish-Jewish literature on the Polish side must be to present a true and authentic image of the Jewish world. This is an abbreviated version of the reasoning behind Szymel's slogan "A true novel about true Jews can only be written by a true Jew,"[37] and behind Samuel Hirszhorn's assertion that "Given our conditions, a Polish novel with a Jewish background written by a Jew is not just a literary event but also a social one. It is intended not only for the Jewish but also for the Polish public which does not know us Jews or, worse still, knows us only from anti-Semitic caricatures."[38]

Thus Polish-Jewish literary circles believed that, for the Polish reader, the value of their creations was primarily cognitive. This is most evident in pronouncements about prose writings, commonly regarded as unique social documents. If an author belonged to the world being presented and indicated this in some way, then this was viewed as a proof of the truth and authenticity of the work in question, as a way of underlining that "writing about Jewish matters the author is solving . . . not just the problems of others but his own as well."[39]

Polish-Jewish critics and writers were of the opinion that the adoption of such a position by writers endowed literary works with documentary value. Thus, in his review of Adam Madler's *Falista linia* (Wavy line), Chaim Löw wrote:

> We sense here not just a struggle with the plot and the rich material but also the wounding battle of one of the heroes for his own worldview. And the author's identification with the novel's heroes (of course, we have in mind not the stylized heroes of the novel but their actual social counterparts) lends it the character of a document written in Polish and thus also intelligible to those who read only works written in Polish.[40]

Stefan Pomer adopted a similar view in his review of the novel *Ludzie którzy jeszcze żyją* (People who are still living) by Czesława Endelman-Rosenblatt:

> Considering Polish conditions, this book is . . . quite exceptional. While describing Jews the author does not separate herself from them but identifies with them. . . . Of course, such an artistic attitude yields results of persuasive sincerity and truth. Because of it, *Ludzie którzy jeszcze żyją* is transformed from a more or less well-written book into a true socio-literary document.[41]

True, these statements contain echoes of the pronouncements of Cohn or Librowicz. But these are just echoes, and not repetitions of nineteenth-century ideas. This is so because the development of Polish-Jewish literature no longer depended exclusively on Polish readers but primarily on a new group of readers that came into being in the interwar period and consisted mainly of Jewish graduates of elementary schools in which the language of instruction was Polish. Located in the cultural borderland, Polish-Jewish literature had a clear awareness of its twofold readership and of its role as a bridge, permanently connecting the Polish and Jewish worlds.

Facing Polish Literary Life

Awareness of the dual reader address of Polish-Jewish literature was one indication of the recognition by Polish-Jewish writers of the multifaceted nature of Polish-Jewish literature. For one thing, this literature developed at the intersection of Polish and Jewish influences. For another, Polish, the language [the literature] relied on, not only led to Polish readers, but also determined the institutional framework of its functioning and its artistic relations, such as its connections with institutions of Polish literary life, its (partial) rootedness in the Polish tradition, and its dependence on the forces controlling the contemporary Polish literary market.

Even the most zealous apologists for Polish-Jewish literature spoke during the interwar period about its Polish aspect. While emphasizing its Jewish face, they did not ignore its Polish reverse. For example, Chaim Löw, who regarded Polish as a legitimate Jewish language, and who welcomed the program of Polish-Jewish literature as a natural and necessary manifestation of cultural changes, asked: "Who of us can, with a clear conscience, call Jewish the works of the poets who consciously assert their Jewishness, who call themselves Polish-Jewish poets?"[42] Thus in the essay *Smok w słowiczym gnieździe* (Dragon in a nightingale's nest, which contains the lines just quoted), he discussed the poetry of Szymel and Brandstaetter—next to the poetry of Tuwim, Słonimski, Wittlin, Peiper, Stern, Wat, Łazowertówna, Kragen, and Mortkowiczówna—as part of the contribution "of Jews to the poetry of Reborn Poland."

Stefan Pomer consistently called attention to the Polish aspect of Polish-Jewish writing. He regarded Polish-Jewish writers as a kind of Jewish school in Polish literature, a school distinguished by a special regionalism that he very clearly viewed as a manifestation of cultural distinctiveness. It was undoubtedly this distinctiveness that Pomer had in mind when he wrote about the "new and unparalleled tone" with which Polish-Jewish writers enriched "the treasure of Polish literature."

[For his part,] Brandstaetter, then an orthodox supporter of Hebrew, excluded Polish-Jewish literature from the future national Jewish culture largely because of Polish "accretions," which he regarded as a considerable flaw. He also emphasized the connection between Polish-Jewish writing and the institutions of Polish literary life, primarily publishing and criticism. He even spoke of "dependence" rather than of "connection." In line with his classicist temperament, he pointed to the Polish tradition this writing presumably [drew upon] namely, the tradition represented by Kochanowski and Mickiewicz.

It should be noted that Brandstaetter's poetry, [however] subordinated [it may have been] to purely Zionist tendencies, at times served critics as proof of the coexistence of Polish and Jewish elements in Polish-Jewish writing. For example, Ozjasz Tillemann claimed that the Polishness of Brandstaetter's Zionist poems "utterly belied the prating of the nationalist rabble run wild."[43] [Tilleman] had in mind primarily, but not exclusively, the language of the author of *Królestwo trzeciej świątyni* (The kingdom of the third temple): the masterfully elaborated classical (or pseudo-classical, as some said) lines that revealed his profound attachment to the Polish word, to the Czarnolesie lips of his muse.

The issue of the dependence of Polish-Jewish literature on the institutions of Polish literary life, an issue raised by Brandstaetter, merits attention and some discussion. An analysis of such institutional ties can show the connections that Polish-Jewish literature had with Polish literary life and the place it occupied in the latter.

Literary life includes "all institutions . . . that form a framework for the activity and mutual relations of persons interested in literature, such as writers, critics, readers, publishers, and patrons."[44] Such institutions appear only after a certain stage of cultural evolution is reached. Thus one can speak of the existence of literary life "only when most contacts in literary communication are intermediary and formal."[45] At this stage we have the producer, the intermediary institutions, and the consumer. Here [I] will discuss briefly the intermediary institutions common to Polish and Polish-Jewish literary life, using the classification proposed by Janusz Maciejewski.[46] I think that, of the relevant institutions the most important were (1) institutions that transcribed literary works and furnished the technical means for their transmission, primarily publishing houses and the press; (2) censorship; (3) institutions that formed opinion [, primarily] literary criticism.

Publishing Houses

Clearly, Polish-Jewish literature had to be associated with publishers who produced Polish rather than Yiddish or Hebrew materials. As a result of the growing popularity of Polish there came into being independent, separate Polish-Jewish publishing houses (e.g. Safrus, Orient, Menora, Wschód, Nowy Wschód, Judaica). It should be noted that Jews traditionally played a significant role in publishing and in the book market.[47]

Was the connection between Polish-Jewish literature and Polish publishing houses "forced" (due to the lack of Jewish publishers or their unimportance) or natural, due to the common language? Here the following facts are relevant. Polish-Jewish writers could associate with small provincial printing houses or (frequently Jewish) publishers, but preferred to work with large, prestigious metropolitan firms known as publishers of Polish literature. (Only the poets of Wzlot (Upward flight) remained faithful to the Stanisławów publishers Przyjaciel (Friend) and Julia Bodek.) Thus Ferdynand Hoesick published the works of Szymel, Pomer, Brandstaetter, and Madler; Gebethner i Wolff, those of Brandstaetter; and *Rój* (Beehive), those of Lewittes.[48]

Copies of Polish-Jewish poetry and prose books from the collection of the Biblioteka Narodowa (National Library) were stamped by the government commissioners of Warsaw. Noted in the stamps was the size of each edition. Here are some of these figures: Maurycy Szymel, *Powrót do domu:* 600 copies, *Skrzypce przedmieścia:* 300, *Wieczór lyriczny:* 600; Anda Eker, *Na cienkiej strunie:* 500, *Melodia chwili:* 500, *Ojców dzieje:* 500; Syda Richter, *Wiry:* 500; Daniel Ihr, *Pożegnanie młodości:* 300; Minka Silberman, *W cieniu życia:* 300; Henryk Adler, *Ariela i Jubal: Palestyńskie opowieści romantyczne:* 2,000; Józef Hartblaj, *Jehoszua: Powieść osnuta na tle "chaluców":* 1,160. These figures show that, during the interwar period, the sizes of the editions of Polish-Jewish literary works were much the same as those of Polish literary works.[49]

The Press

As already mentioned, Polish-Jewish literature was at first closely connected with the Polish-Jewish press. Its "emancipation" began around 1928. Nevertheless, the Polish-Jewish press remained the most important institution of Polish-Jewish literary life. It was a stable daily press that continued to publish throughout the interwar period. When someone wrote for such a paper, he was making a choice of readers and declaring his national and cultural identity. Writers such as [Julian] Tuwim and [Antoni] Słonimski appeared in *Chwila, Nowy*

Dziennik, and *Nasz Przegląd* only when interviewed or when their articles in the Polish press—primarily *Wiadomości Literackie* and *Skamander*—were reprinted. Chone Shmeruk describes the importance of an author's choice of publisher as follows:

> In independent Poland, what most distinguished and determined the Jewish intentions of Jewish writers who wrote in Polish was the place, or places, where they published their works. If a writer published for the most part in Polish-Jewish papers and journals. . . , then it is easy to see that [his works] could not reach the broad Polish public and were not intended to reach it; it is quite clear that they were meant to reach the Jewish public.[50]

The importance of the division of the writers under discussion into those connected with the Polish-Jewish press and those not so connected is attested by the complaint of Mieczysław Braun that "*Skamander* set down the condition for one of its writers [he later disclosed that *he* was the writer in question] that if he wanted his poetry to appear in that monthly then he had to cease printing in a Jewish paper."[51]

Clearly, Polish-Jewish writers were not satisfied with the support of the Polish-Jewish press. Indeed, they very gladly went beyond it. On the one hand, doing so was an attempt to extend their circle of readers and to change its cultural profile. On the other hand, the numerous, willingly established—simultaneous—connections with the Polish-Jewish and Polish presses attested the proximity of the spheres represented by the two kinds of newspapers, the proximity of Jewish culture in Polish to Polish culture.

Value judgments notwithstanding, publication in the Polish press was an activity "on the other shore." How tempting it was is proved by the fact that all of the more eminent Polish-Jewish poets and critics, such as Szymel, Pomer, Brandstaetter, Eker, Dresdner, Fallek, Berman. . . , published in Polish newspapers. Their writings appeared in *Skamander, Wiadomości Literackie, Sygnały, Okolica Poetów* (Poets' region), *Głos Prawdy Literackiej* (Voice of literary truth), *Lwowskie Wiadomości Muzyczne i Literackie* (Lvov musical and literary news), *Głos Literacki* (Literary voice), *Bluszcz* (Ivy), *Tygodnik Ilustrowany* (Illustrated weekly), *Albo-Albo* (Either-or), *Bunt młodych* (Rebellion of the young), *Gazeta Polska* (Polish gazette), *Czas* (Time), *Dziennik Lwowski* (Lvov daily), *Nowa Reforma* (New reform), *IKC, Comoedia,* and *Przegląd Mody* (Fashion review).[52] This shows that they published in the journals of Polish literary groups (*Skamander, Okolica Poetów),* in modern literary magazines (*Wiadomości Literackie),* in illustrated magazines of the older variety (*Bluszcz, Tygodnik Ilustrowany),* and in the daily newspapers of various orientations ranging from newspapers of the "Sanacja" regime (*Gazeta Polska*) all the way to the sensationalist and even rightist newspapers (*IKC, Bunt Młodych*).

Censorship

Censorship affected the Polish-Jewish press as well as book publishers. Indeed, the interventions of censors were especially numerous in the press, and their frequency increased considerably in the late thirties in connection with the government's clear turn to the right and the radicalization and determined anti-anti-Semitic opposition evident in the stance of Polish-Jewish papers. For the most part, censors confiscated texts dealing with manifestations of anti-Semitism: pogroms, the bench ghettos at universities, the economic boycott. Also confiscated were articles critical of the position of the Catholic Church on the Jewish question (e.g., Szymel's article "Recollections, tears, and thoughts of a Christian Jew")[53] or dealing with Catholic concerns in general (e.g., the 1933 confiscation of the issues of *Chwila* containing J[oseph] Klausner's work *Jezus z Nazaretu* [Jesus of Nazareth]).[54] The censorship of Irma Kanfer's small volume *Dwa akordy* (Two chords; 1936),[55] whose tone was that of social radicalism, had loud repercussions. The white blots of censorship could even be found in texts submitted by correspondents of *Mały Przegląd*.

[Literary] Criticism

Another institution of Polish literary life that affected Polish-Jewish literature was criticism. Szymel and Brandstaetter stressed the importance and value of Polish critical reception. Both complained of the weak response of the Polish-Jewish press to their works and to the galling lack of criticism. Undoubtedly, these pronouncements[56] aimed at alarming Jewish cultural opinion, and the references to the range and significance of Polish critical reception were due at least in part to polemical fervor. Also, one must not overlook the fact that Polish critical reception was cited as an important confirmation of the rank and value of Polish-Jewish works, and that one relied on the authority of Polish culture to win over Polish-speaking Jewish readers. (One indication of the respect for this authority was the manner in which *Nowy Dziennik* advertised Maurycy Szymel's second small volume of poetry: "Our permanent contributor is preparing for publication a new volume of Jewish poetry. We recall that Szymel published a year ago a volume of poetry titled *Powrót do domu* [The return home], which was received by the Polish press, on the whole, in a very friendly way.")[57]

The connections with Polish criticism and the kind of reception of Polish-Jewish literature on "the Polish side" can shed new and interesting light on the Polish aspect of the phenomenon under discussion. Above all, it can show which part of Polish-Jewish literature reached the Polish side and how it was perceived on that side.

I have only fragments of the reactions of the Polish press to Polish-Jewish literature. On the other hand, the large variety of newspapers my materials come from (*Wiadomości Literackie, Pion* [Plumb], *Kurier Poranny* [Morning courier], *IKC, Kurier Literacko-Naukowy* [Literary and scientific courier], *Polonista* [Teacher of Polish], *Słowo* [Word], *Gazeta Warszawska* [Warsaw gazette], *Kurier Lwowski* [Lvov courier], *Myśl Narodowa* [National thought], *Sygnały, ABC*) lets me hope that my opinion sample is at least somewhat representative.

There is no doubt that the nature of the contact of a Polish reader with Polish-Jewish literature was different from that of a Jewish reader. Whereas Polish-Jewish publications reached Jewish readers and critics primarily via the press, what "got through" to the Polish side were mainly—if not exclusively—books. How well they sold can be inferred from ads in the Polish-Jewish press: Szymel's first two small volumes (published in 1931 and 1932, respectively) were still available in 1934 and 1935.[58] Of course, [I] do not claim that the Polish-Jewish press had no Polish readers, but the range of its effectiveness in Polish circles was limited and the perception of its contents was very selective. Tadeusz Kielanowski recalled that *Chwila* was an extremely well edited newspaper, with its own foreign correspondents. It was read by Poles although it was primarily concerned with issues of interest to Jews."[59] Michał Strzemski wrote in *Nasze Puławy* (Our Puławy): "The Polish-Jewish *Nasz Przegląd* occupied a singular position. It was virtually perfect when it came to information about political and economic issues. It was the only Jewish paper with many readers among the Polish intelligentsia."[60] This evidence allows us to conclude that Polish readers of the Polish-Jewish press were likely to regard it as a source of political and economic, rather than cultural, information and to overlook texts pertaining to issues of interest to Jews. Regarded by Polish newspapers as a representative exponent of Jewish opinion, *Nasz Przegląd* was undoubtedly the most popular [Polish-Jewish] newspaper, and was frequently quoted in reviews of the press.[61] It was read attentively by *endek*s such as, for example, Adolf Nowaczyński, whose articles (e.g., the collection *Plewy i perły* [Chaff and pearls])[62] frequently referred to information contained in that paper. *Nasz Przegląd* was also read with care—for very different reasons—by the editors of *Wiadomości Literackie,* and most certainly by Słonimski, whose "Kroniki Tygodniowe" (Weekly chronicles) contained refer-

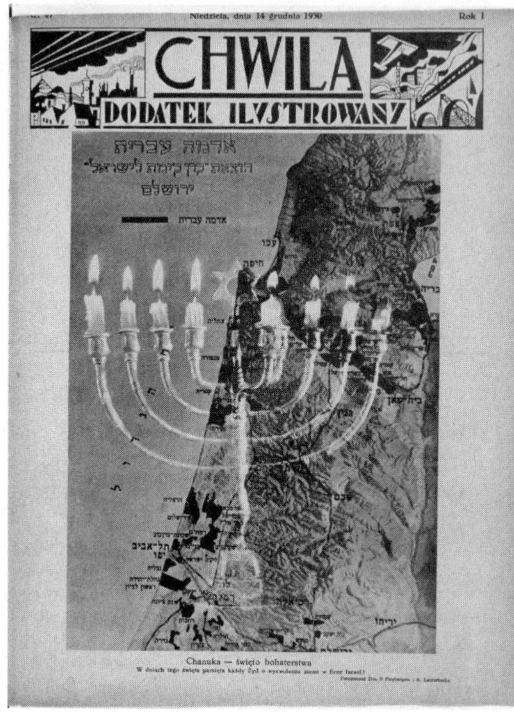
Niedziela, dnia 14 grudnia 1930 Rok I

CHWILA

DODATEK ILUSTROWANY

אדמה עברית
הוצאת "קרן קימת לישראל"
ירושלים

Chanuka — święto bohaterstwa

Polish as the language of Jewish life: holiday issue of the illustrated supplement to the Lvov *Chwila* dating from 1930. *Chwila Dodatek Illustrowany* (Chwila Illustrated supplement) 1930, no. 41, p. 1. Photo A. Musielak.

ences to it.[63] That Polish-Jewish literature reached Polish readers largely through books on the Polish literary market in what may be described as an autonomous manner, books torn out of the context of the Polish-Jewish literary circuit and deprived of the background of Jewish culture in Polish, had a decisive effect on the perception of Polish-Jewish writing in Polish circles. Polish observers noted first and foremost those Polish-Jewish writers who gladly went beyond "the Rubicon," participated more actively in Polish literary life, and published more frequently in the Polish press. It is striking that such writers were viewed as being of the Tuwim and Słonimski variety. Writers such as Szymel and Eker, primarily connected with the Jewish milieu, were not regarded as its representatives. Rather, it was Roman Brandstaetter—a writer charged by lampoonists with having walked "from Czarnolas to Palestine"—who was so regarded. Outside the "home context" of Polish-Jewish culture, Polish-Jewish works were viewed as part of Polish writing. They were systematically registered and discussed by the *Rocznik Literacki* (Literary yearbook) under the heading of Polish literature, and newspapers cited them in their current reviews of literary news. Given the explicitly national Jewish declarations by Jewish poets writing in Polish, some critics (e.g. K[arol] W[iktor] Zawodziński) advanced the hypothesis of "the coming into being, in Palestine, of a part of Polish literature . . . more sophisticated than the émigré literature in the Americas."[64]

Another important factor that determined the reception of the literature under discussion in the Polish press was that most of it was second-rate and even plebeian. Hence the casual nature of the references to it in the bibliographical surveys by important newspapers. Only [newspapers] expressing the opinions of circles especially sensitive to the complex of Jewish problems could be expected to show greater interest in this literature and to discuss it in a more penetrating manner. The newspapers involved ranged from the democratic Left (the Lvov *Sygnały*, which cooperated closely with *Nasza Opinia*), to the elite of the assimilated Jewish intelligentsia (*Wiadomości Literackie),* and all the way to the *endek*s (*Myśl Narodowa, ABC).*

Sometimes the short references and notes ignored the Jewish motifs[65] and Szymel, Pomer, and Brandstaetter were placed on the map of Polish poetry among authors who began to publish in the early thirties, together with their contemporaries from *Kwadryga* (Quadriga), *Kadry* (Cadres), and *Meteor.*[66] That their poetry accorded with the poetry of that generation can be inferred from the favorable reception of the first small volumes of poetry by Szymel and Pomer, respectively. The critic Jan Szczawiej praised them for "honesty," "authenticity," and "noble regionalism."[67]

In general, [Polish critics] noted the "newness of the topic" (a description due to Józef Birkenmajer), [although] of course what was at issue here was not the newness of the Jewish topic but its new treatment. The Palestinian motifs and the manifestation of Jewish national consciousness attracted attention.[68] Thus it was not only Polish-Jewish writers who felt that their choice of topic, combined with their specific position, distinguished their writing from all other writing in Polish. The distinction was noted by Polish critics as well.

The writing in which the distinctiveness of Polish-Jewish literature found expression was not (as Władysław Panas would have it)[69] proof of a shock presumably resulting from the dialectic of foreignness and homeliness experienced in the course of its evolution. On the contrary. The dominant interpretations were not "existential" but sociological, and of a kind that led to the inclusion of Polish-Jewish writing in the ambit of Polish writing. Viewed as just described, this literature became, even before 1939, the object of serious sociological interpretations in the syntheses of interwar literature by Kazimierz Czachowski and Ignacy Fik. Both authors considered Polish-Jewish writing in their discussion of the participation of writers of Jewish origin in contemporary literature. In his

Obraz współczesnej literatury polskiej 1884–1934 (Image of modern Polish literature, 1884–1934), Kazimierz Czachowski devoted to this problem a considerable amount of space. He wrote:

> The truly significant participation of writers of Jewish origin in modern Polish literature is not an isolated phenomenon but one connected with the fundamental transformation of the general social structure. . . . Until the war, Polish literature was enriched by talented individuals drawn largely from the ranks of the gentry. It now has an entirely different social character due to writers from middle-class families, and especially [those from] the proletariat.[70]

Czachowski thought that the participation of Jews in literature was due to changes in the social origins of interwar writers, or rather of the interwar Polish intelligentsia. He called Brandstaetter, the only Polish-Jewish writer he seems to have noticed, a "Jewish poet," and described him as an author who "expresses the yearning of a generation that makes its way to its own fatherland in the Promised Land in beautifully shaped Polish verses quickened by a deep epical-lyrical breath."[71] Thus Brandstaetter's writing was for him a manifestation of a new tendency connected with Zionism, a phenomenon of a clearly generational nature.

Ignacy Fik (*Dwadzieścia lat literatury polskiej, 1918–1938* [Twenty years of Polish literature, 1918–1938]) interpreted the participation of Jews in the interwar literature in much the same way as Czachowski. He regarded them as representatives of the middle class, which increased its activity in Polish culture after Poland's recovery of independence. With Brandstaetter in mind, he also noted the growing number of authors who wrote in Polish but in a markedly Zionist spirit.[72] He included their works in Polish literature and claimed that they proved the attractiveness of its artistic culture and of the Polish language.[73]

More about Criticism: Caught in a Crossfire

Undoubtedly, the strongest response to Polish-Jewish literature came from two groups, namely, the *endek*s and the assimilated Polish-Jewish intelligentsia. The reactions of both were symptomatic and intriguing.

The *endek*s diligently followed developments in the Jewish milieu out of what may be called a "professional" sense of duty. They were the most zealous, but also very special, readers of Polish translations of Jewish literature. Thus Adolf Nowaczyński read avidly I[srael] J[oshua] Singer's novel *Josie Kałb*,[74] and Stanisław Pieńkowski, Józef Opatoszu's [Josef Opatowski's] *W lasach polskich* (In the Polish forests). Pieńkowski's reaction to Opatoszu's novel was a cycle of articles about the "formativity [*plazmatyzm*] of the ghetto" and its destructive effect on the "Aryan soul."[75] Still, there was a paradox here. "It is a paradox, but [it is true that] anti-Semites from Klemens Junosza to Nowaczyński have shown the greatest appreciation of Jewish literature."[76] So wrote J[eheskel] M[osze] Nejman in his reply to a 1938 poll by *Nowy Głos* devoted to Polish-Jewish cultural understanding; he was not entirely wrong.

As expected, the *endek*s' response to Polish-Jewish literature was decidedly hostile. They ruthlessly attacked anything that contained the slightest trace of a connection with Jewishness and regarded Polish-Jewish literature as one more phenomenon in Polish culture that spread "destructive miasmas." They used primitive and vulgar polemical means: their "favorite form" was crude personal attacks. Brandstaetter was most frequently the butt of such attacks. He seemed to irritate old and young leaders of the "cultural self-defense" such as Adolf Nowaczyński, Stanisław Pieńkowski, Zygmunt Wasilewski, and Stanisław Piasecki. In a sample of the style of the *endek* skirmishes with the author of the *Królestwo trzeciej świątyni,* Wasilewski called Brandstaetter a "wanton little Jew," and accused him of "poison-pen antics at the expense of Polish poetry," and even—more pathetically—of a "plot against Polish civilization."[77] He also disclosed in passing another, far from trivial, reason for being indignant with Brandstaetter, namely, his "battle against Polish nationalism [conducted] in *Opinia* and *Nowy Dziennik* using the oratory . . . of spit."[78]

Brandstaetter did not leave these attacks unanswered. Frequently, the clashes went beyond the press. For example, there was the notorious action he brought against Pieńkowski, who imputed to him the wish to convert to Catholicism.[79] Unfortunately, Brandstaetter began gradually but unmistakably to adopt the manners of his adversaries and to specialize in punning invectives of the kind Nowaczyński was a master of. [Brandstaetter's] *Zmowa eunuchów* (Conspiracy of eunuchs; 1936), written in this manner, was received with a certain embarrassment in Polish-Jewish circles because it pointed to the author's adoption of the methods of his opponents and to a drastic lowering of the level of debate. While Brandstaetter was undoubtedly the object of the most violent *endek* attacks, the anti-Semitic campaign did not bypass other Polish-Jewish writers. It may well be that this campaign was the cause of a certain crisis in Szymel's poetry that occurred in the second half of the thirties. In 1935 the *Kurier Lwowski* attacked him for his sentimental "Ballada o złotowłosej panience przy klawikordzie" (Ballad about a golden-haired maiden at a clavichord).[80] The attack ended with an extremely violent eruption of hatred: "Mr. Szymel, why the hell don't you stop littering the Polish language and put your hand to honest work. And if such work doesn't tempt you, then counterfeit dollars, or smuggle saccharine from Germany, or export white slaves to Argentina."[81] I need not comment on the tone and level of these charges. I note only that some Polish newspapers felt obliged to protest against them. Thus the Wilno *Słowo* defended the poem as well as the poet.[82] The attacks were directed not only at original works by Polish-Jewish writers but also at translations, for example, at Izydor Berman's translations from the German.[83] (Berman translated Kafka and Roth.)

It also came to physical attacks, such as the destruction of the offices of Polish-Jewish newspapers (for example, those of the *Nowy Dziennik*) and the wounding of Izydor Berman by "unknown perpetrators" during anti-Semitic riots in Lvov in February 1938. Berman described the incident in an article in *Nasza Opinia* as an example of the descent into savagery and barbarism of *endek* fighting squads, and dedicated the text to "all innocent victims of crime running wild with impunity."[84] The Berman incident acquired such notoriety that Bruno Schulz mentioned it in his correspondence.[85]

Another Polish-Jewish writer affected by the anti-Semitic press attacks was Józef Nacht who wrote for *Nasza Opinia*. When responding to them he used the demonstrative signature "Józef Nacht—Jew."[86]

The attacks on Polish-Jewish writers, classified by the national camp as belonging to the current of "Judeo-Polish poetry," were dominated by phraseology well tested (indeed, from the early twenties on) on Tuwim and Słonimski. Insults rained down, such as "conspiracy against the Polish civilization," "littering the Polish language," and so on. Also, the national camp responded with hatred and aggression to all sociocultural processes that took place in Jewish circles: assimilation, acculturation, and national de-Polonization. For example, what greatly annoyed Wasilewski was that Brandstaetter was "tempted by Polish sanctities" and also that "[he] will remain in Poland. He will be registered as a Polish writer" in spite of being "unmasked" by Wasilewski as someone who "has two countries."[87]

While interpreting assimilation, acculturation, and the birth of modern Jewish consciousness within the framework of their own ideology and worldview, the *endek*s paid considerable attention to all these processes. For example, the belligerently anti-Semitic *Gazeta Warszawska* added the following comment to its "proscription list" of authors of Jewish origin. "Roughly speaking, there are now three categories of Jews who write in Polish:

1. those who lay claim to a position in Polish literature;

2. those who lay no such claim and write in Polish for Jews, for example in the Jewish press;

3. those in a mixed category.[88]

Judging by the list of names, Polish-Jewish writers were primarily included in the second category and described as follows:

> this is for the most part a Zionist who writes in Polish because he doesn't know Yiddish well enough [here the term used for "Yiddish" is *żargon* (jargon)—Trans.] and often has no knowledge of Hebrew. Versed on [*sic*] our literature, he usually torments and murders the Polish language; everything ties him to Jewishness. We include here, for example, Dresdner, Szymel, Pomer, and others. Also, no one would reserve a place in Polish literature for Mr. J[akub] Appenszlak. The columns of a number of Jewish dailies in Polish (*Nasz Przegląd,* and others) swarm with such writers.[89]

Brandstaetter was not included in this group. He was regarded as an author who wrote for Jews and for Poles.

Its aggressive and vicious tone notwithstanding, the national camp was clearly aware of (1) the differentiation of the sense of national and cultural identity in Polish-speaking Jewish circles, and (2) the significance of the Polish-Jewish press in the formation of new Jewish writing in Polish that constituted a distinct literary circuit.

While noticing the new phenomena in Jewish life, the national camp interpreted them by means of its own "classical" stereotypes ("what happens to Polish culture when a worm gnaws at its root")[90] as a manifestation of assimilation, which it fought tooth and nail.

The opposite camp, the camp of supporters of assimilation and assimilationists, was also locked in its own circle of ideals and stereotypes and therefore incapable of a reasonable and objective evaluation of the new phenomena.

The assimilationist camp reacted with considerable consternation to the sociocultural changes in the Jewish milieu, changes chartacteristic of the interwar period, and its attitude toward Polish-Jewish literature was highly differentiated. The polarization of attitudes is well illustrated by the reception accorded Polish-Jewish literature by the former writers for *Izraelita,* a newspaper that at one time was the standard-bearer of assimilation. During the interwar period, this ideologically differentiated group was the source of both positive and negative reactions to Polish-Jewish literature. Thus Andrzej Marek, the creator of the Polish-Jewish theater (who, at the turn of the century, had published most of his "Jewish" dramas in *Izraelita*), was one of the most active supporters of Jewish plays in Polish, and Czesława Endelman-Rosenblatt (whose short stories and prose fragments had appeared in *Izraelita*) published in the thirties a novel (*Ludzie którzy jeszcze żyją* [People who are still alive; 1934]), which young people in Polish-Jewish circles regarded as important for the new trend.[91] On the other hand, the opinions about Polish-Jewish literature expressed by some in the assimilationist circles were so harsh and disapproving that they matched in tone the anti-Semitic attacks. Leo Belmont, once a journalist with *Izraelita,* attacked Brandstaetter and *Opinia* in two rather nasty articles published in *Wolnomyśliciel Polski* (Polish freethinker) with the telling titles: "Obrzydliwy typ hitleryzmu w sosie polskim czyli rasista Roman Brandstaetter" (A disgusting variety of Hitlerism in a Polish sauce or the racist Roman Brandstaetter) and "Klerykalizm we fraku i z cycesem pod narodową kamizelką: Taka sobie maleńka rozprawa z *Opinią*" (Clericalism in tails with zizith under a national waistcoat: Just a wee bit of a debate with *Opinia*).[92]

What outraged Belmont about *Opinia* and Brandstaetter was their disloyalty to the model of identificational assimilation connected with national Polonization. He asked: "What good is it that you sometimes write beautiful Polish if you repudiate (pardon me!) the charge of 'Polonization' as if it were a mortal sin?"[93] He regarded as blatant falsehood the spiritual duality so often talked about by Jewish poets, and poked fun at the juxtaposition of Polish and Jewish cultural props as a ridiculous but widespread mannerism in their poetry:

> One writes "beech" or "willow" and immediately laments that it is not "cedar" or "palm tree." . . . [O]r one takes a simple poplar and hangs from it tefillin with thongs, or finally, one spreads a tallith with zizith on the sand at the Vistula—and all this fills one with a great longing for the wailing wall in Jerusalem, and puts the poet, and possibly also his readers, in a mood of delightful melancholy.[94]

Belmont considered the ideological dimension of Polish-Jewish literature and saw it as the regeneration of the harmful ideas of "clericalism," "megalomania," and national particularism. He regarded it as just an anti-assimilationist phenomenon and called it, accordingly, the "Zionist-Polish" school.[95]

Similar interpretations appeared in pro-assimilationist Polish circles. The position adopted by Władysław Sebyła with respect to Brandstaetter's *Królestwo trzeciej świątyni* was typical. He was obviously surprised, taken aback, and openly indignant at the "Jewish nationalism spreading among our assimilated intelligentsia," at this intelligentsia's "breaking through Polish [cultural] strata to reach the culture of its people," and at the fact that "even individuals strongly identifying with Polish culture give it up in order to build a new Jewish culture in their own state."[96] The combination of Polish and Jewish national consciousness simply shocked all those who were used to the routine of assimilationist thinking and to the old, optimistic prognoses of integration of both groups, an integration presumably to be brought about by the beneficial effect of Polonization. That cultural, or to put it more "safely," linguistic Polonization no longer resulted in customary national self-definitions occasioned surprise and even shock. To quote Sebyła once more:

> It is generally thought that adoption of the language and culture of a given nation indicates acceptance of membership in that nation, of denationalization. Brandstaetter's small volume shows that the criterion of adoption of a language and a culture, that is of everything that determines the national affiliation of an individual and the structure of his mental life, is not synonymous with the criterion of denationalization.[97]

It is clear that what most disturbed Sebyła in Brandstaetter's position was the deviation from assimilationist models, from the model of a Jewish Pole who aspires to admission to the Polish collectivity. Another surprise was the new way of using Polish—no longer in the service of integration. One more element in Sebyła's pronouncement that is impossible to overlook is the—somewhat masked—resentment, whose source is the jolt to the good frame of mind associated with the paternalistic notions about Polish-Jewish relations: "our assimilated intelligentsia," "our Jews." . . . Given this paternalistic posture, it is not surprising that national de-Polonization, combined with acculturation, had an irritating effect. On another occasion, looking for the formula underlying Brandstaetter's poetry, the disoriented and irritated Sebyła asked: "Zionism, racism, or poetry?"[98] His notion of assimilation can be gleaned from the following pronouncement in *Pion:* "It is pleasant to hear from a representative of a people that has found shelter in our land, and has lived together with its stewards for centuries, praise of the adopted fatherland, especially when expressed in beautiful poetic words in the language of this adopted fatherland. This should attest to the complete assimilation of the author of this praise."[99]

It must be said in all fairness that Brandstaetter, who readily used such categories as "noble racism [*szlachetna rasowość*]" and "spirit of the race," undoubtedly supplied reasons for the charges of racism against him. As noted earlier, the use of such categories was connected with the popularity in Zionist circles of romantic and neoromantic notions of national culture, although some thought that the source of these notions was the atmosphere engendered by anti-Semitism: writing in *Lato* (Summer; 1938) of "raging anti-Semitism," [Adolf] Rudnicki stressed its demoralizing effects discernible on the Jewish side. . . . Caught in the crossfire of *endek*s and assimilationists, Polish-Jewish writers were accused by the attackers of utterly contradictory sins: of assimilation and of bad assimilation, of usurping the right to Polish national sanctities, and of refusing to recognize these very sanctities. But in all cases, the sense of outrage was invariably due to the conviction that Polish-Jewish works belonged, or rather "mis-belonged," to Polish culture.

The Complex of Wiadomości Literackie

When writing about the reception of Polish-Jewish literature by assimilationist circles it is impossible to ignore the reaction of the grouping around *Wiadomości Literackie.* During the interwar period, it was a public secret that this weekly, at the time the most popular and influential literary paper, was the voice of the elite of the assimilated Jewish intelligentsia.[100] [Karol] Irzykowski called it "the fortress of brilliant mimicry" and talked about it at considerable length in a long essay in the *Kurier Poranny* devoted to the participation of Jews in Polish literature.[101] The name of the paper was parodied as "Jadąmośki Literackie."[102] ["wiadomości" and "jadąmośki" sound alike in Polish; "wiadomości" means "news," whereas "jadąmośki" is a pseudoword made up of "jadą," meaning "(they) travel," and "Mośki," the plural of "Mośiek," a Polonized version of "Moses" and a contemptuous term for a Jew—Trans.] The paper seems to have suffered from a "Jewish complex," which it could not handle.[103]

In her analysis of the articles devoted to Jewish topics that appeared in [Mieczysław] Grydzewski's weekly between 1924 and 1939, Magdalena Opalski [Opalska] states that the position adopted by the newspaper in discussions of Jewish problems depended to a large extent on the specific social status of the group, the crème de la crème of the Polonized Jewish intelligentsia, that shaped the profile of the paper. And the group's position toward these problems was completely determined by the liberal ideals professed and propagated by the newspaper and derived from positivist and Enlightenment sources. The paper criticized the backwardness of the Jewish ghetto and fought against anti-Semitism and racism; it was critical of the "black continent" of Nalewki* and of "Jewish touchiness" but it also poked vicious fun at *endek* attempts to trace the non-Aryan connections of artists. Briefly, the newspaper fought on two fronts: it defended as an unalterable axiom the Jews' right to assimilation and the belief in the possibility and appropriateness of their complete Polonization.[104]

Wiadomości Literackie took note of Polish-Jewish literature as soon as it went outside the columns of the Polish-Jewish press. Despite its having quoted with

*A street in Warsaw. It was also a loose term for the Jewish quarter in the northern part of Warsaw. [Trans.]

enthusiasm in 1927 the words of Shalom [Szalom] Asz, who objected to "false assimilation, Judeo-Polish superficial assimilation of Zionists who speak and write bad Polish,"[105] the paper discussed Polish-Jewish poetry and prose in a friendly manner. As a measure of this friendliness, one could take the review of the artistically flimsy Palestinian stories in Henryk Adler's *Ariela i Jubal* (Ariela and Jubal): "The exotic locale lends interest to the book, a collection of stories about the lives of Jewish colonists in Palestine. The work is full of great and sincere fondness for the pioneers of this colonization and of sympathy for their idealistic aspirations to create new life forms based on the heroism of labor and on respect for human dignity."[106]

Stefan Napierski [Marek Eigen], K. W. Zawodziński, and Józef Wittlin, the leading critics of the newspaper, wrote about the small volumes of Szymel, Pomer, Eker, Brandstaetter, and Lewittes.[107] To see how they interpreted Polish-Jewish poetry, [let us consider] two opinions of the debuts of Polish-Jewish poets, of great interest from [my] viewpoint: Wittlin's about the debut of Dresdner and Napierski's about the first small volume of poetry by Szymel.

About Dresdner:

> Through these formally uneven poems, there speaks to us with a pure voice the sincere soul of a Polish Jew unafraid of an encounter with itself in a dark ghetto alley. This beautiful, determined posture toward the complex problems of one's own soul [elevates] Dresdner to poet and favorably singles him out from the ever more numerous brigade of the youngest rhymesters who simplify their task by enlisting, en masse, under ready banners and ready formulas.[108]

About Szymel:

> In this volume [*Powrót do domu*], a Jewish poet addresses us with Polish words. To the best of my knowledge, this is done for the first time by a poet with a clear Jewish national sense, who expresses not only (like so many before him) the tragedy of the race but also the tragedy of the Diaspora. . . . The most interesting and powerful is the last cycle: "Noce biblijne" (Biblical nights). Here the dream of the lost East embitters the author's words with a shudder and a cry, colors them bright and iridescent; those cedar nights are purple like the "Song of Songs." It is crystal clear that someone spiritually exiled is singing his boundless grief with helpless words.[109]

The duet of Wittlin and Napierski had a remarkably uniform tone and a single leitmotif. The two interpreted Polish-Jewish poetry in each case as a specific expression of self-definition by the author, as a kind of identity card. The essential spiritual content was worthy of the highest respect, and was more important than aesthetic considerations. Poetry was subordinate to considerations beyond the literary, it was an expression of biography. What Polish-Jewish poetry transmitted, what was recorded in it, was the experience of Jewishness, a new experience of Jewishness. The latter element was of utmost importance. The critics treated the position of the poets very seriously and in a very friendly manner, and it is difficult to resist the impression that this acceptance involved a sincere, one is tempted to say pathetic, understanding that derived from a common fate. . . . If we bear in mind that what was being welcomed were poetic debuts, small volumes that undoubtedly belonged to the area of second-rate literature, then the friendly attitude of the reviewers could hardly escape notice.

True, Napierski evaluated Szymel's second collection far less favorably ("lyricism Semitic throughout, very painful, embittered, somewhat obtrusive, and terribly sentimental"),[110] but in the end the author of *Skrzypce przedmieścia* (Violin of the suburbs) was classified as a member of Tuwim's poetic school, and K. W. Zawodziński (critic extraordinary of the *Skamander* group) extolled his beautiful Polish, his formal virtuosity, and, above all, his use of rhythm.[111]

There is no doubt that Szymel, who was "in the catchment area of *Skamander,"* was more favorably treated by *Wiadomości Literackie* than any other Polish-Jewish writer. On the other hand, Grydzewski's weekly regarded Brandstaetter as the most controversial of all such writers: while it duly noted his poetry (without enthusiasm),[112] he met determined opposition as a journalist. Stanisław Rogoż called *Zmowa eunuchów* "pathological journalism,"[113] and Słonimski did not hesitate to call its author a "Jewish Hitlerite."[114] Above all, *Wiadomości Literackie* sharply criticized Brandstaetter's articles for his liberal use of neoromantic phraseology and his belligerent Zionism.

The relations between Brandstaetter and *Wiadomości Literackie* were rather complicated, even tangled. There are reasons to believe that the conflict involved not only differences of principles and worldviews. It is certain that personal resentments and animosities played a significant role. The misunderstandings had a prehistory that reached back to the time when no one could have predicted that Brandstaetter would become the singer of the "Cedar Fatherland." In 1927, he published an interview with Tuwim in *Gazeta Literacka.* Tuwim objected to the tone of the interview, and the whole thing resulted in comments unfavorable to the young author.[115] Again, in the early thirties, Boy[-Żeleński], the pillar of *Wiadomości Literackie,* took part in the discussion started by Brandstaetter's essay on Mickiewicz's Jewish Legion (*Legion żydowski Adama Mickiewicza* [The Jewish Legion of Adam Mickiewicz]), 1932). After reading Brandstaetter's text, Boy advanced the hypothesis that the bard had been poisoned. This led to a number of misunderstandings and a new wave of attacks, this time by the national camp, on the author of *Legion Żydowski.* Brandstaetter protested against the insinuations of the "national" press as well as against Boy's conjectures.

Before the Tuwim affair, *Wiadomości Literackie* discussed Brandstaetter's debut quite objectively; indeed, it had published his articles.[116] After the incidents connected with the item published in the *Gazeta Literacka,* [however,] relations between the poet and Grydzewski's paper cooled considerably. They took a radical turn for the worse during the period of Brandstaetter's "Zionist conversion," when the writers in the circle around *Wiadomości Literackie* became the favorite targets of his journalistic attacks. [I] may as well say it from the very outset: these were extremely unpleasant personal attacks on Grydzewski, Słonimski, Napierski, and Hemar. Brandstaetter's sharpest attack took the form of a series of articles published in 1935 in *Opinia* and *Nasza Opinia,* in which he condemned both the position of the authors associated with *Wiadomości Lliterackie* and the way it presented Jewish culture. From the position of a converted and ardent Zionist, he spoke loudly about the Jewish complexes of the group around the weekly and called the writers (such as [Marian] Hemar [Hescheles] and Słonimski) "national hermaphrodites." The attack was sharp and, in addition, was conducted using gross means à la Nowaczyński (see the pun insult above). The statement: "*Wiadomości Literackie* is edited by a convert who is ashamed of his Jewish origin and, therefore, constantly and purposefully, passes over in silence all developments in the realm of Hebrew and Yiddish literature"[117] illustrates Brandstaetter's moderately nasty tone. The tone could get worse. "They made ideal and informal friends: the Hebrew carrottop and the Augsburg-reform neophyte. The first an intellectual eunuch showing sick inclinations to talent, the second a shrewd editor, gifted with a racial sense of smell and a splendid sense of what to make money on and how much."[118] Opponents were pelted with insults: "vague cosmopolite," "Jewish renegade," "Warsaw Yid-Pole," "good *Verleger*" [German for "publisher"—Trans.], "Levite-Lachs" [Lach = Pole—Trans.], "Semitic *sarmacisław*" . . . ["*sarmacisław*" is a pseudoword concocted out of "Sarmata" (= Sarmatian) and the ending "-sław" of many Polish first names—Trans.]. It greatly angered Brandstaetter that "Grydzewski relied . . . for years on the devoted Słonimski to spit and poke fun at Zionism in *Wiadomości literackie,*"[119] and that information about [Chaim Nachman] Bialik appeared on the last page of the paper, next to advertisements for toothpaste and White Deer laundry soap. Also, the people who wrote about Jewish matters were—in his view—suspect and incompetent: pitiful "marriage brokers at a barricade."[120] In fact, *Wiadomości Literackie* is just "Mechesówka . . . a traditional Jankiel pub!"[121]

[a "meches" is a Jewish convert to Christianity and "ówka" is a common Polish ending (transl.)]. How much Brandstaetter disliked the milieu of *Wiadomości Literackie* is shown by the fact that he kept up his attacks even during the growing anti-Semitic storm in the late thirties. Thus, in 1938, in an anti-anti-Semitic utopian satire titled "Republika żydowska na Biegunie Północnym" (A Jewish republic at the North Pole), he scoffed not only at Nowaczyński, Piasecki, Rembieliński, and K[onstanty] I[ldefons] Gałczewski but also at Słonimski, Grydzewski, Napierski, Borman, Melcerowa. . . . [122] He did this despite having earlier claimed: "We have no grudge whatever against these Yid-Poles who are assimilated for one reason or another and today, in the face of the great enterprise of the rebuilding of Palestine, are completely indifferent to our national endeavors." [123] The stubbornness, the virtual obsessiveness, of his attacks seems to show that, for him, this was a matter of settling important scores. [Indeed, his] settling of scores with assimilation was his form of condemnation of a road other than his own, his frequently described road of "maturing to Zionism." It was also a form of condemnation of his own earlier position, of doing battle with his earlier sins at a time when he himself could undoubtedly have been considered one of the pilgrims at a "stopover in Mechesówka."

There was a great deal of ambiguity in the arguments between Polish-Jewish writers and *Wiadomości Literackie.* Both sides sensed it. The contest with the assimilated elite of the Jewish intelligentsia was also a contest with the most popular, opinion-molding Polish literary newspaper. (Artur Sandauer commented frequently on the ambivalent status of the paper due to these circumstances.) [124] All this endowed Grydzewski's weekly with an element of exceptional attractiveness for Polish-Jewish circles. If only *Wiadomości Literackie* printed Bialik's portrait on the front page as it printed [Stefan] Żeromski's portrait! Pride in its influence was mixed with regret that it was not an ally in the "national lineup." How badly Polish-Jewish circles needed eminent pro-Zionist European writers in the interwar period, [and] with what gratitude they received them, is illustrated by the reception accorded Franz Kafka.[125]

There was an additional dimension in the contest with assimilation that was present in the arguments between writers for *Wiadomości Literackie* and Polish-Jewish writers. What was contested was "the control of the souls" of the readers. As *Nowy Dziennik* stated in 1935: "It is an open secret that 90% of the readers of *Wiadomości Literackie* are Jews," [126] and [Chone] Shmeruk claims that "it was usual for Jewish youth and intelligentsia who read *Nasz Przegląd* and *Opinia,* or other Jewish periodicals in Polish, to also read literary periodicals such as *Wiadomości Literackie* or *Sygnały.*" [127]

The problem of Jewish readers of the weekly, of Jews who "rejected the

Bible for *Wiadomości Literackie*,"[128] was symptomatic of a broader and more important issue, the issue of the Jewish readership of Polish literature. The growth of this public was noted from the beginning of the century. Thus Wiktor Pordes wrote in 1910:

> Today it is no exaggeration to claim that, in a way, the people that best respond to Polish poetry are members of the Polish intelligentsia of Jewish origin. Eliza Orzeszkowa once said that she wrote novels only for young Jewesses. Much the same could be said about Przybyszewski, Żeromski, Zapolska, and many other Polish writers. The public that comes to lectures, first performances, and meetings, the permanent public of modern Polish culture confirms this striking intellectual participation of the Jewish intelligentsia. Rachela in *Wesele* (The wedding), this half-ironically conceived caricature who bewitches spirits with spells, this innkeeper's daughter possessed by poetry who directs a host of magic visions that shake the Polish manor house, is an unconscious symbol of all this.[129]

An increase in Jewish participation was also noted in the ranks of theatergoers.[130]

The famous theater war of 1859 centered around a small group of the Jewish plutocratic elite that formed an important component of the contemporary theatrical public. But as of the turn of the century, there were increasing numbers of references to Jewish consumers [*odbiorcy*] coming from the ranks of the intelligentsia. This showed clearly that the formation of a Jewish public interested in Polish art had entered a new phase. If we ignore the transparent demagogy of Karol Irzykowski's complaints about the participation of Jews in Polish culture, then these complaints can serve as an important confirmation that awareness of the ever-increasing numbers of Jewish "consumers" was an important element in certain Polish circles' thinking about the cultural status quo during the interwar period. Irzykowski saw Jewish [literary] circles not merely as passive "consumers" but also as active molders of opinion. Also, he seems to have been more troubled by the problem of a Jewish public that would dictate tastes and determine literary fashions than by the problem of writers of Jewish origin. This is confirmed by the following fragment of his article in *Kurier Poranny:*

> What is worse is that the most numerous and fervent consumers [odbiorcy] and readers of Polish literature are likewise Jews. This fact, like the head of Medusa, blinds Polish authors, renders them helpless, and forces them to surrender. Some admit openly that without the interest of Jews they would have no incentive to create. . . . Jews constitute the majority of first-night theater audiences,

> they guillotine some authors, crown others, distribute concessions. It is frightening to think what would happen if one day the Jews decided to boycott Polish literature.[131]

Jewish readers of Polish literary works were also frequently the protagonists in feuilletons by Słonimski.[132]

It is clear that the efforts of Polish-Jewish writers to win readers centered necessarily on those who read exclusively works in Polish or works in other languages as well as in Polish. What prejudiced their position in this contest was that, among linguistically Polonized circles, the status of a Polish writer was much higher than that of a Jewish writer. For example, in a 1937 article in *Nowy Głos* Brandstaetter wrote: "In the consciousness of the broad Jewish collectivity in Poland, a Jewish writer is someone infinitely inferior to, say, a Polish writer. . . . If Tuwim were to start writing in Yiddish and publishing his poems in *Hajnt* [a Yiddish newspaper], his moral and artistic prestige among Jews from Bielańska street would drop to zero."[133]

Adolf Rudnicki shared Brandstetter's view. In his *Lato* (1938), where he depicted the small Jewish artistic world vacationing in Kazimierz, there are the "better"—Polish—and "worse"—Yiddish or Hebrew—writers. These divisions and differences in prestige were undoubtedly connected with the common Jewish conviction of the superiority or "betterness" of Polish, a conviction whose existence has been confirmed by sociological studies.[134]

Thus the position of Polish-Jewish writers intent on acquiring a broad readership was indeed most unfavorable. As (by their own definition) Jewish writers who wrote in Polish, they were located in the middle of the road: armed with the prestige of the Polish language, they did not, however, cross over in a determined manner to the "Polish shore." This context explained Brandstaetter's dislike of Yiddish culture, of the Diaspora, and his apotheosis of Hebrew, [a point] noted by perspicacious interwar critics. Another telling point is that Polish-Jewish writers who wrote about their linguistic situation always placed the "Hebrew language"—not Yiddish—in opposition to Polish. This stance is startling, especially when adopted by eminent poets of this language such as, say, Szymel. In trying to understand this stance one must keep in mind the influence of Zionist dogmas. What makes it difficult to arrive at an unequivocal judgment in this matter is that, in addition to the [anti-Yiddish] sentiments just described, many Polish-Jewish authors openly displayed pro-Yiddish sentiments when functioning as translators and critics.

To come back to *Wiadomości Literackie,* all circumstances contributed to its position as a crucial benchmark for the Polish-Jewish press[135] and to the position of its writers as a corresponding benchmark for Polish-Jewish writers. In Polish-Jewish circles, the case of *Wiadomości Literackie* was a variant of the "issue of assimilation," and thus a most essential problem. The questioning of the presumed "Jewishness" of Grydzewski's weekly in the columns of *Nowy Dziennik, Nasz Przegląd,* or *Opinia* was a kind of ritual,[136] and arguments concerning appraisals of writers for *Wiadomości Literackie* led to pitched battles and to splits in the group of Polish-Jewish writers. For example, Mojżesz Kanfer, editor of the literary section of *Nowy Dziennik,* became Brandstaetter's mortal enemy when [Brandstaetter] attacked Boy[-Żeleński] over the issue of Mickiewicz's Jewish legion. It is interesting that Kanfer unmasked—as it were—his opponent by describing him as a "rebuffed suitor," an author offended by the newspaper's refusal to publish his poetry. In 1935, Szymel launched a determined defense of *Wiadomości Literackie* against Brandstaetter, whose attacks he viewed as detrimental both to the newspaper and to Polish-Jewish circles.[137]

These circles included not only many suporters of the paper but also some of its contributors. Izydor Berman, one of the most meritorious and interesting Polish-Jewish critics, a translator who greatly contributed to the popularity of Franz Kafka and Joseph Roth, published in *Wiadomości Literackie, Skamander,* and *Pologne Littéraire*—in other words, in all of Grydzewski's publishing enterprises. Other Polish-Jewish writers whose work appeared in *Wiadomości Literackie* were Henryk Adler, Jehuda Warszawiak, Artur Prędski, Mieczysław Braun, Emil Igel, Herman Sternbach—and Brandstaetter. *Nasza Opinia,* whose literary section ceased to be edited by the author of *Królestwo trzeciej świątyni,* a newspaper whose profile in the late thirties was clearly anti-anti-Semitic and one which declared that it was against "the parochial spirit of party pigheadedness," treated Grydzewski's paper with gallantry and respect. It discussed the "Jewish" publications of *Wiadomości Literackie* (its 1937 discussion of anti-Semitism, among other things) and condemned the notorious attack on Słonimski.

It seems that Mojżesz Kanfer's article "Czy *Wiadomości Literackie* są pismem żydowskim?" (Is *Wiadomości Literackie* a Jewish paper?)[138] was at least in part representative of the position of the newspaper's Polish-Jewish supporters. The existing differences and ideological antagonisms notwithstanding, this camp's attitude toward the paper became progressively milder in the thirties in proportion to the growing wave of anti-Semitic attacks directed against it. As Mieczysław Braun put it in "*Wiadomości Literackie* w ogniu" (*Wiadomości Literackie* under fire),[139] the [article's] title was a portent of a tremendous conflagration that was dangerous not only for Grydzewski's acolytes.

We and You

The arguments between the Polish-Jewish press and *Wiadomości Literackie,* between its writers and Polish-Jewish writers, were due to differences of worldviews. Grydzewski's newspaper believed in and propagated optimistic liberal ideals,[140] ideas derived from the Enlightenment and from positivism and thus close to those of the Haskalah movement. The Polish-Jewish milieu represented a national movement. This movement had balanced the debit and credit sides of the position based on enlightenment and assimilation and, already at the turn of the twentieth century, had made pessimistic corrections to the nineteenth century's cheerful visions of social progress. From the time of its birth, the Jewish national movement was engaged in a contest with assimilation. This problem was undoubtedly one of the most important topics of Polish-Jewish journalism. References to predecessors whose views one fought against, to a negative tradition, made one's own position more expressive. "The bankruptcy of assimilation" was the starting point of the orientation represented by the Polish-Jewish press as well as the starting point for the formation of the attitude of Polish-Jewish writers. The squaring of accounts with assimilation, with the attitude of writers who supported assimilation, was of utmost importance for establishing the premises of Polish-Jewish literary programs. The manner of thinking about both questions seems to be well presented in Stefan Pomer's cycle of articles dealing with the topic of assimilation in the works of nineteenth century assimilationist writers no longer remembered in the interwar period. Pomer selected texts and writers that would help him to prove as convincingly as possible the thesis that, when talking about assimilation, one should really talk largely (if not exclusively) about the costs paid by the individual who was actually disinherited rather than assimilated.[141] Hence the obvious conclusion that "assimilation is neither . . . possible nor realizable."[142] There is no doubt that this conclusion represented the worldview axiom of the Polish-Jewish milieu.

It is an undeniable fact that the skirmishes between *Wiadomości Literackie* and the Polish-Jewish milieu were contests between assimilationists and Zionists. But this was only one aspect of the problem. Indeed, Polish-Jewish writers regarded the group around *Wiadomości Literackie* as an epigone of a compromised ideology. But behind the clash of ideologies was hidden the conflict of two models of a Jewish identity.[143] The respective positions of *Wiadomości Literackie* and of the Polish-Jewish writers displayed this conflict all too clearly. When the newspaper defended the right of the assimilated to full participation in Polish culture,[144] the writers declared their support for Jewish culture in Polish. When *Wiadomości Literackie* became the center of attraction for Polish writers of Polish-Jewish origin, the Jewish press became the the center of attraction for Jewish writers who wrote in Polish.

It is significant that it was not the older Polish-Jewish writers (those of the Young Poland variety) who manifested the *Wiadomości Literackie* "complex" but the younger ones. This problem deserves to be considered at some length. In particular, the Polish-Jewish arguments with *Wiadomości Literackie* must be viewed in the context of the Polish literary market at the time when they first arose.

Already in the interwar period it was noted that Polish-Jewish writers were for the most part younger writers. In fact, they were the youngest of the generations then entering literature. That is why Chaim Löw regarded Polish-Jewish writing as a new tendency of a distinctly generational character.[145] Indeed, it flourished in the early thirties, and most of the credit for this goes to the 1900–14 generation. According to Ludwik Fryde's map of the literary generations of the interwar period,[146] this was the third, the youngest of the then active generations. Their birth dates made them younger brothers of the Skamandrites, members of the Skamander group. Their dialogue with *Wiadomości Literackie* was a generational dialogue. Brandstaetter's rebellion against the *Skamander* traditions also had some characteristics of a war of the young against the old. For—and this must not be overlooked—the Polish-Jewish poets were the younger brothers of the Skamandrites also in the artistic sense. Mieczysław Braun is classified as a "satellite of *Skamander*." Szymel and Pomer undoubtedly came from Tuwim's poetic school, and Szymel transferred models derived from this school to poetry in Yiddish.[147] Eker openly described herself as a student of [Maria] Pawlikowska-Jasnorzewska. (Brandstaetter seems to have been an exception, although Napierski, for example, thought that he could discern in Brandstaetter a certain dependence on Tuwim even in his pseudoclassical—as he diagnosed it—debut.) If one located the writing of young Polish-Jewish poets on the map of Polish interwar poetry, then it would turn out that it belonged for the most part to the "*Skamander* catchment area"; connections with classicism (Brandstaetter) or with the avant-garde (Wit[kower]) were far weaker.[148] This is not surprising. The Skamander model of poetry was to some extent a model of popular poetry,[149] and thus more accessible and adoptable. As such, it was dominant in second-rate literature, which included most of Polish-Jewish poetry. Of course, all this can explain the particular choice of literary models.

It is not difficult to see that the cult of Tuwim in Jewish circles had still other, quite different motives. For his admirers in these circles (such as Pomer, Szymel, and Berman) Tuwim was a new embodiment of Heine, a new model of a Jew and a writer who went from his own sphere to all of Europe.

The fact that Brandstaetter, Szymel, and Pomer were younger brothers of the Skamandrites had still other consequences. The literary fates of Tuwim, Słonimski, and Wittlin were important elements of the education of the young. They could see that the older writers were "middle-class conquerors" (as Fryde called the *Skamander* generation) who had won an excellent position in the literary market, but they could also see that the splendid careers of Tuwim and Słonimski were from the very beginning accompanied by mutterings or screams of prejudice in circles that regarded themselves as guardians of the "purity" of Polish culture. The anti-Skamander "paseist-rightist"* (Janusz Stradecki's term) opposition was formed at the time when the group was coming into being at the university, at the time of *Pro Arte*† and *Picador*.‡[150] The nasty demonstrations during Skamandrite poetry evenings most frequently took the form of nationalistic, anti-Semitic pranks.[151] Janusz Stradecki's description of the activities of the right wing of the anti-*Skamander* camp shows that the nationalistic offensive lasted throughout the interwar period and that different generations of critics joined the fight. The old—Rabski, Pieńkowski, Wasilewski, Nowaczyński, Cywiński—formed a common front with the young—Hrabyk, Mosdorf, Piasecki, Rembieliński, Gałuszka, Pietrkiewicz—against "Jewcommunism and Jewmasonry [*żydokomuna i żydomasoneria*]." By carefully studying the excellent bibliographical documentation of Tuwim's writing, one can easily find out how persistently he was tormented.[152]

The just mentioned contest in the area of literary journalism is only too well known to historians.[153] But there are less well known, and just as interesting, literary manifestations of this contest that deserve attention. There are two, now forgotten, novels that represent the position of conservative *endek* circles. They were written at the beginning and end of the interwar period respectively, by authors belonging to different generations: Józef Weyssenhoff's *Cudno i ziemia cudeńska* (Cudno and the Cudno land) appeared in 1921 and Agnieszka Osiecka's *Krzyż na piaskach* (Cross on the sands) appeared in 1938. (Agnieszka Osiecka was the pen name of Hanna Chrzanowska, daughter of Ignacy Chrzanowski.)

The plot of Weyssenhoff's novel is simple and unsophisticated. It reflects the author's honest belief in the conspiratorial mechanism of history. It is inter-

*Traditionalists. Innovative writers applied this term to their opponents whom they accused of attachment to past literary models. [Trans.]

†*Pro Arte* (or rather *Pro Arte et Studio*): a literary journal published in Warsaw in 1916–19. Subsequently, many of the people connected with *Pro Arte* became members of the literary group *Skamander* (one of them was J. Tuwim). [Trans.]

‡At the sign of *the Picador (Pod Pikadorem)* was the poets' coffee house in Warsaw in the years 1918–19. Its founders included J. Tuwim and A. Słonimski. [Trans.]

esting that literary-artistic issues are among its more important themes. The book includes a very detailed description of a cabaret, *"à rebours,"* "full of individuals of unknown origin who are nevertheless Polish poets," "specialists at excoriating Russia and the endeks," a cabaret—the cry is finally out—"swarming with Jews."[154] The reference to poetry and the cabaret seems quite transparent: at its beginning, the *Picador* was clearly determined to shock with its newness and revolutionary flair. . . . The allegory in the [novel's] title is also easy to decipher. Thus the Cudno land is simply Poland and Joachim Staropolski, head of the ancient Cudno family, is simply talking about Jews who write in Polish:

> All these Wurms, Hinterstrahls, Fajgenwurcels, together with the pack of "our" Bolsheviks and Judeophiles won over to their faith, this is not Polish literature but one of the Jewish storm squads directed against us and growing from day to day. This gang must be chased out, thrown out of literature. . . . Every historian of literature, every critic, must condemn Jewish literature written in Polish, no honest publisher should acquire it, nor should an honest bookseller sell it.[155]

I have adduced this quotation not only because Weyssenhoff gives here, in a nutshell, the program of cultural self-defense, subsequently developed with alacrity by the national camp throughout the interwar period, but also because it includes the term "Jewish literature written in Polish." This term is of very great interest to us and is similar to the term that appeared in the thirties in Polish-Jewish circles. But Weyssenhoff uses the term in a very different sense, for he has in mind the totality of works by Jews in Polish. This being so, this term played in the endek dictionary the role of a slogan insult, forged in the battle against "Jewinfestation" [*zażydzenie*] of literature and culture.

Osiecka's (Chrzanowska's) *Krzyż na piaskach,* published seventeen years after Weyssenhoff's novel, recapitulates the stereotypes "worked out" in the meantime by the *endek*s. The romantic motif of the book—aptly summarized in the title *Panna ze dworu i wampir z Nalewek* (The maiden from the manor and the vampire from Nalewki)[156] of Chaim Löw's review—is intimately linked with the history of the contest between two models of poetry: the Polish "to the core," rustic, idyllic, and so on, and the "foreign," urban, sensual. The author plays with the reader using black and white pieces: the maiden from the manor is soulful and noble whereas the poet from Nalewki is dissolute and cynical; lofty poetry as against poetry "from the cabaret," and so on. It is characteristic [of her novel] that, as samples of "foreign poetry," Osiecka adduces pastiches of Tuwim's poems. Her romantic and literary story (which, by the way, invites a psychoanalytic interpretation) illustrates the apodictic and naive theses of the superiority of genuineness and purity of the "spirit of culture," of the triumph of virtue, and of the truth of poetry as "the language of the soul."

In the thirties, attacks on the writers for *Wiadomości Literackie* intensified with the increased xenophobia and popularity of the program of the National Democracy [*narodowa demokracja*] Party. One indication of the levels of abuse reached in these attacks is that, on the eve of the war, there were demands to close down Grydzewski's weekly and to put Tuwim and Słonimski in Bereza [a camp for political prisoners].[157] The year 1929 was an important turning point in this *endek* offensive: Karol Hubert Rostworowski promulgated his program of "restoring the health of Polish literature." In it, he formulated his definition of a "genuinely" Polish writer, which subsequently became famous among the *endek*s:

> A Polish author is an author whose experiences, that is his habits, mores, and beliefs, the things that constitute the intellectual and moral essence, grew out of, developed, and matured in a genuinely Polish environment. And conversely: an author brought up in a foreign environment cannot be a Polish writer regardless of how masterfully he handles the Polish language.[158]

It was no accident that [the *endek*s] used Tuwim, who by that time was a very popular poet, as an example of an author who handled the Polish language masterfully and was nevertheless "nongenuine." Rostworowski called him a "native Jew," a "racial Jew," a "tragic Jew," and "a resentful Jew."

In my view, the contest between the nationalistic writers[159] and the liberal-democratic writers for *Wiadomości Literackie* had two important dimensions. The more obvious dimension took the form of xenophobia, of the cult of "nativism" and cultural "purity" in the case of the old, and of anti-Semitism as a component of totalitarianism in the case of the young.[160] The possibly less obvious but equally important dimension was the reaction of the nationalistic writers to the democratization of culture. The attacks of Weyssenhoff and Chrzanowska show clearly that they regarded the *Skamander* model of poetry as an assault on the traditional—exalted!—status of art. The upset of the hitherto unchangeable hierarchy of values and prestige, of the distinction between lofty and popular poetry, was perceived as an outrage. The famous poet who supplied cabaret texts was viewed as an iconoclast, a barbarian, a "foreign invader" trampling on culture, as someone who descended to the cabaret instead of allowing, as in the past, that his lonely, "humble lyre" should buzz above it. . . . The evolution of a new formula for culture was readily blamed on "foreign" elements, and the defense against making art available to the masses was combined with anti-Semitism.

The writers for *Wiadomości Literackie* tried to dispose of the "cultural self-defense" by relying on enlightened-liberal arguments aimed at disqualifying myths such as "soul," "genuineness," and similar stereotypes.[161] On the other hand, the Polish-Jewish writers chose as an answer the Jewish national orientation. The first group never relinquished its full right to create Polish culture, while the second developed the idea of Jewish culture in Polish, thought of as part of a multilingual Jewish culture. It is worth noting that both groups fought for an open culture, the first for an open Polish culture and the second for an open Jewish culture.

The anti-Semitic attacks on the "older brothers" were undoubtedly one of the most important literary lessons for the young Polish-Jewish writers. Recalling Rostworowski's pronouncement, Stefan Pomer wrote:

> There are a very significant number of writers of Jewish origin in modern Polish literature. Since they are distinguished not only by quantity but also by quality, they are all the more visible. But, as noted, they do not admit their Jewishness and assiduously avoid in their works all things close to their origins. Moreover, they are more Polish than the Poles. They propagate genuine Slavism and hark back to Kochanowski and the Czarnolesie Muse, proclaim neo-Catholicism and the cult of Saint Francis. And they exploit their Jewishness, at best, for bits of nonsense for cabarets. Nevertheless, the *endek*s combat these converts as Jews. Of course, this is unjust.[162]

Pomer's pronouncement is a clear manifestation of the aversion to the assimilationist model of Jewish participation in Polish literature. But what also comes clearly to the fore is the significance and severity of the anti-Semitic onslaught against the assimilated.

The writers for *Wiadomości Literackie* were also "caught in a crossfire." Brandstaetter, who certainly did not spare them, admitted in 1937 that Tuwim was "baited by Polish nationalism and all too frequently and unjustly accused by the policemen of Jewish consciences."[163] One such policeman was certainly Marek Turkow, author of an anti–*Wiadomości Literackie* lampoon published in 1930, in which he accused Tuwim, Słonimski, Berman, Wasowski, and Włast not only of "*meches* anti-Semitism" but also of persistently obstructing Polish-Jewish cultural understanding and even of "disgusting renegadism [*renegactwo*]."[164] Brandstaetter had much to answer for as a "policeman": [in his capacity] as literary editor of *Opinia,* he often indiscriminately attacked *Wiadomości Literackie.*[165] [Indeed,] he regarded everything connected with the weekly as being "of the enemy" and was prepared to unmask his ideological opponents, the pseudo-

Zionists, as snobs and . . . readers of *Wiadomości Literackie*.[166] Nevertheless, he maintained that he found the *endek* "lying-in-wait for Tuwim" galling.[167] When [Kazimierz] Wierzynski was appointed academician after the death of Leśmian [Stanisław Bolesław Lesman], Polish-Jewish circles interpreted PAL's (Polska Akademia Literatury [Polish Academy of Literature]) decision as a blow aimed at Tuwim[; it] was said to have "chased him . . . beyond the gates of Polish literature."[168] The young stated openly that "the Tuwim affair," [which showed that] "the opinion of a bath attendant is more important than the dignity of real merits,"[169] brutal mass campaigns aimed at eminent creative individuals, proved the bankruptcy of assimilation. Also, the increasing anti-Semitic pressure showed that, under the circumstances, they themselves could not possibly feel at home in Polish literature which was the scene of a "national" witchhunt.

Casus Brandstaetter, or the Case of the Expelled

It seems that writers of Jewish origin who were younger than the Skamandrites could not enter the Polish literary market as easily as their older brothers. When, at the turn of the twenties, the time came for the debut of the younger writers, their prospects were eminently unfavorable. The reason for this was the growing, organized ranks of—to quote Szymel—"student ruffians as critics" who were delighted to organize "a pogrom against Tuwim's right to Polish literature, which they had no time to master in school because they were busy all the time bashing faces."[170] Which is not to say that no young writers of Jewish origin entered Polish literature in the thirties. Chaim Löw's study of Jews in Polish poetry mentions a number of relevant names. On the other hand, the poetry of, say, J[erzy] K[amil] Weintraub shows that the confrontation with "student ruffians as critics" was a serious matter for the younger brothers of the Skamandrites, and that the growing anti-Semitic atmosphere had serious consequences. Weintraub's poetry was of the two-track variety, comprising, in addition to a visionary stream, a satirical stream that attacked nationalism, racism, and anti-Semitism.[171]

When tracing the reception of Polish-Jewish literature in nationalist circles, I showed that writers who refused to embrace national Polonization and were willing and able to write in Polish ran the same risk of brutal anti-Semitic attacks as writers for whom national identification was of secondary importance and who were not inclined to engage in loud debates of this issue. But while the first group manifested its independence and distinctiveness, the second—attacked and humiliated—had no such spiritual independence to fall back upon. That embracing Polish-Jewish literature could be, and often was, tantamount to refusing to embrace national Polonization is proved by the fate of "converts"—writers who at first were not, or were very loosely, connected with Polish-Jewish circles and who, in time, crossed over decisively to the Polish-Jewish side of the "Rubicon." Here the case of Brandstaetter was the most spectacular[, although] his biography seems to have been typical of young writers who did not initially embrace Zionism but talked ever more boldly about their Jewish roots. Given the growing intensity of anti-Semitism, [however, their position] provoked brutal attacks against them.

When revealing one's Jewish roots, the generational aspect made a difference. To highlight this difference, it is worthwhile to compare the respective positions of Brandstaetter and Słonimski. Even though these two writers fought each other relentlessly, both talked about their Jewish heritage with a certain pride. The reason for their pride was that they came from families that had made signal contributions to the Haskalah. Both fondly remembered their grandfathers, who were eminent *maskil*s. But while Słonimski seemed to assert his Jewishness partly to spite his *endek* foes, to forestall attacks, to "self-unmask," Brandstaetter treated the question of origin with a seriousness that bordered on bombast, without a trace of Słonimski's provocative lack of deference. That Polish-Jewish circles initially regarded Słonimski's bold admission of his Jewish background as intimate and hopeful is shown by the extremely friendly reception of his *Podróż na Wschód* (Journey to the East): "Antoni Słonimski comes from a very respectable old family of Jewish writers and scholars. Unlike the [poetry of the] pleiad of young and talented Polish poets of Jewish origin (Tuwim, Wittlin, Stur), his poetry is marked by sincerity with respect to tradition and a genuine relation to surroundings. . . . His inner dignity guards him against reactions of mimicry."[172]

Henryk Hescheles wrote in a similar vein in 1923, following an evening of the Skamandrites in Lvov: "He knows, and does not want to hide, that he is a Jew whose psyche was shaped by an age-old tradition, a Jew who has acquired the mystery of love of the Polish word."[173]

Roman Brandstaetter, Mieczysław Braun, and Juliusz Wit[kower] were Polish-Jewish writers who most frequently crossed over to the Polish side of the "Rubicon." Brandstaetter was the most ambitious member of this group and one with leadership ambitions. Historians of interwar literature have described on a number of occasions the discussion about the youngest Polish poetry initiated by Brandstaetter in the transition period between two decades (1929–31, a period called by W[iesław] P[aweł] Szymański "the neutral region").[174] Brandstaetter's 1931 pronouncement included an outline of the poet's first literary program, a program—I stress—for Polish poetry. Its merit was a critique of the epigones of Skamander ("as if . . . Polish literature began and ended exclusively with *Skamander*")[175] and a call for a return to the old masters. The "learned poetry" [*poesis docta*] postulated by Brandstaetter derived presumably from solid rootedness in the Polish tradition. He declared in the *Gazeta Polska:* "Frankly, I don't understand how one can write poems without knowing at least the indigenous word formation as well as old literature and its history."[176] These watchwords gained few supporters. Two years later, in 1933, Brandstaetter made known his second literary program, a program for Polish-Jewish literature. Notwithstanding its critical reception, this program brought him far greater fame (on the Polish side as well) than his fight for a distinctive, anti-Skamander, classical expression of the youngest Polish poetry. It seems that the poet's change of basic orientation in his quest for literary affiliation took place between 1931 and 1933.

True, Brandstaetter was always proud of his family traditions, and during the period of his most intense raptures over the idyllic character of the life of the gentry he did not hide his Jewish heritage. (Incidentally, this "idyllic"-rustic tone of his debut was sometimes interpreted "Jewishly": "Some kind of radical transformation must have taken place in the Jewish soul if even Jewish writers who pray to God in the holy Polish tongue, as Brandstaetter does, draw their motifs from a peasant croft.")[177] In the twenties, on the threshold of his literary career, Brandstaetter's Jewish concerns were definitely weaker than his Polish concerns. From 1927 on, he was connected with the Polish-Jewish press as a critic and poet, but the reviews that he published in *Chwila* and in *Nowy Dziennik* were, for the most part, reviews of works of Polish literature and very few of his poems took up Jewish motifs.[178] In the early thirties, such motifs began to appear in his work with increasing frequency, but even then his work retained a clearly two-track character. Thus, in 1932, he presented his doctoral dissertation "Mickiewicz jako krytyk literatury polskiej w okresie wileńsko-kowieńskim," (Mickiewicz as critic of Polish literature in the Wilno-Kowno period) and published at the same time the study *Legion żydowski Adama Mickiewicza,* devoted to Mickiewicz's Constantinople mission, which seems to have contributed significantly to the change in Brandstaetter's literary orientation. Its publication generated a great deal of noise on the "Polish shore." Also, it involved its author in a protracted and sharp controversy with the *endek*s and with Boy[-Żeleński] and resulted in his falling out with his erstwhile allies in the Polish-Jewish circles. (The Polish side of the incident was described by Stanisław Piasecki in a number of essays later included in the volume *Prosto z mostu* [Straight from the shoulder; 1934][179] Piasecki was prejudiced, but his account seems to be rather accurate.)

I think that *Legion* points to a certain essential aspect of Brandstaetter's conversion. The fundamental thesis of this essay asserts that the Constantinople endeavors of Mickiewicz were in some sense precursors of Zionist actions. By invoking the philo-Semitic traditions of Polish romanticism, by regarding Mickiewicz as a pre-Zionist, Brandstaetter remained at peace with his pre—and post-conversion personas. Seen in this perspective, rootedness in the Polish tradition and rootedness in Zionism were in complete harmony with one another. As for Brandstaetter's attitude toward Mickiewicz, the many Mickiewicz-related pieces he published in the Polish-Jewish press until the outbreak of the war[180] show that Mickiewicz remained for Brandstaetter a towering and unquestionable authority, to whom he remained faithful regardless of the ebb and flow of his national feelings. Following the *Legion* affair, Brandstaetter came ever closer to the Polish-Jewish circles. The high point of his progress along this road was the publication of his manifesto for Polish-Jewish poetry. Szymel gave a penetrating analysis of the circumstances surrounding Brandstaetter's "conversion":

> *Jarzma* (Yokes) is a prayer to the Poland of the Kochanowskis and the Klonowiczs, the Poland of the histories of the Chrzanowskis and the Małeckis. Embedded in this appeal to the highest majesty of the nation, to its culture, there is a moving, subconscious, and deeply tragic concern for his literary existence, a yearning for a place for his name. From this appeal there cries out the terrifying homelessness of the Jewish spirit.
>
> Brandstaetter mobilizes the most powerful arguments in favor of his literary affiliation: he arouses all the charms of the Polish language, cherishes the patina of its antiquity, looks for patrons in tradition, and attempts to fathom the depths of the Slavic character. In this way he acquires for his heart an illusory fatherland, of which he can be deprived by any old journalist from the *Gazeta Warszawska.*[181]

In time, the voices of such journalists (the *Gazeta Warszawska* was known for its belligerent anti-Semitism) became progressively more galling for Brandstaetter. [Just] how galling can be surmised from his journalism, poetry, and prose. The evolutionary line of his "post-conversion" work was symptomatic: from praise of Zionism to defense against anti-Semitism. (At the time, this was the direction of the whole Polish-Jewish literature; the differences between the ideological profiles of *Opinia* and *Nasza Opinia* were virtually symbolic.)

Brandstaetter undoubtedly belonged to those for whom Zionism was "a kind of second choice: since they could not be Polish nationalists, they became Jewish nationalists—they could love the Jewish nation and dedicate themselves to the Jewish cause in much the same way as Mickiewicz dedicated himself to the Polish cause."[182] Ezra Mendelsohn claims that one of the reasons why members of the highly acculturated milieu joined the Zionist movement was their desire to preserve personal dignity and to win the respect of Polish society, which opposed Jewish integration.

Spiritual turning points and shifts of ideological orientation similar to Brandstaetter's conversion were not a novelty among pro-Zionist writers. In this respect, Alfred Nossig (acknowledged, as mentioned [in chapter 1], as a precursor of the Polish-Jewish writers) was a predecessor of the author of the *Królestwo trzeciej świątyni.* In 1886, Nossig left the assimilationist camp around the Lvov *Ojczyzna* (Fatherland) for the organization Zion. What is striking is the near identity of the ideological climate of the two conversions. Like Brandstaetter, Nossig was bewitched by the philo-Semitic strands of Polish romanticism and stressed, above all, the political and ideological dimensions of Zionism rather than cultural issues. Already in the nineteenth century, this position was described as typical of those "who lacked genuine ties with Judaism, who approached Zionism solely because they had rejected assimilation."[183] While, in other cases, the first—the Polish—option tended to be suppressed, Brandstaetter's "prayer to Poland" echoed loud and clear.

It seems that we can even speak of a syndrome of drawing on the Polish tradition for arguments for a Zionist conversion. We also find this syndrome in the case of Mieczysław Braun, who left us an interesting record of "maturing to Zionism" in a series of articles "Czarne i białe" (Black and white) published in *Nasz Przegląd* in the years 1937–39. In Braun's case, too, the impulse for the ideological return[184] was the rising wave of anti-Semitism which the author tried to attack with his scathing texts. They were an expression of his initial conviction that he who "in a moment of depression will reach for a bomb of laughing gas will defeat his opponent."[185] In time, altogether nonhumorous notes began to accompany the sneers and puns. These nonhumorous notes culminated in the essay *Syjonizm Adama Mickiewicza* (The Zionism of Adam Mickiewicz), published in the beginning of 1939. Referring to Brandstaetter's study about the Constantinople mission, Braun wrote:

> It will not be a paradox if I say that Adam Mickiewicz, the genius of the Polish nation, was a Zionist. The historical truth contained in these words makes use of a term that came into being a few decades after the great poet's death. The idea of Zionism, two thousand years older than its name, was frequently appreciated and less frequently supported by other nations. . . . Mickiewicz's positive work aimed at the creation of a Jewish Legion was an attempt to solve the Diaspora problem independently of another great aim that it pursued.[186]

Braun's discovery of Mickiewcz's Zionism was accompanied by his critique of the assimilationist position (contained in a feuilleton with the expressive title "Na straconej pozycji" [At a lost position],[187] and especially of the conviction that the Jews are a religious group rather than a nation. Braun stated ever more frequently that the only way to solve "the Jewish question" was for the Jews to acquire a land and to create a Jewish state. He wrote that "the Jewish independence movement is the only powerful motor capable of lifting the best part of the nation out of its torpor and hopelessness."[188] In this view, Zionism could be regarded as a form of a fight for independence ("a fight for an independent Jewish Palestine").[189]

There are further similarities between Braun's stance and Brandstaetter's ideological evolution. In the spring of 1939, Braun formulated his new position, which was a replica of the ideological starting point of Brandstaetter's 1933 manifesto for Polish-Jewish poetry. The problem was the same as in earlier years, namely, the tasks of the Jewish intelligentsia in the new social and political situation. Braun called for involvement in cultural work animated by a national ideology: "Not only are the social activist, the politician, and the journalist working for national liberation and for the creation of a new type of Jewish intellectual but also the writer, poet, musician, artist, and scholar; in fact, anyone who offers what is best in himself and does not distance himself from his nation in a selfish and cowardly manner."[190]

Impetuous and somewhat reckless, Brandstaetter got frequently entangled in actions that, though responding to anti-Semitic attacks, seemed to adopt the modus operandi of his opponents. His reactions were marked by hurt pride, determination—and helplessness. When the *Gazeta Warszawska* published a proscription list of Polish writers of Jewish origin, Brandstaetter published in *Opinia* a supplement to this list.[191] At the time of the intensification of the propaganda of "Polish cultural self-defense," he launched the watchword of Jewish cultural self-defense and popularized it while traveling across the country.[192] If we read carefully the text in which he called for Jewish cultural self-defense, and skip the provocative accents and the controversial description of the state of Jewish culture, then we can see that it is none other than an expression of disappointment in European culture; it is the voice of the Jew expelled from this culture:

> Polish Jewry, staring snobbishly at the literary assets of European culture whose highest modern emanation and dominant factor is fascism, so foreign to the Jewish spirit, refuses to return to the original sources of its own spiritual assets, to the fertile democratic subsoil of its own culture; it thinks that scratching the

> rotting cuticle of European culture is tantamount to progress and enlightenment! . . . [T]oday, in view of the great reevaluation of the values of the fascisized European culture, the only road available to the Jewish society in Poland and to the Jewish writer is a return to the sources of its own culture, to the trenches that enclose Jewry in an impervious ring of fortifications in the face of the pressure of hostile forces.[193]

Here the return to Jewry amounts to hiding behind the shield of Jewishness; it is a return-*cum*-flight from European culture, which has no place for the Jewish newcomers, which has betrayed true values. The metaphors in Brandstaetter's pronouncement—the trenches, fortifications, attack, and self-defense—all these reflect the atmosphere of encirclement and peril. Small wonder that such a climate gave rise in individuals to the tendency to unite with a group that guaranteed a sense of acceptance and affiliation, to the tendency to look for a "we" of which they could safely be a part.

Brandstaetter was not the only one who called for a return to untainted sources of culture. In the late thirties, many in the Polish-Jewish press spoke of the decline of European culture, democracy, and humanism, about the "war epoch," about totalitarianism and dictatorship, and about anti-Semitism as a manifestation of Europe's "spiritual infection." In this situation Braun, for example, thought that the most urgent task for the Jewish intelligentsia was a return "to the sources of national and universal human spiritual culture."[194]

There is no need to prove that the anti-Semitic pressure, the expulsion complex, was a traumatic experience. It suffices to recall the case of Tuwim, on whom the anti-Semitic atmosphere of the thirties had an especially destructive effect.[195] Given that a writer of Jewish origin could expect from the Polish side only attacks and rejection and that the only language he could write in was Polish, it is not surprising that one increasingly encountered in the Polish-Jewish press the names of writers of Jewish origin who had never, or seldom, appeared in these papers before, names of writers of a different ideological orientation. Such writers included Sydor Rey [Izydor Reiss], Henryka Łazowertówna, Włodzimierz Słobodnik, and Artur Prędski.[196] The permanent collaborators with *Opinia* included Leonard Hanin, Leon Pasternak (author of the splendid satirical feuilleton "Figa z makiem . . ." [A fig for you . . .]), Józef Nacht, and Stanisław Jerzy Lec. And—wonder of wonders!—even Leo Belmont began to write for *Opinia,* the same Belmont who somewhat earlier thundered against that paper's "Jewish nationalism" and poked fun at willows that were not cedars and the talliths of Polish-Jewish poetry.

The stories of Rey and Łazowertówna can serve as a commentary on the situation, for they dealt—rather tellingly—with anti-Semitism.[197] Another such commentary is provided by Artur Prędski's novel *Serce bez ojczyzny* (Heart without a fatherland).[198] The metaphorical title, the clearly autobiographical motifs (the hero is a former Legionnaire—Prędski was the youngest soldier in [Piłsudski's] Legions—a Jew, a Polish journalist who prepares a balance sheet of his life), the interruption of the narrative at the moment when the personal and professional affairs of the figures in the story become extremely complicated as a result of the chokingly anti-Semitic atmosphere—all these are highly symptomatic.

Yet another commentary, supplied by Adolf Rudnicki, takes the form of observations made in Kazimierz on the Vistula:

> As we said earlier, all around raged an anti-Semitic hell. Jews, assimilated and nonassimilated, as well as converts, used to come to the small town. That summer, the latter seemed to be, well, ashamed. . . . Having failed to win the approval of the part of society they had joined, they came back and asked forbearance of the silence that gnawed at their souls. They returned to a fate they thought they had cast off forever, and their thoughts, hitherto sharp and sober, must have suffered the kind of dimming, of discouragement, that destroys the faith in the possibility of progress. Having failed to find tranquillity, they returned to the former milieu to look for comfort.[199]

I have no intention whatever of regarding Polish-Jewish literature as a movement of those expelled from Polish literature. But the importance of the expelled for this literature must under no circumstances be passed over in silence: it is these very individuals who contributed significantly to the awareness of the distinctiveness of this literature. And I think that it was no accident that the first manifesto for Polish-Jewish literature came from the pen of a "neophyte."

Anti-Semitism and the Ghetto in Culture

The appearance of a group of writers expelled from Polish literature was the result of a process that had begun before the interwar period. Anti-Semitism in Polish culture has not yet been described in a penetrating and detailed way. I feel, however, that the mechanism that brought about the triumph of xenophobia and nationalism in Poland can nevertheless be outlined without serious error, because the mechanism in question operated throughout Europe. In his *From Prejudice to Destruction: Anti-Semitism, 1700–1933,* Jacob Katz interprets the "scandal of the Jewish artist" as a problem resulting from the coming into being of a free market in cultural goods and of unrestricted competition in that market.

Katz's diagnosis pertains to anti-Semitism in German culture, but it seems very helpful when analyzing the Polish situation: In Poland, as in Germany, the "scandal" in question broke loose when a substantial group of artists appeared on the literary market. This resulted in an increased number of conflicts due to competition for readers.[200]

The equal rights of Jewish writers to participate in Polish literature were always questioned. But while in the nineteenth century this questioning took the form of isolated attacks on particular writers, from the beginning of the twentieth century it translated into a concerted campaign against the "Jewinfestation" [*zażydzenie*] of Polish literature. A few examples will suffice. When responding to [Julian] Klaczko's critique of *Krewni* (Relatives), Józef Korzeniowski reached for anti-Semitic arguments in his drama *Złote kajdany* (Golden handcuffs).[201] In his novel *Ciury* (Small fry; 1904), Wiktor Gomulicki portrayed Aleksander Kraushar as a Warsaw "literary figure" and concentrated for the most part on issues of origin. In the drama *Za cenę łez* (For the price of tears; 1910), [Jerzy] Żuławski depicted [Wilhelm] Feldman in a malicious manner ("the gentleman-expert on literature"). It seems that the campaign against Feldman, launched by writers angered by assessments in his *Współczesna literatura polska* (Modern Polish literature), was the first organized action of a new kind. It took such uncivil forms that part of the literary establishment felt duty bound to defend the attacked critic.[202] In connection with the Feldman case, [Karol] Irzykowski wrote as follows: "There is a natural task for a Jew in Poland. Since he is not spontaneously linked with the past of the nation and is not weighed down by the burden of various national commandments, he can be a sobering factor, can banish needless stupors [*hipnozy*], can be a middleman, and can steer toward firmer contacts with the cultures of other nations."[203] From this position, the author of *Czyn i słowo* (The deed and the word) charged Feldman with trying to be more Polish than the Poles, whereas he could play an extremely positive role if he abandoned the role of a neophyte and made use of his distance from Polishness instead. In the last analysis, this viewpoint, which Irzykowski himself called "culturalistic" and described as a sociological interpretation of the Jewish question, led to the same conclusion as that of the defenders of "genuineness": regardless of the arguments and reasons advanced, the status of a Jew in Polish literature was to be different from, and unequal to, the status of a Pole.

From the beginning of the century, the problem of the ostracism encountered by authors of Jewish origin began to turn up more frequently as a topic in their works. The mood of this group of writers is reflected in Michał Mutermilch's novel *Żydzi* (The Jews; 1905), whose plot deals with acculturizing Jewish circles. One of the novel's key scenes is a discussion of the situation of the artist of Jewish origin in his contacts with the Polish public. The diagnosis is very pessimistic: "Our time has not yet arrived. . . . Our society is not used to the participation of Jews in literary and artistic work. That is why in the press they either kick us or kill us with silence."[204] One of the book's main characters suggests dropping the practice of hiding behind Polish-sounding pseudonyms and other "disguises" [*"zdjęcie przyłbicy"*]. But none of his listeners has any illusions about the response to such a move on the part of readers and of cultural opinion makers alike.

Mutermilch's novel appeared in 1905, before the campaign against Feldman. In 1910, one year after that campaign, Aniela Kallas published the novel *On i oni wszyscy,* in which the literary failures of the young writer Leon Berger elicit the following comment: "They don't want to show this drama because its author is a Jew. The current watchword is 'ridding Polish literature of Jews,' and you, a Jew, had the temerity to write a Jewish drama in Polish."[205]

The Feldman affair, the positions adopted at that time, and the divisions of the literary milieu, all these show that the acculturation and assimilation of Jews greatly frightened certain circles of the Polish intelligentsia. Of course, this was just one manifestation of a more extensive and serious phenomenon. But the following cultural aspect of anti-Semitism must under no circumstances be overlooked: the progress of Jewish acculturation induced on the Polish side an ever more intense tendency to remove the Jews from Polish culture. Moreover, from the beginning of the century, this tendency was given currency in the writings of many journalists connected with the national camp. For example, Stanisław Pieńkowski exclaimed in 1912:

> The Jews in all their multimillion multitude craving the Polish language, for our culture, for fellow citizenship of feelings and spirit with us! Could anyone devise a more monstrous, a more devilish danger for us in this matter?! Truly, that beats all! All we need is this "victory" over Jewish separatism, this mass conversion of Jews to the bosom of our culture. . . . Pyrrhus's victory would pale to zero in its sarcasm in the face of this tragicomical situation for which we would pay with our own [spiritual] life.[206]

The groups represented by Pieńkowski advocated the ideal of a pure, "authentic," "national" culture. That is why Pieńkowski had nothing but praise for the 99 percent of Jews who, he claimed, knew nothing about Polish culture. This is not to imply that the national camp valued Jewish culture. Far from it. It regarded Jewish culture as "twisted" and "organically abortive," much like the "Jewish soul" of which this culture was an expression.

Jewish culture and the "Jewish soul" did not inspire fear as long as they were excluded from the Polish world. But the traces of this "psyche" were pursued obsessively: "A foreign and hostile race of subhumans, straight out of its heders [parochial schools], forced its way into the community center of the Polish tongue and gave in it a purim ball, complete with *marsheliks* [emcees] of the Talmudic art and heroes of a whorish provocation."[207]

The activities of Pieńkowski, Wasilewski, Gruszecki, Weyssenhoff, and other writers of the older, Young Poland, generation prove clearly that, while the tendency to exclude writers of Jewish origin from Polish culture reached its high point during the interwar period, it originated earlier.

The ideas of the older men were picked up and extensively developed by younger men. The best known of those associated with the campaign of "cultural self-defense" were Stanisław Piasecki, Jan Mosdorf, Jan Rembieliński, and Jerzy Pietrkiewicz.[208] The psychotic obsession with an "invasion" of the culture "by strangers" which appeared for the first time in the first decade of the twentieth century, gained greater intensity from decade to decade. Terms that served to delimit the sphere of writing in Polish which was to be the region of "foreignness" appeared and gained currency in the twenties. As noted earlier, Weyssenhoff called it "Jewish literature written in Polish" (1921). Pieńkowski referred to it as "crypto-Jewish poetry" (1926),[209] and Rostworowski as "Judeo-Polish literature" (1929).[210] This sphere was to be a kind of ghetto for all writers of Jewish origin regardless of the topics of their works and of their sense of national and cultural identity. The key criterion was the writer's origin and the verdict was based on the lack of Polish "authenticity."

Arguments suggested by psychological racism were used with great frequency. Thus Zdzisław Dębicki claimed in 1927 that what distinguished writers of Jewish origin and made them "a special group of foreigners writing in Polish" was the lack of a "national link": "Here all masquerades, all mimicry, all hiding behind adopted artificial names are of no avail. The different, non-Polish structure of soul and mind will always show itself. This is the way it must be and the way it should be, for no range of phenomena depends as closely on psychological race as the range of artistic phenomena, whose roots are firmly embedded in the psyche of a nation."[211]

Two other manifestos of xenophobia appeared in the twenties. They created a far greater stir than the pronouncement of Dębicki and were soon included in the canon of writings of the nationalist circles. The earlier of the two was Tadeusz Zieliński's famous *Helenizm i Judaism* (Hellenism and Judaism; 1927), which was an attempt at a radical break with the Jewish heritage of Christianity. In his enthusiasm for de-Judaizing Christianity and making it Greek, the author went to such extremes that he provoked protests from Hellenists, Catholic theologians, and specialists in Judaism. Nevertheless, *Helenizm i Judaism* soon became an inspiration and an important authority, relied upon in many pronouncements of "national" authors. It was cited by such otherwise different writers as Henryk Rolicki (*Zmierzch Izraela* [The decline of Israel; 1931]), Karol Hubert Rostworowski, and Jan Rembieliński. In his (earlier mentioned) project for restoring the health—sanification—of Polish literature, Rostworowski determined, for example, the realm of the truly "native" heritage: "Greece gave rise to Rome, Rome to the papacy, and the papacy to Latin culture, whose eastern redoubt [*"reduta Ordona"* refers to the last stand of one of Kościuszko's generals—Trans.] is Poland. The fact that certain nations did and others did not adopt this culture proves the racial and spiritual kinship of the former."[212]

Rostworowski's project for the "sanification of literature [*sanacja literatury*]," published in 1929, was a signal for the intensification of efforts at "cultural self-defense." It was interpreted as such on the Jewish side and was immediately answered by Samuel Hirszhorn and Samuel Imber.[213] Imber's essay "Co nam i tobie, Tuwimie. . . ?" (What do we and you have in common, Tuwim. . . ?) elicited a considerable response. Imber refuted his opponent's claims point by point in a down-to-earth, civilized manner. He opposed the psychological racism of the author of *Antychryst* (Antichrist) and claimed that the question of affiliation to a particular literature is decided exclusively by the criterion of language, and that Jewish literature consists only of works written in the Jewish languages. He claimed that "Jewish literature is a sovereign territory and not a 'Devil's Island' to which another literature could banish undesirable 'dangerous elements.' "[214] Warm sympathy for those under attack and a friendly defense of their full right to create Polish literature were only one aspect of the position adopted by the author of *Asy czystej rasy* (Purebred aces) [Imber]. Another important component of his position was the conviction of the chasm separating Tuwim and Słonimski from the "Jewish shore," a conviction close to the one that animated Polish-Jewish writers who made a decisive break with the models worked out by the assimilating writers.[215]

The issues that were the subject of the polemic between Rostworowski and Imber were important for the self-definition of Polish-Jewish literature. That is why Brandstaetter joined the debate after the appearance of the essay "Co nam i tobie, Tuwimie. . . ?" in the volume *Asy czystej rasy* (1934). His position in the debate about the boundaries of the national literature and the determination of the criteria of membership of individual authors in it, differed from the positions and proposals of both Imber and Rostworowski. When Rostworowski distributed "citizenship papers" that acknowledged an author's affiliation to a specific national literature he relied on arguments of psychological racism in that he insisted on the decisive role of origins. Imber made use of an objective linguistic criterion and ignored the problem of the writer's identity. But Brandstaetter argued that

> a poet's affiliation to a particular literature is not measured by language or origin but by his awareness of a cultural and historical connection and solidarity with the nation to whose literature he wishes to belong. Here language and origin are irrelevant. Thus Klaczko, Tuwim, and Słonimski are Polish writers because they are not tied to Jewish culture and history by an emotional imperative, whereas Feuchtwanger and Max Brod are Jewish writers because their consciousness is embedded in Jewishness as a historical and cultural concept.[216]

We see that [Brandstaetter's] was a third way: the decisive issue was the writer's national and cultural self-identification.

In the thirties, pronouncements similar to those of Dębicki and Rostworowski became increasingly common. Their authors were not only older and younger *endek* journalists but also older and younger writers and critics. Many of them were respected, eminent, and popular. The voice of the older writers was represented by the open letter to Stefan Pomer ("Żyd to Polak z rezerwą: Do szanownego Pana Kolegi Stefana Pomera, poety, autora *Elegii podolskich*" [A Jew is an undecided Pole: To my respected Colleague Stefan Pomer, poet, author of *Elegie podolskie*]), published by Irzykowski in 1937 in the *Kurier Poranny*. In this article, Irzykowski's stand on the participation of Jews in literature was essentially the same as his stand on the Feldman affair[, although] certain new accents appeared that were undoubtedly a sign of the times. That he wrote, with Jews in mind, of "literature's utter lack of immunity in the face of the Hyksos invasion"[217] shows that the obsession with an invasion of Polish literature by strangers had taken firm hold of this critic. To his horror, these "Hyksos" had not only conquered the Parnassus but had become a significant and influential part of the public. Irzykowski attacked most sharply the writers for *Wiadomości Literackie*—with whom he quarreled for a variety of reasons—but neither did he spare the Young Poland authors, again bringing up the Feldman affair. The one difference between Irzykowski's pronouncement from the beginning of the century and the one from the late thirties concerned assimilation. In 1937, he was definitely opposed to it. And while he gave a penetrating characterization of the assimilating individual faced with the antipathy of the group he wanted to join, he viewed the right of choice of national affiliation, a right which he called "national Anabaptism" [*anabaptyzm narodowy*] as an undeserved Jewish privilege.

He claimed that "a Jew was an undecided Pole." The position of the Jew in the Polish collectivity was exceptional and privileged, he was "above normal from the viewpoint of nationality," and this above-normality was the source of conflict. In other words, the cause of Polish-Jewish misunderstandings was, according to Irzykowski, the free choice of national identity, so frequently debated in Polish-Jewish circles. Small wonder that, under the circumstances, Irzykowski's open letter to Pomer resulted in negative Polish-Jewish comments[218] and its author was dubbed an "undecided anti-Semite."

The loudest and most unpleasant of the younger writers who joined the anti-Semitic chorus was Konstanty Ildefons Gałczyński. His [1937] pronouncement was also contained in [an open] letter, addressed "Do Przyjaciół z *Prosto z mostu*" (To friends from *Prosto z mostu* [published in the literary journal of the same name—Trans.)]. Gałczynski called for "the removal of foreign corpses from the Polish meadow,"[219] cursed "poetic zaddikim," "lice living in the shadow of the Polish sword," "peiperokikes" [*"peiperogudłaj"* is a composite of "Peiper," the name of a Polish-Jewish author, and *"gudłaj,"* one of a number of Polish variants of "kike"—Trans.], "the rabble of pacifists, Socialists. . . , Wellsians, scientifists, friends of the man-in-the-street," and opposed to all this his ideal of a poet: a Pole-Catholic. In its stress on "sunniness, Greek-ness, and Christian-ness" this ideal reflected the spiritual patronage of [Tadeusz] Zieliński.

Stanisław Czernik's essay *Dwadzieścia lat poezji polskiej 1918–1938* (Twenty years of Polish poetry, 1918–1938), published at the beginning of 1939, can be regarded as a kind of crowning touch bestowed on the tendency to remove assimilated and acculturated Jews from Polish literature. The author acknowledged the problem of "two literatures" and the need for their separation as urgent for Polish literature. He wrote: "After 1918, there emerged the problem of virtually two literatures: Polish literature and literature in Polish, the two not being always identical. This is not an isolated phenomenon. It suffices to mention Polish literature in Latin or literature in English."[220]

Notwithstanding Czernik's assurances that it was not a question of creating a literary ghetto, his "Polish-Jewish poetic condominium," in which he placed Leśmian, Tuwim, Wittlin, Słonimski, Słobodnik, Napierski, Jastrun, Jasieński, Peiper, Ważyk, and Brandstaetter, was just such a closed quarter. Czernik's use of phrases such as "the mystique of a nation," "foreignness to the Polish psyche," "sabotage and partisan warfare in literature" disclosed his ideological inspiration. True, [his] essay included attempts at a sociological explanation (likely taken over from Czachowski) of the growing participation of Jews in Polish poetry, but the intentions behind its general premise were beyond doubt: Leśmian formed neologisms because of his lack of "understanding" of the Polish language, Tuwim's poetry was being washed away by "the subsoil water of productions for the stage," the tone of Wittlin's lyricism was "typically Semitic," and so on and so forth. The argument that the creation of a separate island of poets of "Semitic origin" was as justified as the singling out of a group of poets of peasant origin was hardly persuasive. Czernik's resentments and stereotypes about an "invasion" of native culture by "strangers" were far too explicit. His complaints that the new assimilation (called "quasi-assimilation") was not the good, old identificational variant were not based on a positive evaluation of the process as such; Czernik was ready to admit to Polish literature a few barely assimilated writers. But such inclusion was to depend on the acceptance by the Polish side, on its offering the "new arrivals" membership certificates. The issue of who was to be classified as "one of us" was not addressed by Czernik. He wrote about the extreme differentiation of "the Polish-Jewish poetic condominium" and the complexity of all distinctions and classifications in it but was adamant on one point: poetry without a trace of yearning for Polishness—for example, the work of Brandstaetter—was not part of Polish literature. As for the criteria to be used for the determination of the boundaries of the condominium in question, their source was undoubtedly psychological racism; the only thing that linked Leśmian, Tuwim, Słonimski, Wat, Jasieński [Bruno Zyskind], and Brandstaetter, all classified as writers belonging to the Polish-Jewish borderland, was their origin. Like Rostworowski, Czernik believed that "if it is not due to the tactic of adjustment to reality, the adoption of a language has . . . in a way, a substitute significance."[221] This is so because language is sometimes imposed by external conditions, whereas the person, the artist, can retain and save a kind of "national fluid." It was this element—called by Czernik the "mystique of a nation"—that was to decide the affiliation of a writer to one or another national literature. Given the brand of the "national psyche" impressed by the artist on his works, the editor of the *Okolica Poetów* (Poets' region) went so far as to predict that in the future the Jews would "revindicate" Jewish authors and would "single out their literature from foreign literatures."[222]

At this point, it is essential to distinguish the tendency just discussed, a tendency with a well-defined ideological significance, from another tendency which, in a way, also involved a certain limitation of the freedom of writers of Jewish origin, namely, the tendency, to assign to them a "plot of ground" [*poletko*] in the field of Polish literature. Some thought this plot of ground should be that of Jewish themes. The reasons behind such a position, reasons shared by writers such as [Leopold] Staff and [Kazimiera] Iłłakowiczówna, who certainly disapproved of anti-Semitism, were in a sense close to the ideas animating Jewish circles. What was appealed to was the conception of literature as a means of national rapprochement. Staff discussed the idea of Polish-Jewish understanding with Henryk Adler: "It is regrettable that our talented Polish writers of Jewish origin avoid so scrupulously Jewish themes. If we had in our literature someone like Martin Buber, then we would have acquired a deeper notion of the nation that created the *Bible*."[223] This time it was the Polish side which concluded that "only true Jews can write a true novel about true Jews."[224]

Anti-Semitism was part of the social and cultural reality of the interwar period. Some sociologists and historians are inclined to regard it as the most essential influence on Jewish life at the time.[225] How extremely burning an issue it was for the Polish-Jewish milieu can be judged from the literary and journalistic texts of Brandstaetter, Szymel, Berman, Braun, and [Emil] Tenenbaum.[226] A very characteristic motif appeared in a number of stories in which the protagonists—Jews writing in Polish—were subjected to sui generis identity tests during anti-Semitic disturbances.[227]

What is striking is that it was the "expelled" writers who paid the most attention to anti-Semitism. Their Zionist conversions were very clearly linked to setbacks due to anti-Semitism. I think that at this point it is worthwhile to look more closely at the motif of anti-Semitism in the work of Brandstaetter. His most important and longest anti-anti-Semitic pronouncements appeared in the volume *Zmowa eunuchów* (1936); many shorter texts remained newspaper columns. This is true, for example, of the poems "Ballada o pogromie" (Ballad of a pogrom), "Do antysemitów" (To anti-Semites), "Wizja antysemity" (Vision of an anti-Semite), of the autobiographical prose piece "Nad brzegiem polskiej rzeki" (At the shore of a Polish river), and of the essays *Gdzie jest polski Zola? Refleksje na temat polskiej elity umysłowej do kwestii żydowskiej* (Where is the Polish Zola? Reflections on the attitude of the Polish intellectual elite toward the Jewish question), *Gilotyna i elektryczne krzesło: Dzieje dwóch antysemitów* (The guillotine and the electric chair: The history of two anti-Semites), *Niema kwestii żydowskiej, jest tylko antysemityzm* (There is no Jewish question, there is only anti-Semitism), and *Moszkopolis* [literally, "city of Moszeks"; "Moszek" is a contemptuous Polish epithet for a Jew—Trans.].[228] The leitmotiv of these texts was the thought of the dislike, incomprehension, and finally hostility that the Jews invariably experienced in their contacts with Poles. There even appeared the thesis (in *Gilotyna i elektryczne krzesło*) of anti-Semitism as the *general* attitude of Poles toward Jews, an attitude that merely took on different appearances, such as the open anti-Semitism of the conservatives, the "perfidious" anti-Semitism of the liberals, and the "humanitarian," "perfumed," "enlightened," and so on, varieties of anti-Semitism. In this perspective, Prus, Jeske-Choiński, Kraszewski, Jeleński, and others became anti-Semites.

Braun's feuilletons in *Nasz Przegląd* (mentioned earlier) provide a kind of chronicle of anti-Semitic excesses in cultural, political, and academic life in the years 1937–39. The very listing of some of the titles is instructive: "Antysemici na start" (Anti-Semites to the starting line; 1937, no. 256), "Spowiedź antysemity" (Confession of an anti-Semite; 1937, no. 295), "Tragedja antysemitów" (The tragedy of the anti-Semites; 1937, no. 367), "Antysemityzm życia codziennego" (Anti-Semitism in daily life; 1938, no. 29). Braun did not limit himself to describing the symptoms of the phenomenon; he also provided its psychological interpretation and linked it to the crisis of European culture transformed into a European "jungle."

In his work (often cited earlier) on the multilingual interwar culture of the Polish Jews, Chone Shmeruk asked a question pertaining to the press but valid for all Polish writing: "To what extent did the Polish dislike of the Jews and the Jews' inability to publish in the non-Jewish press contribute to the rise of the 'Jewish alternative'?"[229] I am convinced that the tendency of Polish culture to isolate "strangers" was of cardinal importance.

Since they had contacts with the Polish literary market and the Polish public—since they solicited such contacts themselves—Polish-Jewish writers encountered this tendency as an essential component of the Polish cultural reality. This would indicate that an investigation of Polish-Jewish literature as a phenomenon remaining exclusively within the orbit of just one of the cultures of the borderland—the culture from which it arose—and isolated and independent from the influences of the second, would significantly and unfairly narrow the investigative perspective. In other words, a fuller understanding of the phenomenon requires reference to the context of both Jewish and Polish life. Similarly, it is impossible to explain and understand Jewish history without relating it to the lives of the nations in which they led a Diaspora existence.[230]

As a cultural phenomenon then, Polish-Jewish literature must be related on the one hand to the progress of acculturation and the formation of the modern Jewish national consciousness and, on the other, to the Polish anti-assimilationist and nationalistic currents that gave rise to the conception of the "purity" and "authenticity" of the culture and the campaign of "cultural self-defense." The phenomena under discussion were related, and expressed themselves in tendencies that were in a sense convergent: the tendency to include cultural activity in Polish [of certain Jews—Trans.] in the ambit of Jewish culture encountered the wish to remove Jewish writing in Polish from Polish culture.

Of course, I do not forget that these tendencies differed at their foundations because of the different cultural models they were meant to serve (open culture versus pure culture). That the two tendencies were nevertheless convergent is best shown by the fact that the notion of "Jewish literature in Polish" arose on the Polish as well as on the Jewish side. But whereas, on the Jewish side, the term was the name of a phenomenon that marked sociocultural change, and was thus a historical phenomenon resulting from the evolution of the contacts of the Jews with Polish culture, a phenomenon shaped by the influence of historically determined factors of social and cultural nature, on the Polish side, the term was linked to eminently ahistorical conceptions whose tone was clearly that of psychological racism. As a phrase in the *endek* lexicon, the term "Jewish literature in Polish" had a negative meaning and clearly racist connotations.[231]

That the tendencies under discussion had, so to say, a common direction is shown by the commentary with which [Zygmunt] Wasilewski greeted the emergence of Brandstaetter the Zionist and the Polish-Jewish poet. Deploring the fact that Polish spiritual culture was passing into foreign hands, he claimed:

> It is a duty to speak openly about these maneuvers. One can maintain a discrete silence about all manner of conspiracies if exposing them has unpleasant consequences for those involved; but now the conspirators boastfully unmask themselves, openly issue orders to the accompaniment of bellicose shouts. Front lines visible to all have come into being.[232]

Tadeusz Kudliński made a very similar statement concerning the dramatist Leon Wiesenberg:

> Mr. Wiesenberg does not hide his nationality—that some of his plays deal with the Jewish milieu, that he is a Jewish writer writing in Polish—and this is how I react to him. And since I am not a racist, I cannot deny Jews in Poland assistance and the right to create, for not only do I not see in this anything harmful for Polish culture but, on the contrary, I regard such a clear separation as useful in this whole problem.[233]

We see that at the time when the idea of a division of Polish-language literature into "Polish" literature and literature "in Polish" became increasingly popular, the concept of Polish-Jewish literature, of writing in which the author's Jewish identity found expression, could gain unexpected allies.

If we look at the matter in greater detail, then we see that there existed certain more general, worldview-related, sources of convergence. I have in mind the neoromantic pedigree of those convergent tendencies and their anti-assimilationist attitude. It was none other than Imber, who defended Tuwim against Rostworowski's attack, who said that "one cannot praise assimilation as a mass movement, one can and should counteract it, one can fight it in the sharpest possible manner."[234]

The connection between Polish-Jewish literature and Polish nationalist currents in literature were noted in the interwar period. Writing in 1937 about the programs for Polish-Jewish and German-Jewish literatures, Izydor Berman linked the emergence of the idea of Jewish art in these languages with the offensive of nationalism in literary life, an offensive that put in question the sense in which Jewish authors belonged to European literature. The domination of the cultural atmosphere by political tensions forced the reexamination of the problem of the existence of Jewish art. According to Berman, by 1937, equal-rights participation of Jewish writers in Polish literature was out of the question:

> A poet and writer who is a Jew has nothing to say here. What he is or what he should be is decided by other competent persons: the masters of the house. And so one encounters the following views: (1) A Jew cannot be a Polish writer because he creates worthless, "neuter" literature. (2) By way of exception, and in rare cases, a Jew can create works that are valuable from a cultural and national viewpoint. We acknowledge such Jews. (3) It can happen that Jews are good Poles and good writers, but this is a fact we deplore. We can do without such Jews.[235]

Regardless of whether the decree was one of acceptance or of isolation, the artist-Jew was in a sense deprived of his will: dependence on the "hosts," on a public opinion which distributed certificates of affiliation, put him in a situation of clear coercion. If national literature could be created by members of the nation alone, and national membership was based exclusively on the judgment of the collectivity and not on an objective measure of merits, if—in a word—the sense of belonging to literature was not related to the activities of the individual but was linked to something like a favor or to predestination, then it is not surprising that poets with a message, a term bestowed by Chaim Löw on Jewish poets in European literatures,[236] wanted to be free of such humiliating dependence. When their right of belonging to European culture was terminated, they responded by terminating their affiliation to this culture.

The interwar period spelled defeat for the hope of integrating the Jews into European societies, for the coming into being of "a union of common culture created through a common effort." On the eve of the war, Braun set down this balance sheet of the contemporary state of affairs:

The ever deeper process of differentiation has recently resulted in the virtually complete isolation of the Jewish intelligentsia.

Wherever the demarcation line cuts contacts and makes collaboration impossible, there can be no cultural community; but it should be noted that this isolation, sometimes voluntary, has been brought about not by ethnic differences but by anti-Semitism and antagonism due to competition.[237]

3

The Literature of the Cultural Borderland

A Trial Balance

Its programs, the discussions about it, and its reception show Polish-Jewish literature to have been a heterogeneous phenomenon, as much Polish as Jewish, a phenomenon influenced by the changes in both cultures. This being so, Polish-Jewish literature can be considered from two perspectives. On the one hand, it can be included in the sphere of multilingual Jewish culture and, on the other, it can be regarded as an integral part of Polish writing.

At first sight, these two perspectives may seem antagonistic but, far from being mutually exclusive, they complement each other. True, each of these perspectives sees this literature in the context of another whole, against the background of another tradition. These wholes, these traditions, [however,] can be looked upon not only as distinct and independent spheres, but also as spheres related by contacts and mutual bonds. Moreover, the post-Haskalah multilingual (also linguistically Polish) Jewish culture and Polish culture share a certain area, an area of contact, a borderland area. Indeed, the trilingual polysystem of Jewish culture is not an isolated sphere: through its Polish system it forms many connections with Polish culture. One such connection is the partly common institutional framework of literary life.

Chone Shmeruk calls attention to another kind of dependence. He thinks that Polish-Jewish literature and theater "filled gaps" in the literary and theatrical writing of the non-Jewish milieu.[1] This viewpoint considers the connections under discussion in terms of the needs, preferences, and tastes of the Jewish recipients. From this position, Polish-Jewish literature is treated as a kind of supplement to Polish literature contributed by Polish-speaking Jewish circles. To quote Shmeruk:

> Distinctly Jewish literature in Polish played just an accessory and supplementary role in Poland. Its development depended on Polish literature not earmarked in a special way for Jews. It is possible that Jewish readers of just such Polish literature were primarily interested in Jewish topics or in works of Polish authors of Jewish origin who did not write for an exclusively Jewish public.[2]

This supplement can be regarded as a peripheral part of the "housekeeping" of Polish literature, a kind of "literature for . . ." addressed to a particular milieu. But as an element of the multilingual Jewish literature, Polish-Jewish writing was not just a supplement, and its place in that whole was different: "this complex literary sphere had great importance . . . in the polysystem of the culture of Polish Jews in the interwar period."[3]

Clearly, the acceptance of the dual affiliation of Polish-Jewish literature is predicated on the adoption of the model of an open culture. Only thus can Polish be regarded as a language of Jewish culture, and Jewish culture as enriched by elements of neighboring cultures. Only thus can we think of Polish culture as a culture that absorbs values from all its borderlands.

The study of the history of the Polish-Jewish literary circles inclines one to adopt a position that respects the dual affiliation of Polish-Jewish writing. If we adopt, for obvious reasons, the Polish perspective and consider the Polish-Jewish literary circles against the Polish background, then it turns out that there are a thousand links between them and the Polish circles, that people constantly wander between the Polish and Jewish "shores" along the bridge of language.

The Polish-Jewish circles ran the whole extensive gamut of degrees of acculturation stretching from "Polishness" to "Jewishness." These circles included bi- and trilingual writers and journalists who published Hebrew, Yiddish, and Polish texts. There were authors who wrote only in Polish. There was a relatively stable group of permanent coworkers with the Polish-Jewish press, but also a group of authors sporadically connected with that press who published regularly in the Polish press (for example, Bruno Schulz, Artur Prędski, and Henryka Łazowertówna), and a group of writers linked mainly with the Jewish press (Rachela Auerbach, Debora Vogel) who published infrequently in Polish-language papers. There were writers like Braun and Brandstaetter who came from the Polish "shore" and writers like Szymel and Fenster who were on the "Jewish" shore. A substantial group tried to participate in both Polish-Jewish and in Polish literary life. In 1931, Brandstaetter announced a program for Polish "learned poetry." Braun associated with futurists, proletarian poets, and Skamandrites.[4] Wit was [Tadeusz] Peiper's student.[5] Fallek discussed the theory of pure forms with Witkacy. Berman published two variants—one in the *Miesięcznik Żydowski* (Jewish monthly) and another in *Skamander*—of a long essay (the longest in the interwar period) on the work of Franz Kafka.[6] Juliusz Feldhorn published in the Polish-Jewish press only critical texts, and used the pseudonym Jan Las in some of his literary creations. Szymel, regarded as a talented Yiddish poet, was connected with the group of Galician poets.[7] He published some of his poems in two linguistic versions. Many Polish-Jewish authors functioned as translators of works belonging to different Jewish literatures. Brandstaetter deplored the fact that he wrote in Polish. At one time, Braun claimed that "Attachment . . . to the Jewish nation is not at odds with the natural link that ties him to Polish culture and language in an organic whole."[8] How much this milieu was differentiated is also shown by the postwar options of those who survived: Brandstaetter, Safrin, Löw-Przemski, and Stark-Stryjkowski opted for Polish literature while Feldszuh and Dykman chose Israeli literature.

Publication in a Polish-Jewish newspaper meant that an item was intended for Jewish readers. Publication in a book provided an item with a far more "Polish" address. This distinction is easy to observe in the case of the works of Juliusz Witkower-Wit. When selecting items published in the press for inclusion in a book, the poet considered not only their artistic merit but also their Jewish motifs. Moreover, he "Polished" poems originally published in the press before republishing them in book form.[9]

At this point it is tempting to try to give a more detailed as well as a model description of the participation of Polish-Jewish circles in both literary areas in which their activity can be included. Such a model can be constructed if we recognize the milieu in question as a kind of writer ring. Such a category is referred to as a "literary milieu form"[10] and is regarded as one of the institutions associated with literary groupings. Unlike formal and informal literary groups, a ring is a "relatively integrated social milieu"[11] of an ideological artistic nature.

My emphasis on the group nature is not arbitrary: after all, during the interwar period we witness, not isolated instances of Polish-Jewish writing, but the formation of considerable literary groupings. Similar developments took place in the literatures of other language areas. Stefan Pomer put it thus "Roth is a Jew who belongs to a new group of German writers who, like A[rnold] Zweig, Feuchtwanger, Georg, Hermann, Max Brod, and Else Lasker-Schüler, proclaim their affiliation to their nation and consciously and purposely express it in their works: they deal with Jewish problems and shape creatively the fate and history of Jewry."[12]

Janusz Stradecki, who proposed the use of the category of a writer ring in studies of literary life in the interwar period, distinguished during that period rings of nationalist, proletarian, folk, Catholic, and liberal writers. One can add to his map the ring of national-Jewish writers made up of authors who cooperated with the Polish-Jewish press.

I think that the category of a writers' ring reflects well the institutional organization of Polish-Jewish circles considered without reference to the Polish context. In addition to such literary groups as Wzlot (Upward Flight) and the poetic group around *Chwila,* there formed around various Polish-Jewish papers "integrated social groupings" of writers with clear worldview orientations. While each of them had its own literary physiognomy and history, the groupings around *Chwila, Nowy Dziennik, Nasz Przegląd, Opinia,* and *Nasza Opinia* were intimately connected with one another. This being so, we can regard them, with reference to the multilingual Jewish literature, as "the ring of national Jewish authors writing in Polish."

One should add that the category of an artistic-ideological ring agrees with the view—popular during the interwar period—that Polish-Jewish writers were Polish-language authors who "expressed in their works the ideals of the struggling and regenerated Jewish spirit," who adopted "the position of Zionist Jewry."[13]

Regardless of whether [it is included] in Polish or in Jewish culture, the ring of Polish-Jewish writers and Polish-Jewish literature [can be] seen as a region with a clear center and an indistinct periphery that abuts on the system of Jewish culture in Yiddish and Hebrew as well as on Polish culture. As such, it can be regarded as the area common to all these spheres.

When [I] write about the differentiation of Polish-Jewish literary groupings, about their Polish, Yiddish, and Hebrew connections, and finally about a certain indistinctness of the boundaries of Polish-Jewish culture, [I] must emphasize that this view of the phenomena in question depends on their being seen from a close perspective. Viewed from a more distant perspective, their contours become sharper and more definite: the Jewish ring stands out in the Polish-language literary groupings. Few Polish authors, such as Tadeusz Hollender, Paweł Hulka-Laskowski, Tadeusz Zaderecki, Franciszek Gil, Antoni Gronowicz, and Stanisław Vincenz, published in Polish-Jewish newspapers. Also, this ring was certainly not representative of all Jewish groupings whose members wrote in Polish. Outside this ring were *Wiadomości Literackie* as well as many other groupings, including leftist writers such as Andrzej Wolica and Rafał Len [Lichtensztajn]; democratic writers not definitely connected with a particular party such as Halina Górska, Maksymilian Cheyfec (pen name Maks Wit), and Helena Neufeldowa (pen name Helena Maty); and writers shunning all ideological engagement such as Zygmunt Pufeles and Helena Sokołów.

A striking thing, noted by Chone Shmeruk, is that Polish-Jewish literature was largely created by second-rate authors; such first-rate literary talents as Schulz, Wat, Rudnicki, Ważyk, Stern, and Peiper functioned outside its purview. Irving Howe observed a similar phenomenon in the American setting: Jewish immigrant groupings created in the twentieth century a rich literature which was, for the most part, "of little literary value, because writing about man's urgent needs results in the narrowing of the area of observation, in trifling outpourings of feelings, and a defensive posture."[14] The reference to American experiences is neither unfounded nor arbitrary; sociologists relate the processes of acculturation that took place in Poland in the interwar period—especially linguistic Polonization—to analogous phenomena taking place in American society.[15]

The indistinctness of the contours of Polish-Jewish literature manifests itself also if we regard the Polish-Jewish texts (whether published in the press or as books) as a coherent corpus. The whole so constituted turns out to be thematically nonuniform: the clear center is made up of works with Jewish topics, but a considerable area is taken up by reflective lyricism and by erotica. We also encounter rather frequently texts based on quintessentially Polish motifs (such as the November uprising, Piłsudski, or the regaining of independence).

This being so, I propose to make the subject of my description the thematic core of Polish-Jewish writing. As is usual in the case of second—or third-rate writing, we encounter here a significant amount of conventionalization of literary means. Thus I will make it my task to provide a description of the "literary language," the collection of motifs and images that served to draw the Jewish self-portrait.

PART TWO

The Jewish Self-Portrait

4

I, a Jew; We, Jews

Genealogy

I, Roman Brandstaetter, a Jew from the tribe of Judah,
Bearing within me the holy heritage of prophets and kings,
of desert wanderings and of the temple

(R. Brandstaetter, "Psalm goryczy i gniewu" [Psalm of bitterness and anger], *Kts,* p. 31)[1]

These are the names of my sisters and brothers,
Hatched in the dark houses of the suburbs:
Abraham the knife grinder who lost an arm,
And Dan of whom no trace is left
. . . .
My old mother's name is Chana [Hanah]
And Zev is the name of my grandfather from Toporów

(M. Szymel, "Genealogia" [Genealogy], *Sp,* p. 7)

In an old podolian manor house
. . . .
lay at rest a manuscript
by a friend—the Jew Lewittes

(J. Lewittes, "Geneza następnych wierszy" [The genesis of the subsequent poems], *P,* p. 67)

Such confessions constitute an autobiographical seal that Polish-Jewish writers applied with alacrity to their texts. Confessions of Jewishness appeared in the middle of the nineteenth century in the writings of the first generation of writers of Jewish origin[2] (for example, A[dolf] J[akub] Cohn, "Głos Żyda polskiego" [The voice of a Polish Jew], A. Kraushar, "Handel! Handel!" [Business! Business! (a literal translation of "Handel! Handel!," the "business" cry of secondhand clothes peddlers—Trans.)]. During the interwar period such confessions were not unusual, even on the part of authors outside the Polish-Jewish circle. Relevant examples [can be found in the works of] Wittlin, Tuwim, Słonimski, and Hemar.[3] The problem of Jewish identity, though incidental elsewhere, was central in Polish-Jewish literature.

Polish-Jewish writings were saturated with the autobiographical element. Nevertheless, this element did not always appear as openly, [and] did not always assume a form as intimate and concrete as that in the quoted poems of Brandstaetter, Szymel, and Lewittes. For the most part, the autobiographical tendency was reflected in a gesture rather than in [a full-blown] autobiographical declaration.[4] It is significant that such a gesture invariably referred to the "I" of Jewish identity, seldom as, say, "I—Brandstaetter," or "I—Jakub Lewittes," [far more] often as "I—a Jew."

In lyric poems, the confession of Jewishness took on still other—intermediate—forms. One of them was the family saga—the genealogy—as in the Szymel poem quoted above, in which the family history was the history of a few generations, derived from the memory of a single individual. In Brandstaetter's case, the prose and poetry family saga reaches far deeper into the past and is undoubtedly an inheritance from the forefathers:

> My forefather Isaac from Frankfurt . . .
> . . . .
> . . . was a duke's factor [Jewish middleman]
> And perished at the stake on German soil
> . . . .
> My great-grandfather Chaskel [Haskel] . . .
> . . . .
> . . . was a merchant
> And died on a cloudy day
> And rests in the Brzesko cemetery.
> My grandfather Mordekhai David . . .
> . . . sang of the Diaspora
> And died on a May afternoon
> On foreign soil.
>
> (R. Brandstaetter, "Dzieje mojego rodu" [The history of my family], *Kts*, p. 11)

Genealogical tales played an indispensable role in the process of self-identification. In these tales, the "I" conceived itself as a link in a chain jointed for centuries; it conceived its own fate by comparing it with the pattern repeated for generations. The collectivity was cemented by the awareness of bonds of blood and by respect for the heritage bestowed by the ancestors. This heritage had more than a private dimension, for the history of a family was also the history of the Diaspora: Frankfurt and Brzesko; factors [Jewish middlemen] of princes, merchants, and writers . . . Thus family histories were records of the historical experience and the historical fate of the Jews, records of varied experience. In Pomer's "Elegia o moich praojcach" (An elegy about my forefathers)[5] there are references to innkeepers and merchants in small borderland towns praying in "dreary little houses of prayer," bent over "a yellow page of the Gemara by the glimmer of brass candlesticks." In Celina Meerson-Becker's "Do mowy żydowskiej" (To the Jewish tongue)[6] there is mention of routes from Estonia and France to Mazowsze, wanderings in the course of which the family abandoned its mother tongue . . .

The memory of the dead ancestors and the memory of the spiritual heritage bequeathed by them were important elements that strengthened the chain of Jewishness. And so the dream of this chain could be expressed in the vision of father and son united in the prayer for the dead at the grave of the grandfather who went to the land of Israel shortly before his death:

and maybe God will grant,
my son, that we,
healthy and robust,
and not yet tired
at noontime—
should stand together
at the grave of my grandfather
and in a soft, inaudible
whisper utter in unison
"El moleh rakhmim."

(J. Lewittes, "Do syna" [To my son])[7]

Due to the dominance of the sense of collectivity, the history of the family was seen as a triumph of continuity based on blood ties stronger than generational differences. The strongest bond was the connection between generations, which clasped hands and formed a chain that stretched across centuries. This emotion is very frequently present in Polish-Jewish lyric poetry in single poems (S. Pomer, "Grób mego ojca" [My father's grave],[8] K. Dresdner, "Czemu?" [Why?]) as well in cycles of poems (by, for example, Szymel and Rosenfeld) devoted to the memory of near ones. In addition to elegiac recollections and lamentations we also find here the "Kaddish," the Jewish prayer for departed parents:

God,
Let Your golden dawns
Light the peace of Her grave,
In Her cold grave
Let Her rest
After life and toil.
. . . .
Let Her in Her grave
Dream of Your power,
Let my Kaddish rock her to sleep
(K. Rosenfeld, "Kadisz" [Kaddish], *Wcl,* pp. 30–31)

The sequence of generations was not always sharply depicted in its successive historical links. Sometimes the "I" identified with all the forebears, with all the biblical ancestors, and regarded itself as the heir of their "golden and bitter blood." Sometimes it failed to mention the names of its brothers and sisters. It was often a Jewish Everyman, the brother "of every . . . simple believing Jew."[9] We find this kind of identification in Roman Brandstaetter's "Psalm 1933," his thanksgiving song of Jewishness:

. . . Glory to Thee, O Lord
That there burns in my veins, like an angel in an olive lamp,
The fire of my forefathers, who conquered the land of Canaan with the sword,
That there flows in me the blood of the vengeful Bargiora,
That my family derives from tents,
Which you visited
("Psalm 1933," *Ktś,* p. 29)

In addition to autobiographical confessions, genealogical accounts, and praises of Jewry with all of whose generations the "I" feels connected, we encounter in Polish-Jewish lyric poetry declarations of identity that are definitely in a category of their own. These are testimonies of connection with Jewishness rather than with Jewry. One such involves the invocation of Jehovah's names in a poetic prayer:

Before You, oh Lord
I bend my knees

Adonai
Elohim
Adonai
Echad!

(J. Lewittes, "Modlitwa" [Prayer], *P.*, p. 63)

Another quotes the beginning of a Hebrew prayer and follows it with a paraphrase of the text in Polish:

Avinu Av Ham'rahem Harahmani
In Your name, O Father, merciful Lord

(N. Füllenbaum, "Aszer Jacar" [Asher Yatzar])[10]

Hebrew titles of poems are steps in the same direction; they occur most frequently in paraphrases of prayers (for example, in "Boreh Pri Hagafen" of Natan Füllenbaum)[11] and in poems of the hymn variety (for example, "Maasseh berejszit" of I. Deutscher)[12]

In these texts, the "I" was placed in the midst of cultural signs, in the symbolic area created by rituals and holidays, populated by biblical heroes, by figures from East European folklore, and persons belonging to the pantheon of assimilated greats. In a word, the "I" faced the many forms of the age-old Jewish tradition with which it declared its spiritual connection. Here, side by side, stood the Second Temple and the East European house of prayer; the shepherd's tent and the shtetl; King David, Shulamite, Mother Rachel, and the Ba'al Shem Tov, the prophet Elijah, the Prague Golem, Heine, Disraeli . . .

Bonds with Jewishness could also be established *à rebours*—by distancing oneself from European culture or even demonstratively cutting oneself off from it. An example of such an act is Roman Brandstaetter's ode "Do litery łacińskiej" (To a Latin letter), a kind of anti-ode, a hymn of revenge of a Jew, a descendant of a people conquered and enslaved by Titus. The conquest of "the Latin letter" ("you must sing through my mouth the fame and greatness of Jerusalem / And humbly prostrate yourself before the land full of myrrh, acacias and turtledoves") is a form of revenge: "sinking the spear of victory" (*Kts*, p. 28) in the enemy's culture.

Declared in different forms, the Jewish identity was synonymous in Polish-Jewish literature with finding a place in the row of generations and with taking root in the symbolic space of Jewishness; a matter of ties of blood and of symbolism.

The Eternal "I," Eternal Jewishness

In the writings of the Jewish milieu the experience of Jewishness comes to the fore in its private as well as in its universal dimension, hence the possibility of a dual lesson that derived from its dominant autobiographical component. Treated as a kind of historical source, this literature yields biographical testimony representative of two generations of Polish-Jewish writers. It documents radical social and cultural changes, for it includes stories of nonreligious sons of rabbis (Bertisch); of poets writing in Polish born in homes where Yiddish was spoken, homes that lived the rhythm of traditional life (Szymel); stories of grandchildren of *maskil*s returning to Jewry (Brandstaetter); and of pioneers rebelling against the hopeless vegetating in Poland (Mayer). In this literature, attention is focused on the individual and on the historical: the son of the "head of the Jewish community," a boy from the shtetl, a *halutz*, a gymnasium student, a university student, an official, a poet living the life of his time. Obviously, these writings are primarily prose, marked by an emphasis on the truth and authenticity of the stories they tell, that can lay claim to documentary status. Thus Henryk Adler wrote in the introduction to his Palestinian stories: "The first [stories] were written during moments free from pioneer work or during periods of post-malarial convalescence" (*AiJ,* p. 5), and Rubin Feldszuh described himself as "a worker from Kiryat Anavim" on the occasion of the publication—by the Lvov *Chwila*—of the cycle of his Palestinian images.[13] There is a close connection between the autobiographical pact with the reader and the referential pact, according to which "a work contains information about the reality beyond the text, it is its image, it aims not at simple plausibility but at verisimilitude."[14] Literature is just "recorded reality."

While autobiographical threads vary from author to author, taken together they give a general image of collective Jewish history. Individual fates and historical fates contain a national, a historical core. Thus the biographies I have been talking about can be thought of as crystallization points for the purely collective and universal.

Moreover, the tension between the individual and the collective, the historical and the metahistorical, always accompanies the autobiographical threads of Polish-Jewish literature. In this literature, the "I" invariably sees in personal histories signs of the Jewish fate, signs of Jewishness. In Szymel's "Rozmowa ze starym Eljaszem" (A conversation with old Eli), *Pdd,* pp. 36–37, this universal pattern is found in the biographies of the young poet who writes in Polish and of the old milk delivery man. In his "Namioty Izraela" (The tents of Israel; incidentally, a paraphrase of the morning prayer "Ma tovu"), the "I" acknowledges

Wilhelm Wachtel's cover for Henryk Adler's *Ariela I Jubal: Palestyńskie opowiesci romantyczne* (Ariela and Jubal: Palestinian romantic stories).

the kinship that ties its lot to the lot of peddlers from poor Warsaw neighborhoods, to brother Jews: "How sad are your tents, O my brother Israel" (M. Szymel, "Namioty Izraela," *Pdd,* p. 70). In this text, we come across an instance of the use of a poetic device characteristic of Polish-Jewish poetry, a device that aims at creating a hero or a lyrical "I," which is at once the figure of the eternal Jew:

Brother, who with trembling hands
touches the holy Torah rolls,
'tis you who for many ages
with saddest face has been repeating:
"How beautiful are thy tents, O Israel."
(M. Szymel, "Namioty Izraela"
[Israel's tents], *Pdd,* p. 69)

In this poem, the changelessness of the hero who prays to God for centuries with the same words is a sign of loyalty to the Covenant and of the permanence of fate.

Far more frequently, the figure of the eternal "I" adopts a different stance: it maintains its identity, not through changelessness, but in the multiplicity of experiences in time and space. This is how it appears in, for example, the poetry of Brandstaetter, Safrin, and Baumberg.

Roman Brandstaetter was especially fond of this device. His, in a sense, programmatic poems "Autoportret Żyda" (Self-portrait of a Jew) and "Mesjasz" (Messiah) are monologues of an "I" whose existence is timeless:

I was your betrothed, You made a Covenant with me
By the seven-color arch of the rainbow and the warm blood of circumcision;
And so you have never left me on the scorched desert dunes,
Even when I staggered in worldly sin and low pride,
Setting up golden calves on sands plowed by thunder.

(R. Brandstaetter, "Autoportret Żyda" [Self-portrait of a Jew], *Kts*, p. 13)

The history of Israel, from the Covenant to twentieth-century contemporaneity, is for such an "I" personal history. "The beloved of the Lord" and brother of Christ tells his story that reaches back to a mythical past: the Burning Bush, the Exodus from Egypt, the wandering in the desert, the joy of "free life in the fatherland," the destruction of the Temple, slaughters and pogroms in Europe, the Polish era . . . The "I" is eternal like God, who has elected it. Its past is at once heroic and bucolic; slavish and commercial. Its biography encompasses all of Jewish history. It is an elect transformed into a pariah:

You have slowly changed my face, blurred the sharpness of my features,
You have taken the swarthiness of my cheeks, the strength of my copper arms,
From my shape the noble loftiness of slimly growing cypresses,
You have given my back the shape of a bow and haste to my exhausted chest.
And on my face froze the whiteness of sepulchral marbles,
And my full lips froze in a line silent and thin,
And instead of a costly garment I dressed in a black gabardine,
Marked with a shameful badge, as if by your thunderlike hand.

(R. Brandstaetter, "Autoportret Żyda" [Self-portrait of a Jew]; *Kts*, p. 14)

Elect or exile, the "I" retains a sense of identity in all situations. Shepherd and Hebrew warrior, merchant and inhabitant of a ghetto, these are just its different embodiments.

The figure in question comes through with special sharpness, in the rhetoric of a declaration, in Brandstaetter's "Mesjasz" (Messiah):

It was about me that lips spattered with foam sang,
It was my heart that trembled in the hands of Cossacks reeking of the heavy odor of vodka,

It was my blood that glistened on the splendid cassocks gorgeous in gold,
And in palaces on the Tiber, full of marble, lapis lazuli, and pools.

It was me whom the lean crusaders slaughtered,
And their knives glistened in the dark, like narrow slits in the dimmed pupils of cats,

It was about me that a German wind, full of Rhine vineyards and blood sang,
Blowing in dry bones like flutes.

It was about me that the fire hissed,
When the pitchy kindling of the stakes I died at caught fire from the inquisitor's red cassock and the purple lightning of the bishops,

It was my name that burned in the flames of little Galician towns,
It was my name that was fouled under the heels of the Beilis judges.
("Mesjasz" [Messiah], *Ktś,* p. 33)

Here the "I" is at once Messiah and the Eternal Jew; it experiences through centuries all the suffering of the Diaspora, dies many times at the hands of the crusaders, the Inquisition, the Cossacks, but it is also privy to the knowledge of future events: the vision of rebirth.

Another expressive creation of the eternal "I" is found in Mieczysław Braun's "Rapsod" [Rhapsody]:

The Philistine's poisoned arrows,
the hail of stones from Amalek's hands,
The swish of the Egyptian's whip,
Roman cohorts at my gates!
And again the spilled blood is foaming
And Torquemada reddens his coat
And in the fire the blood congeals into ice.

Under Prague's wall from the Middle Ages
I walked wretched and half naked,

And the free wind blowing in the field
Furtively cooled my face.
The guards at the gates sneered at me
And pushed me, and called me "Golem!"

When in Kiszyniów, in Proskirów
The red slaughter stained the pavement
I stood amid smoldering ruins of towns in mourning,
And looked within me for leftover tears,
I waited in vain for a brotherly hand,
And only a wounded dog
Bestowed on me the alms of his favor.
("Rapsod" [Rhapsody])[15]

The biblical past and modern history; the Philistines, Amalek, the Spanish Inquisition, medieval Prague, pogroms in Russia . . . the protagonist's lot is suffering and pain, loneliness and encirclement by hatred.

By wandering in time and space, the "I" identifies with the totality of historical experiences forming the Jewish heritage. In this situation, the personal memory absorbs the collective memory; the eternal "I" becomes the universal subject of Jewish history, the universal carrier of Jewish fate.

Going through centuries and countries, the "I" can be Ahasuerus, who walks—as in Władysław Szlengel's *"Nihil Novi"*[16]—"down its sad road / for two thousand years." In Lewittes's "Ahaswer" (Ahasuerus), the protagonist shows his own face, and looks in the eyes of his son through which "speaks / a track . . . / of twenty centuries" (*P*, pp. 56–57): Titus's captive in Rome, Rambam's student in Spain, a fugitive in Flanders . . . in both poems under discussion the beginning of the wanderings of the "I" is marked by an encounter with Christ. But Ahasuerus can remember what happened before this encounter.[17] The curse of exile pronounced by the bearer of the cross turns out to be a repetition of an earlier curse, the curse of the Babylonian exile, and the fate was sealed by Jehovah:

In the marshy meadows the homeless birds play and trill for me:
my harps abandoned on the willows of Babylon.

I walk on into the unknown—the brim of my hat
links me to distance and makes me one with the horizon.

I threw my shadow behind me: ancient tales, myths, stories . . .
I, Ahasuerus, the Eternal Jew, stepson of Adonai
(H. Safrin, "Ahaswer" [Ahasuerus])[18]

As a result of its union with the personal "I," there is a certain modification of the figure of the eternal "I" described earlier. Szymel's "Modlitwa do mego Boga" is offered to Jehovah, Lord "of my mother who died young" and Lord of the Land "I have loved for centuries." Every Jew is an Eternal Jew. This eternal Jewishness is an awareness of the heritage of centuries and of its changelessness through centuries based on the certainty that the same God speaks from Sinai and enters "a small, smoky house of prayer" ("Modlitwa do mego Boga," *Pdd,* p. 45). The "I" does not wander through ages and lands; it discovers in its personal memory a layer of the collective memory. In Safrin's "Pieśń o sobie" (Song about myself) it recollects past incarnations:

I caress weird visions, I fumble in my sleepy memory,
I remember: way back then my ur-father Abraham led me from the land of Haran.
It seems that I stood trembling at the cistern in the morning, rash youth,
And served Laban seven toilsome years for a wench.
Then I sold my flesh-and-blood brother to the Midianites,
Built Ramses and Pitom on Pharaoh's estate . . .
. . . .
I dream of olden times in a seven-colored cloak of rainbows—
("Pieśń o sobie" [Song about myself])[19]

Here the "I" is one of the group led out of Haran by Abraham; it is Jacob, brother of Joseph—and the poet from whose memory emerge all the figures and events of the past. The vision of the Promised Land and of the national history slumbers in it and waits for resurrection:

whole worlds slumber in me,
I need only, like one moonstruck,
break through the darkness
and wake the confounded soul.
(H. Safrin, "Judaica")[20]

We encounter a similar séance of reminiscence in Karol Dresdner's dialogue *Heine i nieznajoma* (Heine and the stranger). In a setting of symbols of Jewish culture (a rainbow, a menorah), Heine encounters the phantom of the Stranger—

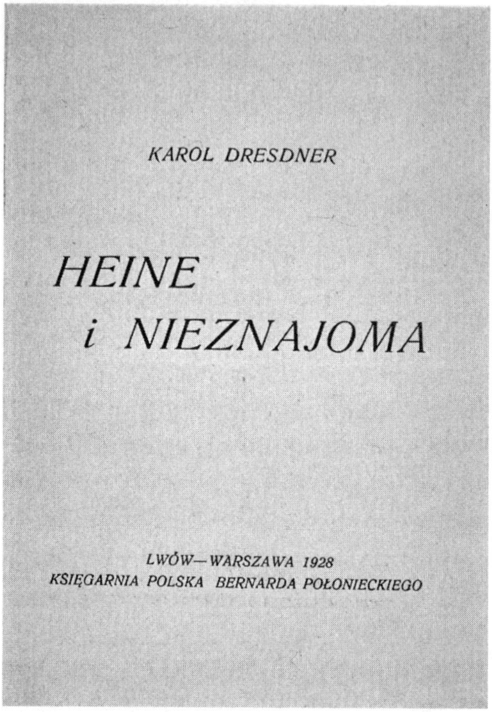

Reproduced by A. Musielak. Title page of Karol Dresdner's *Heine i nieznajoma* (Heine and the stranger). Photo A. Musielak

the incarnation of Jewishness: Shulamite and the Princess Shabbat in one. The protagonist—a cynic, a renegade, a *"meches"*—has retained the memory of his Jewish roots and Jewish experiences:

> The Lord saved my ancestors in Mitzraim
> From the hands of Pharaoh's myrmidons,
> My name was originally Chaim [Haim],
> Which to them presumably means "life."
>
> Have I not heard the crash of beams
> When the blasphemous crowd set the temple on fire?
> In that candelabrum from Titus's arch
> The oil still seems to hiss and sputter . . .
>
> (K. Dresdner, *Heine i nieznajoma*
> [Heine and the stranger], *Hin,* p. 10)

Here the past is alive and almost palpable. The conversation with the Stranger intensifies the memories and yields new ones. It also helps disclose to the protagonist his own fate: "your name was originally Haim / Which to us means eternal life!" The dialogue is a debate between partners who exist beyond time. Jewishness is from-ever and for-ever. Thus Heine cannot escape it or completely forget it. [He] pays with his life for recognizing the Stranger, for recognizing in himself the stigma of eternal Jewishness. Other Dresdner heroes, for example Disraeli (in the poem "Disraeli"), also frequently become aware of this stigma, albeit in less dramatic form.

The eternal "I," Ahasuerus, persists in the main current of Jewish history. The memory of this history has fallen to the lot of every Jew. It is the source of understanding of each individual fate. It is a kind of "heavenly burden" (L. Baumberg, "Brzemię niebieskie" [Heavenly burden]) and stigma: the bedrock of Jewish identity.

Outcasts, Exiles, Wanderers

When the "I" tells the story of its people, when it identifies itself with past experiences and determines its place in the chain of generations, it appeals to Jewish history. It seeks in it—in the voice of Jehovah who speaks in it—the truth about itself and a sense of the national fate. Sometimes it is guided in this search by Jewish holidays that commemorate events of the national history: Pesach—the Exodus from Egypt; Purim—deliverance from Haman; Hanukkah—the miracle of the Maccabean revolt.[21] The cycle of holidays that make up the Jewish year is a sequence of national monuments set in time. We find a sketch of the history fixed in this sequence in, for example, the sonnets of Karol Rosenfeld ("Menorah," "Judas Maccabee," "Purim," "Pesach," "Shavuoth," "Credo," "Tisha b'Av," "Rosh Hashana," "Al Het," "Yom Kippur"). In Rosenfeld's work, the Jewish year is a priceless guide, the compass "of the shattered boat of a homeless people," and the historical memory is the only national treasure:

> . . . At Hanukkah the Menorah burns with the sad fire of memories
> In the light of its rays, in the night of the Diaspora,
> It dreams the glorious dream of Zion.
>
> Let us watchfully guard the golden lights of its arms
> For if they go out—the deep sea will bury
> Our boat lost in abysmal shadows.
>
> (K. Rosenfeld, "Menorah," *Wcl*, p. 55)

Prayers, tales about heroes, historical and legendary events commemorated by holidays, all this is a peculiar lesson of the Jewish fate. Following the rules of the sonnet, Rosenfeld juxtaposes in holiday images scenes from two eras: the eras before and after the Diaspora. This device always serves to bring to light the dramatic change of the status of the Jews: from freedom to slavery; from greatness to decline and fall; from election to abandonment by Jehovah. Pesach, once a joyous holiday of liberation and salvation, does not allow one to forget the exile:

They left Mitzraim. At Jehovah's will
Moses led the chosen people across the Red Sea
To the gates of Jerusalem, to the Promised Land,
Where golden dawns burn with the eternal Fire of Freedom.

Today the children of the ghetto tearfully read the Haggadah
Suppressing prayerful sobs at the Seder,
And yearning for the Ancestors' past in their own land.
(K. Rosenfeld, "Passah" [Pesach], *Wcl,* p. 58)

The confrontation of holiday joy with Jewish contemporary reality discloses the yawning gap between the past and the present:

O my brothers, so serious, so absorbed in life
Do you rejoice in God's law?
Where is the law? Where are the priests?
Woe to you!

You have hidden the law in airless synagogues
And holiness in little grotesque sheds
(M. Szymel, "Święto Szałasów"
[The feast of Tabernacles], *Wl,* p. 72)

From the lesson of Jewish history recited constantly in Polish-Jewish literature, there emerges the image of a people unhappy, suffering, homeless, persecuted, permanently threatened, and alone among nations:

Poor, wretched nation of exiles
(M. Silberman, "xxx")[22]

You once had your own land,
You had a house and kings,

You had might and power of the Spirit,
You were once a free people!

Your house is burned, your land is ravaged,
The radiance of your temples' domes is extinguished,
Your might is nought!
Perished is the great nation of nations.

(K. Rosenfeld, "Wizja" [Vision], *Wcl*, p. 20)

"A chosen people—a bastard among nations," "a history of dejected pride"[23]—this is the mystery of Jewish history. The question of this mystery is present in all comparisons between images of the sublime past and scenes of life in the Diaspora. The moral is hidden in the antinomies: a charismatic collectivity, Jehovah's chosen [versus] a collectivity of outcasts; Hebrew warriors and shepherds [versus] European merchants; elevated [versus] degraded; chosen [versus] cursed. Braun's "Ahaswer" is a catalogue of such antinomies: "alive and pure" [versus] "weak and dead"; "the quiet and melodious psalmist" [versus] "Shylock consumed by greedy desire"; entering into a Covenant with Jehovah [versus] bowing before the golden calf; "everywhere near" [versus] "everywhere far."[24] The lot of the Jews is the realization of a scenario of tragic events: God's protection as against the suffering in the Diaspora; powerful Israel [versus] Israel fallen and vanquished.[25]

What is the Diaspora? In Polish-Jewish literature, it is interpreted in different ways. In the first place, as slavery:

. . . like our shadow, secretively,
The cruel fate of slavery
Follows Judah throughout its life

(K. Rosenfeld, "Motto," *Wcl*, p. 5)

The motifs of manacles and "fetters of the Diaspora" turn up repeatedly in [Karol] Rosenfeld's poetry. Life in the Diaspora is for him a "bloody house" ("Ze snu się porwij" [Awake from your sleep]), "bondage and shame" ("Ahaswer"). In Rosenfeld's poems, the "I" is often "a helot of the ghetto" ("Zmartwychwstanie" [Resurrection]) in "fetters of bitter bondage," mourning its people who "melted the sword into chains" ("Wizja" [Vision]). With the "cry of a slave," the "I" takes leave of the disappearing phantom of [Theodore] Herzl, who calls for a deed of resurrection The poet invariably links the Diaspora with emptiness, numbness, and death. It is a "bloody grave" ("Ahaswer"), a silence of tears. He sometimes makes use of the symbolism of resurrection in the Tyrtaean threads which appear in his songs of freedom. If the Diaspora bondage is death and the grave, then liberation brings "glimmers of awakening life," the "dawn of resurrected freedom" ("Wizja," *Wcł,* p. 22) presaged by "dawns of resurrection" (this is the title of a cycle of poems in the volume *W ciszy łez* (In the silence of tears):

The disk of the morning star is shining,
And past is the night of exile
From our flowering meadows
Flows the song of resurrection!
(K. Rosenfeld, "O wstań na bój . . ."
[O rise to battle . . .], *Wcł,* p. 47)

The breaking of the chains of bondage turns up in [Jakub] Appenszlak's images of Jewish liberation:

I will break the chains
Before I march to the battlefield
For Judah's future!
("Mowie polskiej" [To the Polish tongue], *P,* p. 7)

The martial element is sometimes expressed in Old Testament form. Liberation will be an exodus from the house of bondage, and will be preceded by signs employed by Jehovah on a previous occasion:

To arms, O Israel
The Lord is with you, and the Lord is one!

Defend yourself!
Flare up with the fiery bush
And the crimson cloud!
(R. Brandstaetter, "Psalm 1933," *Kts,* p. 30)

For the Diaspora bondage is another version of the bondage of Israel. Its images are often ahistorical and even archetypal. For example, in Braun's "Fragmenty dziejów" (Fragments of history) there are "underground existence in mines," "millstones that crush against the ground," "clay worked with the fingers."[26] The motif of Psalm 137 often turns up in Polish-Jewish poetry, sometimes as a paraphrase of that lament of outcasts (as in, say, K. Rosenfeld's "Nad wodami Babylonu" [At the waters of Babylon], *Wcl*, p. 39).

This motif symbolizes all forms of bondage and exile. Polish rivers are also Babylonian:

It is not the rivers of Babylon that flow turbidly into the empty distance,
The rapid stream flows in the Vistula valleys;
We sit on the low banks, under gray willows,
And watch the ripples subside,
And the willows above us rustle and sough.

It is not priests' harps that hang on the willows,
This is not Babylon, this is Polish land;
The wind blows, it strikes the leaves, they tremble
And utter whispers, which our vigilant hearts hear.
As if, with covered face, Jeremiah sat
Under this wilted weeping willow.

It is not the prophet crying, it is the weeping willows
Oozing grief with the dry whisper of wilted leaves;
It is we who sit at the bank, listen with rapt attention,

In will-less mourning, as if in evil dimness,
We wait, bent by pain and worry—
And the wind blows in our eyes the eternal Jewish sadness,
Like smoke.

(S. Pomer, "Nad rzekami Babilonu" [By the rivers of Babylon])[27]

The landscape near the Vistula speaks with signs of mythical bondage. The willows speak with Jeremiah's whisper. Pain, worry, sadness, and mourning weigh on those by the Vistula and by the rivers of Babylon alike. Free Jewish song cannot sound in a foreign land with a "foreign moon" (M. Szymel, "Nad rzekami Babilonu" [By the rivers of Babylon])[28]

Polish-Jewish literature sometimes adduces the Egyptian period as a symbol of national enslavement: the "specter of Pharaoh hovers over Europe" (K. Rosenfeld, "Herzl w świątyni" [Herzl in the temple]); in Brandstaetter's "Psalm 1933," the tale of persecutions in Germany, of "locking in the fetters of the Diaspora," is transformed into a prayer for a second exodus, for a Pesach of the future:[29] "Lord of Hosts! Pass through the land of crime / And pass me by" (*Kts*, p. 29).

The Diaspora is not only bondage but also a dream and a "night of exile" (K. Rosenfeld, "O wstań na bój . . ." [O rise to battle . . .]). The abandonment of the fatherland is like the erstwhile abandonment of Eden: "O God, since the *galuth* [exile] is so much pain / restore the lost paradise" (Rosenfeld, "Psalm," *Wcl,* p. 44). The punishment raises the question of guilt. According to some, the punishment is meted out to sinners who fail to fulfill the obligations of the Covenant, or even hesitate to fulfill them. According to others, it is a mystery, an unpredictable fate, an omen whose meaning remains to be deciphered. In the poetry of Rosenfeld and Braun the symbol of Jewry is the outcast Ahasuerus whose fate is supposed to redeem his sins:

> Now quarrelsome, now silent
> You haven't noticed where the lost item fell.
> Where the Burning Bush is blazing?
> Where Jacob's ladder reaches?
> Let your pain absolve you of your sins,
> Let the fire of torments purify you—
> (M. Braun, "Ahaswer," *Wp,* p. 152)

The theme of the Diaspora exile is linked with the themes of homelessness and exile:

> To the East, the West, the North, and the South we are, like leaves, of no account
> . . . we flow, a black procession amid squares of towns that are not ours
> (M. Szymel, "Żydzi" [Jews]) [30]

> . . . a Jew is roads, roads, distant roads covered with snow
> (M. Szymel, "Ballada o życiu i śmierci Jehudy Halevy'ego" [Ballad on the life and death of Jehuda Halevi], *Pdd,* p. 92)

The outcasts are wanderers. The Succoth huts, which commemorate the wanderings in the desert, become symbols of Jewish homelessness and life on the road (W. Szlengel, "Szałasy" [Tabernacles]).[31] Moses was an exile when he led the Jews out of Egypt (Szymel, "Droga na Nebo" [The road to Nebo]; R. Friedmann, "Opowieść o lasce Mojżesza" [The tale of Moses' stick]) [32] "so that they could go on, fall, and triumph again" (M. Szymel, "Droga na Nebo," *Pdd,* p. 62). Thus the wandering in the desert to the Promised Land was also an image of the Diaspora.

The Jews are brothers of other wanderers: "brothers of Odysseus / Older brothers of the great exile" (M. Braun, "Assimi: Fragmenty poematu" [Assimi: Fragments of a poem]).[33] The peddler pulling his cart along the street personifies the exile, the Wandering Jew:

The sky above you has fallen silent,
but the earth shouts denial of your words
and chases you along the spreading distance of tracks
from town to town,
from land to land

(M. Szymel, "Namioty Izraela" [Israel's tents], *Pdd,* p. 69)

The "errant wandering" (M. Braun, "Ahaswer") takes place in threatening, dangerous, enemy surroundings. Szymel's tale about Jews and dogs is an allegory of just such a road:

God bade us follow a difficult road;
The thorniest of all roads
For sore and age-old legs.

Dogs blocked that road;
They wrinkle their snouts. They bare their fangs!
Each big, each strong, each evil.

What do these dogs want of us weaklings?
Do their paws hurt? Their abscesses? Their teeth?
No paw. No abscess. No tooth.
What these hungry dogs are missing is our bodies.

(M. Szymel, "Żydzi i psy" [Jews and dogs], *Wl,* p. 68)

Israel is an old, weak, tired exile persecuted by strong and evil dogs. The same allegory is used by Braun in "Ahaswer":

On the roads, huge dogs bark
And shred my clothes.
I fear, I fear the dogs!
They attack in a furious pack.
I escape. I escape again,
I escape through all hell.

("Ahaswer" [Ahaswerus], *Wp,* p. 153)

The road through hell leads through the "garden of the world." Ahasuerus is the only one who experiences suffering unknown to others.

The situation of being trapped in a circle of hatred, similar to the one in the allegorical tales related earlier, recurs frequently in Polish-Jewish literature. The "Jewish road" is "the thorniest of all roads," and "the Jewish spring" is the gloomiest of all springs. A song about this spring is a song by someone trapped:

> Birds, and flowers, and the like are already here—
> But what good is all this to us,
> When the ground is burning under our feet!
>
> O God, show us the way to open fields,
> Where the winds wield no clubs,
> Where the trees don't break windowpanes,
> And the moon does not peer ominously through the window.
> (M. Szymel, "Wiosna żydowska" [Jewish spring], *Wl,* p. 63)

In Szymel's case, the threat hides in every—anthropomorphized—element of the landscape. In Rosenfeld's case, all existence is hostile to the Jews: "Man and earth / beast and flower / Breathe envy at us" ("Herzl w świątyni," *Wcl,* p. 13). In *"Nihil Novi,"* Szlengel sets down a catalogue of transgressions the Jews are charged with. It is a long list. It ranges from collusion with evil spirits, well poisoning, blasphemy, profanation of Catholic churches, and ritual murder to being an "anonymous world power," to Jewmasonry, Communism, atheism . . . The prayers found in Polish-Jewish poetry are filled with resignation: "we cannot escape infamy, blood, and torments" (M. Szymel, "Jankiel Cymbalista" [Yankel the Dulcimer Player], *Wl,* p. 56). It is impossible to fill the yawning gap between "Zion and Golgotha" (K. Dresdner, "Gdyby tak można" [If it were possible]). Christ's death, this testimony of God's love, brings no peace. The brothers of the Crucified One beg in vain for mercy (K. Dresdner, "Świadectwo miłości" [Testimony of love]).

Loneliness of the roads of the Diaspora, the ever-present menace, exclusion, and entrapment result in a vision of the Jew as a person who "stands all alone in the gale of the world."[34] These views inspire a succession of interpretations of the Diaspora. Its history is one of suffering: "the Gehenna of the ghetto," "the ocean of tears," "the bloody chasms of exile," "the black depths of the *galuth.*" All these characterizations, drawn from [Karol] Rosenfeld's poetry, are symbolized by his image of sailors who sail an ocean of tears and blood:

. . . the drowning boat of the nation
Tossed by the hurricane frenzy of the waves
On a sea of tears and blood
Into the boundless distance . . .
("Herzl w świątyni" [Herzl in the temple], *Wcl*, p. 12)

From the port of bloody Fate the sea's waves
Carry the straying broken boat of a homeless people.
("Menorah," *Wcl*, p. 55)

The crowd of straying
Exiles . . . life's seamen
On a sea of tears whipped by a storm
("Rosz Haszanah" [Rosh Hashanah], *Wcl*, p. 63)

Poets frequently avail themselves of Christian symbolism: liberation will be resurrection and the Diaspora is Golgotha ("Rosz Haszanah" [Rosh Hashanah]). The wanderings take place against a background of cosmic scenery: they are a passage through the unbridled elements of fire and water.

Bondage, exile, a life of wandering, homelessness, entrapment . . . in Polish-Jewish literature, the Diaspora is, above all, an era of suffering. The ages of the Diaspora are "steps dripping with blood" (R. Brandstaetter, "Mesjasz" [Messiah]). They are ages of martyrology: "Utter exhaustion from the ultimate strain," "stoning with defeats" (M. Braun, "Ahaswer" [Ahauerus]), defenseless death: "they perish defenseless like shivering gazelles" (R. Brandstaetter, "Psalm 1933"). They are an unbroken kiddush that sanctifies the name of Jehovah. Including in its fate the experiences of the Diaspora, the eternal "I" identifies with pain and death. Election is predestination for suffering:

God of my fathers,
tormented,
and maltreated,
. . . .
God
chosen by the people
to take upon himself
the passion of the whole world,
. . . .
and to be present everywhere in suffering—

Adonai
Elohim
Adonai
Ehad!

(J. Lewittes, "Modlitwa" [Prayer], *P*, p. 63)

The prayers and songs of the Diaspora are always "sad songs of exile" (M. Braun, "Fragmenty dziejów" [Fragments of history]), laments, threnodies, psalms of pain. Martyrdom is a Jewish stigma: "they need only look at one another to know they are brothers / The living brotherhood of martyrdom hidden in the look" (M. Braun, "Fragmenty dziejów").[35] To be a Jew is to identify oneself with all Jewish suffering, to be one in pain with the brothers:

A stone thrown unexpectedly hits you in the back,
Brother—it hurts me.
They chase you in the streets and whip you.
I am marked with the stigmata.

With the rest of your strength you tore your fetters and above your sunny ship,
Sailing east white gulls flutter—
I fly with them.

You die alone in a dungeon, unlamented, because you are a Jew,
I am proud to die with you.

(D. Ihr, "Bracie" [Brother])[36]

From this perspective, understanding fate, arriving at the sense of the Diaspora is, above all, seeing into the sense of Jewish suffering. The interpretations are extreme. They range from suffering as punishment (K. Rosenfeld, "Rosz Haszanah") to suffering as election, that is, a metaphysical mission. The idea of the Jew as a revolutionary of the spirit recurs in Szymel's poetry:

God chased me out of my fatherland, marked me with wounds
so that I, debased in body, heroic in soul,
should plant burning dynamite under your wretched peace

("Ghetto," *W7*, p. 52)

Here suffering is a weapon in the battle for a new face of the world: "We set nights on fire with pyres and shouts / We want to exchange the earth for heaven" ("Żydzi" [The Jews], *W7*, p. 53). In the introduction to the volume of

Awrohem Ptaszkin's poetry that he translated, Szymel stated that he regarded the Jew as "the most authentic symbol of all restlessness."[37] And he ended his Psalms of hope with a utopia of harmony of the world and of universal love, and a vision of mankind following the "word of the priests," who brought it from Zion. The mission of the Jews is to proclaim God's truth:

> . . . our lips brought the world
> From the most distant, highest clouds
> The bronze word, the golden word—
> The reflection of God's face
>
> ("Psalmy nadziei" [Psalms of hope])[38]

Feldszuh saw the Jews as eternal revolutionaries, as "the world's walking restlessness, a flaming torch that cannot be extinguished" (*Czd,* p. 168). He saw them as guardians of truth and justice who thirst for progress and development, as "repairers" of the world, seekers for a better tomorrow, for perfect man, for higher forms of existence. The word revealed to the world by the Jewish voice is often identified with the biblical ethos, carved on tablets "corroded by the desert wind" (L. Baumberg, "Brzemię niebieskie" [The heavenly burden]).[39] Then there is the message of love that is sometimes interpreted as close to the word of Christ. Thus in Brandstaetter's "Autoportret Żyda" (Self-portrait of a Jew) Christ is a brother of the eternal "I":

> Then you took from me my brother. You gave him the sweetest words,
> Hewn in the heart of the fatherland, in its toil, defeat, fatigue,
> You nailed Him to a dark cross! So that in his winged shadow
> The crowd of reasonless believers should spit at me and murder me.
>
> ("Autoportet Żyda" [Self-portrait of a Jew], *Kts,* p. 13)

The suffering Jesus had the face of the "murdered in the districts of the pogrom" ("Psalm 1933"); his teaching does not oppose or contradict the Jewish word but is its noblest emanation.

Polish-Jewish literature did not interpret the sense of the Diaspora exclusively in terms of the collective fate. The suffering of the exile is not just a national martyrology. The Diaspora does not signify exclusively the stateless and landless condition of the Jews. It also signifies the human experience of endangerment and homelessness. For those who wander among foreign peoples, for those who cross the lands of strangers, for the slave, the persecuted, the world is not home. In Polish-Jewish literature, the portrayal of the situation of the Jews living in the Diaspora has very clearly two dimensions: the historical—collective and universal—and the individual. Hence the constant tension in this literature between the private and the national, the individual and the collective. The history of the group is realized through individual biographies. The question of the sense of the national fate is also a question of the sense of the individual fate. An inquiry into the sense of the Diaspora is also an inquiry into the sense of one's own existence. The Jews are outcasts, exiles, wanderers. The Jew is an outcast, exile, wanderer. The Jews are suffering, homeless, strangers. The Jew is suffering, homeless, a stranger. They are full of sadness and despair. He is full of sadness and despair. *Judenschmerz* is a variant of *Weltschmerz*. History seems to turn into existence.

This existential syndrome is easily found in the poetry of Szymel, Brandstaetter, and Dresdner. It is especially clear in the poetry Dresdner, whose small volume *Heine i nieznajoma* (Heine and the stranger) is a collection of variations on the theme of foreignness ("Boże Narodzenie" [Christmas], "Gdyby tak można" [If it were possible]), homelessness ("Sądny Dzień" [The Day of Judgment]), and suffering ("Świadectwo miłości" [Testimony of love]).

The analysis of the predicament of the Jew leads at times to diagnoses close to the existential descriptions of "the Jewish situation"[40] found later in the work of, say, Sartre. More specifically, Szymel's dialogue "Nie chcę być Żydem" (I don't want to be a Jew; 1935), which is an account of the idea of the universal, metaphysical mission of Jewry, contains a formulation of the dual dependence and imprisonment of the Jew by Others, which is identical with that of Sartre in his *Reflections on the Jewish Question:*

> I must pay the world double for everything. In addition to the fixed payment for the right to live as a human being, I must pay the same amount over again for the right to live as a Jew. When others take one step, I must, in the same time, get ahead of them by two steps. It is only then that the judges declare that the line has been evened out. They regard my liter as half a liter and my two hands as one.[41]

The situation of the Jew is an important theme in the poetry of Maurycy Schlanger. The title *Idę* . . . (I walk . . . ; 1936) of his slender volume of poetry has a symbolic dimension:

> I walk into the night and the winter,
> I walk into the dark gale,

I walk,
because walk I must,
. . . .
I walk
because I am a Jew
("Idę . . ." [I walk . . .], *I,* p. 5)

In Schlanger's poetry, it is not only the "I" that views wandering as its destination, that lives "under way," but also the sons of Israel, the whole nation stepping "with naked feet on the stony roads of the Diaspora" ("Juda verecke!" [Perish, Jew!], *I,* p. 8).

In the case of Irma Kanfer, this fate is personalized by Jewish actors:

Sick with nostalgia
they tramp, tramp
By day and by night—Jews—exiles—actors
("Żydowscy aktorzy" [Jewish actors]) [42]

Schlanger and Kanfer explicitly link Jewishness with exile, wandering, and homelessness. This linkage is the first step toward the universalization of the experience of the Diaspora. The next stage on this road seems to be the adducing of symbolic situations of the kind we are discussing without the addition of a national commentary. This is so, for example, in the lyric poetry of Syda Richter, where the motifs of wandering and wanderer are related to the Jewish context implicitly rather than explicitly:

Who are you wanderer, eternal exile
. . . .
Whose curse or sacrifice
Chases you into the distance—devoid of joy?
For whose guilt so terrible a punishment?
For what crimes the centuries of atonement?
("???") [43]

Similar devices are found in the poetry of Fryderyk Bertisch:

We have neither shelter nor home,
We have neither friends nor relatives,
Even if you devoted rows of volumes to the sufferings of eternal exiles,

Who will grasp the fear of hunted people,
who will listen to their mournful complaints?
("Bezdomni" [The homeless], *Knu,* p. 44)

Here the exiles and the homeless are as much the collectivity of all wanderers and strangers as they are Jews. In Juliusz Feldhorn's "Zwycięstwo Ahaswera" (Ahasuerus's victory) Adam, the Wanderer, and Ahasuerus are the same figure in different disguises.

The existential note present in the interpretation of the Diaspora exile can be perceived in certain cultural themes that actualize the tension between the national and the private. It is strongest in the images of Rosh Hashanah and Yom Kippur, the most important Jewish holidays, filled with lofty ethical content. It is here that the proximity of the historical to the existential comes to the fore. These holidays, whose fundamental feature is the "change in man, the abandoning of mundane life, and the return to perfection,"[44] take on a national value in Polish-Jewish literature, in the sense that they refer not only to the individual but also to the collectivity. Existential and national threads coexist in the Yom Kippur prayers:

All our lurking fear, all our dreadful, ravaging homesickness,
The burning shame of humiliations and bitterness of favors gained
Despair, sorrow, humble torment, must be wept out in a raucous voice
Must be sent to You, to the stars, today, in the hour of judgment.

Our festering pain erupts from the depths of the body
And chokes us in the throats until it finally explodes in a cry, in sobbing
As if we suddenly felt in impotent and laughable anger
That we who are puny, we who are nothingness and dust, are the only ones
who are human.

For centuries we have been standing in these benches unmoved and alone
All those who sob in the houses of prayer in hamlets and towns echo us.
The candles crying with golden, bright drops echo us
For the crying is to reach high, to You—Lord in the stars.

Oh where are you, where are you, dearest, unknown, holy Fatherland?
Why always far away?—Such a long time has passed . . .
To you alone, oh God, we may today confess all,
You alone listen to us in the glorious crown of stars.
(A. Eker, "Jom Kipur" [Yom Kippur], *Mch,* p. 41)

The praying people are a crowd of suffering, desperate, complaining, and frightened people who experience the insignificance of man's condition. This crowd is also a crowd of eternal Jews, mourning "for centuries" the lost fatherland, humiliated, "lashed by the winds" of the Diaspora.

In Karol Dresdner's "W Sądny Dzień" (On the Day of Judgment), the situation of the "I"—which describes itself as homeless, a wanderer, a Jew—has its source in the fate of the collectivity. Thus here, too, the Yom Kippur reflections are as much private as national in character:

Black-striped mourning clothes,
Stearine sobs of candles
A defensive prayerful mound,
Behind the earthwork a rally of supplicants
. . . .
If I get together boards and logs
To build a small house
What fatherland
Will grant me a true sonship
What fatherland? . . .

And if I will want to take a wife
To my well-earned bed
What girl will want to marry me,
Me, the exile, me the Jew,
What girl will want to marry me?
. . . .
Black-striped mourning clothes
God bids us atone for sins,
He gave us exile and tabernacles
And Tituses a triumphal arch.

(K. Dresdner, "W Sądny Dzień"
[Judgment Day], *Hin,* pp. 16–17)

It turns out that the determination of one's private existential situation is closely connected with reflections on the mystery of the fate of the collectivity.

Confronted by the terror of the trial and the sentence, the "I" becomes one with the collectivity in prayers, such as "Unetaneh tokef," which proclaims the power of Jehovah (H. Safrin, "Unetaneh tokef . . .";[45] S. Dykman, "Netane tokef"). In Dresdner's "Elul," the collective "we" confesses its Elul fears and asks for intercession:

Oh, how sad are the days of the month of Elul . . .
With pale face, with tearstained cheek,
With prayers of lament let us make a round of the synagogue
And dressed in colors of mourning
Let us go and measure our fathers' graves . . .

Oh, how sad are the days of the month of Elul . . .
The cemetery stones drip with blood and tears
O good dead, O holy dead,
Pray for us!
("Elul," *Hin,* pp. 19–20)

Thus Yom Kippur is the time of union of the living and the dead,[46] the time of linking the symbolic chain of generations in front of Jehovah's throne.

But above all, this holiday is a time of confronting the truth of one's own existence. The experiencing of this truth is realized in a special setting and involves culturally determined forms; the "I" expresses this experiencing in paraphrases of prayers and marks the ritual text with the mark of privacy (H. Safrin, "Kol Nidre"; I. Deutscher, "Kol Nidre").[47] Confrontation of the mystery of fate, the encounter with a God who judges and sentences, ethical self-knowledge, the experience of the fragility of existence—all these are an act that is fundamental for the sense of humanness. This act is repeated by the "I" that is aware of this repetition and of its sense:

Here I am, ashes and dust
Here I am, wretched reptile
I come to You again,
I come once more—
I will keep nothing from you.
(M. Hochberżanka, "Jom Kipur"
[Yom Kippur])[48]

The existential note, the attempts to universalize the experiences of the Diaspora, the manner of description of the condition of the Jew—all these did not result in an equal sign between the condition of the Jew and the condition of man in Polish-Jewish literature. Such an equal sign is found, for example, in the thirties, in the writings of Max Brod, who regarded the condition of the Jew in the Diaspora as a special case of the human condition. In Max Brod's view, to be a Jew is to be a human being in a particularly intensive manner; it is to be the essence of a human being:

> the Jewish condition is just a symbolic image, intensified and therefore endowed with great explanatory power, of the general human condition. The Diaspora Jew is lonely, deprived of support, uneasy. But isn't everybody essentially lonely? Isn't it true that all alliances, all states of peace turn out to be endlessly, permanently fluid, trivial? Within a certain range of feelings, which is palpable at least every now and then (I do not claim that these feelings are optimal, final, decisive), everyone is a Diaspora Jew. (*Hin,* p. 270)[49]

The reason no such equal sign was introduced in Polish-Jewish literature was that, in this literature, the Jewish "I" was very strongly linked with the Jewish "we," with the historical experiences of the collectivity and its memory. The existential condition is an offshoot of the historical condition: the Jewish person wears the stigmata of Jewishness.

To Be in the Diaspora, To Be in Poland

The experience of the Diaspora comes to the fore not only in the biography of the eternal "I," in Jewish history—biblical, Roman, Spanish, and German. It also has a modern, Polish, variant. The Polish landscape, the Poles, and "Polishness" take part in the Jewish fate. The sequence is not accidental; the ties of this fate to the landscape were extremely strong. For many generations of Jews the land of exile had been a fatherland. "Wherever you are—there is the land dear to your heart / It has borne you, it has nurtured you" ("Jankiel Cymbalista" [Yankel the Dulcimer Player], *Wl,* p. 56) says the Szymel figure, Yankel the Dulcimer Player. Polish-Jewish literature often bears testimony to this truth. Home is Podole ("at home in Podole"—S. Pomer, "Złota Lipa" [The golden linden]),[50] Lvov, Cracow, Warsaw . . . The Vistula flows among the fields of Mazowsze "like a tear on a yellowed Talmud" (R. Brandstaetter, "Ballada o rabinie z Płocka" [Ballad of the Płock rabbi], *Kts,* p. 19). The shadow of Rachel appears in the corn:

> Through Polish corn fields, through golden rye,
> In eternal milky whiteness,
> Flows quietly, into time, at dawn,
> Rachel's slender shadow.
>
> (K. Dresdner, "O świcie" [At dawn], *Hin,* p. 22)

The Wandering Jew takes with him in his "exile's bundle" the landscape of the small home town with its crooked little house of prayer and roadside willow (W. Szlengel, "Tobół tułaczy" [The exile's bundle]).[51] The dream of Palestine may end in tears because of the imagined leavetaking of Cracow (E. Silberstein, "Golusowy sen" [A *galuth* dream]).[52]

The Polish land is a private fatherland.[53] Eretz Israel is the spiritual fatherland. The "I" belongs to both:

It makes no difference—here or not here,
It makes no difference—in the last concern
I dream of you,
Jerusalem, as I dream of Poland.
(M. Braun, "Ahaswer" [Ahasuerus])[54]

Henryk Sztrom, the protagonist in Jakub Appenszlak's *Piętra* (Stories), also invokes Jerusalem and Poland as his two fatherlands. For this young Zionist, Warsaw was just as holy as the memory of the city of David: "he is linked with this city to the end of his days. Nothing will break this bond. He remembered the words full of primeval terror: 'If I forget thee, O Jerusalem' . . . a stigma of memory in the Jewish soul. But it is just as true that I will never forget thee, my native town."[55]

Even Palestinian *shomrim** discover the truth of the two fatherlands. Feldszuh says that the "nights of guard duty," "the Eastern nights," are also nights of dreams about Poland. "[the *shomer*] has two fatherlands. Here is the fatherland of his soul, there of his body. Here is the cradle of his Yesterday and Tomorrow, there his Today" (*Np,* p. 9).

The motif of two fatherlands[56] played an important role in the writings of Maurycy Szymel, especially so in his first small volume of poetry *Powrót do domu* (The return home):

Two fatherlands—two lands and two skies
Fate gave the heart in penitential wanderings
("Dwie ojczyzny" [Two fatherlands], *Pdd,* p. 90)

The first fatherland is the Polish landscape, which Szymel usually praises and delights in:

Why do you have springs I won't forget
Why do you have fragrant mountain summers—
Behold, I walk drunk with huge wonder,
For your charm oppresses me with the sweetest of burdens.

*In Hebrew a Jewish guard or scout. [Trans.]

My blood is full of the song of your orchards,
It throbs like the Vistula—wholesome with delight—
And, truth to tell, choked with happiness—I don't know
how to make my joy flutter with words.

("Ziemio . . ." [O land . . .], *Pdd,* p. 89;
original title "Polsko!" [O Poland!])[57]

We find a similar note in the poems of Brandstaetter, who is deeply attached to "the holiest fields of Podkarpacie." What is striking is that both poets recall on such occasions rustic landscapes pervaded with the spirit of an idyll and with Slavic characteristics. Their private fatherland is a land "of wheat," silvered by the "deeps of the Vistula," "white with the clattering of storks," gray with thatched roofs (R. Brandstaetter, "Autoportret Żyda," *Ktś,* p. 15). For Appenszlak's protagonist, too, the covenant with Polishness is understanding "Polish snow," the mood of the fields on the banks of the Vistula, Rejmont's villages, Tetmajer's Podhale . . .

In Szymel's "Wieczór na wsi" (Evening in the country; the original title was "Polska" [Poland]),[58] it is just the landscape of the Polish village that evokes the sense and avowal of "family feeling" and rootedness:

For, sitting on this bench, here, on Polish land,
Whose mists climb to distant stars,
I absorb the universe through your words
And I begin here.

("Wieczór na wsi" [Evening in the country], *Wl,* p. 57)

But the memory of Eretz Israel is inseparable from the attachment to the private fatherland:

I bless you my unknown meadows,
Strewn across my distant fatherland,
I bless you, walking in a buff-colored Polish cornfield
That smells of milk and honey.

(M. Szymel, "Woń miodu i mleka"
[The fragrance of milk and honey], *Wl,* p. 70)

Sometimes this twinning inspires a kind of mirror image: the Polish landscape evokes the Palestinian landscape, and the work of the peasants—that of the *halutzim* (D. Ihr, "Błogosławieństwo" [Blessing]).[59] The "here" in Poland is a model for what is "there," "in Palestine":

Just as here, when ripe fields of coarse grain
Kneel before the sickles, so too on the swarthy earth
Of the Emek buff-colored stripes of corn bend,
And so, pitchers of cold water for Jewish peasants.

Let the hot sky hide behind the threatening weight
Of clouds; straw ropes will crackle in the sheaves
Just as here when the rack wagons are chased off the fields
And the rain chatters on the harnesses and in the roadside ditches.

(R. Brandstaetter, "Żniwiarzom żydowskim spoczynek po pracy"
[Rest after work for Jewish reapers])[60]

But far more frequently there is no propinquity between the landscapes of the two fatherlands. Here—the North; there—the Orient. Here the dominant characteristics are Slavic, Piast-related; there—those of the Bible. Szymel's "Poetom ziemi walczącej" (For the poets of the fighting land) was intended as a confrontation of North and South:

Live nights, fiery nights
Throb over your head—
with a hot breath—
with crimson passion—
you breathe them in with the native word
. . . .
I don't know if you still remember
the snowy polar sunsets
and the tender winter nights,
black nights.

("Poetom ziemi walczącej"
[For the poets of the fighting land], *Pdd,* p. 79)

Flame and snow, "burning nights" and "polar sunsets" are, of course, hyperboles in the service of contrast.

This mirror-image quality and the contrast of images may have a common source. The "cedar," "swarthy" [earth], "Hebrew" fatherland, so referred to by Brandstaetter, [belong to] a dreamland, a land of the imagination. It is the fatherland called forth by the power of the imagination from the books of the Torah, in which it lies "hidden in the branches of wide Hebrew letters," "the fatherland I have not seen":

Even though I don't know how colors rise in your sky
or the aroma of bread gotten from your soil,
I call you on lonely evenings
with sad words

(M. Szymel, "Ojczyzna, której nie widziałem" [The fatherland I have not seen], *Pdd,* p. 82)

Such exercises of the imagination are not always successful. The theme of Szymel's "Wiersz smutny" (Sad poem) is the impossibility of "building a fatherland out of words," "out of nothing," the making of its sky and land out of a dream:

O ancient beautiful God, ruler of word and earth,
cast a spell over me, envelop me in a shady dream of palms.

It's no use covering the windows, it's no use dimming the lights,
It's not David's chariots rumbling, it's trolleys, red trolleys.
It's not the thunder of trombones, not a flame fluttering in the dusk of the altar—
It's just words, words I repeat in the darkness

("Wiersz smutny" [Sad poem], *Pdd,* p. 74)

The contrast between the biblical vision and the image of interwar Warsaw (the realia include Smocza street scenery) deepens the chasm between word and objects, between word and world.

The motif of building a fatherland—as well as oneself!—out of a book, out of the Bible, is also used by Brandstaetter. His "Biblia" (The Bible)[61] is the fertile soil from which the cedar grows; it is the cedar from which the house is built; it is the house "standing in God's shadow"; it is the mother from this house; it is the fatherland and state which defend this mother; it is the body and blood of the Jew; it is his grave and ashes. Thus Jewishness is understood as a state of being totally enclosed in the life-giving, indestructible biblical cycle, in its eternal rhythm. The Bible land grows cedar, house, fatherland, and the man who fertilizes this land with his "fertile ashes"—a man who draws on Jewishness as well as enriches it.

Sometimes the tension between the private fatherland and the spiritual fatherland takes on a rather dramatic air: the blessings directed to the Polish landscape are accompanied by a prayer to Eretz Israel, but the sense of the proximity of the blessed land is linked with a sense of alienation described in Szymel's "Elegia do ziemi polskiej" (Elegy to the Polish land):

> You gave me Your bread and peace, You gave me the sky over my head—
> My cradle was of Your firs, my coffin will be of Your lindens—
> But not of You do I sing with Your beautiful word
> Fatherland not mine yet dear—earth I'll die on.
>
> I see You at night, outside the window, in the gentle light of your stars
> Tossing wavy shadows with a line of dark fields—
> You will forgive my eyes which could not tear themselves away
> From another, distant land . . .
>
> ("Elegia do ziemi polskiej" [Elegy to the Polish land], *Pdd,* p. 89)

There is a sense of connection with the Polish land in life and in death, sealed by a kind of dissolving in its juices, and there is eternal yearning after Eretz Israel. Both are part of one's fate. The tone of the praise of the Polish landscape is elegiac . . .

The motif of "not my fatherland," so important in the quoted poem of Szymel, appears frequently in Polish-Jewish poetry:

> I would praise the stars of the fatherland that is not mine
>
> (R. Brandstaetter, "Elegia" [Elegy], *Kts,* p. 9)[62]

> You praise the charm and beauty of the land that is not yours
>
> (M. Szymel, "Jankiel Cymbalista"
> [Yankel the Dulcimer Player], *Wl,* p. 55)

Moreover, the opposed terms, mine [versus] not mine, are often displaced by the harsher, mine [versus] foreign. The private fatherland becomes a foreign land:

> I love you, blue sky dissolving in blackness,
> and you, old moon with your silver glitter.
> Oh, rustling bushes on fragrant banks,
> evenings at the Vistula flickering with illusions.
>
> . . . and I run furtively to the airless little room,
> full of melancholy and anxious toil,

for here nothing but my old cradle
must I love. Nothing here is mine.
(M. Schlanger, "Obczyzna" [Foreign land], *I*, p. 14)

In the foreign, distant Fatherland I will remember
This town, so close, so familiar—not mine.
(M. Füllenbaum, "Więdnące korzenie" [Withering roots])[63]

As can be seen, the sense of foreignness takes a very special form. It is not that the land seems foreign to the "I," which loves it dearly. It is that the "I" feels a foreigner, an intruder deprived of the right to love the land . . . The source of the split mine [versus] not mine is rejection. The nineteenth-century myth of a "shared land," a myth of solidarity and optimism, has been brutally shattered by the triumphs of hatred. Srul from Lubartow, the hero of a popular short story by Adam Szymański, a man who embodied the love for "our land," was introduced by Brandstaetter into the interwar reality to state the truth that "nowadays you won't find Poland in the golden flowers of lupin or in bean pods,"[64] that the land is foreign, bitter, and sad. Szymel's Yankel the Dulcimer Player, returning from Zosia's wedding, is the "brother in bitterness" of the homeless, homebred musician, convinced of the unavoidable Jewish shame and martyrdom. The situation of the expelled is an important motif in the poetry of Szymel, Brandstaetter, Dresdner, Ihr, Kanfer . . . It is especially affecting in Szymel's late poems: "Rozmowa o ludziach i drzewach" (A conversation about people and trees), "Rozmowa z Panem Mikołajem" (A conversation with Pan Mikołaj), "Śpiew Żyda polskiego" (Song of a Polish Jew), and "Wspomnienie" (Recollection),[65] whose leitmotiv is the sense of indissoluble bond with the land in spite of experienced wrongs.

My enemies batten on hatred
And the times are dreadful
Yet no one can break the love
The Polish forest planted in me.

My dignified grandfather used
To sit on this bench, next to the crooked hut—
One precious atom of this earth
Is worth to me as much as the whole wide world

I can't help it. If I knocked my poor head
Against the wall and shouted: No!
The bitter love would come back again
No matter how sad and unhappy I am.

A wrong hurts. Every wound hurts.
Rebellion hurts and every shout and shame—
Dear land, beloved land,
A Polish Jew prays to you.

Every bush that slumbers in the dark knows me
Every path knows my sad song—
There is so much space on the Polish earth,
So much shadow under the leaves of the trees.

A man can give as much of himself,
As a tree, bush, and flower—
Take my hands too to build
Your bridges, houses, roads, and huts.

Don't believe those who are screaming—they,
Their words are dark and evil;
In the weave of human arms my hands
Will not be missing, harnessed to your yoke.

The noble yoke of harmony and freedom—
I don't want to be like a detached lump of scrap—
I hereby put my young hands
In the sweet yoke that is our house.

Restore the hearts of those who strike at me
The way you restore the greenness of grass;
Save from pointless hatred
And wrongs—save the oppressed!

(M. Szymel, "Śpiew Żyda polskiego" [Song of a Polish Jew])

Prayer to the land—the home, the only ally of the oppressed by hatred—is an appeal to collectivity, to kinship through the land. The homely, rustic landscape counterbalances; it nourishes the hope of future amity and peace. The goodness and gentleness of nature bring consolation:

The hatred of crowds run wild
Breathlessly rushing into the madness of blood
Won't silence the rustling of birches at the water's edge
The croaking of frogs or the silence of mosses . . .

Nor will thunder suddenly dropping out of the sky
Silence my love—
Calm will again come after the storm
To my beautiful forest. My quiet home . . .
(M. Szymel, "Wspomnienie" [Recollection])

The conversation with an anti-Semite ("Rozmowa z Panem Mikołajem" [A conversation with Pan Mikołaj]) is a similar discourse on the goodness and fairness of gardens and clouds, which give fruit and shade to everybody without exception.

The sense of foreignness is not the result of hatred alone. It persists even in love. In Szymel's love poem "Do . . ." (To . . .), it is love and foreignness that bind the lovers with a fascinating bond:

I must not write about you with my own words—
my mother could not pronounce your name—
although we share bread in the same land,
. . . .
You'll never love my brothers on sad streets,
you'll never understand the nervous speech of my sisters
(M. Szymel, "Do . . ." (To . . .), *Pdd,* p. 33)

Their worlds are foreign to each another, and the "haughty, huge, cold cross," a symbol of this foreignness, separates them irrevocably.

The image of Eretz Israel is at least a partial antidote to foreignness and a compensation for it. It is the promised land of rootedness. The mechanism of its construction is transparent: here—"land that is not nine"; there—"the motherland"; here—pain; there—joy; here—"the shadow of the cross"; there—prophets and kings; here—"Pan Mikołaj" and others like him; there—Hebrew sisters and mothers," "good, quiet shepherds," "Hebrew knights," "biblical people" . . .

These descriptions are drawn from Szymel's poems, which are replete with scenes of ideal life in Eretz Israel. Usually rustic in tone, they take place in the vineyards, gardens, and meadows of the Galilee, Samaria, and Judea, where "the shepherds' pipes play quietness and peace" ("Kołysanka" [Lullaby], *Pdd,* p. 86). The "I" dreams itself into this world, renews the covenant with the land of its ancestors, and experiences the mystery of rootedness:

> Let my fatherland sweep over me
> With crimson dawns—
> this is the hum of my land,
> the glimmer of my sky.
> . . . .
> For this is the bread of my land,
> And the wine of my fruits—
> . . . .
> Good are silence and peace
> under the shadow of one's own tree—
> (M. Szymel, "Przymierze" [Covenant], *Pdd,* p. 56)

The presence [in the Polish original] of all three gender forms of "mine" provides a transparent leitmotiv that leaves no doubt about the true source of the joy of the covenant.

The search for rootedness and peace is a dominant element of the posture of the "I" of Szymel's slender first volume of poems, of the "I" surrounded by images of "my fatherland," "going to meet" "the fatherland of prophets," turning up among "Hebrew knights," awaited by "Hebrew" mothers, sisters, and lovers; of the "I" that confirms itself repeatedly in the belief that "it is good in one's own land"; of the "I" full of love and delight:

> Let us go to our fields, our rocking meadows—
> let us sow with kisses love fervent and young—
> O stars, beloved stars—
> O meadows, O water—
> ("Miłujmy się . . ." [Let us love each other . . .], *Pdd,* p. 86)

The idyllic quality of some of the poems is reinforced by their pastoral or lullaby form ("Kołysanka" [Lullaby]; "Sielanka" [Pastoral]).

The Promised Land, the land of the Kingdom of the Third Temple and of "Jerusalem of Light," was also an important theme in the poetry of Roman Brandstaetter. But instead of intimacy and coziness, the dominant tones of his poetry are those of the pathos and monumentality of the "land of the ancestors." For example, "Autoportret Żyda" ends with the following prayer "to the bosom of my fatherland":

That you should let me rest under the crown of a slender palm
Amid Jordan bulrushes and in the silence of a golden field,
And breathe in the fragrance of cedars flowing from the peaks of Lebanon
And listen intently to the gurgling of the water in Heshbon's light blue ponds,
And gaze for a long time at the herds of goats
Descending from the darkening mountains into the valleys teeming with people.
(R. Brandstaetter, "Autoportet Żyda" [Self-portrait of a Jew], *Kts,* p. 15)

This image is obviously of biblical origin. The stylizing element penetrates the spheres of language, poetic imagination, and symbolism. Brandstaetter's "songs about the fatherland" are made with printing plates inspired by the Book, often selected in accordance with an allegorical or symbolic key suggested by tradition. These devices can best be seen in texts in which patriotic themes are combined with the symbolism of the Song of Songs. The result is a kind of patriotic "Shir hashirim" (Song of Songs) that extols the Jew as the Bridegroom and the Fatherland as the Bride:

In your swarthy arms turned like ivory
In your palms as sweet as a Hebrew pomegranate
In your slender neck, which is like David's tower,
In your slender figure, which is like Hermon peaks
In your girlish body
I found the sweetness of my fatherland.

When the white turtledoves fall silent at night
And we—completely lost in one another—
In the shadow of birches and golden stars
Join ardent lips in a fervent covenant
On your lips I feel the heat of lush earth and flowering orchards,
And in your eyes
I see the depth of the Kineret,
And I know that you are for me an open vineyard
In which an angel is on guard a day before the vintage.

My cedar fatherland and Hebrew state
Charmed into eyes shaded by long eyelashes, and into the quietest hands!
(R. Brandstaetter, "Ojczyzna" [The fatherland], *Kts,* p. 25)

The images derived from the Song of Songs—a swarthy bride, a bride [and] a vineyard, love [and] a seal, conventions for describing people ("pomegranate," "tower of David"), place-names[66]—are supplied with an interpretative key: the lovers are, at once, Israel and the fatherland; the covenant is a union; and passion is a patriotic passion. Erotic symbolism frequently turns up in Brandstaetter's poetry in just such concatenations: the memory of the fatherland is the memory of love caresses ("Dzieje mojego rodu" [The history of my family]), the regaining of the fatherland is an act of love ("Jerozolima światła i mroku" [Jerusalem of light and dusk]) that will bear new life . . .

Szymel's bucolic Eretz, Brandstaetter's "cedar" "Eretz" and "Bride-Eretz," Pomer's legendary "Eretz beyond the seas" ("Ziemia Święta" [Holy Land])[67]—all these are fantasies about a land that is happy, beautiful, and safe . . .

Do you know the land
Where slender cedars bloom
Where the color of the sky
Is forever blue?

(L. Jamer, "Czy znasz ten kraj?"
[Do you know the land?])[68]

Living in the Diaspora, the "I" not only inhabits two fatherlands but is also "under the spell of two languages." The motifs of "not mine," of a "foreign tongue" and of "our tongue"—Hebrew, Yiddish—are among the formulas of Polish-Jewish poetry. It is clear that these are manifestations of threads that are not only cultural or existential but also purely artistic. One indication of the importance of language for Diaspora writers is that there is hardly a lyric Polish-Jewish poet who did not write an "elegy about the Polish tongue," or an "elegy about the Hebrew tongue."[69]

Yet another important symbol of the Diaspora in Polish-Jewish literature is the motif of two languages. The drama of language, characteristic of the Diaspora and experienced by every Jew in exile acquired special poignancy for the artist. Thus the following description of a Polish lesson in a Hebrew school, taken from Jakub Appenszlak's *Piętra* (Stories), is also characteristic of life among strangers:

> a curse lies heavy on the Jewish school, on every school that is not in a Jewish land but in the Diaspora. Everywhere children pore over some Talmud of Yiddishism or Hebraism or a forced assimilationist lesson. They cannot live a full life in one language, simply, naturally. School always takes from them one language and gives them a substitute language, it transforms, changes, and forces

> into a new form. . . . "Window"—says the Jewish child and thinks in Yiddish: "Dus fenster"; and in Hebrew: "Halon." The windows are usually barred with multilingual names. And only after having understood their meaning is it possible to look out the window and see the world.[70]

Multilingualism is yet another affliction of the Diaspora, another thorn on the Jewish road. Its experience takes an interesting form in Szymel's lyric poetry. Here the "I" always addresses someone in a foreign language: the mother who speaks no Polish—in Polish ("Połóż mi dobre ręce swe na włosach" [Put your good hands on my hair]); and the beloved who speaks no Yiddish—in Yiddish ("Do . . ." [To . . .]). Initiation into many languages is "a treasure that lies as heavy as a curse." The fate of laboring for strangers is the fate of every poet in the Diaspora, of every Jew in exile. This fate is present in Szymel's "Rozmowa ze starym Eljaszem":

> You cart the manorial milk so as not to starve to death—
> And I must sing this sad poem in a foreign tongue.
>
> ("Rozmowa ze starym Eljaszem"
> [A conversation with old Eli], *Pdd,* p. 36)

The Diaspora and Eretz, Polish and the "free Hebrew tongue," "poets of the Diaspora" and "poets of the fighting land"—all these can coexist. In Szymel's "Poeci ziemi walczącej" (Poets of the fighting land), images of a "free Hebrew land" are at the same time visions of meetings of poets:

> youths in the stadiums of the fatherland
> will speak your poems,
> the daughters of Jerusalem will shade your head with garlands
> in the free Hebrew land
> in the free Hebrew tongue.
>
> ("Poeci ziemi walczącej" [Poets of the fighting land], *Pdd,* p. 79)

Anda Eker described being in the fatherland as "laughing in Hebrew" ("W ojczyźnie naszej" [In our fatherland], *Mch,* p. 111).

The "two-language spell" is, of course, another variant of the tension between one's own and the foreign. Polish is a "northern dialect," "soft, Slavic word" (Pomer), "from above pines and snow / northern speech, not mine, one and only" (Füllenbaum), "doleful and larklike word," "a language woven from flowers of the field," "of the Vistula and of linden" (Ihr), "entwined with azure like stocky apple trees" (Brandstaetter). On the other hand, "hymns to Hebrew song," "elegies on the Hebrew tongue" (just once, exceptionally, there is a reference in C[elina] Meerson-Becker's "Do mowy żydowskiej" (To the Jewish tongue; meaning, I think, both Jewish languages): "I heard that you are the tongue / of fanatics and of the damned, that you are a wretched jargon"[71] extol "the word . . . one's own, near" (Ihr), "ancestral" (Szymel), "free speech," "ancestral shout" (Schlanger), "mild, sweet, melodious, soft" song (Safrin), "the only mother" (Ihr). The languages, characterized in this way, represent opposite worlds. Polish evokes the rustic and the Slavic; Hebrew—the biblical and the Jewish historical experience. Ihr depicts the spell of Polish as the experience of wandering among Slavic deities and fireflies ("Do polskiej mowy" [To the Polish tongue]),[72] while the word flowing from Rachel's grave conceals the image of all of Canaan, its vineyards and streams ("Do mowy hebrajskiej" [To the Hebrew tongue]).[73] Brandstaetter contrasts the coziness and "Vistula quality" of Mazowsze Polish with Hebrew, which "pulses with the pain . . . of the ancestors and with their blood" ("Pożegnanie muzy czarnoleskiej" [A farewell to the Czarnolesie muse], *Ktś,* p. 7). In Szymel's case, we have "Piast words" ("Ziemio" [O land]) and the "branchy Hebrew letters" out of which emerge Hebrew landscapes and men. The motif of Yiddish plays a marginal role: in addition to Celina Meerson-Becker, whose "Do mowy żydowskiej" I mentioned earlier, Szymel alludes to Yiddish in "Rozmowa ze starym Eliaszem" as "restless" and "sad" "words of one's own."

Yes, there is Hebrew, but it is "far" and "unknown" (Szymel), whereas Polish is intimately close:

> . . . the day greets me with a bright murmur in Polish,
> the muse plays an Aeolian harp in Polish,
> lilac wilts in Polish, corn smells in Polish.
>
> Hey! Ring angelic sounds
> of an ageless maternal lullaby,
> of a melancholy Cracow song.
>
> (M. Schlanger, "Wyznanie moje" [My confession], *I,* p. 26)

Polish is often, literally, a mother tongue: "I heard you in the cradle / from my mother's mouth" (D. Ihr, "Do polskiej mowy"). It is also, literally, the most intimate language, the language of professions of love.

Thus when it comes to language, the relationship between "mine" and "foreign," tends to be disturbed. The language of strangers is one's own and one's own is strange. This reversal of emotional ties is the theme of Celina Meerson-Becker's "Do mowy żydowskiej":

A hundredfold sad heritage! Tired by the long road
I approach you today on bumpy fallow ground.
O my unknown tongue, tragically squandered,
Perhaps more foreign-sounding than any foreign tongue.
("Do mowy zydowskiej" [To the Jewish tongue])

"Unknown," "foreign," "strangest," and yet one's own . . . The disturbance of natural ties results in ambivalence toward both languages:

fatally in love with a tongue not my own
(M. Szymel, "Genealogia" [Genealogy], *Sp,* p. 7)

You gave me a tongue woven of golden chamomile
Interspersed with poppies, but foreign to my chapped lips
And you bade me sing in it pain with an utterly broken soul
And give holy vent in it to my most secret complaints.
. . . .
And in a tongue which one day will disown my heart
To set my whole heart on fire and sing out all of my heart
(R. Brandstaetter, "Autoportret Żyda"
[Self-portrait of a Jew], *Kts,* p. 14)

A curious union of nearness and strangeness, indeed, of intimacy and enmity. Like the expatriation from the private fatherland, this is due, as well, to external causes:

And I—write this poem in a foreign tongue,
in a tongue that hisses at me like a snake: Jew! Jew! Jew!
(D. Ihr, "List" [A letter])[74]

The motif of a hostile language turned up with particular frequency in Ihr's poetry, and became a virtual obsession in his late poems, such as "Do polskiej mowy" (To the Polish tongue), "Do mowy hebrajskiej" [To the Hebrew tongue], "Kołysanka" (Lullaby), and "List" (A letter), all written after the publication of his "Pożegnanie młodości" (A farewell to youth). They are a farewell to Polish—a mother tongue and an intimate tongue—and document the shock of rejection:

> . . . to stop at thresholds
> To knock at doors in vain
> And instead of bread
> Take for a viaticum
> A bloody insult and a curse for the night's journey
> (D. Ihr, "Do mowy hebrajskiej" [To the Hebrew tongue])

The crisis in the relations with Polish is due to humiliation—by the language and in it. The violence of Ihr's reaction is rather exceptional in Polish-Jewish literature, where the tone of farewells was usually milder, as in the case of Schlanger: "tomorrow I'll kiss the moss on the holy wall / tomorrow I'll choke on the homeland shout" ("Wyznanie moje" [My confession], *I,* p. 26)

Despite Hebraistic and Hebrew yearnings, Polish remained a value the "I" was permanently connected with and a language allied with the Jewish experience: "in this my Polish tongue trembles Jewish sadness" (R. Brandsaetter, "Elegia" [Elegy], *Kts,* p. 9). An ideological reason was often given as a justification for writing in a "foreign" language. Thus Mayer-Arieh, author of "Pieśni chaluca" (Songs of a *halutz*), referred to himself as a Jewish poet fulfilling a national mission:

> I admit that I sometimes write Jewish
> Poems in Polish
> But I am really a Jewish poet
> . . . .
> . . . until the last Jew awakens
> From the night of the Diaspora in a bright fatherland
> And until the last pauper will swim to the shore of the land
> From the sea of apostasy
> And will shout "I am a Jew"
> Until then the Jewish poet will last
> And will write in all tongues of Babel
> And call in all the world's tongues
> On Jews to be Jews.
> ("Pieśń o poecie żydowskim" [Song about a Jewish poet], *Pch,* p. 24)

As long as the Diaspora endures and Jews live in the Diaspora, poets in the Diaspora must address them in the "tongues of Babel."

Notwithstanding ideological reasons and sentiments, ignorance of Hebrew was felt to be a kind of lameness. The image of the mute Hebrew poet appeared in Polish-Jewish literature in a number of variants:

Until palms throw the shade of a menorah
On my head—full of happy toil—
I—a Polish poet, a Hebrew mute
Will be sad and sick
(M. Schlanger, "Wyznanie moje" [My confession], *I,* p. 26)

Across the fear of midnight's evil hour,
Across the expanse of earth and sky
I stretch out my hands to your motherly hands—
Mute and blind.

I go groping across silence and darkness,
I know that you will fold your bad son to your heart,
And that you, Hebrew tongue, the one and only mother,
Will give words to the mouth and sight to sightless eyes.
(D. Ihr, "Do mowy hebrajskiej" [To the Hebrew tongue])

Szymel's poet has no "words of his own" ("Żydowscy trubadurzy" [Jewish troubadours]);[75] he speaks "the language of his fathers' stuttering" ("Rozmowa ze starym Eljaszem" [A conversation with old Eli]). In Brandstaetter's "Elegia na mowę hebrajską" (Elegy on the Hebrew tongue)[76] "a stranger," "a vagabond," prostrates himself before Hebrew in love, pain, and silence. The motif of consolation to be found in Hebrew, thought of as a mother, of rest in it by the exhausted "stepson from the distant North," the "unworthy son," "the illegitimate successor," of gaining rootedness after wandering and straying, is a kind of therapeutic prescription. The clearest of such prescriptions were due to Brandstaetter and Safrin. In Brandstaetter's "List z Palestyny" (Letter from Palestine), *Kts,* p. 17, "Hebrew gives the yearned-for peace and shade / and joy." In Safrin's Hymn to Hebrew song,[77] Hebrew "rocks to childlike dreams." The Hebrew word is the word of salvation, the guide of the perplexed:

And you are calling me, mother—I hear, I hear—
Amid the groan of Slavic winds
Across the silence of closed homes and hearts
I walk, your homeless son—and ownerless dog
(D. Ihr, "Do mowy hebrajskiej" [To the Hebrew tongue])

The admission "I—a Jew" is synonymous with speaking about the Jewish collectivity. For the "I" of Polish-Jewish literature regards itself as the carrier of the universal Jewish fate, the representative of eternal Jewishness. The existential diagnosis grows out of the historical diagnosis: to understand oneself, one must understand the sense of Jewish history. One's identity turns out to be a function of solidaristic collective memory. The situation of an individual's identity expresses the situation of the collectivity. Living in the Diaspora is living not only in national slavery, but also in the slavery of one's humanity, experiencing the foreignness of the world and remaining homeless in it.

5

"The Return Home"

Childhood

One of the rudimentary experiences of the "I" of Polish-Jewish literature is leaving home and returning to it—in reality or in a dream—years later. The parts of its symbolic formula—"about the things I leave behind" and "the return home"—are found in the titles of the small first volumes of poetry of Awrohem Fenster and Maurycy Szymel, two authors in whose work this experience constitutes one of the central motifs.

Recollection and return determine a particular perspective of the Jewish world—a perspective of loss that, while promoting idealization, also prompted confrontation of the remembered with the actually experienced. It is a privilege of memory that it can embrace opposing emotions. The actual return provided the opportunity for superposing a new version on the remembered version of one's world.[1]

Images of leaving home occur far less frequently in Polish-Jewish literature than images of returning home:

> With father's blessing
> and mother's warm, languishing glance
> I left the house . . .
>
> (F. Bertisch, "Wyprawa po złote runo"
> [Pursuit of the golden fleece])[2]

> even if you crossed the whole wide world,
> you are bound to return to the same spot.
> and yet: I am setting forth in the world.
>
> (H. A. Fenster, "O tym co opuszczam"
> [The things I am leaving behind], *Otco,* p. 21)[3]

Usually, one leaves not only the physical home but also the home of Jewishness:

> The volumes of eternal books,
> The quiet, sad God of dark small houses of prayer were left behind somewhere—
> White Slavic nights cast a spell on us
> And visions of glittering roads running into the distance.
>
> . . . .
>
> Fed blood and milk of foreign words
> we fell away—green, young leaves—
> Our grandparents—gray Talmudists—
> Cried, their heads sadly lowered.
>
> (M. Szymel, "Żydowscy trubadurzy" [Jewish troubadours]) [4]

The time between leaving and returning includes two experiences. One is the end of childhood, the "farewell to youth"; the other is a kind of identity test, the reexperiencing and reevaluating of the Jewish tradition. The two are not disjoint. Childhood and Jewishness form a composite—the Jewish childhood. This is not just a biographical term but a state of existence.

Indeed, for the "I" of Polish-Jewish literature this state is a kind of existential asylum. At the beginning of youth, the "I" writes invocations to "Childland" (J. Wit, "Okręt Andersena" [Andersen's boat]) [5] and wants to return to school. For the child, school is both one of the most important settings and an institution representing life as ordered by others, an institution in which every step, every deed is weighed and evaluated. "I want to be a child—not a grownup," asserts the hero of H. A. Fenster's "Słowo o dorosłych synach wiecznie młodych matek" (A word about grownup sons of eternally young mothers), *Otco,* p. 11. Sometimes, leaving school provides an opportunity for elegiac reflections:

> Who bade us leave the school bench, the classroom, the schoolhouse
> . . . .
> There was a schedule in school,
> I knew what followed what
> And now everything comes as a surprise
> And while I know nothing, no one fails me.

And so I don't know what I do well, and what badly
And no one rewards me, no one punishes

(M. Szymel, "Elegia na początek roku szkolnego" [Elegy on the start of the schoolyear], *Pdd,* p. 88)

Eker sees her childhood as a house, a space of happiness: "My childhood was / Like a good white house." ("Moje dzieciństwo" [My childhood], *Mch,* p. 11). Its end marks the point when everything in the life of the "I" begins to go wrong. The world ceases to be ordered, ceases to be bright and cozy:

When I wore very short dresses
The snow was really white and soft
And the world was childlike, like snow
So pure, naive and different

(A. Eker, "Tamte zimy" [Those other winters], *Mch,* p. 14)

One's life story is sharply divided into two halves and amounts to knowing two worlds: the first bright, friendly, and harmonious; the second dark, chaotic, and hostile. Growing up marks a transition to the dark side of the universe.

Thus regression into childhood is also the choice of a particular image of the world. Stories about the "golden age" of innocence and harmony of existence constitute a ritual of Polish-Jewish lyrical poetry:

Let me, once more, take in my cool empty hand
The warm charm of childhood, the singing time that's passed,
Once more believe everything, question nothing,
And lock myself in this happiness.

(M. Silberman, "W zimowy zmierzch" [A winter dusk])[6]

. . . I wish that my childish complaints
vibrated once more with sad speech,
that the sky were sweet, that the lips were mother's,
and that the world cooled into happiness under the gas lamp.

(R. Brandstaetter, "Wspominanie Cezara nad Rodanem" [Remembering Caesar at the Rhone])[7]

The world of childhood is a world of warmth, happiness, and trust. Its climate supports existence.

The idealization of childhood occurs with particular frequency in the work of Anda Eker:

> It would be nice to be a child again
> and live in an old-fashioned house,
> in a tiny house with a motley garden
> and take leave of my old sadness.
> In a tiny house with a gate and fence,
> without worries and yearning
> It would be nice to be little again,
> as if nothing had yet happened,
> as if life held
> no sorrows, loneliness, or grief
> as if what had happened
> had been just a bitter dream,
> as if what had happened
> had been a scary fairy tale.
>
> (A. Eker, "O pewnym domku"
> [About a certain little house], *Mch,* p. 46)

Eker's lyrical poems show clearly the motifs of the mythicization of childhood. The almost frenzied attempts to create a bright and simple world are interspersed with complaints about being lonely and lost.

Adulthood is a "scary fairy tale." Childhood, its opposite, is seen by the worn out hero as a refuge, a period of order, peace, and happiness:

> Look how sad it is outside the window, look how white
> So little joy is left for us,
> . . . .
> Maybe my eyes will again dream of my warm home
>
> (M. Szymel, "Zapal świeczkę chanukową"
> [Light a Hanukkah candle], *Wl,* p. 69)

The return to this era is an expression of evasive tendencies: "childhood returns to the eyes of a simple, sad man" (M. Szymel, "Przyjdzie Eljasz prorok" [The Prophet Elijah will come], *Pdd,* p. 16).

For the "I" subject to such tendencies, the "I" facing the past and recollecting, the image of home is the center of the described world. Stories about the family collectivity and the home space are the most frequent motifs in the poetry of Szymel, Eker, Dresdner, Ihr, Silberman, Pomer, and Fenster. In these stories,

Anda Eker. *Wiadomości Literackie* 1938, no. 29, p. 5. Reproduced by A. Musielak

the physical space of the "beautifully white house" becomes the symbol of the motherly milieu in which the "I" was immersed in childhood. And this milieu was motherly in the fullest sense of the word. The home collectivity centered around the mother, the Jewish mother, the poor, Yiddish-speaking Jewess with whom the poet-son conducted awkward conversations—in Polish: "I set down in this poem the simplest words / so as to be able to talk with you—" (M. Szymel, "Połóż mi dobre swe ręce na włosach" (Put your good hands on my hair), *Pdd,* p. 12).

There is mother singing the old Jewish lullaby about raisins and almonds (M. Szymel, "Kołysanka mojej matki" [My mother's lullaby]). There is mother making a fire, peeling potatoes, buying on credit in the little store, grumbling (a cycle of poems in Szymel's *Skrzypce przedmieścia* [Violin of the suburbs]: "Moja matka" [My mother], "Matka w sklepiku" [Mother in the little store], "Matka rozpala ogień" [Mother is making a fire], "Matka obiera kartofle" [Mother is peeling potatoes], "Matka w kinie" [Mother at the cinema]). Fenster's collection of "farewells"—*O tym, co opuszczam* (About the things I abandon)—is an individual record of conversations with mother ("Słowo o dorosłych synach wiecznie młodych matek," "O tym, co opuszczam," "Elegia o sobotnim wieczorze" [Elegy on a Sabbath evening]).

It is surprising how infrequently fathers turn up in the childhood world of Polish-Jewish poets. In his "Genealogia" (Genealogy), Szymel mentions his mother Chana [Hanah], his grandfather Zev, his brothers Abraham, Dan, and Efraim, and his sister Ruth. But his father's place is empty. In "Moja siostra" (My sister), first the brothers and then the mother mourn the sister who died in Eretz. In his "Notatki autobiograficzne" (Autobiographical notes), mother, brother, sisters, and grandmother form a solidary family ring. The father is outside it. The chain of Jewishness, traditionally formed by fathers and sons, is formed by grandfathers, mothers, and children in Polish-Jewish literature. It is very unusual for fathers to play a leading part (as, for example, in the poetry of Bertisch).

The Jewish home is remembered as an idyll of children, women, and old people. Thus the introduction into the space of Jewishness is a function of mothers rather than of fathers. It is striking that, in all of Polish-Jewish poetry, there is not a single image of a father guiding his son's hand over the letters of The Book. The Jewish God emerges from the tales and prayers of the mother:

When my mother put me to sleep
And led my soul into the night's darkness,
She chased away evil phantoms
And nightmares and spells.

She charmed with ancient words,
She bewitched with a magic whisper,
And I repeated her incantations
With a child's fervor.

Already then I believed
Not in little angels that protect us,
Not in the good "Lord God"—
But in him, in all his glory and terror . . .

For the quiet wings of
Michael, Raphael,
Uriel, and Gabriel
Brush away phantoms from before my eyes.

And when my head
Sinks with the weight of lead,

The immortal glow of the Shechinah
Blossoms on my pillow.
(K. Dresdner, "Szechina" [Shechinah])[8]

It is impossible to return to the past, impossible to return to the childhood home. And so the "I" describes its ruins and recollects the former idyll. The image of home that is either destroyed or being destroyed is one of the topics of Polish-Jewish poetry:

The walls of the house scattered
(R. Friedmann, "Matka" [Mother])[9]

And I waited and waited,
Until the walls of my home scattered,
And the fall winds carried off the roof—
(M. Szymel, "Powrót do domu"
[The return home], *Pdd,* p. 5)

Sometimes the home is still standing but it is empty and forsaken:

I return to an empty house
(M. Szymel, "Powrót do domu"
[The return home], *Pdd,* p. 5)

an abandoned house stands under the lonely moon
and the rooms of the house are empty
(A. Eker, "Moje dzieciństwo" [My childhood], *Ncs,* p. 79)

The ruin of the physical space symbolizes the dissolution of the human collectivity. In Szymel's "Genealogia" (Genealogy), mother and grandfather rest in the cemetery and brothers and sisters are scattered around the globe. One of the main themes of his small first volume of poetry is mourning for his mother. The poems, "Notatki autobiograficzne" (Autobiographical notes), "Matka w mroku" (Mother in the dusk), "Obudź mnie rano" (Wake me in the morning), "Śmierć mojej matki" (My mother's death), and "Przyjdzie prorok Eljasz" (The prophet Elijah will come), are a threnody of a Jewish son, a poetic kaddish. "Powrót do domu" (The return home), the opening poem of the threnody, is a pilgrimage of the memory in which images of the former intimate collectivity mix with images of the present poignant lonesomeness:

I return home—
nobody's hand will shake mine
and no one will come and meet my heart—
(M. Szymel, "Powrót do domu" [The return home])

The return is a return to a void. The uninhabited physical space does not soothe the sense of homelessness.

The Small Town

The home space described in Polish-Jewish literature has real dimensions. The childhood homes are located in market squares and in narrow streets of small, provincial towns, and in the suburbs and alleys of towns. For example, such scenery is dominant in the early poetry of Juliusz Wit:

I am a little boy and I live at the market square
("Syn handlarza winem" [Son of a wine seller])[10]

Lunatics, small-town madmen
Roaming the narrow streets of spring and winter,
I remember you from the time I was a child
("Wariaci" [Lunatics])[11]

For Szymel's lyrical heroes, the familiar, homey landscape is the landscape of a poor suburb with narrow alleys and old, little houses. The picture that emerges from his "Notatki autobiograficzne" is that of a one-story brick house in a crooked alley with a little grocery. The family described in the "Genealogia" (Genealogy) stems from "dark houses" somewhere on the periphery of the town. The childhood scenery of the "I" of "Skrzypce przedmieścia" (Violin of the suburbs) includes a low, blackened ceiling, wet and peeling walls, an oil lamp, and a water bucket.

The childhood locale[12] described in Polish-Jewish poetry is frequently the shtetl, the small Jewish provincial town. The "I" of the lyrical poetry of Szymel, Pomer, Fenster, and Wit is often a man of the people, a "simple, believing Jew" living in a small town. Hence the "I" 's return home is a return to a shtetl:

I return to you, small town
Whose unchanged visage includes the memory of things past;
. . . .
For at close quarters you are an ugly Jewish hamlet,
Reeking of gray, dirty, evil poverty by day;
Glistening at night with stars,
Whose yellow glimmer glows on your pointed roofs like sabbath candles.
(S. Pomer, "Powrót" [Return], *Ep,* p. 7)

I returned to the town,
the town of colorful childhood
the town I am no longer in
the town I am always in.
(J. Wit, "Zwycięstwo" [Victory])[13]

It is easy to see that the shtetl occupies an affectionate and tender place in the memory of this "I," that it is a place filled with personal experiences and memories. The shtetl is a homely, private area, mine or our small town. (The title of one of Fenster's poems is actually "Nasze miasteczko" [Our little town].) The phrases "our little town" and "in our little town" recur like a refrain in Cz[esława] Endelmanowa-Rosenblattowa's "Ludzie którzy jeszcze żyją" (People who are still living).

Pomer's poem quoted above is a kind of introduction to his *Elegje podolskie* (Podolian elegies), in which the shtetl provides the scenery for lyrical events. Its role is ambivalent, for it is a place at once pleasant and obscure [*locus amoenus* and *locus obscurus*], both paradise and jail:

Again, when sleepy sameness pours like gray powder,
To see you in the noontime heat, to hate you, to curse you—
You—Podolian hamlet—for being reality and illusion,
A godforsaken prison and a magical cradle.

. . . .

O ugly, evil, sad nest of my youth,
The only lost, Galician paradise!
The power of recurrent longing, the ripe power of love
Joins your destitution and beauty into a rainbow of charms.
(S. Pomer, "Powrót" [Return], *Ep,* p. 8)

Pomer's small volume, referred to during the interwar period as a "lyrical geography of a small Jewish town," is a very carefully constructed story of a return to such a town. The introduction (quoted earlier) is followed by two groups of poems. One describes the scenery of the shtetl (the cycle "Miasteczko" [The little town]: "Zaułek" [An alley], "Studnia" [The well], "Bożniczka" [The little house of prayer], "Szynk" [The saloon], "Rozstaje" [The crossroads], "Wólka"). The other describes a number of shtetl characters ("Ostatnie życzenie" [The last wish], "Stara panna" [The old maid], "Życie i śmierć Jonatana grajka" [The life and death of Jonathan the klezmer], "Miłość wieczna" [Eternal love], "Moja matka" [My mother]). The scenery and people provide the setting for a particular lyrical activity of actual or recalled emotional adventures of the "I" that wanders all over the little town by day, dusk, and night; in sunshine, rain, and snow; in summer, fall, winter, and spring:

> The cloudy sky hangs over the small town,
> Like a leaden nightmare
>
> (S. Pomer, "Deszcz pada" [It is raining], *Ep,* p. 41)

> The little town is asleep under a quilt of snow
>
> (S. Pomer, "Naprzeciw" [Across the street], *Ep,* p. 45)

> . . . the sun luminously suspended over the small town
> The bright joy of life, hope and love
>
> (S. Pomer, "Inaczej" [Otherwise], *Ep,* p. 58)

From these wanderings emerges an image of the space which is a palimpsest whose two layers have contrasting aesthetic and emotional values. The first layer is scenery subject to the aesthetics of charm: the little Jewish houses of prayer, the little Orthodox churches, the old little houses, the little streets, the little market stalls against the background of the little hills and the little river—the bucolic shtetl:

> I can see you again from afar on a flat hill, next to the white tape of road
> Enclosed by the green band of trees—
> Like a color illustration of a classical eclogue . . .
>
> (S. Pomer, "Powrót" [Return], *Ep,* p. 7)

Perceived in this way, the shtetl can be the hero of a love scene in a shepherd idyll:

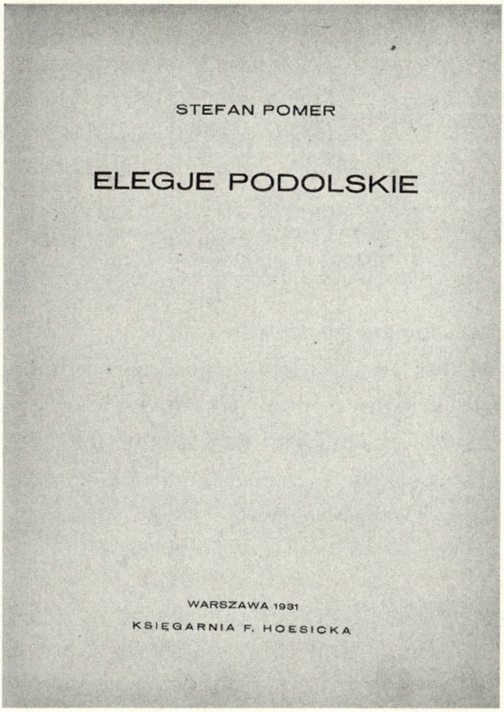

Title page of Stefan Pomer's *Elegje podolskie* (Podolian elegies). Photo by A. Musielak

The moon has knelt on a bent ray like a shepherd in an idyll
And luminously sings a starry serenade
On the huge stage of the sky, above the proscenium of clouds

And the moon's mistress is the quiet street in the small town,
In bed in the white and pink shirt of cherry orchards:
She plaits the flowery hair of trees and passionately presses and nestles
A love picture of the moon close to her fragrant cheek.

(S. Pomer, "Teatrum księżycowe" [Moon theater], *Ep,* p. 56)

But it can also undergo a Chagall-like metamorphosis:

The colored wings of the window shades
Hang above the show windows like butterflies above a pond:
The shingled roof of the town hall is a blooming field,
And the digits on the clock crawl like beetles in the grass.

The green dome of the little church floats down like a ship from space
On the hill bathed by the golden sea of nasturtium

And beyond it the roofs of the town, and above it
The streaming flag of slender birch twigs flutters in the green wind.

And the town hall—the well—the narrow streets—and the red houses amid the orchards
And one's own lifeless heart, float in the air
Like silhouettes cut out of paper.
(S. Pomer, "O piątej po południu" [At five in the afternoon], *Ep,* p. 27)

All the elements of the town landscape are perceived as rustic props. The whole space is caught in a moment of motion and flight that changes its initial layout into a fantastic, surreal, Chagall-like composition. "Charming," "sweet," "tender" are the epithets the "I" bestows on the bucolic image of the shtetl.

The second layer of the palimpsest is subject to the aesthetics of ugliness: mud, dust, puddles, a rotten railing, a freakish synagogue, wretched trees, crooked lampposts, rusty signs:

The stench of sauerkraut escapes from the uncorked little basement windows,
. . . .
Mud in the street lies like a drowned body with swollen and glutinous lips
(S. Pomer, "Ślady" [Traces], *Ep,* p. 48)

Outside the window, naked trees like black teeth in a mouth
Protrude at the road turned into slush by the foul March weather
(S. Pomer, "Nocturn" [Nocturne], *Ep,* p. 47)

Sometimes, in images of the daily existence of the common people, the ugliness of the Jewish milieu is depicted by Pomer with a kind of naturalistic frenzy. These images are constructed (and evaluated) in a uniform tone of defeat by the hopelessness of extreme poverty. For example, in the poem "Rachela i katarynka" (Rachel and the barrel organ)[14] the little street and the alley are "blind," the little houses are "gray and crooked," the thresholds are "worn and dirty," the girl is "thin and pale," the organ grinder is crippled, and

The rotten odors of the gutter, the musty smell of dishwater
Envelop the world in a cloud of ugliness and poverty.
(S. Pomer, "Rachela I katarynka" [Rachel and the barrel organ])

The contrasting images, now mild and bright now sharp and dark, are sometimes brought together in a single text. The resulting effect is one of representational and emotional ambivalence, of undulation of the mood emanating from the landscape and experienced by the "I":

Warmed by the sun, the narrow streets smell lazily of violets,
Like the nude body of a woman dewed with the sweat of pleasure;
Sad old people look out of open windows as from a painting in a wide frame,
Old maids comb thin hair.

In the marketplace, round the well with a shrine and a consumptive square
Run breathless brats, barefoot, in scanty pants.
Trees blossom. The wind sucks the mud like a lollipop
(S. Pomer, "Cień sztachet" [Shadow of railing], *Ep,* p. 49)

Sometimes this ambivalence of delight and dislike, of love and hatred, is the theme of a poem:

Small town of my boyhood years, paradise lost,
Why can't one now wade in your mud!
. . . .
Feel your charming ugliness in one's heart, like a sharp spit,
The former loathing and the former fervor.
(S. Pomer, "Powrót" [Return], *Ep,* p. 8)

The ugly landscape is also near and precious. The aesthetic evaluation is at odds with the emotional evaluation.

The tone of the presentation in Pomer's volume changes also with the time of the year. The sad fall images get brighter in the winter and sunny in the spring. But the small town of memory, the shtetl of mother and childhood, is always bright:

Good fairy, enveloped in the mist of children's folk tales,
in an enchanted small town, at a pond lulled to sleep.
The little town, the pond and the childhood form a bright background
Against which you'll always remain in my memory serene and bright.
(S. Pomer, "Moja matka" [My mother], *Ep,* p. 24)

The shtetl of the *Elegje podolskie* is stashed away somewhere in the hills of Podole, in a "backwater provincial area" ("List" [Letter]). It is actually a "half village" and is set in opposition to the large town ("Złota lipa" [The golden linden]).[15]

Similar accents in the image of a small town are found in Adam Madler's novel *Falista linia* (The wavy line), where the landscape, though barely sketched and echoing the protagonist's moods, is always quiet, mild, and pretty. There is the market square, the little main street, the little store; there is the "tiny light" at night, the "tiny school lantern." The sleepiness and virtual absence of people are contrasted by visitors from a large town with the animation and feverish activity of the industrial "city of chimneys."

Hersz Awrohem Fenster depicts the transformation of the provincial, half-village home landscape into the big city landscape:

my house was once
at the boundary of town and village,
now houses have surrounded it,
have stolen its sun, its flowers and its sky,
and have transferred it
to the middle of a street in a big town.
("Mój dom" [My house], *Otco,* p. 7)

When it loses its provincial, rustic character, the childhood space becomes an unfriendly, strange landscape. Our little town becomes a strange city. The city scenery strikes the shtetl outcasts as always strange, and the provincial scenery as always cozy:

it knocked down our old small houses but built nothing for us on the ruins
. . . .
and many a time one is tempted to run from the cylinders of reinforced concrete to these houses, out of the way but familiar and small.
(H. A. Fenster, "Elegia o sobotnim wieczorze"
[Elegy on a Sabbath evening], *Otco,* p. 18)

This mood is only a step away from the hope of regeneration of the little town, the second blooming of the Jewish provincial town:

Children will grow into boys and sprightly girls—
Will fill with noise the narrow streets, the prayer houses and market square
With noise and life, toil and hope—
So the grandfathers laugh and the fathers laugh,

When life is done—substantial gains—
The children will fix the roofs and renew the houses

And just like snow in the spring,
sadness and fear will vanish.
A beautiful brand-new roof will sparkle in the moonlight
(M. Szymel, "Na prowincji żydowskiej" [In the Jewish provinces])[16]

Provincial characteristics and homely rusticity are not always dominant in depictions of the little town. They are not present in the poetry of Ihr, who contrasts the "resounding thunder of the town," its "globe lamps" and "noise of sin," with the white childhood house in an alley ("Ballada o zaułku" [Ballad about an alley].[17] Nor are they found in the poetry of Szymel, who is quite willing to depict the wretched side of the milieu of the shtetl. Like Pomer's *Elegje podolskie,* Szymel's *Skrzypce przedmieścia* is a "lyrical geography"; in this case, of Jewish suburbs. Here the mother wanders on a "crooked street of one-storied houses" ("Matka w kinie"), on a "Crooked, bumpy little street full of bird noise" ("Moja matka"). In the evening, the Jews sit in front of their houses and await the Messiah ("Mesjasz"). The old people, sitting next to the house of prayer, yearn for Jerusalem ("O staruszku tęskniącym" [About a yearning old man]). The God of the suburbs is the God of poor people, the God of rubbish and ruins:

O God of crooked streets, abandoned carts,
Broken shafts, dung hills, and manure—
God of crumbling walls, wet with mildew
(M. Szymel, "Wieczór na mojej ulicy"
[Evening on my street], *Sp,* p. 15)

It is striking that the small towns of Polish-Jewish literature remain anonymous. The name of the space of childhood is of no significance. It is just a little town. "Łask, Gawrolin, Żgów, or Kałuszyn—what is the difference? They are all alike, like nameless anthills strewn in the woods" says Cz[esława] Endelmanowa-Rosenblattowa in the introduction to her volume of daguerreotypes from the life of the shtetl.[18] The small town emerges from recollections and accounts of return as a universal space of Jewish biography. Its topography is determined by the market square, the house of prayer, the saloon, the grocery, the crooked little street, the blind alley, and the cemetery. The most Jewish element of this space is the house of prayer. It is usually old and about to fall into ruin:

A sweet shudder shook the old house of prayer!
(M. Szymel, "Skrzypce przedmieścia"
[Violin of the suburbs], *Sp,* p. 26)

Grown into the ground up to the moldings of its dusty windowpanes,
Covered by a pointed roof of blackened sheet iron,
It sticks up in the narrow lane like a grotesque mushroom
In a dried-out yard, surrounded by a rotten railing.

One descends to its dark depths by two sunken steps,
One stops at the door. It is scorching hot outside.
It is cool and shady here. It smells of mold.
Children's thin voices reciting the Talmud resound melodiously.
(S. Pomer, "Bożniczka" [Little house of prayer], *Ep,* p. 13)

The whole landscape of the shtetl is usually the domain of old-age ruin. The little houses, the little house of prayer, and the stones in the cemetery are falling down. The moss-covered walls crumble. Polish-Jewish poetry is replete with variants of such images:

The old man is walking, the house is caving in
(A. H. Fenster, "Nasze miasteczko" [Our small town])[19]

In a large quadrangle of little old houses,
Bent, with peeled-off plaster, overgrown with moss and horsetail,
Babbles a transparent spring, its casing crumbled
(S. Pomer, "Studnia" [The well], *Ep,* p. 12)

The huts shake like lunatics,
Panic-stricken lanes stampede down the market square
In clouds of dust—
Fathers and grandfathers are asleep in alcoves.

The plaster is peeling off the walls.
The hut feels insecure under its roof—
At night, grandparents think:
"One should patch the roof."

They think . . . meditate . . . fall asleep . . .
Stars fall down on the crooked roof like hot tears.
(M. Szymel, "Na prowincji żydowskiej" [In the Jewish provinces])[20]

Night hides this scenery of ruins and favors its metamorphism into fairy tale or phantom.

The note of wretchedness, present in the image of the landscape of the shtetl, also dominates the representation of shtetl characters. Polish-Jewish poetry abounds in literary forms of image or ballad that use small-town folklore motifs, introduce common people as protagonists, and record generic scenes of shtetl life. Their topic is the life of "brothers—simple, believing Jews"; birth, love, work, the death of porters, tailors, shoemakers, tinsmiths, beggars, merchants, secondhand clothes peddlers, salesmen, tenants . . . ; less frequently of cabbalists, Talmudists, rabbis. To this milieu belong most frequently the heroes of Szymel, who tells of the death of a beggar's son ("Śmierć Arona" [Aaron's death]), the birth of a child in a porter's family ("Miriam rodzi" [Miriam gives birth]), an anti-Semitic brawl in a Jewish alley ("Antysemici" [Anti-Semites]), dusk on a "crooked" little street ("Wieczór na mojej ulicy" [Evening on my street]), and Friday evening in the provinces ("Gdy w małym miasteczku zapada sobota" [Sabbath eve in a small town]). Pomer also likes to depict this milieu: the crippled organ grinder in a Jewish alley ("Rachela i katarynka" [Rachel and the barrel organ]), a tubercular Jewish woman ("Ostatnie życzenie" [The last wish]), an old klezmer ("Życie i śmierć Jonatana grajka" [The life and death of Jonathan the klezmer]), the unhappy engaged couple ("Miłość wieczna" [Eternal love]), and Passover in the basement apartment of paupers ("Pesach nędzarzy" [Passover of paupers]).

These images of life in a small town are sometimes close to a type of poetic report (for example, Szymel's "Miriam rodzi" or Pomer's "Ostatnie życzenie"). Sometimes they are recollections from childhood:

He died. In a moonlit summer evening.
The son of a beggar. The thirteen-year-old Aaron.
Fumbler. Drudge. Stutterer.
Not even his mother mourned him.

But in the yard his *payess*-framed face rose
Livid and swollen like the moon,
Its black eyes raised to the stars,
It shone in the rough recesses of the walls.

Fear cobwebbed the hallway and yard.
A big boy, I was afraid to leave the room
Because the evil, smelly corpse, swathed in white,
Grabbed by the throat with cold, bony fingers.

While he, like all sons of Israel,
Listening intently to each melodious "Amen" and sobbing "Selah,"
Lay on the ground, smiling amid the light of the candles,
In the cramped and airless room, hot with featherbeds.

Also, his father's hump grew, its shadow trembling on the wall
When he praised death and God with devout chanting.
(M. Szymel, "Śmierć Arona" [Aaron's death], *Sp,* p. 22)

The horror of death is intensified by the fears of a child's imagination: the deceased seems to fill all of space, to lie in wait in the dark, to listen to the mourning prayers.

Unlike their predecessors from the turn of the century, Polish-Jewish writers do not try to capture the phenomenon of Jewish small-town life in terms of a society with a particular set of customs. It is striking that the principal genre used in writing about the shtetl is poetry. If and when it appears in prose works (such as Adam Madler's *Falista linia* or Emil Tenenbaum's *Tła* [Backgrounds]), the shtetl is not the protagonist; it merely provides the setting for events. Thus when Czesława Endelmanowa-Rosenblattowa, a contemporary of Feldman, well regarded by Polish-Jewish circles (but not connected with them), published in 1934 a cycle of images from the life of the shtetl, it was composed as a "photographic album" of small-town characters. This record of the milieu of the small town was not meant to lead to social diagnoses. Rather, its aim was to register the distinctness of customs and to preserve folkloristic variety and colorfulness. Despite the author's assurances that the portraits presented were those of people still firmly rooted in the life of the small Jewish town, the depicted characters undoubtedly belonged to the past. The action of the stories was taking place before World War I, in the region under Russian occupation. In the foreground are characters connected with traditional life: the matchmaker [*shadchan*], the Jewish schoolmaster [*melamed*]; folk heroes: the fishmonger, the featherwife, the tailor, the cook. Next to them, the assimilated: the actor, the medical attendant, the boarding-school girl. As indicated by the book's title, the daguerreotypes gave permanence to people who were still living. The pre-World War I shtetl continued to exist as a cultural and social form, but was definitely receding into the past. The world of the small town was composed as a kind of mosaic of characters and scenes of daily life. These daguerreotypes and images were held together solely by the narrator.

The landscape and people of the shtetl are enveloped in a particular emotional aura. Polish-Jewish lyrical poetry relies on artless emotionalism: the "I" names feelings and attaches value judgments to the depicted world; it is saturated with the tenderness of the small town:

> I stand in a dream within your crooked lanes
> And an unbidden melancholy grabs me by the throat with tearful affection.
> (S. Pomer, "Powrót" [Return], *Ep.,* 7)

The characteristic mood of melancholy, sadness, and tearful emotion is often evoked by music: tangos and waltzes of the record player, the maudlin tones of the street organ, and the sounds of klezmer orchestras. In Szymel's "Skrzypce przedmieścia" the violin of the suburbs plays a "tender, tearful, Strauss waltz." Its sad melody flows through the small town in Wit's "Na skrzypcach grać" (To play the violin).[21] Brandstaetter regarded melancholy as the main characteristic of the shtetl, and made his stylized Kasrylówka (a locality created by the Yiddish prose writer Shołem Alejchem) dissolve in laughter through tears and in flute and piano music ("Kasrylówka" [Kasryluvka], *Kts,* pp. 21–22).

Sabbaths and Holidays

The home and the small town lived a traditional life. The "I" recalls holidays and rituals that mark the rhythm of the Jewish world: Hanukkah, Purim, Pesach, Lag B'omer, Simchat Torah . . . [22] It sees tradition as a refuge from a threatening reality:

> On my table lies a Bible,
> In the Bible cedar forests murmur—
> I immerse my tired head
> In the warm fragrance of its lights.
> (M. Szymel, "Biblia na stole"
> [The Bible on the table], *Pdd,* p. 59)

The attributes ascribed to the Book—warmth, fragrance, brightness—are characteristics of a safe and beautiful space. Especially in Szymel's poetry, immersion in tradition is a soothing procedure. The Jewish heritage is a source of hope, joy, light, and life:

> O my ancestors!
> You have left in your words
> So much silence, so many lights, so many trees for my eyes,
> For my thoughts
>
> (M. Szymel, "Dziadowie Biblii" [Biblical ancestors], *Pdd,* p. 46)

The "I" of Szymel's poetry frequently allays unease, sadness, and weariness by recalling rituals remembered from childhood, such as lighting Hanukkah candles in memory of the cleansing of the Temple at the time of the Maccabean revolt. Their light has a therapeutic, existential value. It evokes memories of a happy childhood:

> Look how sad it is outside the window, how white . . .
> So little joy is left us
> You have good, womanly hands,
> Light, light the Hanukkah candle!
>
> You see, formerly my grandfather, a tailor from Toporów,
> Used to lead me on this evening to the window and kiss me—
> And used to light with his yellowed hand, one by one,
> Eight lights of sadness and hope.
>
> At night, when the house was fast asleep,
> The Maccabee would appear before my astonished eyes
> And the priests looking for oil,
> How happy was I then, how very happy.
>
> Now it is sad outside the window, it is white now . . .
> Nothing is left of the yellowed hand . . .
> You have good, womanly hands,
> Light, light the Hanukkah candle!
>
> Maybe my warm home will come in a dream before my eyes,
> Maybe dreams will come, distant and huge,

Maybe my grandfather from Toporów will rejoice
When a Hanukkah candle shines in our window

(M. Szymel, "Zapal świeczkę chanukową" [Light a Hanukkah candle])

A characteristic feature of Polish-Jewish poetry is the association of childhood with tradition. This is achieved in a number of ways. A frequent device is to look at the holiday through the eyes of a child (S. Pomer, "Przyśpiew purymowy" [Purim intonation]). Another is to present scenes of rituals in which child participants are given special prominence (M. Szymel, "Purymowy wieczór" [Purim evening], "Simchat Tora" [Simchat Torah]). Yet another is recalling childhood memories.

The last device has a splitting effect: the temporal distance emphasizes the contrast between the idealized scene from the past and the present. Sometimes this contrast is the main theme of a poem, as in Szymel's cycle of Pesach poems: "Przyjdzie Eliasz prorok" (The Prophet Elijah will come), "O Proroku, który nie przyszedł" (About the Prophet who failed to come), "Pascha samotnego" (Passover of a lonely man). The poet invariably associates Pesach with the mother as protector and priest of Jewishness. The holiday brings "joy to the eyes of children and to mother's hands" ("O Proroku, który nie przyzedł"). The mother is the central figure of the Seder feast:

On this night, when the unleavened bread and bitters lie on the table,
I hand myself over to you, Mother; I believe in everything.
Place the piety of your wrinkled hand on my eyes—
through you and for your sake miracles are wrought on this night.
. . . .
How sweetly you pronounce the yellowed words of the Haggadah, Mother

(M. Szymel, "Przyjdzie Eliasz prorok" [The Prophet Elijah will come])

Jewishness and motherhood are virtually synonymous: "I will eternally believe in your eyes, in our prayers" ("Przyjdzie Eliasz prorok"). But the image of the Seder celebrated by the mother turns out to be just a memory, and her invitation to wait together for the prophet's arrival—a conversation with the departed. The story "O Proroku, który nie przyszedł" (About the Prophet who failed to come), which begins with the joyous mood of preparations for the holiday, ends with an admission of loneliness after the death of the mother.

The Jewish holidays presented from a child's perspective have no clear historical or national content. They are rituals performed by a small collectivity. Transmitting an historical injunction, this collectivity transforms the ritual into a legend, a fairy tale told in the family circle. In such a fairy tale, angels and Judas Maccabee belong to the same legendary reality of Israel's history:

Grandma tells the children curious fairy tales
And praises the deeds of the fathers of Israel
With eyes of the soul immersed in the past.

Before the eyes of the children looking at the candlelights
Marvellous angels line up
And the Maccabee's armed ranks
On this wonderful night of Hanukkah whiteness
(J. Werfel, "Chanukowa biel" [Hanukkah whiteness])

The story of Esther, told at Purim time and celebrated in memory of the deliverance of the Jews from their enemy Haman, is not a national legend. Rather, it is a fantastic tale of "ancient miracles" (M. Szymel, "Purymowy wieczór"). In accounts of many holidays, there recur scenes reminiscent of the one in Werfel's quoted poem, where grandmothers, grandfathers, and mothers bring one into the space of Jewishness and tell Jewish fairy tales and legends (images of Purim, Pesach, and Hanukkah are found, for example, in A. Eker's "Elijahu" [Elijah]). The obvious objective of interspersing the private with the national and the mythical with the historical is the creation of a private myth. National history becomes a family legend, and Jewishness the most intimate heritage.

Beneath the layer of realistic descriptions of traditions in scenes of Jewish rituals lies a representation of a universal festive state. This state is associated with childhood and has a clearly existential dimension. The Jewish holidays bring a sense of safety, quiet, peace, and happiness, a profound sense of being at home in the world, of belonging to an intimate collectivity. That is why this state is often invoked by the sad and solitary "I":

On this melodious spring evening
It is hard for the lonely and I am sick at heart—
The stars shine ominously
Above the dark domes.

It is Passover. The pots and wine
Ring and smell in the dusk.
Why has Elijah passed by
My sad, solitary room.

I open the window and call:
Mother, come! Light candles here—
The dense silence all around
Sighs with lights on the river.

But my mother hesitates to come,
And the silence denies the voice—
Whom should I ask the questions
And who will answer me?

There is only the dark noise of the river
And the crooked branches of trees
And your eyes are far away,
And your eyes will not be here.

And there is the moist windowpane
And the sky heavy with gilt—
How is this solitary night different
From so many of my other nights?

(M. Szymel, "Pascha samotnego"
[Passover of a lonely man])

Here the youngest child's ritual question, "How is this night different from all other nights," which is answered with the story of the Exodus from Egypt, the story of national liberation, is travestied in a characteristic way. Here the holiday—a kind of monument in time—refers not to the history of the nation but to the biography of the "I." It is a memorial to the state of happiness and safety at home, under Mother's protection. The darkness and enmity of the world, the sadness and loneliness, give rise to the wish to be soothed by the light of the candles lit by her.

The happy holiday state is associated with the motif of light. There are lights at home and lights at the house of prayer. All holiday lights are friendly: "On the white table the Seder bloomed with lights" (M. Szymel, "O Proroku, który nie przyszedł"). The light motif is expansive. It transforms the holiday night into a night of brightness and radiance:

And the little town lies under the twinkling stars
Like a huge Purim cake strewn with raisins.
Grotesque little houses glow rosy and golden
With candles burning in all the Sabbath candlesticks.

(S. Pomer, "Przyśpiew purymowy" [A Purim intonation])

The burning candles transform and make familiar the ugly and wretched milieu:

In swept corners, in the dark basement,
In little rooms, in outbuildings, in holes and dens,
The glimmer of slender candles in brass candlesticks
Will make warm, happy brightness and a pious glow.

(S. Pomer, "Pesach nędzarzy" [Passover of paupers])

Among the descriptions of Jewish holidays in Polish-Jewish literature, descriptions of the Sabbath, the fundamental Jewish ritual prescribed by the Torah, occupy a very special position. Here too we can discern two layers of the image, the generic and the symbolic. The Sabbath image occurs frequently in the poetry of, say, Maurycy Szymel, who likes to describe Sabbath scenes in poor suburbs, in a small town, and in a village ("Notatki autobiograficzne," "O staruszku tęskniącym," "Świąteczny wieczór na wsi" [Holiday eve in the country]):

They'll sweep the room clean, set up the Torah scrolls in the inn,
Tables and stools in zigzag will pile up in chaotic lines—
Soon mystical white candles will blaze up in menorahs
For at night the dead ancestors will form a minyan here.

In the hut one can smell the holiday broth,
Boys hurriedly polish their fathers' Sabbath boots.
Mothers plait blue ribbons into the girls' hair.
It is late. The peasants return from their daily work at the manor.

. . . .

In a little while, the hammer will hit thrice the low door frame,
Time to hurry to prayers to Yankel's old inn,
And so a quick farewell. Supper is on the table:
Challah and wine blessed and holy.

("Świąteczny wieczór na wsi" [Holiday eve in the country])

Generic Sabbath scenes are also found in Polish-Jewish prose works such as Szymel's *Krawiec z Białegokamienia* (The tailor from Białykamień) and in Adam Madler's novel *Falista linia.* But the Sabbath theme occurs far more frequently in poetry than in prose.

The Sabbath period is sometimes used for compositional purposes. It often marks the beginning of sudden changes in the action, a turning point or a decisive break in the fate of the protagonists. The solemn mood is made to collide with events that destroy the prevailing order. In Emil Tenenbaum's novel *Tła* (Backgrounds), Sabbath is the time of a pogrom that destroys the hitherto peaceful existence of a small borderland town. Szymel's tailor from Białykamień is possessed, on the Sabbath, by the idea of making the Messiah come. He begins to make clothes for him and thereby desecrates the Sabbath.

The symbolic layer of the image of the Sabbath is extremely interesting. First, its most important sense: the Sabbath is a symbol of the Jewish tradition interpreted in a special way, a symbol of the heritage to which the "I" of Polish-Jewish literature wants to return. Such return was already depicted in European art at the beginning of the century: Wilhelm Wachtel's well-known painting "Friday evening," contains an anecdote many variants of which have been told by Polish-Jewish writers. In Wachtel's "Friday evening" a man dressed in European clothes is looking pensively through the window of a poor Jewish home lit by Sabbath candles. The Sabbath is synonymous with Jewishness: it is the symbolic sense of the Sabbath that Polish-Jewish authors point to. In Szymel's "Żydowscy trubadurzy" (Jewish troubadours), the leaving of the collectivity and the returning to it is synonymous with the receding and approaching of the Sabbath: "Sabbaths called us from bright windowpanes / with eyes of golden fluttering candles."

In the poem just quoted, Jewishness—identified with the Sabbath—is a kind of "archaic home." For it is significant that the "I," anxious to return to harmonious forms of existence associated with childhood, home, and tradition, makes a significant choice within the purview of tradition. In most cases, it associates the "archaic home," the idyll, with the Sabbath. Comparable associations with other holidays—Purim, Hanukkah, Pesach—are far rarer. The Sabbath is the most private and intimate heritage. It is often the only hallmark of Jewishness of key figures in Polish-Jewish literary works: "The flash of Sabbath lights is not all extinguished in me" (K. Dresdner, "Piątek" [Friday]).

The Sabbath—here I am anticipating subsequent reflections—is a very special component of tradition that has the power of creating harmony in the minds of men as well as in their midst. It signifies that there is a kernel of sense, order, and peace in the chaotic world and in the disharmonious individual. Permanently allied with home and mother, the Sabbath in Polish-Jewish literature is the archetypal idyllic state, the state of idyllic Jewishness. Tradition equips the "I" with principles that order and interpret the universe and assign a place to the individual. That is why it can form an idyllic center, a return to which has a peculiar therapeutic effect. Turning the Sabbath idyll into a synonym of Jewishness is a significant device: everything that its sphere encompasses—and thus everything Jewish—is harmonious and mild. Upon returning to the Jewish home, the "I" retreats into a primeval idyllic space.

In Jewish culture, the Sabbath is often associated with the figure of a young woman—a queen, a princess, a bride. Such metaphorical exemplifications[23] of the idea of the Sabbath are readily found in Polish-Jewish literature, for example, in Anda Eker's "Bajka o Sobocie" (Fairy tale about the Sabbath). Horacy Safrin paraphrases the ritual song "Lcha dodi" in accordance with the prototypical version and develops the chain of associations: the Sabbath—the bride—the queen. The emotional dimension of welcoming the Sabbath has the tension of a love encounter:

> Come, beloved, toward the princess
> Let us greet the Sabbath eve with song!
> . . . .
> Enter the room, husband's crown.
> A circle of friends is awaiting you.
> (H. Safrin, "Lcha dodi" [Come, beloved])

But the traditional metaphorical exemplification is displaced in Polish-Jewish poetry by a new personification: the Sabbath becomes the mother. As a bride, a queen, a princess, the Sabbath was a young woman. As a mother, she is an old woman. Szymel's poem "Sobota" (The Sabbath) is based on this chain of associations: the waiting old woman—the Sabbath ("the old woman the Sabbath is waiting in a glow of candles")—the waiting old woman—the mother, whose eyes reflect the flames of the Sabbath candles—mother-Sabbath. This personification makes the holiday blessing of the candles a melancholy gesture of an old person: "mother will cover her eyes with wrinkled hands / and cry bitterly over the trembling candles."

The figure of the old Sabbath-mother indicates that the home tradition is both near and ancient. The Sabbath is a part of the past; surrender to the present is synonymous with the destruction of the ritual.

Sometimes the figure of the Sabbath-mother is linked with other images. In Anda Eker's fairy tale "The Princess Motherland will stand on a mountaintop, will stretch out her hands like a mother blessing the Sabbath candles, and will utter just two words: God bless!" ("O Teodorze Herzlu, gdy był małym chłopczykiem" [About Theodore Herzl when he was a little boy], *Odz,* p. 87). This imagery blends the image of the Princess Sabbath with that of the motherland. The blessing of the lights is at once a pathetic and patriotic gesture.

The connection between the Sabbath and the mother figure goes beyond personification. It is the mother alone who re-creates the holiday idyll and is the sole priestess of the rite:

> The whisper of Your lips called her, Your whisper over the candles!
> Only You are able to call her, mother!
> (A. Eker, "Wiersz o sobocie" [Poem about the Sabbath])

At the center of the remembered Sabbath, the Sabbath seen through the eyes of a child, is the figure of the mother blessing the candles. Kiddush, the blessing of the wine, is pronounced by men. It is mentioned just twice in Polish-Jewish poetry: "The 'kiddush' has died away—father is dozing" (M. Szymel, "Sobota" [The Sabbath]).

Neither father nor grandfather enter the fully developed scene of the Sabbath motherland. The prayer is recited by the "I":

> In a trembling voice, deep as the sea,
> I repeated the words—sweet fruit, words that rustle and flow:
> Bless You, Lord God,
> Who has created wine—
>
> Bless you for drawing bread from the earth
> And for ordering us, among so many nations,
> To sanctify the Sabbath eve with your words,
> With words of the land full of milk and honey—
>
> and for giving the holiness of the Sabbath to enraptured eyes
> (M. Szymel, "Gdy w małym miasteczku zapada sobota"
> [Sabbath eve in a small town])

In Polish-Jewish poetry the Sabbath is a private and intimate holiday. It is never an expansive crowd scene. It is limited to the small mother-and-children circle. There is little doubt that the choice of the child perspective in the description of such scenes intensifies the idealization of the "archaic home."

The intimate image of the Sabbath ceremony, full of an aura of tenderness, turns up so frequently in Polish-Jewish literature that it can be considered one of its main themes [topoi]. The Sabbath is the kingdom of mothers and light:

> And I always see you bright and beautiful in the glory of candles,
> Blessing the Sabbath, your hands covering your face—
>
> (S. Pomer, "Moja matka" [My Mother])

> The fingers of my mother's hands flutter over the candles,
> A warm radiance shines through them. They become transparent.
> . . . .
>
> O fingers of my mother's hands! O you tears, jewels that lightly flow from under the hands down the face!
> O dusk that sings for us the Sabbath in the room!
> O star that shines brightly in the dark window.
>
> (A. Eker, "Wiersz o sobocie" [Poem about the Sabbath])

> And your figure, mother, enveloped in the gauze of memories,
> Approaches me slowly, an ethereal, tender image.
> You enclose the two lights with the thin muslin of your hands,
> And open the gates of heaven with the voiceless prayer of your lips,
> With the pair of white wings, like a bird in sky-high flight
> You bless the two of us: your son and the Sabbath.
>
> (K. Dresdner, "Piątek" [Friday])

> I would clasp your hand
> Rosy with the light of Sabbath candles
>
> (M. Szymel, "Matka w zmroku" [Mother in the dusk])

> On Fridays, when the little grocery stall was closed from the street,
> My mother prayed over small, crooked candles
>
> (M. Szymel, "Notatki autobiograficzne" [Autobiographical notes])

> Pining after Judean suns,
> My mother hid the charm of her eyes in her hands
> And dissolved in silver tears
>
> (K. Rosenfeld, "Sabbat" [The Sabbath])

The two prose quotations below confirm what I just said: the image of the mother, fixed in the gesture of blessing the Sabbath candles, is one of the main topoi of Jewish culture. Here is the recollection of the Sabbath by the eminent Yiddish poet Itzik Manger:

> The Sabbath nights, when our mothers uttered in an undertone, in the dusky rooms, "God of Abraham," will last in our memory unforgettable and charming. Nostalgia, nostalgia for the passing of the Sabbath, has left a profound mark on our characters and cannot be forgotten. All Jewish homes were then splendid Rembrandt paintings, compositions of light and shadow with our mothers at the center.[24]

Manger provides the image in question with a psychological motivation (present as well in Polish-Jewish literature): it is a picturesque and moving scene that no Jewish child would ever forget. And here is interesting confirmation of Manger's opinion in the response of J. A. (Appenszlak?), to Wachtel's painting:

> There is a lovely painting from that time . . . "Friday Evening." The young man seems to have come from far away, yearning brought him from far away. . . . He is standing quietly and modestly at the window of a small Jewish house as if recalling a distant childhood. . . . He is looking through the window at a tidy little Jewish room, there is the warm holiday glow of the Sabbath candles on the table, the mother of the house is offering ritual prayers over them while covering her face with her hands. . . . She is praying with devotion . . . the little Jewish mother. . . . All week long she is intimidated, overworked, always on the run, she is praying on Friday.[25]

Rather than describe the painting, the author presents his own associations and moods evoked by the painting. Concentrating on the figure of the returning person, Wachtel focuses on the scene in front of the house. But the core of the writer's impression is the story of what is going on inside the house. It is a story of childhood memories, with the mother playing the main role.

The motif of light, so essential in images of Jewish holidays, plays an important role in the image of the Sabbath as well. The representation of the Sabbath is usually composed of light and bright colors, and sometimes of light alone: "Sabbaths called us from bright windowpanes / with eyes of golden fluttering candles" (M. Szymel, "Żydowscy trubadurzy"). The Sabbath appearing in the form of a young woman is a shining, luminous figure (A. Eker, "Bajka o sobocie").

Associated with the mother figure, the Sabbath is a land of feminine mildness, warm and motherly: "in the little house of prayer heaven opened above me / The ancient Sabbath heaven of mother, warm and feminine—" (M. Szymel,

"Gdy w małym miasteczku zapada sobota"). The word "Sabbath" denotes the quality of friendliness as well as the holiday quality. Stanisław Vincenz, an expert on the home life of Polish Jews, claims that the Sabbath is one of the most significant spiritual experiences of the Jewish child, for the Sabbath ritual combines a sense of the sublime with a sense of coziness and shelter.[26] If we take Vincenz's idea a step further, then we can say that the adjective "Sabbath" is synonymous with "safe" and "home." Thus it is not surprising that the space of "at-home-ness" symbolized by the Sabbath is a space of homeliness reminiscent of Bachelard's space of happiness.

In Polish-Jewish literature the Sabbath is not only a symbol of idyllic Jewishness but also a symbol of a mythical time and of a mythical state of the harmony of existence. This traditional idea—which appears, besides others, in the description of the special Sabbath order of the universe in the Zohar—is also popular in twentieth-century Jewish thought represented by, say, Abraham Joshua Heschel or Erich Fromm.[27]

Many Polish-Jewish authors extol the Sabbath aura of quiet and peace. It brings with it a special state of mind experienced by the "I": "now the Sabbath strokes me and gently caresses my soul" (H. A. Fenster, "Elegia o sobotnim wieczorze"). It denotes consolation and peace:

Holy Sabbath of our hearts!
We are waiting . . . come on a winter night.
The room is quiet—bright—golden
The candles tremble and flutter on the table . . .
When I look at my mom's smile
I feel that there is peace on earth
(M. Szymel, "Sobota" [The Sabbath])

For Anda Eker the Sabbath world is clearly an idyllic world-home presented with tenderness and delight:

And I don't know why suddenly the world is as quiet
Bright and good as our home on the Sabbath.
. . . .
I don't know why during the evening Sabbath hour
The world is different: sincere, cheerful, and pure.
("Wiersz o sobocie" [Poem about the Sabbath])

In images of the Sabbath, the contrast between the holiday time and spirit and the everyday is one of great intensity. For example, in Szymel's case, this contrast is sometimes the compositional axis of a poem:

> The quiet time of Sabbath lights arrived
> But the noisy evening continued to rumble above our heads.
> ("Sobota" [The Sabbath])

Here the "peace of holiness" and the "quiet of Sabbaths" are contrasted with the "noise of breathless streets"—order—with chaos.

The sense of the harmony of the world mediated through the Sabbath can hardly stem from remembered childhood experiences. Indeed, the image of the Sabbath is, for the most part, a recollection of the ceremony, sometimes an imaginary ritual, and seldom the real rite. For the most part, the Sabbath theme takes on an elegiac shape and is developed as a form of melancholy reflection on the bright and mild image of the ritual, whose recollection is coupled with the realization that the former idyll cannot be regained. During the interwar period, "Elegies on the Sabbath evening" and "poems on the lost Sabbath" were written by Maurycy Szymel, Hersz Awrohem Fenster, Anda Eker, and Karol Dresdner. The return home, to the little town, to tradition, is in Polish-Jewish literature a return to ruins. All idyllic spaces in which the "I" would like to take root again are destroyed. The house has fallen apart. The little town has declined. The tradition can no longer create the cosmos. The harmony of the world can no longer be experienced through the Sabbath. The ritual's power was tied to the motherly milieu. The collapse of the house is the death of the mother, together with the loss of the sense of the orderliness of the universe experienced in childhood:

> Today one cannot, in this very simple poem,
> Return to the home which has distanced itself,
> One cannot sit down at a table, next to brothers and sisters,
> When there is no one here to light the Sabbath candles.
> (M. Szymel, "O sobocie utraconej" [About the lost Sabbath])

The Sabbath idyll is a precious but distant image:

> Years later, in other cities and among other people,
> Among foreign words and events, one often thinks of this:

Would that one could wake in one's heart a dear, distant image:
A table, a tablecloth, a menorah, hands, the whisper of your lips, the Sabbath dusk.
(A. Eker, "Wiersz o sobocie" [Poem about the Sabbath])

The Sabbath symbolism is invoked not just for the purpose of rendering the spiritual harmony of the "I," the state of love, happiness, delight in the world, and confidence in existence. Sometimes the motif of the Sambatyon, the legendary restless river that subsides only on the Sabbath, is used as a representation of the protagonist's inner chaos, or of the experience of the disorder of a threatening universe. In Daniel Ihr's poetry, the Sambatyon is the threatening world-river that defeats the individual, whose liberation and consolation can only come with death, death likened to the Sabbath:

In the river of days you roll God's heavy, boiling
Rocks of cares. The surf rumbles and flows and burns.
We stand at the shores blinded by the foam, rendered mute
By the noise. There is no peace in our Sambatyon.

But You, good God, also know the core of
Trembling hearts. You bring an end to thoughts, advice to yearnings.
There is a moment when the Sambatyon lies down
Quietly at one's feet: After life there is death, and after toil—the Sabbath.
("Sambation" [Sambatyon])

It is clear that the archetypal idyll cannot be realized in such a world. The building of a sentimental utopia of the "archaic home of Jewishness" betrays its own therapeutic and escapist character, shown most trenchantly in H. A. Fenster's "Elegia o sobotnim wieczorze." The poem is a request to the mother for soothing Sabbath stories. The quest for a comforting utopia is mixed with the impossibility of believing in it, and the desire to immerse oneself in a soothing tradition, with the realization that such therapy can no longer work. The Sambatyon symbol is clearly presented, and so, too, is the opposition between the past and the present. The "I" has experienced a painful expatriation from an idyllic world that is now collapsing:

I want to believe; today I will believe anything, so tell of miracles and unbelievable witchcraft,
about biblical fathers and forefathers; parables and legends heard seven times.
". . . that all week long it froths, doesn't rest, spews rocks, the old Sambatyon,

his deafening voice reaches heaven, he squirts snowy freezing foam to the stars."
(oh yes, Mother, now I believe, I saw the Sambatyon with my own eyes;
I know that he never knows peace, that he keeps on tossing and frothing),
". . . but on the Sabbath he rests, and throughout the holy Sabbath day
he is silent, does not squirt foam and does not spew rocks from his depths."

oh Mother, Mother, I believe you that it was so in former times,
but tell me why the old tired Sambatyon nowadays fails to rest even on the Sabbath?
I know that we are the Sambatyon, but why is our road now so slippery, so steep,
that our bones never experience rest

(H. A. Fenster, "Elegia o sobotnim wieczorze" [Elegy on a Sabbath evening])

In a chaotic world, the holiday is lightless, it turns into a Sabbath of darkness: in Fenster's "Elegia," the conversation between mother and son takes place in the dark . . .

Praise of tradition, the cult of the community of family and culture, the importance of remembrance, the turn toward childhood, all these combine in Polish-Jewish literature to form a very clear complex of motives. This complex encloses equal shares of biographical and symbolic experience: the return to the Jewish home is at once a return to the home of Jewishness. The reason for the return is a sense of crisis in relations with the world experienced by an "I" deprived of the support of the collectivity and of the guarantee of safety given by the tradition. In place of sacrally ordered time, there is chaos. In place of rootedness, there are splits and loneliness. In this perspective, the Jewish childhood appears as an ideal period of existence and the family as an intimate collectivity which is an oasis of Jewishness and an existential asylum. The world seems to be a palimpsest: under the layer of ruins and chaos there persists a model of sense and harmony. The "I" turned to the past remembers the experience of the order of the universe. Tradition, the key to the covenant with existence, was given to one in childhood; it was tradition as manifested in family rituals regulating East European daily life. The daily East European Jewishness had soothing power and existential value.[28] There is always an idyllic core hidden in the "elegies on a lost Sabbath" and the "elegies on a little town."

The complex of the discussed motives can be interpreted as an expression of evasive tendencies and was so interpreted in the interwar period. Chaim Löw wrote the following about Szymel's debut: "Each poem resounds with yearning after childhood; the poet wraps himself in it and in this way protects himself from the roughness of stormy life. Of course, this is a romantic stance; the poet escapes from the difficult, unsolvable present which is further complicated by the national-racist element."[29]

In the poem "Do przyjaciół poetów" (To poet friends),[30] Daniel Ihr did not hesitate to call the attachment to the past an attachment to cemeteries. He regarded it as a negative cult, as an exploration of dead regions with no living content that might be used by the present.

But one can look differently at the yearning after the idyll of Jewishness and its apotheosis, namely, as an attempt to find the necessary counterweight to the sense of crisis and disharmony, an attempt to sanctify order against chaos.[31]

6

A New Life

Zionist Education

The building of a sentimental utopia, of a world of harmony, and the idealization of traditional life were undoubtedly means of allaying the sense of the world's enmity and chaos. Much the same purpose was served by the building of a vision of a new life, a life of freedom and of rebirth in one's own land, in Eretz Israel, in a Palestine that was acquiring real shape, color, and smell.

This vision was shaped in Polish-Jewish literature under the influence of Zionist ideology. In previous chapters I stated critical observations that I considered to be indispensable for the understanding of interwar Zionism, of the reasons for its popularity, and of its significance for Polish-Jewish culture. My primary concern was to view Zionism as a cultural phenomenon of signal importance for twentieth-century Polish Jewry and as one of the approaches to the modernization of traditional Jewish life, and to overcome in this way the stereotypes of Polish thinking about Zionism.[1] Now I want to point to its social aspect, to Zionism as a movement for social change and an expression of the will to national rebirth, an aspect also stressed by recent Polish studies.[2]

Polish-Jewish literature, especially prose works from the period 1928–33, supplies important arguments for the social interpretation of Zionism. This literature also provides excellent proof that the supporters and followers of Zionism saw it as a kind of religion of a fatherland and of a new life. The wave of prose in question could be called Zionist and Palestinian, for its main topics were life in Zionist settlements and the rebuilding of Palestine. Its main themes were the maturing to Zionism and the search for true Zionism, thought of as a project for a new world order based on foundations other than the known, European ones, and different from all other movements aiming to build a new world. The first of these themes is reflected in what may be called "novels of Zionist education," such as—to name the best—Bernard Zimmermann's *Tirsa* (1930),

Adam Madler's *Falista linia* (Wavy Line; 1932), and Jakub Appenszlak's *Piętra* (Stories; 1933). The second theme is reflected in the frequent surfacing of the motif of confrontation with Communism, in novels such as Zimmermann's *Tirsa* and Feldszuh's *Czerwone dusze* (Red souls; 1932).

Thought of as a search for a new life, Zionism was nevertheless a product of the Diaspora, a project for a new life based on the experience of the old. This motif recurs in the fates of the protagonists of Polish-Jewish prose works, which are replete with characters who arrive at ideological Zionist conclusions after following a long and arduous road full of hesitations and disappointments—characters who mature to the acceptance of Zionism, who experience a spiritual transformation. This transformation turned Diaspora Jews into new Jews, the enslaved into the free, the disappointed into believers. It is striking that, through such spiritual rebirth, many Jews who had left Jewry and Jewishness in an attempt to blend into the non-Jewish world returned to their Jewish roots.

As early as the interwar period, this phenomenon of Zionist metamorphosis had acquired a rich tradition and even classical and hallowed models. The archetypal model was, of course, Teodor Herzl, frequently referred to by Polish Jews as the man whose "name was forty-four*." It is interesting that Herzl was not a popular figure in Polish-Jewish literature and that he appeared only in a few lyrical poems by [Karol] Rosenfeld and [Szymon] Wolf and in a story by Anda Eker. A biography of Herzl, titled *Mojżesz współczesny* (A modern Moses), was written by Leo Belmont. This was commented on unfavorably by Jews, who regarded Belmont's work as a desecration of Zionist sanctities by the "hands of a profane" and a "convert."[3]

But the Herzl model was nevertheless essential in Polish-Jewish prose. It was especially explicit in Appenszlak's *Piętra,* whose protagonist Henryk Sztrom describes himself as an imitator of Herzl and points to parallels between his biography and the biography of the leader. One such parallel is Herzl's historic encounter with Baron Hirsch and Sztrom's encounter with the rich Warsaw man Leiter. Sztrom hoped to persuade Leiter to give him funds for a Hebrew people's school. In *Piętra,* the famous Paris scene (described in detail in Herzl's diary) is woven into the contemporary Warsaw scene, with Sztrom loudly specifying to his interlocutor all points of convergence between the two situations (*P,* pp. 59–62).[4] Of course, it is a far cry from Appenszlak's hero to the author of *Alt-*

*Refers to the numerological interpretation of the name of the "governor of freedom" (*namiestnik wolności*) in visions of the future based on the Bible and the Apocalypse of Saint John in Part III of A. Mickiewicz's famous drama *Dziady.* (The word *dziady* [forebears] refers to an ancient fold ceremony of calling forth the ghosts of the dead.) [Trans.]

neuland and from the Warsaw financier to the famous philanthropist. The core of the novel is not just the contrast between the dreamy idealist and the cynical pragmatist. What was important and universal in the Herzl model was that it expressed the disappointment with assimilation, with life on the old continent, and with European culture. The sources of many Zionist conversions were the bankruptcy of the nineteenth-century faith in the harmonious brotherhood of peoples, the flourishing of nationalisms, and a sense of life's emptiness and lack of ideals. Such motifs recurred stubbornly in the fates of protagonists leaving Europe on boats bound for Jaffa or Haifa. Most of them were young members of the intelligentsia who left behind unfinished university studies, rich homes, and artistic careers. This is not to imply that Polish-Jewish writers did not portray emigration in a realistic manner, or that their undeniable tendentiousness ruled out a sober and critical evaluation of what was happening in Palestine. These writers also saw among the arrivals in Eretz Israel people interested in a better life, in a career, or just in daily bread. But for most of the protagonists the abandoning of Europe was a choice dictated by ideals. For them, Zionism was a worldview rather than an ideology, a spiritual rather than a political stance.

The Polish-Jewish didactic novels referred to earlier can be used to construct a kind of triptych depicting the maturing to Zionism as a worldview and stance. What I have in mind when constructing such a triptych is that [the narratives of] its component novels supplement each other in the building of a social panorama. The protagonists are young men and a young woman. The locale is Warsaw, a small Jewish town near Lodz, Vienna, Tel Aviv, Jerusalem, Palestinian kibbutzim. The main ideological themes are the overcoming of assimilationist attractions, the decision to emigrate, and the experience of Palestinian life that promotes rebirth. The typical common characteristic of the otherwise individualized and colorful heroes is the sense of emptiness and hopelessness in Europe and the search for recovery, rebirth, and spiritual salvation in Palestine.

Take, for instance, Henryk Sztrom, the hero of *Piętra.* He is "dejected, wretched, stern," "abandoned in the world, surrounded by a hostile, dull darkness" (*P,* p. 119), he "must contend with himself" (*P,* p. 150), must look "for a way out" (*P,* p. 189) of the hopeless situation, of the hopeless existence in the house on Bielańska Street. The house is on the boundary between the Polish and Jewish parts of the town and forms a kind of Jewish microcosm. The apartment house stories are like social strata. Sztrom's biography was meant to be typical. He represented a generation whose members were "straining to move ahead, stopped at the boundary of the ghetto, consumed by doubts, derided by cynics, overworked, exhausted, always pursued by thoughts, always in the thick of battle, chased out of workplaces, lecture rooms, libraries, and dissecting rooms" (*P,*

p. 150–151). A generation on the boundary of two eras—a name by which it referred to itself. Henryk comes from an assimilated family, from a milieu with ambitions for social advancement. He is "a cosmopolite and a citizen of the world." He graduates from a Polish gymnasium and from the humanities division of Warsaw University. He goes through the war of 1920. The result of the intensifying nationalistic atmosphere, combined with its associated anti-Semitism and the complex of rejection and humiliation, is a traumatic experience that makes him realize that his situation is one of "a man without a country." It is this situation that is discussed—in Polish—by the teacher of Polish in the Hebrew gymnasium during Zionist meetings, attended by young people from orthodox homes. An erotic intrigue, political disappointments, family complications—all these conspire to make Sztrom, a man who saw himself as lost and homeless, realize that Zionist education is relevant to his inability to find a place for himself in the world and to his disgust with his past life; that it is a worldview option rather than a political option; and that Zionism offers him the only chance of anchoring in life. It is significant that Sztrom, who is at best an observer and certainly not a political activist, is made to see the brutality and amorality of preelection political manipulations in the house on Bielańska street. The watchwords about the will to action and self-liberation conceal the vicious rules of the fight for power and influence. Rich cynics and ideologically neutral individuals alike are recruited to follow the Zionist banner. Party opposition is silenced and tamed. The ideologically pure are manipulated. The dreamers and idealists do not stand a chance when confronted by skillful pragmatists ready to strike a bargain. It is clear that Appenszlak wants to unmask the Zionist party elite. The young, captivated by the vision of the golden table from the Jerusalem Temple, pursuing the "luminous ideal of Palestine" and forming "a separate world unlike the world of the old" (*P,* p. 146), probably did not understand the hard realities of the political game. But it was precisely the dreamers who abandoned Europe for work in Palestine.

Sztrom's generation are contemporaries of the older Polish-Jewish writers (one of whom was Appenszlak). They experience the end of the war and the anti-Jewish incidents of the years 1918–1919 as young people; they understand very well that the "assimilationist illusions [are] being extinguished" and that the "annunciation of Palestine" is taking place (*P,* p. 21). This new generation draws the ideational consequences of the Great War, which put an end to the optimistic social utopias of the nineteenth century. It abandoned the "humanitarian Vulgate"[5] of enlightenment and positivism, and saw its only chance within the framework of a national collectivity. Appenszlak has no doubt about the sources of this ideational transformation: the lives—the former lives—of the protagonists are deeply involved with it. For them, Zionism is not a question of a mere political program but a personal issue, an issue of hope, of meaning, and of the purpose of existence. Sztrom exclaims: "Where can I find a place for myself in a Jewish world where people deafen themselves with noise and blind themselves with worthless gewgaws? . . . Restless, feverish, breathless, in constant pursuit of the means of a wretched, insecure existence! Zionism! True, profound Zionism is born out of disgust with such a life" (*P,* pp. 225–226). A student of his, the son of an engineer executed in Moscow during the revolutionary turmoil, will be writing compositions on the beauty of nature in *Pan Tadeusz* while thinking of emigration to Palestine . . .

Sztrom's generation includes the protagonists of Adam Madler's *Falista linia,* young people who, at the end of World War I, ended up in a shtetl near Lodz. One of them is Wiktor Merk, an arrival from the "city of chimneys" and an ideologically perplexed man from the borderland. Merk hesitates between the Polish and Jewish sides, between the ideals of equality and justice for all and the dream of a Jewish home. He tells a Zionist enthusiast who wishes to "convert" him:

> All I know is that when I approach the one side they surround me with invisible ties but don't gather me in. The others invite me, want to treat me with tender care, and rejoice in the return of the prodigal son. . . . When all is said and done, when I am to decide where I am—here or there—I can say: neither here nor there; but I can also say: both here and there. (*Fl,* pp. 15–16)

After the Lvov incidents, such an undecided person tended to become one of those who "returned to the nation" (*Fl,* p. 67) and dreamed of the road to Jaffa. And while Merk does not leave the Diaspora, many of his friends do, because they regard Palestine as synonymous with liberation, as an "asylum," "a shelter": "an escape from unresolved life situations" (*Fl,* p. 179).

The protagonist of Zimmermann's *Tirsa* motivates her departure in exactly the same way. She, too, is running away from the aridity of life, from a lack of opportunities for work, and from a sexual scandal involving her father: "I tried in different ways to fill the void that opened around me wherever I entered. . . . I studied at the university, at the academy of fine arts, and I even attended for a year a course for nurses. But I could not stay very long in one place. . . . I wanted to go abroad no matter where, just to find a source of interest." (*T,* p. 80)

Thus, initially, the choice of Palestine is not based on a profound ideological motivation. But such motivation is to come, as a result of getting to know the land and the people "who harnessed themselves to the chariot of a sublime idea" (*T,* p. 138), who "sacrificed their careers, their professions, and their health for the good of the nation, for the good of society, for higher human purposes" (*T,* p. 139). After getting to know the new Palestinian life, Tirsa wants to be part of it. Her aims and aspirations become clear. She acquires independence, freedom, and a sense of dignity and emancipation of which, at home in Vienna, she could not dream. Although Palestine in the process of rebuilding is a far cry from dreams about it, on balance, Tirsa finds in herself much that is good and new. These gains are so essential that, faced with the prospect of losing them, Tirsa commits suicide on the eve of her return to Europe.

My three-part scenario of Zionist education outlined earlier can be found in the life stories of many of the protagonists of Polish-Jewish prose works. All of them are "disgusted with the world and its order, look for improvement, higher forms, repair" (*Czd,* p. 136). True, some of them arrive at the Zionist conclusion after the most extreme experiences: the horror of wartime pogroms. But others just leave home, leave "physical and spiritual rot" and the old life for Palestine, "where a new Jewish society is being built on new social and moral foundations" (*T,* p. 490). This is where "they find the direction and aim in life" (*Czd,* p. 120).

In addition to prose records of conversions to Zionism, Polish-Jewish literature contains also intimate, lyrical testimonies of such changes. One example is Jakub Appenszlak's poem "Mowie polskiej" (To the Polish tongue; 1915). Another is Bronisław Mayer's little volume *Pieśni chaluca* (Songs of a *halutz;* 1934). The first of these testimonies is a kind of confession of faith of "one who is returning" ("I am coming back to you, my nation, after a prodigal journey").[6] The other is an interesting lyrical notebook of a *halutz* poet of an explicitly autobiographical nature:

> And I, Bronisław Mayer, a well-known man of letters
> Squat on a sack of corncobs and with difficulty wake in my brain the talent for peeling potatoes
>
> ("Przy obieraniu ziemniaków" [Peeling potatoes], *Pch,* p. 10)

The form of the volume is that of an autobiography. There is his family: his mother, a teacher and a "townswoman," his unemployed father, his old grandmother. The gymnasium. The hopelessness and lack of opportunities. The anti-Semitism. His response is rebellion, trampling on the past ("Moja hachszara" [My *hachsharah**]), and the conviction that "I must follow the track of my own

*In Hebrew, a kind of agricultural or trade course for prospective halutzim who intended to go to Palestine. [Trans.]

roads" ("Powrót z hachszary" [Return from the *hachsharah*], *Pch,* p. 13). Many of the poems in *Pieśni chaluca* echo with the proud "we threw away":

> We tossed out anatomy books, pandects, wise philosophies of medieval monks
> (B. Mayer, "Rzuciliśmy" [We threw away], *Pch,* p. 7)

> I threw away my elegant navy-blue suit, the stiff collar of city conventions
> Theaters, museums, movies, trolleys, electric bulbs, marbles, picnics
> (B. Mayer, "Moja hachszara" [My *hachsharah*], *Pch,* p. 8)

> to abandon home, and her, and the parents
> (B. Mayer, "Wspomnienie" [Recollection], *Pch,* p. 16)

This is not, as might seem, a question of abandoning culture but of abandoning the fight for a place in the given social order: instead of following his parents' dream, a course of study and a career as a lawyer, the son chooses the *hachsharah* and the role of a "poet and worker in Israel" ("Pieśń o poecie żydowskim [Song about a Jewish poet], *Pch,* p. 24). The cycle "Obrazki plugowe" (Images of a work group) describes the details of the *hachsharah:* work in a sawmill, illness, guard duty in the orchard, the kitchen, the laundry, digging a pond ("Tartak 'Foresta' " [The sawmill "Foresta"], "Chory w pludze" [Sick in a work group], "Strażnik sadu" [Guarding the orchard], "Przy obieraniu ziemniaków" [Peeling potatoes], "Przy balii" [At the washtub], "Przy kopaniu stawu" [Digging a pond]).

Mayer gives a very clear account of the political circumstances underlying the choice of ideological orientation: the growth of fascism in Europe, the Poland of anti-Semitic screams . . . *Halutzim* became those at whose "feet landed the *endek* shouts: Beat the Jews!" ("Rzuciliśmy" [We threw away], *Pch,* p. 7). The poet also declares emphatically that he seeks a new social order that will oppose exploitation and oppression in Europe with Palestine's "joy of the collective" and "liberated machine" ("Pieśń o naszych i waszych maszynach" [Song of your and our machines], *Pch,* pp. 19–20). Thus the search for the new need not be exclusively a search for the sense and aim of life, but can also be, say, an escape from enslavement: "Pierzcham stąd, gdzie żyję pod batem" (I run from where I live under the whip) wrote Mayer, describing the road to Palestine as a migration to the sun.[7]

As can be seen, in all variants of the story of Zionist education, there appears the motif of negation of the old order, of maladaptation, and of suffering:

Wait for me, fatherland!
When the world here gives me bitterness to drink,
When people spatter venom in my soul
Then I will come to Your holy feet—
(M. Hochberżanka, "Czekaj na mnie . . ." [Wait for me . . .])[8]

The more real were the prospects of war, the more it seemed that reaching the Palestine shore of Jewish life was tantamount to salvation. In Mieczysław Braun's poem "Assimi," published in *Nasza Opinia* in August 1939, the boats carrying emigrants were

[l]arge rescue boats
A flotilla of salvation
Looking for the last haven.
("Assimi")[9]

In his "Fragmenty dziejów" (Fragments of history), published a week earlier in the same periodical, Braun referred to escaping from Europe as escaping "annihilation that knows no hope . . . [10]

"Jerusalem of Light and Dusk"

The Fatherland

The images of the Diaspora and the liberation from it constituted a metaphorical whole. There was the sailing on a sea of blood and tears, and the reaching of land:

I would dream like Moses, an infant, on the Nile . . .
I would dream of conquering the mainland . . .
I would dream of land for my feet and the feet of my brothers . . .
I would dream of a proud, toilsome freedom
(S. Spund, "Tak bym chętnie" [I would so gladly])[11]

In descriptions of Zionist pilgrimages, it is obviously not just a question of reaching land: the intended port and haven had to be Eretz Israel, the Holy Land—the land promised anew to the Jews of the Diaspora. To Merk, the protagonist of *Falista linia,* "the ship carrying emigrants seemed . . . like a gangway leading to land, where the homeless retrieve a home, where those thrust away from the plow and the workshop find their due place" (*Fl,* p. 70). A home, a place, and thus rootedness.

For Jewish homelessness is sometimes interpreted as "pain of the earth":

In cold, dark houses of prayer the pain of the earth preys on us
We stand bent, fearful and dumb
(I. Deutscher, "Modlitwa o deszcz" [Prayer for rain])[12]

This pain is the permanent memory of loss. Thus, for Deutscher, the Jews are

like a peasant deprived of a span of land that came to him from a long line of
ancestors; while this field, once his, is hardly worth a care
he keeps stopping at the balk and talking to the field
("Modlitwa o deszcz" [Prayer for rain])

Palestine turns out to be a land that was "once theirs," the land of the forefathers, part of the Jewish heritage. Going to it was a dignified and noble enterprise:

We are going
Serious and proud
To our land
(M. Schlanger, "Synowie Izraela"
[Sons of Israel], *I,* p. 9)

The arriving Jews are "returning home"; after thousands of years, they recognize "outlines of landscapes retained in dim memories" (M. Braun, "Assimi"). They are "sons who strayed," arriving on "cedar ships" at "hearths long extinguished, at altars levelled to the ground" (J. Werfel, "Hajfskie wybrzeże" [The Haifa shore]).[13] They find in modern landscapes traces of biblical images. What is stressed is the antiquity of the connection with this land, an antiquity weakened by the Diaspora but now being strengthened anew.

A weakened but never broken connection. The memory and myth of Eretz Israel, described in previous chapters, were important elements of the syndrome of exile. Hence the encounter with the land was also a confrontation of dreams with reality:

finally they were to see Eretz Avotenu which called them with a sweet voice all life long—in stifling heders, in the yeshiva, in the Beth Hamidrash, where in the darkness of night dotted with yellow flames of tallow candles the yellow pages

> of the holy books were frames surrounding the biblical landscape. For so many years they smelled esrogs in search of its aroma, . . .so many times they kissed the sand placed in little sacks under the heads of the dead. (*P,* pp. 343–344).

Crying, prayers, joyful dances on the decks of the ships arriving at Jaffa and Haifa are scenes frequently described in Polish-Jewish literature. [Indeed,] feverish, tense waiting for the emergence on the horizon of the first outlines of the Land is a fixed point of emigrant biographies: "They stayed all the time on the deck and spent the last night before arriving in Eretz Israel in feverish waiting and watching. When someone went to sleep, utterly exhausted, he implored another to wake him as soon as the ship came near the beloved fatherland" (*Czd,* pp. 81–82). The land about to appear is for the travelers an "ancient land" (M. Silberman, "Kadimah"),[14] "true," "harsh," "last" (M. Braun, "Fragmenty dziejów"), "free," "Hebrew" (M. Szymel, "Poetom ziemi walczącej" [To the poets of a fighting land]), "paternal," "fatherly" (R. Taubenschlag, *"Judea resurrecta:* Pieśń bólu i radości" (*Judea resurrecta:* Song of pain and joy),[15] "good," "one's own" (D. Ihr, "List" [A letter]). It is also—and this image recurs a number of times—the waiting Mother-Land:

> And I know, Mother Earth, that you are waiting for me
> And will forgive my sin when I return
> (D. Ihr, "List" [A letter])

The vision of "mother Eretz Israel" (M. Korn, "Modlitwa o deszcz")[16] is sometimes accompanied by an introduction of "wandering sons," "foundlings radiant with joy who, after years of wandering, had found the true mother" (*Czd,* p. 158).

The next stage of the road—a kind of mystery of greeting and rootedness—can be found in the Palestinian poems of Anda Eker. Here the patriotic exaltation is expressed in litanies of emotional epithets so intense that the author did not hesitate to call one of the poems "A near erotic":

> How will I enfold You all, O my beautiful, lovely,
> O my one and only, dearest, beloved.
> How can I absorb You all, with what caresses should I caress you
> O my own land, awaited with such fervent yearning
> (A. Eker, "Prawie erotyk" [A near erotic], *Mch,* p. 106)

The ritual of greeting the land reminds one of greeting a beloved person, and is enriched with the insertion of a number of patriotic-sentimental gestures: "the only thing I can do is pick up a black lump of You with my fingers / Lift it slowly to my mouth and kiss it quietly."

Incidentally, in her Palestinian poems, Eker frequently resorts to love lyrics as models. For example, the rhetoric of a lovers' farewell is found in "Odjazd z Ojczyzny" (Departing the Fatherland):

> You have bewitched my heart. You have appropriated my soul.
> You have seduced me, O earth, forever. I must be Yours for all time.
>
> . . . .
>
> For I know that from now on it will be impossible to forget You,
> Don't allow, don't let them take me! I love you so tremendously!
>
> (A. Eker, "Odjazd z Ojczyzny" [Departing the Fatherland], *Mch,* p. 110)

The essence of this mystery seems to be the restoration of the natural order of emotional values, the transformation of the strange, distant fatherland into one known, near, and one's own:

> You are no longer a stranger to me, no longer unknown,
> O sweet, dear, dearest, most beloved!
>
> (A. Eker, "Słowa szczęśliwe" [Words of happiness], *Mch,* p. 109)

In Eker's case, the tonality of the regaining of the fatherland is invariably joyful and lofty: the litany of emotional epithets is accompanied by strings of exclamations; the descriptions of the Palestinian landscape are saturated with delight in the beauty that emanates from it; and the "I" is full of a sense of consolation, peace, and happiness. There is the stark contrast between the previous state of wandering and the present state, which is "good," "quiet," and "sweet." The world of harmony and quiet ("as if all the world were of this fragrance and quiet") is a world in which "one need no longer wander" ("Wieczór w Tel-Awiwie" [Evening in Tel-Aviv], *Ncs,* p. 19). The very recollection of the experience of this world, the dream of Palestine dreamed in Europe, can be soothing:

> The names of your settlements call alluringly at night.
> And the fans of soft grasses sough gently above my head—

Colors, memories, tones, and smells come to me—
Take me away good fatherland, take me, shelter and save me.
(A. Eker, "Wiersz bez tytułu" [Untitled poem], *Mch,* p. 116)

The regaining of a home, the regaining of a land, the regaining of a fatherland was sometimes also the regaining of one's identity, a covenant with the Land, a covenant with one's own history:

> A land full of memories. . . . Open like a *chumash* volume, like a Talmudic *"nigun,"* like a childhood legend. They sensed that here walked Saul and Gideon, David and Bar Kochba and the Maccabees, and centuries of people small and great, cohorts of fathers and forefathers. Relatedness, connection. Not all the world is foreign. There is yet a stretch of land that understands rather than spurns them, that is, proud rather than ashamed of them. A land that retains, deep inside, the memory of their heroes, dreamed of in messianic expectations, in Davidic promises, in heder melodies sung on a winter night before returning home. . . . They discovered their worth in the land of their yearning. (*Czd,* p. 42)

This long quotation from Rubin Feldszuh's *Czerwone dusze* makes an important attempt to interpret the significance of the new Jewish covenant. The most important element of the connection with the land is undoubtedly the taking root, the overcoming of the sense of foreignness. Palestine is also a place where Jews can make a covenant with one another, can give expression to collective memory, can affirm and strengthen their identity. Images of a union with the mythical biblical past through the tie with the Land can also be found in Brandstaetter's work: the same "land smelling of myrrh," and "the same . . . evening" greeted the "tents of slender Israel" and the steam mills of the Haifa port ("List z Palestyny" [Letter from Palestine], *Kts,* p. 16). The resulting effect is very close to Herzl's *Altneuland* formula: the old-new land, an alliance between the past and modernity.

For the "old land," the "land of the forefathers" is an ally of the Jewish today and of the Jewish tomorrow. Coming to it from Europe resembles "Day One" (M. Braun, "Fragmenty dziejów"), the beginning of a new world and a new life—new in part because of the covenant with the land. The vision of rootedness, even of union with the land, is an important motif of Polish-Jewish literature:

I know—I believe:
One must grow into the earth
(M. Hochberżanka, "Święto" [Holiday])[17]

In a quiet golden evening
I will again fall to the ground,
I will listen to the breathing which dozes—somewhere—in my breast

And I will cease being me and blend with this earth—
(I. Deutscher, "Orka" [Plowing])[18]

In Deutscher's case the covenant is realized through work, through plowing. Szymon Bart, one of the protagonists in *Falista linia,* thinks likewise: this arm will plow the fallow land. I will be one with the land, it will be my friend" (*Fl,* 180). The happy plowman is the "I" in Lutwak's Palestine[19] and the protagonist of Brandstaetter's "Elegia cedrowa" (Cedar elegy):

Once a gray innkeeper, tenant of another's land which you could not will
to your sons,
today heir to a rich property you till
knotty chunks of land with your own plows in the cedar fatherland.
("Elegia cedrowa" [Cedar elegy])[20]

Szymel's *halutzim* plow "with bleeding hands." Another character that appears in Polish-Jewish literature is that of the *halutz* sower, who symbolizes not only brotherhood with the land or rootedness but also the beginning of a new life:

In the black, fragrant earth, in the scarified earth,
In the holy earth breathing hard with maternal conception
He throws golden grains with a pleading incantation
That it grow up a yearning prayerful flute
(A. Eker, "Chaluc" [*Halutz*], *Odz,* p. 52)

To sow is to build. Those working in Palestine "are sowing for the Future" (Z. Schenker, "Nad grobem ofiar palestyńskich" [At the grave of Palestinian victims]).[21]

The motif of barren land, of fallow restored to life through the deeds of the pioneers, recurs frequently in Polish-Jewish literature. It is more than a reflection of reality. For the new life is viewed as a covenant between the land and the people as well as a transformation of the latter. The desert coming back to life, once stony but now fertile (A. Eker, "Zabawa w szomrów" (The *shomrim* game), *Odz,* p. 97), is one of the symbolic images of national regeneration. Death is conquered by life, barrenness by fertility, old age by youth. It comes down to this:

the boys came to the rocky soil,
They hit the rock with a pickax and a spring squirted from the rock!
The life-giving streams of water soaked the parched soil
And the land awoke
(M. Braun, "Fragmenty dziejów" [Fragments of history])

Orchards blossom in the desert!
Fresh greenness bores an ancient wall!
(M. Braun, "Assimi")

You sent to the desert hosts of *halutzim* so that the Lord's vineyards would blossom with clusters of grapes.
(M. Korn, "Modlitwa o deszcz" [A prayer for rain])

Images of the soul as reclaimed barren land also appear in lyrical poetry that has recourse to the technique of the inner landscape:

From souls the stones of infirmity were tossed out
From fallow hearts the weeds of illusions excised

And from souls newborn gushed the harvest of the sowing.
(Z. Schenker, "W narodową rocznicę" [A national anniversary]) [22]

The desert that greets those who liberate themselves from the slavery of the Diaspora is sometimes associated with the biblical land of the forty-year trek to Canaan. For this desert, like the biblical one, is meant to be a space of transformation and cleansing:

Don't say that it is promised, that the land promised ages ago
Is just a desert in which fate raised you from the dead.
Before you are born in it, proud and free man,
You will die here of death, so that you can forget the humiliation . . .
(M. Braun, "Fragmenty dziejów" [Fragments of history])

Bernard Zimmermann thinks of the pioneers as people born "in a desert pass between two eras" (*T,* p. 95) But the land is not just a cleansing desert. It is also frequently a Providing Mother, and

like a mother, it will softly give, but not without a battle,
The reviving power of your fathers, the power of faith, milk, honey, and dates
(A. Marc, "Ziemia" [The earth])[23]

Dresdner ("Do chaluca" [To a *halutz*]) compares the *halutz* to Antaeus who draws strength from the life-giving mother earth. Feldszuh draws this image of the covenant:

> As if tossed by the strength of the wind, we fell to the ground, nestled close to her with our whole bodies, and embraced her with our arms. Her, our soil. Her, the one and only, who can restore our peace, honor, . . .self-assurance, tact, and soul, true, sincere, healthy soul. The soul of Israel and Palestine, full of faith and sublimity. (*Np*, p. 90)

Here undergoing change means regaining through the land the former spiritual countenance.

Building the New

Yet another version of the transformation is sometimes encountered in Polish-Jewish literature:

A new people is born in the ancient land
And hoists new flags.
Young people rise on the old Land
And new fanfares resound—
Risen from the dead on a new and stronger throne
Arise Zion!
(M. Silberman, "Kadimah!")

In the images of the covenant with the land, of regeneration through the connection with it, the key issue was rebuilding, restoring of the old. Here the stress is not on regaining the old, not on an old-new synthesis, but on creation of the new. This idea was so popular in Polish-Jewish literature that we can even speak of a kind of exaltation with the new.

The Cult of the New is especially clear in the prose of Henryk Adler and Rubin Feldszuh. Adler's heroes frequently repeat the watchword of building life "beginning with the foundations" (*AiJ*, p. 14), with the substructure. In Feldszuh's work, there appears a vision of Palestine as a "land in the making," as the "batter for a new Tomorrow" (*Czd,* p. 133). As Herzl's translator, Adler presented a Polish version of his *Altneuland* formula, which he rendered as "at the gates of a new life," thus subverting the stresses of the original. He also wrote an introduction to the Polish edition of Herzl's utopian novel in which he presented his own interpretation of the work. The new society presented in *Altneuland,* a society that equates happiness with work and learning, that dispenses with an army and the dictatorship of the clergy, and that is tolerant and justly rewards the merits of its members, is, for Adler a "new, ideal form of collective human life,"[24] one that radically rejects the "old, rotten model of the European state with its classes of rulers and slaves, with an army, militarism, and class and national chauvinism."[25] In the view of the commentator, the most important thing was basing the state on the idea of justice, justice that does not lead to an "artificial equality" of all but guarantees freedom, full development and happiness of the individual.

The tone of journalistic commentary is frequent in literary texts. Feldszuh's heroes declare: "We will try to create there a new world, a new people. Without rotten foundations. A world of truth and faith. A world of sweat and blood" (*Czd,* p. 59). The desire for the new is sometimes so strong that it calls for a "revaluation of values" (*Czd,* p. 115), for a fight for a "beautiful and wholesome world," for a new society, for a new culture, for a "luminous vanguard" of civilization.

The revaluation touches the very rudiments of the social structure: the family must disappear and its place must be taken by the collective. Some of the watchwords of the young are: "what is the family compared with the *kvutza*?*," and "together we will go through life." They are found in Mayer's "Pieśń chaluca," which also opposes the "true warmth of the *kvutza*" to the coolness of the family home ("Wspomnienie" [Recollection], *Pch,* p. 16), and the joyful life of "happy *kvutza* children" and "happy children of collectives" to the suffering of Jewish children in Europe ("Pieśń o sabrach" [Song about sabras], *Pch,* p. 21). The symbol of the new, exuberant collective life is often the image of a group dancing the hora:

> The circle is getting ever larger,
> Faces radiant with happiness—glowing eyes,
> Dishevelled heads—unplaited braids
> And legs prayerfully dancing
> Flicker

*In Hebrew, a group of Jewish pioneer settlers in Palestine. [Trans.]

. . . .
And with the steady din of the leg on the floor they sound a hymn of happiness, a hymn of labor, a hymn of power
(B. Mayer, "Hora," *Pch,* p. 17)[26]

The new society and the new culture are to be created by the new people, the vanguard of a "happy tomorrow" (*T,* p. 95), by pioneers-*halutzim.* It is through their labors that deserts come to life with—one might say—the flower of newness:

They left
behind
home, parents and brothers,
the harsh unhappy Diaspora,
to lose the cursed past
and build a new world.
They created,
built . . .
Their hands gave rise to bright houses,
radiant with the happiness of a better future,
sands changed to gardens
heavy with the fruit of a better tomorrow.
(J. Kleinberg, "Chalucim" [*Halutzim*])[27]

[Jan] Kleinberg's style is very expressive: a new world, creativity, the fruit of the future. Also, my use of the Mickiewicz phrase* was premeditated. Familiar echoes sound not only in the poem just quoted. Even an inexperienced reader will note them in, say, the following:

Hey, forward! Onto the road of life!
Forward, young *shomrim!*
Hey, forward! . . . forward, young friends!
(L. Krasucki, "Hej naprzód" [Hey, forward])[28]

The new values, of which there is so much talk, are: freedom, dignity, strength, courage, perseverance, honor. They are represented by these very

*A reference to the term "with the flowers of newness" (*nowości kwiatem),* taken from Mickiewicz's Ode to Youth (*Oda do młodości).* This poem is a romantic apotheosis of youth and a call to a complete transformation of reality (motifs that appear in the Polish-Jewish poems interpreted here). [Trans.]

builders. These are the new Jews. Anda Eker calls them "white-and-blue" Jews. They are proud and happy:

> It is we who have finally got our own fatherland.
> It is we in whose veins flows hot new blood!
> (A. Eker, "Biało-błękitni" [The white-and-blue]; *Mcb,* p. 107)

The mystery of the birth of the new man is one of the favorite themes of Palestinian prose. One of its recurrent motifs is the transformation of the Diaspora Jew into a proud Palestinian; of a homeless wanderer into a "son of the soil and of the fatherland"; of a slave into a free man; of a Nalewki peddler into a Judean shepherd.[29] Sometimes the process is paid for with a life (as in Adler's story *Tchórz* [The coward]). Sometimes, as in Feldszuh's "Noce straży" (Guard nights), it is accomplished in one night. The narrator comments: "A ward of Diaspora fear died and a free son of an (almost) free fatherland was born; a shomer of Palestine was born" (*Np,* p. 21). There emerges a model of a Palestinian, a Zionist model of a spiritual metamorphosis, a model of the *obiit . . . natus est* [dies (and) is born (again)] kind. Feldszuh is especially fond of this model. He often contrasts the frail and fearful Diaspora Jew with the brave and physically strong *halutz* or *shomer* (as in the short story *Rachel*), and describes the "regaining of the soul" (*Np,* p. 21) resulting from the covenant with the land.

The ideal that emerges from the dreams about the new life is that of a "free Jew in the free land of Israel." He is an "independent engineer of his own life. He draws up the plans and lives according to them, he creates his edifices of Truth" (*Czd,* p. 158). The life of the *halutzim* and *shomrim* is described as romantic in the deepest sense of the word, as full of adventure and meaning, as—to quote Adler—a "song of storm and love": "the shomer's life is a paean of Love and Storm, and the song of Storm and Love is more powerful than all storms and stormier than all experiences" (*AiJ,* p. 46). One possible explanation for the appeal of the sensational and melodramatic to Polish-Jewish prose writers is that (on a certain level) they may have regarded erotic incidents or fights with the enemy as synonyms for the fullness of life.

Thus the positive heroes of Palestinian prose are strong, decisive men and courageous, independent women. Put differently, they are responsible and worthy individuals, able—a key characteristic—to reject European conventions. Their antitraditionalism is most spectacular in the area of social conventions, and is supposed to lead to a new quality in interpersonal relations. In this connection, the obvious fascination of Polish-Jewish prose writers for the erotic freedom of Palestinian life is significant. Thus Adler wrote a number of stories and essays devoted to free love against the background of nature—"the Kineret, the Sky, and the Galilean sun" (*AiJ,* p. 23)—love viewed as an oasis of pure joy and true human freedom. He regarded the "new mode of loving" as "one of the foundations of our new life" (*AiJ,* p. 176). "The new Eros" (the title of one of his texts) meant for him primarily life in threes, which he interpreted as the rejection of the old world's law of ownership that encumbered the sphere of even the most intimate relationships. For Adler, life in threes was a rejection of egotism in favor of community. He included the following commentary in his story about the "wife of two husbands" ("Zahrura"): "From this time on I looked at these three with the trembling of high regard. Their beautiful spiritual faces projected rays of brightness on the distant, unknown future of the new culture" (*AiJ,* p. 97). In his "Księga Ruth" (Book of Ruth), a paraphrase of the biblical theme, Adler cast an old worker as Boas and made Ruth the Venus of the commune, a "vestal," a "priestess of the community" "guarding the holy fire of loving" (*AiJ,* p. 81). From their union was born a son named symbolically "Oved," that is, "Worker."

The will to create the New was inseparable from the determination to abandon or destroy the old, which was treated with dislike and often with contempt and even hatred. Those intent on breaking the ties with the past thought even of destroying the Wailing Wall, which to them was a "monument of shame" (*T,* p. 161), a symbol of impotence and national lethargy. The iconoclastic enthusiasm of the followers of the religion of the New was not directed against all of the Jewish tradition. What was the object of a relentless attack was the Diaspora. What could help in the overcoming of the Diaspora was the biblical heritage.

The biblical heritage was also used to create models of men. For example, the new men would resemble Palestinian knights. This is especially clear in the case of *shomrim* and Żabotyński's legionnaires, "knights with iron bodies and noble souls" (*Np,* p. 139), guarding the peace of Jewish settlements with "carbine, quiver, and revolver" (*Czd,* p. 106). Feldszuh overtly propagated models of the knightly biblical past. In *Czerwone dusze,* he told the story of the contemporary Brotherhood of the Gideonites, a kind of knightly order that was at the same time a secret conspiracy and an association of Nazarites. Its members saw themselves as inheritors of Gideon and his select three hundred warriors, heroes of the battles against the Midianites related in the Book of Judges. Whereas the traditional Nazarites swore allegiance to God, the contemporary knights-monks swore allegiance to the fatherland: "Our land is our cloister, our call is the Jewish nation, we vow to gain freedom by Deed" (*Czd,* p. 175). They were also a conspiracy of avengers, of "brilliant desperados" (*Czd,* p. 195) and terrorists, ready to destroy all those who would stand in the way of the rebirth of Palestine: "Expelled from the land, a band of avengers, we will produce gases and bombs to choke the world in torment. . . . We will do this if those who have everything take from us, who have nothing, the last sliver to which we are attached with soul and hope" (*Czd,* p. 196).

The use of biblical motives (without Feldszuh's sensational modifications) in Palestinian subject-matter, as well as in the symbolism of rebirth, was quite common in Polish-Jewish literature. Thus in Rudolf Taubenschlag's *"Judea resurrecta:* Pieśń bólu i radości" (*Judea resurrecta:* Song of pain and joy), the "miracle in Canaan" is the rebirth of the "spirit of the Hasmoneans," the resurrection of the Maccabees, who send "golden messengers" of liberation:

Hoofbeats are heard . . . are these birds . . .
Young braves dash along with the wind
With a song resounding on their lips
The youth of Judah sings powerfully
Of freedom and brotherhood,
Of reborn heroism.
A thousand lances of the knightly party
Augur safety for the land.
(*"Judea resurrecta:* Pieśń bólu i radości"
[*Judea resurrecta:* Song of pain and joy])[30]

Given these biblical and revival associations, the new life appears as an awakening from a dream of slavery—Diaspora (M. Silberman, "Kadimah"), or as a resurrection ("a people risen from the dead"—F. T. Aszkenazy, "Hasmonea").[31]

One finds in Polish-Jewish literature yet another interpretation of the heroic models we are discussing. A young Zionist in Madler's *Falista linia* says: "We want to be Maccabees. But we will fight with the plow and not with weapons" (*Fl,* p. 34). The title of one of the chapters in Feldszuh's *Czerwone dusze* is "W okopach pracy" (In the trenches of labor). Adler's heroes "went to work with the feeling of soldiers marching to the battlefield" (*AiJ,* p. 117). Eker's "Wiersz o dawnych chalucach" (Poem about the *halutzim* of long ago) is based on contrasting the lot of a group of soldiers to that of a group of *halutzim* in such a way that the battle of labor is seen to be more onerous than armed battle, and the lot of the pioneer harder than that of the soldier.

At this point it is appropriate to comment at some length on the Maccabees of work, on the cult of "work—the mother of culture" (*Fl,* p. 81), and on "life with work and through work" (*Np,* p. 73). Judged in artistic terms, Palestinian prose of the turn of the thirties was largely the work of amateurs. But these were some of the actual builders of the new Palestine. As such, they stressed the authenticity of their "romantic Palestinian stories" by describing them to their readers as notes of *halutzim.* This was done, for example, by Adler, who noted in the introduction to *Ariela i Jubal* (Ariela and Jubal) that it was "written in moments free from pioneer work or during post-malarial convalescence" (*AiJ,* p. 1). Both Adler and Feldszuh, whose work included the most intense apotheosis of the New, came to Palestine in the early twenties as part of the so-called third aliyah. Hence their essays, images, short stories, and novels can be regarded as a literary record of the consciousness and worldview of the generation of builders, whose arrival in the land shortly after World War I was—generally speaking—a response to the ideology of the halutz movement.

According to Ezra Mendelsohn, the eminent modern student of Zionism in Poland, the idea of work was one of the key categories of contemporary pioneer programs. He writes: "It is well known that the pioneer idea . . . meant the creation of vanguard groups whose dedicated work in Palestine was to promote large-scale immigration to that country."[32] Such an understanding of the role of work—and of their own role in the task of rebuilding—was characteristic of Adler's and Feldszuh's heroes, members of the intelligentsia, whose patron saint was Aharon Dawid Gordon (Feldszuh's "Gordon" of *Noce palestyńskie*), who were convinced that work could indeed, could in fact be poetry, and that life filled with work could be beautiful, elevated, and rich in meaning.

Gordon, who can be thought of as a disciple of Tolstoy and who was regarded as one of the most eminent philosophers of Zionism, made the cult of work part of his philosophical system. His system emphasized man's spiritual transformation, man's connection with all Creation, the Cosmos, and Nature, achieved by dint of physical effort. Faint traces of this philosophical position can be found in Polish-Jewish literature, where only a popular version of Gordon's ideas appears, the version assimilated by pioneer ideology. Nevertheless, we find in it motifs of rebirth through work and through contact with nature (for example, in Feldszuh's *Rachel*) and of taking root through work: "Mother-Soil, cultivated by us, plowed by us, bedewed with our sweat and blood" (*Np,* p. 84). An important role is also played by production work, by "productivization": the white-and-blue Zionist flag is "woven from the sky of Palestine / and the white holiday shirts of workers" (B. Mayer, "Jiskor" [Yizkor]; *Pch,* p. 22). The gallery of heroes includes figures such as Adler's Szrajber—fanatic of work—who totally "dedicate themselves to the ideal of pioneer work. Not for a little moment do they want to busy themselves with anything else" (*AiJ,* p. 124). The ideal form of work is agriculture: of it sing the Palestinian idylls of, say, Brandstaetter and Szymel. The work of the farmer is a kind of return to nature. Dreaming of it, the virtuoso violinist becomes a gardener and the student of philosophy a plowman and sower.

Yet another interpretation of the role of work, besides Gordon's, is that work is a sacrifice whose value is the same as, and possibly greater than, the struggle for the land. [From Polish-Jewish literature,] it is easy to put together a rich panorama of work-related scenes of superhuman, murderous efforts and death: the draining of marshes, the building of roads, work in quarries . . . Hospitals for those sick with malaria, victims of deadly accidents . . . The forward march of work and rebirth continues in spite of—indeed, because of—suffering and death. Adler's *Inwalida* (The invalid), the story of a dreamer-pioneer who commits suicide when sick and therefore presumably useless for the country, ends with a scene of triumph: an uninterrupted construction project, uninfluenced by the deaths of a few individuals. "In the quarries pioneers blasted hard basalt rocks with dynamite and broke them with hammers into smaller rocks, and girls broke them with small hammers into little stones. Invalids ended up in gorges, and on the new roads, on the slopes and tops of mountains, a young generation of pioneers conquered a new life" (*AiJ,* pp. 131–132).

Death in Palestine was sometimes interpreted as a kind of redemption, as a blood offering for the sake of rebirth: "Only blood will redeem the destruction—the blood of young people who crave a better tomorrow" (*Czd,* p. 16). Some died of disease, some in skirmishes with Arabs, some during riots . . . "Before I die for the fatherland," says the "I" in Brandstaetter's "Psalm goryczy i gniewu" (Psalm of bitterness and anger, *Kts,* p. 32).

The cult of sacrifice, the tone of the mourning prayer "Jiskor" (Yizkor), permeate the martyrological stream of Polish-Jewish poetry, where poems dedicated to the memory of the victims of bloody riots and pogroms occupy a special place. In these poems, death in Palestine is invariably the nucleus of a new life, the death of free people for the freedom of the fatherland, a blessed sacrifice:

> Glory to You, Brothers fallen in a distant Fatherland!
> The nation's foundation, strengthened by Your blood,
> On which will rise a State praised for centuries
> In Your and our prayers offered to the Lord.
>
> (Z. Schenker, "Nad grobem ofiar palestyńskich"
> [At the grave of Palestinian victims])[33]

The chain of builders is never broken and the place of the fallen is taken by new volunteers:

For one pair of dead hands, ten that live;
For one silenced heart, ten that beat.
(D. Ihr, "List" [A letter])[34]

Some relevant specifics. Szymel ("Moja siostra" [My sister], "Powrót do domu" [The return home]) tells of a brother who runs away from home to go to work in Palestine in place of his sister who died. Hochberżanka tells of the *kvutza* Bamaaleh that sent new people to an outpost where five *halutzim* had been murdered. Hersz Fenster's "Ballada o młodych synach starej ziemi" (Ballad of the young sons of an old land) tells of a mother's farewells to a succession of sons departing for Palestine:

Yellow fever swallowed Efroim Sztejn
and Arab hands killed my oldest Jejkyl;
don't go there son, for death awaits you
("Ballada o młodych synach starej ziemi"
[Ballad of the young sons of an old land])[35]

These stories of heroes and martyrs "consumed by a desire to offer their blood on the altar of the fatherland and of honor" (*Np,* p. 166) are, of course, part of the Palestinian pantheon erected in Polish-Jewish literature.

The tone of these stories is sometimes surprisingly familiar to Polish readers. The protagonist of [Józef] Hartblaj's *Jehoszua* (Joshua) says that, for the sake of Palestine, one should "renounce even one's own mother." Another echoes this sentiment with "I must sacrifice my own happiness for the good of the cause."[36] Arie Weissman in Zimmermann's *Tirsa* renounces love and the idea of starting a family because he is convinced that "[i]n Palestine the private life of an individual comes to an end and social and national duty begins" (*T,* p. 182). Service to the fatherland, put ahead of private, personal concerns, turns out to be an important imperative and motivation for many individual actions.

For many of the protagonists, the question of the proportion of national and universal content in the New presented a dilemma just as essential as the conflict between patriotic duty and personal desires. Thus the settling of accounts with Communism,[37] a system that attempted to build the New on other than national principles, was not something that appeared in Polish-Jewish literature (in Zimmermann's *Tirsa* and in Feldszuh's *Czerwone dusze*) by accident, or owing to the great attractiveness of the political theme. Obviously, in all such squaring of accounts Zionist tendentiousness won out and guaranteed the triumph of national feelings.

As if to compensate for the victories of particularism, there were attempts to fashion out of the Palestinian experience a model for the "new existence," the "melody of the new Tomorrow" (*Czd,* p. 166), or even the new Word, issuing like its ancient predecessor from the Land of Israel. The protagonists dream of the realization in Palestine of the eternal mission of Jewry: of the "religion of Love and Brotherhood," of the struggle for "more perfect forms of existence, of "freedom, equality, and brotherhood" (*Czd,* p. 215). When fulfilling this mission the Jews were red souls, intent on "justice, solidarity, and the cooperation of nations" (*Np,* p. 215) and on combining "work, ethics, cooperation and mutual respect with just sharing" (*Czd,* p. 217). Visiting missionaries saw in the *halutz* communes a "Christian brotherhood among Jews" (*AiJ,* p. 184). I have quoted the original terms used in expressing these dreams because the phraseology says a great deal about its authors' consciousness.

When they universalized the Palestinian experience in this way, Adler and Feldszuh, the two main practitioners of this genre, were not Zionist heretics. Rather, they were diligent readers and disciples of Herzl. In Herzl's vision of the New Society, sketched in [his] utopian *Altneuland,* the new life in Palestine was to be open to all, regardless of nationality and religion. Of course, Herzl motivated this idea very differently. In his view, the New was to be based on "thought, the common property of all cultured nations,"[38] hence the moral duty of rejection of separatism and of acceptance of the watchword "let the stranger be comfortable in our midst." With this understanding, the raising of the New could be called the raising of the "Jerusalem of light": Radiant Jerusalem—herald of love and brotherhood.

Dusk

It would be a considerable simplification to represent the Palestinian stream of Polish-Jewish literature as completely optimistic and utterly dominated by tendentiousness and didacticism. True, the vision of the new life, its main values and particular form, is assigned a central position. But the tendentiousness and utopianism are accompanied by critical threads. The New Jerusalem emerging from this literature is—as in Roman Brandstaetter's poem—a "Jerusalem of light and dusk." In the poem there are two fatherlands. Opposed to the ideal—"pure and angelic," "laureled and angry"[39]—fatherland is a (possible rather than really existing) replica of a well-known European order: hatred, brute force, and suffering . . .

The critical threads are strongest in Zimmermann's *Tirsa,* although they are far from absent from the work of Adler and Feldszuh, the most fervent eulogists of the New. Also, these threads are not exclusively the result of the disappointment due to the confrontation of dreams with reality; they are not only—as Feldszuh puts it—"a cold shower on the heads of pioneers full of wild pretensions" (*Czd,* p. 115). Of course, the romantic images of roads strewn with roses, of dropping stars, of "tents of Hebrew knights"—of which there are many in Szymel's and Brandstaetter's visions of Eretz Israel—could not possibly have anything in common with Palestinian reality. Nor could the vision of a colorful life, full of adventures and joy. For Palestinian reality was a "steady, quiet, unending sacrifice of a gray weekday" (*T,* p. 347), a life full of hardship, care, and suffering.

In the case of both pioneer-writers, the more critical tones are found in their later texts which, as Adler explained, were expressions of the "retrospective attitude to the directly experienced Palestinian reality" (*AiJ,* p. 1). In fragments of Adler's *Ariela i Jubal,* written from such a perspective, the "Song of Love and Storm" is no longer triumphant and the squaring of accounts with the watchwords of the pioneer movement is more frequent. There is criticism of the cult of physical work: it wastes the talents, knowledge, and abilities of many people who are diverted from creative and useful pursuits and unable to support the burdens of the New (the fragments "Śmierć Chany" [Hanah's death], "Wariaci" [Crazies]). There is also criticism of the ideal community and of the concept of equality of all, which is hardly possible among strong and weak, healthy and sick . . . Finally, there is an attack on the Zionist party elite, the "activists" who retreat from the labor ranks of the pioneers to comfortable bureaucratic positions.

As noted earlier, the squaring of accounts with the New is most emphatic in Bernard Zimmermann's *Tirsa,* the most extensive Polish-Jewish panorama of Palestinian life. The novel's protagonist comes from Vienna to Palestine and gets to know the country and the society in the making, first as a well-disposed but ideologically uninvolved observer and then as a participant. This format offers a convenient opportunity for presenting Palestinian reality. Zimmermann describes in detail the structure of the *gdud** and the kibbutz and subjects their organization to detailed criticism. He is especially critical of points that seem to him to rely too much on Soviet models. His reasons are clear. The new social forms, which are supposed to realize the idea of community and freedom, restrict rather than develop the individual's freedom and impose standardized solutions without creating opportunities for free choice. These social forms are

*An organizational unit of some of the Zionist youth organizations. [Trans.]

also far from realizing the so insistently declared equality of all members. After all, there are always personal sympathies and antipathies, friendship and dislike, spiritual proximity and foreignness, love and hatred. Complete and perfect community does not exist. The sphere of privacy, of intimate family life, is irreplaceable; but it singles out, it disconnects from the group.

Zimmermann objects most emphatically to the rejection of the traditional institutions of marriage and family. The lack of "civil law ceremonies" (*T,* p. 121), a manifestation of the New, does not strike him as a salvational remedy for the ills of the old world. Freedom in this sphere can degenerate into irresponsibility and become the cause of personal tragedies. And while the system of collective rearing of children is a nucleus of the New and frees one from parental burdens, it also deprives one of the most wonderful and intimate human joys.

The protagonists of *Tirsa* claim that "work and an idea are the two factors that can be a refuge in life" (*T,* p. 134). But work is not a universal key to personal rebirth and inner transformation. Hard and uncreative work can be a torment and an ordeal. This is especially clear in the case of working women. In Zimmermann's writings we find a number of scenes similar to the one below, which involves a group of girls building a road:

> They sat astride a pile of small stones with wide-brimmed straw hats on their heads. Their legs were wrapped in rags or covered with a sack and their fingers were bound up. The sun's heat was unbearable. . . . They sat in total silence and lifted and dropped their hammers mechanically on the chunks of stone from which the blows splintered off sharp fragments. Some of the girls were quite young and physically underdeveloped, like children. (*T,* p. 133)

A sad and hopeless sight. Zimmermann's implied moral is obvious. Work must be satisfying, it must correspond to a person's predisposition, and it must strengthen the conviction of the importance of the person's effort devoted to the building of Palestine.

There is no reference in *Tirsa* to an exalted covenant with the land. There is instead a description of hunger for land. Some wait for an opportunity to work on the land for years, years full of disappointment.

Disapproval of the New is not the only element that gives *Tirsa* its pessimistic tone. What deepens this tone is the author's linking of the Palestinian crisis of 1926 with the personal story of the protagonist whose father, a businessman, went bankrupt and had to return to Europe. In a sense, [Tirsa] had to lower herself in the social scale by giving up her job as a volunteer nurse in a

Hadassah hospital and by joining a kibbutz. There were also economic problems, unemployment, and a lack of opportunities.

One other issue that darkened the vision of the "Jerusalem of light" was the Arab question. The theme of bloody riots and pogroms in Palestine appeared in Polish-Jewish literature, not only in the variant of the "blessed sacrifice," the redemption of the Land by young blood, or the apotheosis of the New Warrior-Jew, but also in the stereotype (of varying intensity) of the enemy with a "vengeful nature" ([J. Hartblaj,] *Jehoszua* [Joshua]), the wild, evil, and cruel opponent of building.

The Orient, The Orient

The image of the new Palestinian life would certainly be incomplete if one ignored its oriental background. The obvious fascination with the East was quite natural. The arrivals in Palestine were Europeans, "sons of the North" at home in a Slavic landscape. Like Appenszlak's heroes, they imagined the Orient in terms of an Arabia about which they read in . . . Mickiewicz's *Farys* (*P,* p. 209).

Many lyrical notebooks (I have in mind primarily Eker's lyrical poems), as well as Palestinian recollections written in prose, give special emphasis to oriental exoticism. They contain a great many variants of "Easternness": "tumult of the East" (*Czd,* p. 11), "Eastern contemplation" (*Czd,* p. 62), "Eastern lyricism" (*Czd,* p. 169), "Eastern soul" (*Np,* p. 38), "man of the East" (*Np,* p. 11), "eastern facial features" (*AiJ,* p. 31), "eastern July," "balms of the East," "fragrances of Arabia," "sky of the Levant," "exotic trees" (A. Eker, "Ballada o Tyberjadzie" [Ballad about Tiberias]), "elegy from the Orient" (A. Eker, "Elegia z Orientu do Lwowa" [Elegy from the Orient to Lvov]), "oriental melodies" (A. Eker, "Wspomnienie o cukierence arabskiej" [Recollection of a little Arab café]), "oriental night" (A. Eker, "Noc orientalna" [Oriental night]), "oriental sky" (A. Eker, "Film kolorowy" [Color film]) . . . The litany of "Easternness," of "Orientalness," and of exoticism could be considerably extended.

The images of the Orient are stereotypes. A "son of the desert, a wild Arab takes a beautiful maiden, the flower of Canaan, by the waist" (*Np,* p. 8). A *shomer* is on guard duty in an "orange vineyard at the waves of the Kinereth" (*Pn,* p. 9). The Arabs are "sons of the desert and of freedom" (*Np,* p. 56), "children of the East" "full of wild passion" (*Np,* p. 59). Eastern nights are full of "eternal mystery, blood, crime, love" (*Np,* p. 60). The East entices with a charm that is "devilishly dark" and "divinely mysterious" (*Np,* p. 22) and with the promise of hearing the "symphony of utter wildness" (*Np,* p. 62). It is the antithesis of the

West. Lilien, the protagonist of *Czerwone dusze,* gives a detailed account of the diametrically opposed characteristics of the Orient and of Europe: here, depth, romanticism, and soul; there, superficiality, rationalism, and classicism. In a word, all is as it should be: the Arabs are wild and vengeful, the Bedouin women are unbelievably beautiful and sensual, and in the voices of the hyenas rings the grim music of the desert . . .

The reason for frequently quoting Feldszuh's texts is that the myth of the Orient appears there in its purest and most conventional form:

> Myth of the desert, of Bedouins, odalisques, crocodiles, harems, eunuchs, loves, betrayals, fights, revenge, of noblemen's horses, of charming nights, jackals, hyenas, mosques, dervishes. A safe with a thousand fairy tales, princesses, treasures, carpets, camels, hetaeras and servants of love. The eternity of monotony, ecstasy, rapture, faith. The wild projectile from god's bow for the rush of blood, heroism, the knightly stance and sensual women. (*Czd,* p. 64)

The wild, the primitive, the sensual, the mysterious—Feldszuh resorts to strong and banally sensational effects to spice his Palestinian essays and short stories.

Feldszuh makes rather frequent use of the device that holds together the fragment of text just quoted. It comes down to putting together a catalogue of stage props, of exotic signs, and of evocative stereotypical watchwords. By delighting in otherness [40] and by presenting synopses of exotic images, [he] parades exoticism before the reader and dazes with the rate at which he displays the various requisites: "Carpets, eunuchs, male servants, female servants, narghiles, depth of thought, contemplation, desert, whispers, flashes of eyes, Arab stoicism" (*Czd,* p. 90); "cedars, cypresses, stone pines, villages, groves, gardens, vineyards, mud huts" (*Czd,* p. 101).

Feldszuh is not alone in the use of this technique for constructing images of the Orient. A similar approach is used by Eker, who presents Palestine from the viewpoint of a tourist dazed by the noise of the East and depicting it:

> I love a colorful crowd, heart-warming, pleasant,
> Of noisy shoeshine boys, the braying of mules and asses
> thrilling lanes, narrow and twisted bazaars brownly overgrown with dates.
>
> Old tarbooshes, red, rainbow-colored turbans,
> hookahs in the little coffee houses and sweet cool drinks
> and the shepherds wailing their long "Shvo-ye! Shvo-ye!"
> recesses, gates, vaults, minarets, little steps—
> I love the loud talk, noise, traffic, racket, hum, Eastern fruit,

vases, colorful dresses, carpets, turbans
black burnouses, soft like the nights of the Levant,
magic, the beauty of the Orient—its tremendous charm.
("Żywa Jerozolima" [Living Jerusalem], *Ncs,* p. 22)

Thus it is the Oriental, Levantine, and Eastern qualities—to use the epithets in the poem—that attract and bewitch.

The perspective of delight in the East, so clear in "Żywa Jerozolima," dominates [Anda] Eker's cycle of Palestinian poems whose form is that of a notebook from a trip. What distinguishes this notebook is its fantastic, fairy tale tone, present also in Eker's visions of Eretz Israel. This tone is especially pronounced in her recollections of Palestine ("W ojczyznie naszej" [In our fatherland], "Wspomnienie o cukierence arabskiej," "W nocy wołają wabiąco . . ." [They call alluringly in the night . . .], "Ballada o Tyberjadzie"):

In the warm and golden settlements the red wine sparkles,
The palms sway in the radiance, the fragrant almond trees are in bloom.
And in the sapphire bay sailboats float quietly into the distance
(A. Eker, "W ojczyznie naszej" [In our fatherland], *Mch,* p. 111)

The perspective of exoticism is also easy to spot in Zimmermann's and Feldszuh's images of Palestine. There is the fondness for generic oriental scenes and for Eastern landscapes, for prayers to the otherness of Palestine, and there is the use of Eastern intrigue as a plot element (Feldszuh's *Selim: Noce dzikich skał Galilei* [Selim: Nights of the wild rocks of the Galilee] and Adler's *Zemsta Beduinki* [Revenge of the Bedouin woman]). Also, there are open declarations in favor of this way of perceiving Palestine, of sensing in it the "direct breath of the exotic East, with its unlimited variety of colors and expressions, with its originality of dress, language and song" (*T,* p. 10).

The fascination with the exoticism of the Orient, and above all with its wild and primeval strains, is especially striking in the works of Feldszuh. His *Czerwone dusze* is a Palestinian gutter novel based on a sensational and melodramatic Eastern intrigue. (This was probably the reason for its tremendous reader appeal, compared with, say, the little volumes of Polish-Jewish poetry, and for its having gone through two editions in a short time.)[41] When resorting to devices of questionable artistic value (such as the use of eroticism in a manner bordering on pornography), Feldszuh claimed that he merely wanted to depict the particular tone of the Orient. Accordingly, he described orgies and sadomasochistic practices in oriental brothels, attractions offered to Europeans interested in "tasting the East." All this fitted the stereotype of a sensual and voluptuous Orient breathing "utter wildness."

Curiously enough, these very stereotypes corresponded in some way to the dreams of the new life—a life that was to be colorful, full of adventures, even stormy. Hence descriptions of oriental scenery in Polish-Jewish literature featured not only "wild Bedouins" but also *halutzim* or *shomrim,* strong, pleasure-seeking men avid for life, heroes of Eastern masquerades. They join Bedouin tribes and take part in intertribal warfare (*Tirsa).* They don kaffiyehs and burnooses and change from *halutzim* to "Jewish sheiks." Suitably disguised, they steal Bedouin secrets (H. Adler, *Zemsta Beduinki* [Revenge of the Bedouin woman]).

Such masquerades were, of course, obvious manifestations of Orientalism. But they allowed an interpretation other than that of the triumph of a convention of popular literature. The East, with all its wild and primeval flair, was also supposed to be an oasis of life close to nature. Arabs were brother Semites in happy harmony with nature. Adler presents one of his heroines in this way: "the primitive soul of a girl in whom everything was natural, untouched by a distorted civilization, always original and great in its essence" (*AiJ,* p. 62).

Thus being under the spell of the Orient was to some extent a manifestation of the yearning for nature. Jews born in Palestine were presumably natural, primeval, and wild; with these traits in mind, Polish-Jewish writers referred to them as Palestinians. Hebrew songs were "full of the East and of desire" (*Np,* p. 47), and the erotic freedom characteristic of the new life manifested the true nature of the "children of the East."

Another important aspect of Eastern masquerades was that they were attempts to take root in the Orient. This aspect is also most explicit in the writing of Feldszuh, whose heroes often discover that they are people of the East consumed by "ur-Eastern desires of the senses" (*Czd,* p. 80) and think that they hear in the music of a Bedouin caravan the melody of their own soul: "These tones sound strangely close to him; why, these are the sounds of his soul, of his ur-soul, foreign songs had sounded in the sad Diaspora, foreign melodies had rocked him to sleep. But these are the youthful sounds of his self, and they woke his soul and rocked it to bliss and peace" (*Np,* p. 10). On another occasion, the writer did not hesitate to juxtapose the prayer of an old Talmudist and the chant of the muezzin and to claim that they contained similar tones.

One of the consequences of the search for oriental roots was the exoticizing and orientalizing of the biblical past and the imparting to it a style in harmony with the directives of "primevalness," "naturalness," and "wildness":

> Memories and images woke deep inside him. . . . In this land, next to the Judean hills, hundreds of generations of his forefathers had tilled their soil by the sweat of their brows, hundreds of generations had lived their lives. Here were performed the joyful dances of the beautiful daughters of Canaan, and swarthy bodies had swayed to the rhythm of love. Here the wild eyes of the sons of Eretz, full of lusts, had flashed rainbows of passion and had shone with the might of their battles and victories. (*Np,* p. 35)

This stylization implied a revaluation of the biblical tradition and the discovery in it of new dimensions.

This getting used to the East was also an attempt to overcome the foreignness of Palestine and to make its otherness and exoticism near and one's own. It was an expression of the hope that the home being built would endure, and that there would be a brotherhood between "Israel, the old son of this land," and its "younger son the Arab" (*Np,* p. 40). When he is host to a Bedouin caravan in a pardes, Feldszuh's hero, a *shomer,* is filled with a "sense of nearness to this nation, whose wild looks and fearsome eyes had initially so alienated and repelled him. He felt that we come from the same race, that we share the same richness of soul and the same love of all that is noble" (*Np,* p. 38).

The Zionist and Palestinian threads in Polish-Jewish literature formed a distinct and well-defined stream. At its foundation was a challenge to European culture, to the postwar European order, and to the place of the Jewish collectivity in it. This challenge led to a vision of a new life, or rather a new Jewish situation, one opposed to the Diaspora as well as to the European order. It brought with it national and personal rebirth, and it promoted the building of a new society that emphasized the values of community and of labor.

7

The Jewish Self-Portrait

A Trial Balance

Looking at Polish-Jewish literature from the viewpoint of themes and images that recur in a rather intense and conventionalized form, though only one of many approaches, allows us to uncover the fundamental topics of this literature more effectively than other approaches. In accordance with the principles of thematic criticism, these fundamental topics are to be thought of as the record of singularly vital experience. If we peruse the Jewish self-portrait and look beyond the tangle of its constituent motifs and images without losing sight of its sources, then we discover two such topics, namely, identity and rootedness. They provide a platform for the key Jewish experience: the search for the shape and sense of Jewishness in its private and collective dimensions and the search for a real and symbolic space of rootedness, a fatherland both geographic and spiritual.

What is gained from other ways of reading the Polish-Jewish literature? Suppose we adopted the historico-literary approach and looked at the literary genres—poetry, prose (novels, short stories, journalism), and drama—represented in it. The immediate observation is the dominant role of poetry, from the viewpoint of quantity as well as quality, and the relative insignificance of drama. This phenomenon can be explained at least in part by the character of Polish-Jewish literary life: for a poem to be effective it was enough to publish it in a newspaper, whereas the possibilities for staging Polish-Jewish dramas were few and far between.

Now suppose we looked at Polish-Jewish literature with a view to apprehending its characteristic ideational and artistic tendencies. The [two] clearest tendencies turn out to be opposed to one another: the sentimental stream relied on traditional culture, the culture of the shtetl, whereas the broadly interpreted Zionist stream was linked with the old-new culture of rebuilding Palestine.

These two streams also differed radically in their artistic forms. The poetry-dominated sentimental stream was characterized by its rootedness in traditional culture and by its reliance for inspiration on folklore and on Yiddish literature. Here we come across frequent parodies and paraphrases of folkloric threads whose form is a stylized version of such folk genres as the ballad.[1] Szymel gave (splendid!) artistic shape to Chełm motifs.[2] Safrin used Hasidic threads.[3] Dresdner availed himself of local Lvov Jewish legends.[4] The sentimental stream bequeathed to Polish culture an array of traditional Jewish topics, especially those that constitute the folk treasury of Jewishness: beliefs pertaining to the Messiah, legends about the prophet Elijah, and tales about the Golem.[5] It also assimilated images and motifs derived from Yiddish literature, for example from the works of I[cchak] L[ejb] Perec, Szołem Alejchem, An-ski, and P[erec] Hirszbein.[6] In the sentimental stream, characterized by its turn to the past and its clear evasive tendencies, tradition is regarded as a tool for a covenant with the world; in association with childhood, it evokes a state of existential safety, peace, and harmony.

The opposing stream reflected a variety of threads of Zionist ideology embodied in more or less radical Zionist positions. The more radical position echoed the watchwords of the pioneer movement: the apotheosis of the New and the demand to build a new world, a new social order, and a new order of relations among people. The far less radical position emphasized primarily the national tasks of Palestine-related work. We find in this stream a fair number of occasional and propagandistic texts, such as songs of Zionist and pioneer organizations[7] as well as a considerable number of prose writings permeated with reportage and marked by tendentiousness. The reportage derived from various authenticating devices frequently employed by Polish-Jewish prose writers. The tendentiousness led to the elaboration, within this stream, of a model of the Zionist educational novel. This stream was characterized by a critical attitude toward traditional culture and a turn toward the future, a future that was to be marked by the triumph in Jewish life of new forms reconstituting in part biblical models.

If one looks at the two streams in question against the background of contemporary developments in Polish and Jewish literatures, then it turns out that analogies can be found in both. For example, Chone Shmeruk finds in interwar Yiddish literature a conservative movement of adoration of tradition, marked by "condemnation of large towns and a call for a return to the shtetl to strengthen and continue the now threatened traditional mode of life."[8] This points to the possibility of linking the attachment to the values of traditional life, so characteristic of the sentimental stream of Polish-Jewish literature, with the traditionalist tendencies in Yiddish literature. Here it is significant that the praise of provinces and suburbs and the antiurban tone are found in the writings of bilingual Polish-Jewish authors. Two such authors were Szymel and Fenster, both of whom wrote in Polish and in Yiddish. The traditional Jewish topics were the main raw material for Horacy Safrin, author of the little volume *Fun mencz un fun got* (Of man and god; 1926). The developing Palestinian life, its new order, and the ideology of the *halutz* movement were an important topic of Hebrew literature, created by authors of the third aliyah, who came to Palestine in the early twenties. This topic was also picked up by Yiddish prose writers.[9]

Polish-Jewish literature had strong worldview links with Jewish literature, but artistically it looked to Polish literary models. I think that this division between its worldview and artistic dimensions is significant. While it is true that quintessentially Polish topics turned up in the writings of certain Polish-Jewish poets (Szymel wrote about the ensigns of 1830 and about Słowacki; Ihr about the Mickiewicz figure Gustaw; Dresdner about Słowacki; and Brandstaetter's interests included Kochanowski), they were only used occasionally and were outside the mainstream of Polish-Jewish literature. In fact, polemics against Polish literary conventions for viewing the Jewish world (for example, Mickiewicz's Jankiel or Adam Szymański's figure of Srul from Lubartów) were more frequent than reaching for "Polish topics."

But matters were radically different when it came to the tradition of artistic speech. In the introduction to the posthumous little volume of Anda Eker, [*Melodia chwili,*] the poet's father noted that her writings showed "echoes of Tuwim, Wierzyński, Pawlikowska-Jasnorzewska" and an absorption in the "golden tones of Lenartowicz, Konopnicka, and Kazimiera Zawistowska."[10] As a literary critic, Szymel was strongly in favor of the Skamander model of poetry,[11] which he realized in his literary practice. These tastes were shared by Stefan Pomer, who was definitely an apprentice in Tuwim's school. Rosenfeld's writings show traces of the poetic conventions of Young Poland. Brandstaetter appealed to Polish classical and pseudoclassical traditions. Wit was to be a follower of Peiper.

The convergence of tone between Polish and Polish-Jewish literatures is also clear in reflective lyricism (which I have not discussed extensively in this book). Young Polish-Jewish poets who debuted in the early thirties, just like their Polish contemporaries from the dark second decade of the interwar period, were "facing the night" (this is what Szymel wanted to call one of his collections of poems). The dark, pessimistic tone, conversations with a Hidden God, intimations and visions of death, moods of "autumnal fears," the popularity of the nocturne and elegy as forms—all these seem to point to a certain connection between Polish-Jewish poetry and the atmosphere of Polish lyrical poetry in the thirties.

There is no doubt that a comparative study of Polish-Jewish literature against the background of Polish and Jewish literatures would be of greatest interest. Unfortunately, such studies cannot be undertaken in the present state of research on Polish-Jewish literary connections. Comparative studies in this area are extremely rare,[12] for they require competence in three cultural areas, namely, Yiddish, Hebrew, and Polish. Thus it is clear that the development of such studies is a matter for the future. On the Polish side, such studies would be aided by a detailed investigation of Jewish motifs in older, mainly nineteenth-century, literature. While it is true that interest in this range of problems increased in the eighties, few monographs written at that time deal with Jewish motifs or threads.[13]

My own modest attempts to study Polish-Jewish literature from just such a perspective[14]—of course, with reference to the Polish tradition—show the considerable distinctiveness of that literature's linguistic conventions. For example, when it comes to the motif of the Sabbath, the language of Polish-Jewish literature turns out to be very close to the linguistic conventions of Jewish literature.[15]

If one refers Polish-Jewish writing to the tradition of Jewish topics in Polish literature, then it turns out that its distinctiveness consists not only in its appeal to topics of Jewish culture but also in its specification of the topography of the familiar and the alien, which is different from that of Polish culture when the latter tries to deal with Jewish topics. As is well known, such topography is an expression of the opposed terms "familiar" and "alien," [in effect, "ours" versus "theirs"—Trans.] which is fundamental for the identity of every culture. In Polish literature, the Jewish world is, for obvious reasons, an alien sphere ["theirs"], whereas in Polish-Jewish literature it is a familiar one ["ours"]. But this sense of belonging is expressed in Polish. To some extent, the resulting tension is dissolved by the biographical element—with which Polish-Jewish writing is permeated—which supports and emphasizes a belonging conceivably diluted by Polish. The autobiographical pact with the reader is also a pact of authenticity: what is at stake here is the truth of the description of the Jewish world, the importance and reliability of art as a cognitive means to master reality.

This brings us to yet another possible way of reading Polish-Jewish literature. If we treat it as a record of Jewish reality, then it registers this reality at a moment of vast transformation, midway between the declining home of traditional life and the new Palestinian life. For a modern reader, the following description of an apartment house on Nalewki street, written by Maurycy Szymel in the summer of 1939, is piercingly moving:

> everything here breathed temporariness. Much as at departure time, or prior to a journey, straw mattresses were dragged out of rooms, put down anywhere, cups of coffee, of tea, were brought out for people lying on litter. This is what the Hebrews must have looked like on that memorable night before escaping from Egypt—black, bearded, drenched with sweat and tired to death after building Pithom and Rameses.[16]

The world on the eve of leaving yet another home of slavery. Jews waiting for the sign of liberation, for the words of a new Book of Exodus, for the next crossing of the Red Sea . . .

Appendix

Polish-Jewish Writers and the Primary and Secondary Literature

This appendix contains information about writers, critics, and journalists omitted from the existing dictionaries of Polish writers and from the Polish biographical dictionary. A list of these information sources may be found on pages 158–160 of this appendix.

Henryk Adler (?–?)

Pen names: Hanan Neszer, Neszer (Eagle), ha

Journalist, prose writer, literary critic, translator. Spent the years 1920–24 in Palestine as a pioneer. Lived in Warsaw from the mid-twenties. Published in the Polish and Polish-Jewish newspapers *Comoedia, Wiadomości Literackie, Chwila, Nowy Dziennik,* and *Nasz Przegląd.*

Works

Ariela and Jubal: Palestyńskie opowieści romantyczne, Warsaw, 1931.

Translations

U wrót nowego życia: Powieść-utopia (Altneuland) by T. Herzl. Warsaw, 1928.

In preparing this appendix, I made use of the following special materials: questionnaires, translated by Ruth Szenfeld and kept in the House of Writers; materials scattered throughout the interwar Polish-Jewish press; publications in the Polish-language Israeli press; and information based on conversations with and letters from Janina Altman, Mariona Andre, Arie-Leona Bauminger, Michał Borwicz, Roman Brandstaetter, Natan Gross, Irena Kanfer, Ryszard Loew, Julian Stryjkowski, and Abraham Suckewer [Sutskever]. [E. P.-J.]

Secondary Literature

On *Ariela and Jubal:* Piwiński, L. *Wiadomości Literackie* 1931, no. 395.
"Książka z życia palestyńskiego." *Chwila* 1931, no. 4286.
On translation of T. Herzl, *U wrót nowego życia:* Hirszhorn, S. "Ideał żydowski w szacie beletrystycznej T. Herzl, *U wrót nowego życia* po polsku: Przekład H. Adlera." *Nasz Przegląd* 1929, no. 45. Nussenblatt, T. "Altneuland: U wrót nowego życia." *Chwila* 1930, no. 4037.

Jakub Appenszlak (1894–1950)

Pen name: Pierrot
Journalist, poet, prose writer, translator, literary and theatrical critic. Publisher of *Nasz Przegląd* and its editor in chief in the years 1923–39. Established the Polish-Jewish club "Tłumackie 13."* Contributed to many Polish and Polish-Jewish papers (*Izraelita, Złoty Róg* (as editorial secretary), *Prawda, Echa Literacko-Artystyczne, Widnokręgi, Głos Żydowski, Przegląd Codzienny, Nowy Dziennik, Chwila, Nasz Kurier, Kurier Warszawski*). Traveled extensively in Europe and in Palestine. Just before the outbreak of the war, he ended up in the United States, where he spent the rest of his life. He lived in New York, editing its Polish-language newspaper *Nasza Trybuna* from 1940 to 1950.

Works

Mowie polskiej: Poemat. Warsaw, 1915.
Piętra: Dom na Bielańskiej. Warsaw, 1933.
The Black Book of Polish Jewry. New York, 1943.

Translations

Państwo żydowskie by T. Herzl. Warsaw, 1917, 1929, 1934.
Notatki komiwojażera by Shołem Aleijchem. Warsaw, 1925, reprinted 1958.
Motke ganew by Shalom Ash. Warsaw, 1925.
Pamiętniki by T. Herzl. Vol. 1. Warsaw, 1932.

Secondary Literature

On *Mowie polskiej:*
"From literature." *Izraelita* 1915, nos. 14–15.

*The address of the association of Jewish writers in Warsaw in the interwar period and center of literary life. [Trans.]

On *Piętra:*

Advertisement. *Nasz Przegląd* 1930, no. 78.

Kanfer, M. [pen name M. K.]. *"Piętra* Jakuba Appenszlaka." *Nowy Dziennik* 1933, no. 79.

Szymel, M. *"Piętra żydowskiej Warszawy." Opinia* 1933, no. 8.

"Głosy krytyków o powieści *Piętra." Nasza Opinia* 1933, no. 181.

Hirszhorn, S. "Momenty społeczne w *Piętrach." Nasz Przegląd* 1933, no. 43.

Paulina Appenszlak [Appenszlakowa, Fogiel] (?–1976)

Pen name: Jamajka

Journalist, translator, poet. Wife of Jakub Appenszlak. During the years 1928–33, she was the editor of *Ewa,* a weekly for Jewish women. She traveled extensively in Palestine (in the company of Anda Eker, among others) and in Europe (including a trip to Yugoslavia in the company of Maria Dąbrowska, among others). In 1939 she went with her husband to the United States. She returned to Poland on the eve of World War II but managed to leave for Palestine. She remarried. Her second husband was a journalist who worked in the sports section of *Nasz Przegląd.*

Translations

Cylka z lasu: Romans by Z. Segałowicz. Warsaw, 1929.

Życie bez tajemnic by V. Baum. Warsaw, 1933.

Wilhelm Berkelhammer (1889–1934)

Journalist, political and social activist. After graduating from gymnasium in Tarnów, he studied law in Vienna. Worked as a lawyer in Tarnów and in Cracow. Was one of the editors of the monthly *Moriah* (Vienna). In the years 1919–20 and 1925–34, he was editor in chief of *Nowy Dziennik.* In 1922, he published *Nowiny Codzienne* in Warsaw. Worked for the Lvov *Chwila.* Member of the Zionist party Hitachdut. Active in the Centralna Organizacja Syjonistyczna [Central Zionist Organization] and in many Jewish cultural and philanthropic organizations. Vice president of the syndicate of Cracow journalists. Died suddenly of a heart attack.

Works

My i narody świata. Cracow, 1922.

Secondary Literature

Fallek, W. "Stosunek Żydów do narodów świata." *Chwila* 1922, no. 1284

Obituaries

Chwila 1934, no. 5545.

Tygodnik Żydowski 1934, no. 34. Fallek, W. "Berkelhammer: Drogowskaz dla obecnych i następnych pokoleń." *Nowy Dziennik* 1934, no. 224.

Schiper, I. "Wilhelm Berkelhammer: Wspomnienie pośmiertne." *Opinia* 1934, no. 35.

Izydor Berman (ca. 1898–1942)

Pen names: Adam Niedźwiedzki, Iber

Poet, prose writer, satirist, translator, literary critic, journalist. Doctorate in Germanic studies. Gymnasium teacher in Lvov. Associated with the artistic circle around Ostap Ortwin. A foremost Polish-Jewish critic and translator. Contributed to many Polish and Polish-Jewish papers *(Skamander, Wiadomości Literackie, Pologne Litéraire, Sygnały, Kamena, Opinia, Nasza Opinia, Lektura, Chwila, Nowy Dziennik, Nowy Głos).* Editor of the satirical weekly *Chochoł.* Meritorious translator and popularizer of Franz Kafka, Joseph Roth, Max Brod, and Józef Wittlin, whose *Sól ziemi* [Salt of the earth] he translated into German. Perished in the Janów death camp.

Translations

Hotel Savoy by J. Roth. Lvov, 1928.

Borgia: Rasputin by A. Henschke [pen name Klabund]. Warsaw, 1930.

With Broniewski, W. *Car Piotr: Powieść* by A. Henschke [pen name Klabund]. Warsaw, 1930.

Banda zbójecka by L. Frank. Lvov, 1933.

Śmierć made in Germany by H. Liepmann. Lvov, 1934.

W poszukiwaniu wolności by H. Kesten. Lvov, 1936.

Historia nocy 1002 by J. Roth. Warsaw, 1937.

Kariera Doris Hart by V. Baum. Lvov, 1937.

Miłość Doris Hart by V. Baum. Lvov, 1937.

Młodzież bez Boga by Ö. von Horvath. Lvov, 1938.

Anula by M. Brod. Lvov, 1939.

Berman was also one of the first translators of Franz Kafka's *Lekarz wiejski: Studio* 1936, no. 9.

Fryderyk Bertisch (ca. 1913–1941?)

Poet. Son of Godel Bertisch, the rabbi of a progressive synagogue in Stanisławów. Member of the artistic group Wzlot. Published poems included in the group's collective volume of poetry *Wieczór i myśli* (1936). Contributed to the Polish-Jewish press *(Nasza Opinia, Słowo).*

Works

Kwiaty na ugorze. Stanisławów, 1939.

Secondary Literature

Bujnicki, T. "Ach, poeci." *Słowo* 1939, no. 19.
Kowalkowski, A. "Nowości poetyckie." *Kultura* 1939, no. 29.
Sinko, T. [pen name R.]. "Wśród nowych książek." *Kurier Literacko-Naukowy* 1939, no. 19

Maksymilian Jakub Bienenstock (1881–1923)

Critic, translator, teacher, social activist. After graduating from gymnasium in Tarnów, he studied German at the Jagiellonian University, receiving his doctorate in 1904. Worked as a teacher in Wadowice, Stryj, and Lvov (where he was the director of a Jewish gymnasium). Associated with the Zionist movement. Contributed to the Polish, Polish-Jewish, and German press *(Nowe Tory, Chwila, Nowy Dziennik, Xenien).*

Works

In Polish

"O wpływie niemieckim na twórczość Słowackiego uwag kilka: Schiller i Goethe." In *Sprawozdania dyrekcji c. k. gimnazjum w Wadowicach za rok szkolny 1909.* Reprinted as vol. 3, *Księga pamiątkowa ku uczczeniu setnej rocznicy urodzin Juliusza Słowackiego.* Lvov, 1909.
"Ze studjów nad historią oświaty w Polsce: Klementyna z Tańskis Hoffmanowa." In *Sprawozdania dyrekcji filii c. k. gimnazjum w Stryju za rok szkolny 1913.* Stryj, 1913.

In German

Das jüdische Element in Heines Werken. Leipzig, 1910.
Zur Theorie des modernen Dramas: Henrik Ibsen. Leipzig, 1913.

Translations

"Z. Krasiński, Die ungöttliche Komödie: Einleitung und Übersetzung." In *Sprawozdania filii c. k. gimnazjum w Stryju za rok szkolny 1912.* Stryj, 1912.
Wybór pism by S. Kierkegaard. Lvov, 1914.
Księga Jizkor poświęcona żydowskim strażnikom poległym w Palestynie. Lvov, 1920.

Obituary

Chwila 1923, no. 1450.

Zygmunt Bromberg-Bytkowski (1866–1923)

Dramatist, poet, essayist, theoretician and critic of art, social and political activist. One of the founders of the political party Hitachdut. Teacher. Director of the Jewish gymnasium in Lodz. Contributed to the Polish, Polish-Jewish, and German press *(Życie, Chimera, Lamus, Wiedza i Życie, Dziennik Krakowski, Krytyka, Nasz Kraj, Nowe Mody, Nowe Słowo Polskie, Nowe Życie, Postęp, Przegląd Tygodniowy, Przemysłowiec, Rocznik Samborski, Światło, Bohemia, Der Jude, Beiträge zur Ästhetik).*

Works

In Polish

"Stanisław Przybyszewski." In *Charakterystyki literackie: Żeromski, Przybyszewski.* Lvov, 1902.
Ines de Castro: Dramat w 4 aktach. Lvov, 1906.
O monologu w dramacie. Lvov, 1909.
"Słowacki jako dramaturg: Fragment." In *Księga pamiątkowa ku uczczeniu setnej rocznicy urodzin Juliusza Słowackiego, vol. 2, edited by W. Hahn, Lvov, 1909. Reprinted as* Juliuszowi Słowackiemu grono nauczycielskie Gimnazjum II we Lwowie. Lvov, 1909.

In German

Zur Kritik der Anwendung des Naturalismus in Drama: Das naturalistische Drama Hauptmanns: Eine Vorstudie. Lemberg, 1905.
Gerhart Hauptmanns Naturalismus. Hamburg, 1908.
Kontemplative und ekstatische Kunst. Lvov, 1910.

Translations

Natan mędrzec: Poemat dramatyczny w 5 aktach by E. G. Lessing. Złoczów, 1893.
Intruz by M. Maeterlinck. Lvov, 1902.
Ślepcy by M. Maeterlinck. Lvov, 1902.
Pieśń nad Pieśniami (Song of Songs). Illustrated by A. Szyk. Prepared for publication and with an introduction and commentary about the Song of Songs by W. Fallek. Lodz, 1924.

Secondary Literature

On *Charakterystyki literackie:* Chrzanowski, I. "Krytyka." *Książka* 1902, no. 9.

Sarnecki, Z. "Książki i czasopisma." *Przedświt* 1902, no. 81.

On *Ines de Castro:* Hahn, W. "Z literatury dramatycznej." *Myśl Polska* 1 (1906), no. 21.

Mianowski, T. "Dramat schematyczny: Kilka uwag z powodu dramatu p. Z. Bytkowskiego." *Nasz Kraj* (Lvov) 2 (1906), no. 15.

Flack, J. "Kronika literacka." *Przegląd Polski* (Cracow) 1 (1906–07).

On *Gerhart Hauptmanns Naturalismus:* Kretz, J. "Recenzje i sprawozdania." *Pamiętnik Literacki* 1910, no. 2.

On "Słowacki jako dramaturg": Zaleski, Z. L. "Krytyka." *Książka* 1910, no. 1.

On *Pieśń nad Pieśniami:* Bienenstock, M. [pen name M. B.]. "Recenzje." *Nowe Życie* 1924, no. 2.

Berkelhammer, W. "Przepiękna książka": Z. Bromberg-Brytkowski *Pieśń nad Pieśniami. Chwila* 1924, no. 2005.

Recollections

Fallek, W. "Twórczość i działalność Z. Bromberga-Bytkowskiego." *Nowy Dziennik* 1924, no. 79.

———. "Twórczość i działalność Z. Bromberga-Bytkowskiego." *Chwila* 1924, no. 1814.

———. "W dziesiątą rocznicę zgonu Z. Bromberga Bytkowskiego." *Nowy Dziennik* 1933, no. 86.

Zangen, B. "Z. Bromberg Bytkowski." *Chwila* 1933, no. 5086.

Brandstaetter, R. "Z. Bromberg-Bytkowski: W dziesiątą rocznicę zgonu." *Opinia* 1933, no. 1.

Izaak Deutscher (1907–1967)

Pen names: Krakowski, I.J.D., J.D., i.d., d-r

Poet, translator, Polish-Jewish critic. Born into, and grew up in, a religious family in Cracow. His early education was religious. He contributed to *Nowy Dziennik, Moment, Nasz Przegląd, Kurjer Wieczorny, Miesięcznik Literacki, Literarisze Bleter* (where he was for some time secretary of the editorial board). He came to Warsaw in 1925 and initially worked as a proofreader for *Nasz Przegląd.* At first a Zionist sympathizer, he was a member of the KPP [Communist Party of Poland] in the years 1926–32, publishing its publications until he switched his allegiance to Trotsky. He went to London in 1939 and became an English journalist *(Economist, Observer).* He was a historian of Marxism.

Karol Dresdner (ca. 1908–1943)

Poet, translator, critic, historian of Polish literature. Member of the group of poets associated with *Chwila.* One of his gymnasium teachers was Józef Wittlin. Studied Polish at the Jan Kazimierz University and obtained his doctorate in 1932 for a dissertation titled "Udział Żydów w poezji polskiej XIX wieku" [Participation in Polish poetry of the nineteenth century], written under the supervision of Professor J. Kleiner. Gymnasium teacher in Lvov. Contributed to the Polish and Polish-Jewish press *(Chwila, Nowy Dziennik, Opinia, Nasza Opinia, Nowy Głos, Filary, Miesięcznik Żydowski, Słowo, Dziennik Lwowski, Lwowskie Wiadomości Muzyczne i Literackie, Tygodnik Ilustrowany, Tęcza, Trybuna Akademicka, Nowe Widnokręgi)* and to scientific periodicals *(Filomata, Pamiętnik Literacki, Przegląd Humanistyczny, Kwartalnik Klasyczny).* Murdered in the Janów death camp.

Works

Heine i nieznajoma. Lvov, 1928.

Translations

Wizerunek własny żywota by U. Acosta. Warsaw, 1933, reprinted in 1960 (with an introduction by L. Kołakowski).

The History of Literature and of Folk Art

"Brat Gerszon: Jan Andrzej Ram." *Pamiętnik Literacki* 1928, no. 2.
"Z korespondencji J. I. Kraszewskiego: Listy Armanda Levy." *Przegląd Humanistyczny* 1931, nos. 1–2.
"Udział Żydów w poezji polskiej XIX wieku." *Miesięcznik Żydowski* 1932, no. 5.
"Krasiński a przechrzci." "Zjednoczenie." Lvov, 1932. Reprinted in *Chwila* 1932, nos. 4623–4624.
"Żydzi w powieściach Korzeniowskiego." *Przegląd Humanistyczny* 1933, no. 3.
"Listy Matiasa Bersohna do Augusta Bielowskiego." *Miesięcznik Żydowski* 1 (1935).
With Goldstein, M. *Kultura i sztuka ludu żydowskiego na ziemiach polskich.* Lvov, 1935.
With Charszewska, Z. *Wypisy z literatury polskiej dla klasy V.* Kiev-Lvov, 1940.

General Secondary Literature

Brandstaetter, R. "Między Syjonem a Golgotą," *Opinia* 1933, no. 20.
Löw, Ch. *Smok w słowiczym gnieździe: Żydzi w poezji Odrodzonej Polski. Warsaw, 1934. First appeared as* "Żydzi w poezji Odrodzonej Polski: Part 5. Poeci polsko-żydowscy." *Miesięcznik Żydowski* 1934.

Loew, R. "Przypomnienie Karola Dresdnera." *Nowiny-Kurier* 1975, no. 85.
———. *"Karol Dresdner."* Typescript. N.p., n.d.

Secondary Literature

On *Heine I nieznajoma:*
Wolf, Sz. "Dwaj młodzi poeci lwowscy." *Nowy Dziennik* 1928, no. 277.
Barbasz, W. "Wśród młodych poetów." *Chwila* 1928, no. 3367.
Wittlin J. [pen name j. w.]. "K. Dresdner, *Heine i nieznajoma."* *Wiadomości Literackie* 1928, no. 248.
On translation of U. Acosta, *Wizerunek własny żywota:*
Tillemann, O. *"Exemplar vitae humanae." Miesięcznik Żydowski* 1933.
Ihr, D. "Autobiografia Uriela Acosty." *Nowy Dziennik* 1933, no. 194.
On "Udział Żydów w poezji polskie XIX wieku":
Schipper, H. "Wśród pism i książek: K. Dresdner, 'Udział Żydów w poezji polskiej XIX wieku.' *Zjednoczenie* 1932, nos. 7–9.

Salomon Dykman (1917–1965)

Poet and translator. Born into a rabbinical family with Hebrew literary traditions (the writers Sz. Kantorowicz and A. Frank were close relatives on his mother's side). After graduating from a Hebrew gymnasium in 1934, he studied at the Instytut Nauk Judaistycznych [Institute of Judaic Studies] in Warsaw. Debuting as a translator in *Chwila* in 1934, he also contributed to *Nowy Dziennik, Chwila, Ster, Nasza Opinia,* and *Filary.* During the war, he lived in the Soviet Union. On his return to Poland in 1956, he resumed literary activity and, in particular, edited Edward Mezrycer's interwar translation of I. J. Singer's novel *Josie Kałb.* Soon thereafter, he emigrated to Israel.

Biographical Materials

"Salomon Dykman: Polski tłumacz Bialika." *Opinia* 1934, no. 29.
Dykman, "Nota autobiograficzna." *Nowy Dziennik* 1934, no. 244.

Anda Eker [Ekerówna] (1912–1936)

Poet. Member of the literary group associated with *Chwila.* Daughter of a Zionist activist who settled in Israel in 1933. Graduated from gymnasium in Lvov and studied at the Jan Kazimierz University. Traveled extensively in Europe (England, Switzerland, Italy, Holland, Denmark) and in the Middle East (in particular, in Egypt and Syria). Stayed for a time with her family in Palestine but returned to Poland because of poor health. Debuted with poems for children when she was still a teenager. Contributed to the Polish and Polish-Jewish press, especially with their supplements for the youngest readers *(Przegląd Mody, Chwila, Nowy Dziennik, Nasz Przegląd, Opinia, Nasza Opinia, Ewa, Okienko na świat).*

Works

Na cienkiej strunie. Lvov, 1936.

Melodia chwili: Poezje. Lvov, 1937.

Ojców dzieje: Dla dzieci i młodzieży. Lvov, 1937.

Mama śpiewa kołysankę: Bajki ilustrowane dla milusińskich. Lvov, 1937.

O świerszczyku muzykancie: Bajki ilustrowane dla milusińskich. Lvov, 1937.

Posthumous Recollections

Appenszlak, P. "Anda Eker." In *Almanach żydowski wydany przez H. Stachla.* Lvov, 1937.

Hirszprung, M. [pen name M. H.]. "O zmarłej poetce—wielkiej przyjaciółce dzieci: Pamięci Andy Eker." *Okienko na świat* 1937, nos. 7–8.

"W drugą rocznicę śmierci Andy Eker." *Nasza Opinia* 1937, no. 75.

Silberman, M. "W rocznicę śmierci Andy Eker (23 Jan. 1936–23 Jan. 1937)." *Słowo* 1937, no. 93.

———. "Anda Eker: Po drugiej rocznicy śmierci." *Nasza Opinia* 1938, no. 125.

S-r. "Kilka słów o spuściźnie błp. Andy Eker." *Nowy Dziennik* 12 June 1937.

Hirszprung, M. [pen name H. M.]. "Wspomnienie: W 3 rocznicę śmierci Andy Eker." *Okienko na świat* 1939, no. 3.

Berman, I. "Z teki pośmiertnej Andy Eker." *Nasza Opinia* 1937, no. 121.

Obituaries

Nasza Opinia 1936, no. 25.

Appenszlak, P. "Nad grobem Andy Eker." *Nasz Przegląd* 1936, no. 62.

Markus, N. "Błp. Anda Eker." *Nowy Dziennik* 1936, no. 64.

Kanfer, M. [pen name M. K.]. "Błp. Anda Eker." *Nowy Dziennik* 1936, no. 33.

Hirszprung, M. "Anda Eker nie żyje!" *Nowy Dziennik* 1936, no. 36.

Herzberg, N. "O umarłej poetce." *Chwila* 1936, no. 6115.

Secondary Literature

On *Na cienkiej strunie:*

Boruchowicz, M. [pen name m. b.]. "Między książkami: *Na cienkiej strunie:* Poezje Andy Eker." *Nowy Dziennik* 1936, no. 8.

Zawodziński, K. W. "Liryka i epika wierszem." In *Rocznik literacki za rok 1936,* edited by Z. Szmydt. Warsaw, 1937.

On *Melodia chwili:* Hulka-Laskowski, P. "Literatura piękna: *Melodia chwili.*" *Nowa Książka* 1939, no. 2.

Zawodziński, K. W. "Dwie poetki." *Wiadomości Literackie* 1938, no. 29.

———. "Liryka i epika wierszem." In *Rocznik literacki za rok 1937,* edited by Z. Szmydt. Warsaw, 1938.

Jaworski, W. "Nowości poetyckie: *Melodia chwili.*" *Sygnały* 1937, no. 32.

On *Ojców dzieje:*

Fraenkl, G. "Słoneczny światek." *Chwila* 1937, no. 6540.

Rubin [Reuwen] Feldszuh (1900–)

Pen names: Ben Szem; Benszem

Prose writer, journalist, publisher, political activist, teacher. Graduated from gymnasium in Czortków. In Palestine from 1919 to 1921, he worked as a pioneer building roads and preparing land for cultivation and was associated with the labor movement. In Vienna, he studied philosophy (receiving his doctorate in 1923) and psychology (especially interested in psychoanalysis). Graduate of the Wyższa Szkoła Rabiniczna [Advanced Rabbinical School] in Vienna. Married the pianist Perla Richter in 1928. Beginning in 1924, he taught at Hebrew gymnasium in Warsaw (and later became its vice director). He was a Zionist activist. Initially a sympathizer of the leftist Haszomer Hacair, he subsequently became a follower of Grossmann's revisionist Betar group. Publisher and editor of the Polish-Jewish papers *Nowa Era* (1928), *Nowy Czas* (1931), and *My sami* (1935–36). President of the Warsaw branch of the Związek Pisarzy i Dziennikarzy Hebrajskich [Association of Hebrew Writers and Journalists] and its national vice president. Founder of the Liga Mandatowa Polski nad Palestyną [League for a Mandate of Poland for Palestine] and of the Legion im. Berka Joselewicza. Contributed to the German, Hebrew, Yiddish, and Polish-Jewish press *(Wiener Morgenzeitung, Der Tag, Die Stimme, Die Neue Welt, Hacfira, Hayom, Bederech, Haboker, Herut, Hamaszkif, Derech Haszomer* (as editor), *Hajnt, Moment, Unzer express, Warszawer express, Chwila, Nowy Dziennik, Nasz Przegląd, Nasz Głos, Ster, Trybuna Literacka*). After the war, he was a member of the Centralny Komitet Żydowski [Central Jewish Committee] in Lublin and Warsaw. Left for Palestine in 1945. Teacher. Director of Laor gymnasium in Jaffa. Published recollections of the occupation period and a number of works in psychology, in Yiddish and Hebrew, respectively.

Works

In Polish

Noce palestyńskie. Warsaw, 1928.

Czerwone dusze. Warsaw, 1932.

In Hebrew

Me'al hakwarim hadomim. Tel-Aviv, 1946.
Bejn chomot ha'getto. Tel-Aviv, 1947. (Tales of the Warsaw ghetto.)

In Yiddish

Pojln brent . . . Buenos Aires, [1960?] (Recollections.)

Secondary Literature

On *Noce palestyńskie:*
Lector, "Palestyna w zwierciadle poezji," *Nasz Przegląd* 1929, no. 55.
On *Czerwone dusze:*
Note in *Ilustrowany Almanach Żydowski,* edited by J. Zineman. Warsaw, 1933.

Hersz Awrohem Fenster (1908–1942)

Poet, prose writer, translator. Graduated from gymnasium in Złoczów and then (according to L. Bauminger) studied at the Instytut Nauk Judaistycznych in Warsaw with a view to teaching. Contributed to the Polish-Jewish and Yiddish press *(Chwila, Nasza Opinia, Fołks cajtung, Arbeter cajtung, Wochenszrift far literatur, Literarisze bleter).* Stayed in Złoczów during the occupation and was taken to the Bełżec death camp from the Złoczów ghetto.

Works

In Polish

O tym, co opuszczam. n.p., 1932.

In Yiddish

Di lewone gejt unter: Lider. Warsaw, 1938.

Biographical Materials

Chwila 1932, no. 4641.
Nasza Opinia 1937, no. 85.

Riwka [Regina] Gurfein (1908–1983)

Polish-Jewish and Hebrew writer, journalist, teacher, literary critic, translator. Born in the village of Żarnowa in the Rzeszów region. After graduating from gymnasium in Sanok, she studied agriculture at the Jagiellonian University then literature and education at the Hebrew University. Debuting in Polish in *Chwila* in 1925, she also contributed to *Nowy Dziennik*. She published a great deal of correspondence from [her new home] Israel (under pen name of Rywka z Karkur). Beginning in 1934, she also wrote in Hebrew. Contributed to the newspapers *Dwar Ha'poelet, Ha'miszmar, Dawar, Moznaim,* and *Hedim,* among others. Translated into Hebrew Julian Stryjkowski's *Austeria* and *Sen Azrila* and a volume of poetry by Anna Kamieńska. She served as a diplomatic representative of Israel in Poland from 1948 to 1951.

Works

In Hebrew

Neurim be'szemesz. N.p., 1954. (Novel for youth.)
Taam szel bchira. N.p., 1975. (Story about kibbutz Ejn Szemer.)
Le'ever chof alum. N.p., 1981. (Literary essays.)

Józef Hartblaj (?–?)

Prose writer.

Works

Jehoszua: Powieść osnuta na tle życia "chaluców." Warsaw, 1928.

Secondary Literature

Rosenzweig, B. "Józef Hartblaj's *Jehoszua," Chwila* 1928, no. 3338.
Warszawiak, J. "Nowa książka polska o nowej Palestynie," *Nowy Dziennik* 1928, no. 14.

Henryk Hescheles (1886–1942)

Pen names: Henryk Trejtwart, Jerzy Zglicz, H.H.

Prose writer, translator, literary and theatrical critic, journalist. University studies in Vienna. Literary debut in 1912 (translations of poetry, articles devoted to literary criticism, reports from Germany to Polish papers). During World War I, served in the Austrian army and then in the Legiony* (1914–15). Editor in chief of the Lvov

*A military formation created by Józef Piłsudski. [Trans.]

Chwila from 1920 to 1939. His articles on public issues appeared also in other Polish-Jewish and Polish papers (such as *Nasz Przegląd* and *Przegląd Literacki*). Social and political activist. Member of the Emigration Society "Jeas" of the Żydowska Rada Emigracyjna [Jewish Emigration Council] and of many economic institutions (such as Warsztaty Rękodzielnicze im. A. Korkisa [A. Korkis Handicraft Workshops] and Związek Żydowskich Spółdzielni Mleczarskich [Association of Jewish Milk Cooperatives "Chema"]). Took part in the Wszechświatowy Kongres Żydowski [Jewish World Congress] in Geneva. Took an active part in the social and cultural life of Lvov as a member of the Lvov Rada Miasta [Lvov City Council], of the Rada Nadzorcza Miejskiego Muzeum Przemysłu Artystycznego [Supervisory Council of the City Museum for Industrial Art], and of the Syndykat Dziennikarzy Lwowskich [Syndicate of Lvov Journalists]. Traveled extensively in Palestine and in Spain. When the war broke out, he escaped to Romania but returned to Poland to resume the publication of *Chwila.* Murdered by the Germans in 1942.

Maria Hochberżanka [Hochberg-Mariańka] (1913–)

Poet. Contributed to *Nowy Dziennik, Okienko na Świat, Czyn, Ilustrowany Kurjer Codzienny,* and *Kurjer Literacko-Naukowy.* During the war, she took part in the work of the Rada Pomocy Żydom [Council for Aid to Jews] under the name of Maria Mariańska. In Israel after 1948.

Works

Mariańska, M., and Mariański, M. *Wśród przyjaciół i wrogów: Poza gettem w okupowanym Krakowie.* Cracow, 1988.

Daniel Ihr (?–1942)

Poet, feuilletonist, critic. Member of the literary group associated with *Chwila.* Graduate of Jewish gymnasium in Lvov. Studied Polish at the Jan Kazimierz University under Professor J. Kleiner. Winner of the 1934 literary competition of the Żydowski Fundusz Narodowy [Jewish National Fund]. Contributed to the Polish and Polish-Jewish press *(Ilustrowany Kurjer Codzienny, Chwila, Nowy Dziennik, Opinia, Nasza Opinia).* Perished in Lvov in 1942.

Works

Pożegnanie młodości. Lvov, 1934.

Secondary Literature

Lauterbach, A. "List do poety." *Chwila* 1934, no. 5376.
Boruchowicz, M. *"Pożegnanie młodości." Nowy Dziennik* 1934, no. 125.
Hulka-Laskowski, P. *Nowa Książka* 1935, no. 5.
Brandstaetter, R. *"Pożegnanie młodości." Opinia* 1934, no. 24.
Berman, I. [pen name I. B.]. "Debiut poetycki D. Ihra." *Miesięcznik Żydowski* 3 (1934).

Irma (Irena) Kanfer (1920–)

Poet, translator, journalist. Daughter of Mojżesz Kanfer, head of the literary section of *Nowy Dziennik*. Contributed to the Polish and Polish-Jewish press *(Naprzód, Nowy Dziennik, Nasz Przegląd, Nasza Opinia)*. Studied political science at the Wolna Wszechnica Polska [Free Polish University] in Warsaw. In France after 1937. Studied French literature in Paris and Geneva. Became French writer and journalist.

Works

In Polish

Dwa akordy. Cracow, 1936.
W mleczną drogę. Cracow, 1937.
"Bariery: Powieść." Manuscript.

In French

Avant—Être. N.p., 1966. (Poems.)
Contes du milieu de la nuit. N.p., 1972. (Short stories.)
Le luth brisé. N.p., 1968. (Anthology of poems about the Holocaust.)

Secondary Literature

On *Dwa akordy:*
Fleischman, I. "Udany debiut." *Nowy Dziennik* 1936, no. 26.
b. (I. Berman?). *"Dwa akordy." Nasza Opinia* 1936, no. 33.
Putrament, J. *"Dwa akordy." Poprostu* 1936, no. 14.
Zawodziński, K. W. "Liryka i epika wierszem." In *Rocznik literacki za rok 1936,* edited by Z. Szmydt. Warsaw, 1937.
On *W mleczną droge:*
Zawodziński, K. W. "Liryka i epika wierszem." In *Rocznik literacki za rok 1937,* edited by Z. Szmydt. Warsaw, 1937.

Mojżesz Kanfer (1880–1942)

Pen names: Moassi, -assi, -si, M.K.

Journalist, literary and theatrical critic, translator. For many years editor of the literary section of *Nowy Dziennik*. Son of the well-known Hebraist Mark M. Kanfer, who contributed to *Syrena*. Contemporary and friend of Szmuel Agnon (Czaczkes), the eminent Hebrew writer and Nobel prize winner. Dismissed from the Buczacz gymnasium for anarchist activity, Kanfer obtained his gymnasium graduation certificate [*matura*] in Brzeżany. Studied law in Vienna and in Lvov, where he was granted his doctorate in 1908. Socialist sympathizer and member of student socialist organizations. Married Gizela Waleria Stern in 1910. Fought as an Austrian army officer in World War I. In the early twenties he taught Polish literature in Wilno. In Cracow, after 1923. Contributed to a number of Polish-Jewish newspapers *(Nasz Przegląd, Chwila, Nasza Opinia, Nowe Życie)*. Founder of Towarzystwo Przyjaciół Teatru Żydowskiego w Polsce [Friends of the Jewish Theater in Poland]. Vice president of Związek Dziennikarzy Polskich Zachodniej Małopolski [Association of Polish Journalists of Western Małopolska]. Murdered in the Bełżec death camp.

Translations

Siedem przygód Odyseusza by H. Frank. Warsaw, 1931.
Zaczarowany kraj miłości by M. Brod. Cracow, 1932.
Matka by Sh. Asz. Warsaw, 1933.

Lucjan Krasucki (1902–1923)

Poet. Active in Zionist youth organizations in Kalisz.

Works

Wiersze wybrane. Kalisz, 1923.

Artur Lauterbach (?–?)

Poet, critic, translator, reviewer of literature, theater, and the fine arts. Connected with the Lvov *Chwila,* he contributed to the Polish and Polish-Jewish newspapers *Comoedia, Głos Literacki, Tygodnik llustrowany, Chwila, Nasz Przegląd,* and *Nowy Dziennik.*

Jakub Lewittes (ca. 1892–1942?)

Poet, journalist. Began to write while still a gymnasium student, under the "literary patronage" of Władysław Orkan. Soldier in the Austrian Army in World War I. In Warsaw, after the twenties. Lawyer (doctorate of law). Contributed to *Nowy Dziennik* and *Nasza Opinia.*

Works

Posthumus. Warsaw, 1930.

Secondary Literature

(h). "Poetycka gawęda i faktomontaż: Zbiór poezji Jakuba Lewittesa." *Nowy Dziennik* 1930, no. 277.

Napierski, S. "U poetów." *Wiadomości Literackie* 1932, no. 36.

Anzelm Lutwak (1877–?)

Poet, journalist, social and political activist. Graduated from gymnasium in Cracow in 1895. Studied law at the Jagiellonian University (doctorate in 1900), where he was one of the organizers of the Zionist academic societies Libanon and Haszachar-Przedświt. In Vienna from 1901 to 1903, he was a member of the Jung Jüdischer Klub. Among his friends were Martin Buber, Stefan Zweig, Natan Birnbaum, and Ephraim Moses Lilien. Debuted in the Lvov Zionist weekly *Przyszłość.* Published his work in the Polish, Polish-Jewish, and German newspapers *Wschód, Chwila, Nowy Dziennik, Nasz Przegląd,* and *Welt.* Played an active role in lawyers' organizations (member of Lwowska Izba Adwokatów [Lvov Chamber of Lawyers] and Stowarzyszenie Adwokatów Żydowskich [Association of Jewish Lawyers], among others). Published in professional law journals such as *Palestra, Gerichtshalle,* and *Geller's Zentralblatt für die juristische Praxis.* Editor in chief of *Głos Prawa* after 1924.

Adam Madler [Marek Bauman] (?–?)

Prose writer and dramatist. Contributed to *Nowy Dziennik, Opinia, Głos Poranny, Ilustrowana Rewia Tygodniowa.*

Works

Falista linia. Lodz, 1932.
Cienie zdarzeń. Warsaw, 1936.
Droga: Dramat w trzech aktach. Warsaw, 1937.
Irena Munk: Powieść. Warsaw, 1938.

Secondary Literature

On *Falista linia:*

Dudziński, B. "A. Madler, *Falista linia.*" *Wiadomości Literackie* 1934, no. 3.

Löw, Ch. "Adam Madler, *Falista linia.*" *Nowy Dziennik* 1934, no. 2.

Fallek, W. "Łódź w literaturze pięknej." *Nasz Przegląd* 1934, no. 42.

———. "Łódź w literaturze polskiej." *Nasza Opinia* 1936, no. 10.

Stolarzewicz, L. *Literatura w Łodzi w ciągu jej istnienia: Szkic literacki i antologia.* N.p., n.d.

On *Cienie zdarzeń:*

Drogoszewski, *Nowa książka* 1937, no. 9.

Andrzejewski, J. "Recenzje z książek." *Prosto z mostu* 1936, no. 24.

Kucharski, Z. "Pisarz, książka, czytelnik." *Tygodnik Ilustrowany* 1936, no. 24.

On *Droga:*

Dudziński, B. "Nowe książki." *Naprzód* 1937, no. 45.

On *Irena Munk:*

Dudziński, B. "Nowe książki." *Naprzód* 1939, no. 66.

Putrament, J. "Wśród nowych powieści." *Sygnały* 1939, no. 70.

Bronisław Mayer (?–?)

Pen name: Arieh

Poet. Member of the Stanisławów group Wzlot. Contributor to *Chwila.* Emigrated to Palestine around 1935, living in Kfar Hachoresz, from which he sent letters to the Polish-Jewish press.

Works

Pieśni Wertera. Stanisławów, 1934.

Pieśn chaluca: Poezja i proza. Stanisławów, 1934.

Secondary Literature

On *Pieśni Wertera:*

Sinko, T. [pen name R.]. "Wśród nowych książek." *Kurier Literacko-Naukowy* 1932, no. 134.

On *Pieśn chaluca:*

Zawodziński, K. W. "Liryka i epika wierszem." In *Rocznik literacki za rok 1934,* edited by Z. Szmydt. Warsaw, 1935.

Stefan Pomer [Pomeranz?] (?–1941)

Poet, prose writer, literary critic, translator. Member of the group connected with *Chwila.* Probably born in Borszczów. Studied Polish at the Jan Kazimierz University in Lvov. In Warsaw after 1930. Editor of Polish-Jewish daily *5 Rano* (1931–39). Contributed to the Polish and Polish-Jewish newspapers *Bluszcz, Gazeta Polska, Głos Literacki, Okolica Poetów, Głos Prawdy, Kurier Literacko-Naukowy, Tygodnik Ilustrowany, Chwila, Nowy Dziennik, Opinia, Nasza Opinia, Ster, Lektura, Nowy Głos,* and *Nasz Przegląd* as well as to the Yiddish newspaper *Globus.* After the outbreak of the war, Pomer ended up in Lvov, where he presumably died before the Germans entered the city (information supplied by J. Stryjkowski).

Works

On *Elegie podolskie.* Warsaw, 1931.

Translations

Trzy pary narzeczonych by Z. Segalowicz. Warsaw, 1935.
Bracia Aszkenazy by I. J. Singer. *Nasz Przegląd* 1935, nos. 105–189.

General Secondary Literature

Löw, Ch. *Smok w słowiczym gnieździe: Żydzi w poezji Odrodzonej Polski.* Warsaw, 1934. First appeared as "*Żydzi w poezji Odrodzonej Polski:* Part 5, Poeci polsko-żydowscy." *Miesięcznik Żydowski* 1934.

Secondary Literature

Sinko, T. [pen name R.] "Wśród nowych książek." *Kurier Literacko-Naukowy* 1931, no. 36.
Eker, A. "*Elegie podolskie:* Lyriczna geografia żydowskiej mieściny," *Nowy Dziennik* 1931, no. 312.
Ihr, D. "Elegie prowincji: Poezje Stefana Pomera." *Nowy Dziennik* 1931, no. 200.
Birkenmajer, J. "Poezja." *Polonista* 1932, no. 4.
Szczawiej, J. "Na młodym warszawskim Parnasie." *Kurier Literacko-Naukowy* 1934, no. 34.
Dresdner, K. "Z młodej poezji: *Elegie podolskie.*" *Chwila* 1931, no. 4431.
Note in *Chwila* 1931, no. 4431.

Jerzy Reitman (1888–?)

Polish-Jewish poet and social activist. Graduated from gymnasium in Lvov. Studied law at the Jan Kazimierz University, where he was a member of academic organizations of Jewish youth (such as "Judea"). Co-organizer of the Żydowski Dom Akademicki in Lvov. During World War I, he fought on the Italian front as an officer in the Austrian Army (and was awarded *Signum Laudis*). Lived in New York, Vienna, and Lvov. Served as director of Browary Lwowskie [Lvov Breweries]. In 1933, he started a tourist settlement, called "Zaświecie," in Korostów near Skole, which soon became popular with the "Galician" Jewish intelligentsia (one of the guests was Bruno Schulz). In the twenties, he contributed to *Chwila.*

General Information

Igel, E. "Korostów: Żywy poemat," *Chwila* 1935, no. 5939.

Runa Reitmanowa [Próchnik] (1890–?)

Journalist and social activist. Graduated from the Queen Jadwiga gymnasium in Lvov and then studied at the Jan Kazimierz University. Active in academic organizations of Jewish youth. From 1910 to 1912, she chaired the Związek Żydowskich Słuchaczek UJK [Association of (Female) Jewish Students of the Jan Kazimierz University]. After 1916 she devoted herself to social and philanthropic work. Besides other things, she organized a day nursery, an orphanage, a shelter for Jewish children, a Dom Pomocy Społecznej [Social Assistance Home], and the "Farma Ogrodnicza" ["Garden Farm"] society in Sygniówka. She spent the years 1921–1925 in Vienna. From 1925 to 1927, she was the editor of *Chwilka* (a supplement of the Lvov *Chwila* for children and youth); from 1928 to 1933, also the editor of *Dzienniczek* (a supplement of the Cracow *Nowy Dziennik*); and from 1931 to 1932, publisher of *"Kalendarz Społeczny."* After 1936, she was the co-organizer—with her husband Jerzy—of the tourist settlement "Zaświecie" in Korostów.

Syda Richter (?–1941)

Poet. Member of the Stanisławów group Wzlot. Contributed to the Polish-Jewish newspapers *Chwila, Słowo, Okienko na Świat.*

Works

Wiry. Stanisławów, 1932.

Karol Rosenfeld (?–?)

Cracovian poet and satirist. Took part in World War I. After the thirties, lived in Vienna. Galician collaborator of the Zionist press before 1918 *(Moriah, Wschód).* Contributed to the *Nowy Dziennik* in the twenties.

Works

Amori canto: Poemat o Sfinksie-Erosie. Cracow, 1918.
Kokota: Sketch z życia paryskiej elity. Cracow, 1918.
Piosenki kabaretowe: Strofki zza kulis ucieszněj nadscenki. Cracow, 1918.

Pożar krwi: Poezje z okopów wielkiej wojny. Cracow, 1919.
Na falach życia: Erotyki i inne poezje. Cracow, 1920.
W ciszy łez: Poezye golusu. Cracow, [ca. 1920].

Secondary Literature

On *Pożar krwi:*
Bienenstock, M. "Z najnowszych wydawnictw," *Chwila* 1919, no. 265.
Sinko, T. *Czas* 1920, no. 33.

Maurycy Schlanger (ca. 1915-ca. 1942)

Cracovian poet and journalist. Belonged to the Cracow circle of contributors to *Opinia* (together with Z. Königsberg, J. Greiwer, and M. Bornstein). Member of Zionist youth organizations. Graduated from gymnasium in 1934. Took part in a *hachszarah* that prepared the participants for life in Palestine. Published his works in the Polish and Polish-Jewish papers *Nasz Wyraz, Nowy Dziennik, Chwila, Słowo, Kontratak,* and *Opinia.* Perished during the occupation.

Works

Idę . . . Cracow, 1936.

Secondary Literature

Boruchowicz, M. [pen name m. b.]. "Wśród poetów." *Nowy Dziennik* 1936, no. 107.
Sinko, T. [pen name R.]. "Wśród nowych książek." *Kurier Literacko-Naukowy* 1936, no. 18.
Greiwer, J. [pen name Jotge]. "Debiut Schlangera." *Nasza Opinia* 1936, no. 38.
Silberman, M. *"Idę . . ." Słowo* 1937, no. 97.
Zawodziński, K. W. "Liryka i epika wierszem." In *Rocznik literacki za rok 1936,"* edited by Z. Szmydt. Warsaw, 1937.

Biographical Information

"Krakowskie koło współpracowników *Świata Młodych." Opinia* 1934, no. 9.
Schlanger, M. "A imię ich . . . cztery." *Nasza Opinia* 1935, no. 21.

Minka Silberman (ca. 1912–1941)

Poet and translator. Cofounder of the Stanisławów literary group Wzlot. Published poetry in *Chwila, Nowy Dziennik, Słowo, Nasza Opinia,* and *Okienko na Świat.* Perished in Stanisławów after the invasion of the Germans.

Works

W cieniu życia. Stanisławów, 1937.
Dzień matki. Stanisławów, 1938.

Secondary Literature

On *W cieniu życia:*
Safrin, H. *"W cieniu życia:* Poezje Minki Silberman." *Chwila* 1937, no. 6554.
———. *"W cieniu życia." Słowo* 1937, no. 112.
On *Dzień matki:*
Es. Am. "Wydawnictwa młodej literatury: *Dzień matki." Słowo* 1938, no. 156.

Władysław Szlengel (ca. 1914–1943)

Poet, satirist, songwriter. Author of cabaret texts. Collaborated with the small theatrical company "Ali Baba," among others. Published his writings in the Polish and Polish-Jewish newspapers *Nasz Przegląd, Chochoł, Szpilki,* and *Sygnały.* Took part in the September campaign and the defense of Warsaw. Was the poetic chronicler of the Warsaw Ghetto and an organizer of its cultural life (the café "Sztuka," "Żywy Dziennik"). Perished during the uprising, in April 1943.

Works

Co czytałem umarłym. Collected and prepared for publication by I. Maciejewska. Warsaw, 1977. (Poems of the Warsaw ghetto.)

Secondary Literature

Kwiatkowski, J. "Felieton poetycki." *Twórczość* 1983, no. 8.

Dow Sztock [later Dow Sadan] (1902–1989)

Poet, critic and historian of literature, folklorist. Born in Brody. Studied in Polish gymnasium in Lvov from 1914 to 1918. Member of the Zionist organization Hechaluc, which he helped manage (1923–1925). In 1925, he became the secretary of the Światowy Związek Młodzieży Hebrajskiej [World Society of Hebrew Youth] in Warsaw and the editor of the paper *Haatid.* Emigrated to Palestine in the same year. Represented the Palestine trade unions in Berlin (1928–33), where he also studied political science and economics. Lecturer in Yiddish at the Hebrew University after 1949; head of the department of Yiddish after 1958; and professor after 1963. Member of the Israel Academy of Science (1962). Wrote in Polish, Hebrew, German, and Yiddish. Connected with the Lvov *Chwila* in the twenties; editor of *Dawar* (1933–44). Translated into Hebrew the poetry of Brandstaetter, Ihr, and Szymel *(Dawar).*

General Information

Gross, N. "Dow Sadan po polsku." *Nowiny-Kurjer* 1976, no. 290.

Maurycy [Mosze] Szymel [also Schimmel, Schimel] (1903–1942)

Pen names: Jerzy Sorkin, M. Sch, Sch.

Poet, prose writer, translator, critic, publicist. Member of the poetic group associated with *Chwila.* Graduate of the Żydowskie Gimnazjum Humanistyczne [Jewish Humanistic Gymnasium] in Lvov. Lived in Warsaw (1930–39), where he probably studied Polish. Contributed to the Polish, Polish-Jewish, and Yiddish papers *Gazeta Warszawska, Ster, Hajnt, Globus,* and *Szriftn.* After the outbreak of the war he returned to Lvov. Worked in an office in the Judenrat during the German occupation. Wartime and occupation-time poems appeared in the press *(Sowietisze Literatur* 1940, no. 3) and in anthologies *(Lid dos iz geblibn).* Murdered in the Janów death camp.

Works

In Polish

Powrót do domu. Warsaw, 1931.
Skrzypce przedmieścia. Warsaw, 1932.
Wieczór liryczny. Warsaw, 1935.
Gdzie jesteś Ewo? Novel published in installments in *Nowy Głos* 1938, nos. 44–76.

In Yiddish

Mir iz umetik. Warsaw, 1936, reprinted 1937.
Wartime poems collected in *Lid dos iz geblibn: Lider fun jidisze dichter in Pojln umgekumene bejs der hitleriszer okupacje: Antologie,* edited by B. Heller. Warsaw, 1951.

Translations

O Zusmanie Segałowiczu: Zbiór artykułów. Warsaw, 1936.
Ani sobie, ani muzom by A. Ptaszkin. Warsaw, 1936.
Wczoraj śpiewałem by Z. Segalowicz. Warsaw, 1936.
Historja syjonizmu by J. Heller. Warsaw, 1936.
Ukryty skarb by G. Nachum. Warsaw, 1939.
Pierwsze walki w Palestynie by A. Smali. Warsaw, 1939.

General Secondary Literature

Löw, Ch. *Smok w słowiczym gnieździe: Żydzi w poezji Odrodzonej Polski.* Warsaw, 1934. First appeared as *"Żydzi w poezji Odrodzonej Polski: Part 5. Poeci polsko-żydowscy."* Miesięcznik Żydowski 1934.

Loew, R. "Maurycy Szymel." *Od Nowa,* 10 May 1960.

Słucki, A. "Przypomnienie Maurycego Szymla." *Nowiny-Kurjer,* 24 Oct. 1969.

Istner, F. "Miasto poetów." *Tel-Aviv* 1974, no. 34.

Gross, N. "Spóźnione spotkanie z Szymlem." *Nowiny-Kurjer* 28 Feb. 1968.

Secondary Literature

On *Powrót do domu:*

Napierski, S. "M. Szymel *Powrót do domu." Wiadomości Literackie* 1931, no. 48.

Schneiderman, Sz. L. "Żydzi i 'żydzi' w poezji polskiej." *Nowy Dziennik* 1931, no. 186.

"Na młodym warszawskim Parnasie." *Kurier Literacko-Naukowy* 1934, no. 34.

Syga, T. B. "U poetów." *Gazeta Warszawska* 1932, no. 97.

Pomeranz, M. "Poezja polsko-żydowska: M. Szymel." *Nowy Dziennik* 1932, no. 330.

Pomer, S. "Niezwykły debiut poetycki: Maurycy Szymel, *Powrót do domu." Chwila,* 1931, no. 4396.

Löw, Ch. "Wśród poetów." *Miesięcznik Żydowski* 1931.

On *Skrzypce przedmieścia:*

Napierski, S. "M. Szymel, *Skrzypce przedmieścia," Wiadomości Literackie* 1933, no. 25.

Arnold, B. "Drobiazgi." *Tygodnik llustrowany* 1932, no. 42.

Brandstaetter, R. "Poeta żydowskiej ulicy: M. Szymel, *Skrzypce przedmieścia." Opinia* 1933, no. 21.

Zawodziński, K. W. "Lirika." In *Rocznik literacki za rok 1932.* Warsaw, 1933.

Schorr, A. "Poeta księżyca." *Miesięcznik Żydowski* 1931, nos. 1–2.

On *Wieczór liryczny:*

Sinko, T. [pen name R.]. "Wśród nowych poezji." *Kurier Literacko-Naukowy* 1935, no. 24.

Eker, A. "O trzecim tomie wierszy rasowego liryka." *Chwila* 1935, no. 5755.

Feldhorn, J. "Poeta małego miasteczka: M. Szymel, *Wieczór liryczny." Nasza Opinia* 1936, no. 26.

Sebyła, W. "Lirika." In *Rocznik literacki za rok 1935.* Warsaw, 1936.

Sztycer, M. "Twarzą ku nocy." *Opinia* 1935, no. 15.

Emil Tenenbaum (1897–1943)

Prose writer and journalist. Graduated from gymnasium in Tarnopol. Medical and pharmaceutical studies in Vienna. Worked as a pharmacist, first in Skałat, then in Żydaczów, and finally in Lvov, where he owned a drugstore on Bernardyński Square. From 1936 to 1939, he published an anti-anti-Semitic weekly, *Kontratak.* After the

German invasion, he worked in the drugstore run by the Judenrat. Murdered in the Janów death camp.

Works

Na początku było kłamstwo: Komedia. Lvov, 1932.
Tła: Powieść. Lvov, 1935.

Secondary Literature

Diamand, J. "E. Tenenbaum *Tła,*" *Nasza Opinia* 1935, no. 13.
Sinko, T. [pen name R.]. "Wśród nowych książek." *Kurier Literacko-Naukowy* 1935, no. 21.
Kucharski, Z. "Powieśc." *Pion* 1935, no. 21.

Saul Wagman (?–?)

Poet, journalist, translator. Publisher of *Nasz Przegląd.* Contributor to *Tygodnik Nowy.* May have committed suicide in the Soviet Union during war.

Translations

W lasach polskich by J. Opatoszu. Warsaw, 1923.
Płomienie i zgliszcza: Antologia. Warsaw, 1925.

Bernard Zimmermann (1885–1931)

Journalist and prose writer, political and social activist. Completed gymnasium in Bochnia and polytechnical studies in Bern and Vienna. Employed as a building inspector by the city of Cracow. A municipal official in Tel-Aviv between 1924 and 1929. Returned to Cracow because of wife's illness. Member of the Hitachdut Party and of the management of the Keren Hajesod. Played an active part in Jewish sports organizations. Coauthor of the building plans of the Jewish gymnasium Żydowskie Towarzystwo Gimnastyczne and the Mizrachi School in Cracow. Contributed to the newspapers *Moriah* and *Nowy Dziennik.* Died suddenly of complications following surgery.

Works

Tirsa: Powieść z życia współczesnej Palestyny. Cracow, 1930.

Secondary Literature

Kanfer, M. [pen name M. K.]. "Powieść o Palestynie: *Tirsa* Bernarda Zimmermanna." *Nowy Dziennik* 1930, no. 135.

Pomer, S. "Trzy ciekawe książki." *Chwila* 1930, no. 4154.

Wagner, J. B. "Powieść o życiu żydowskim w Palestynie: *Tirsa* Bernarda Zimmermanna." *Nasz Przegląd* 1930, no. 180.

"*Tirsa* Bernarda Zimmermanna jako premia dla prenumeratorów *Naszego Przeglądądu.*" *Nasz Przegląd* 1932, no. 13.

Obituaries

Nowy Dziennik 1931, no. 256.

Other Biographical Materials

"Akademia ku czci Bernarda Zimmermanna." *Nasz Przegląd* 1931, no. 269.

Sources of Biographical Information

Bibliographies

Polska retrospektywna bibliografia literacka (Polish retrospective literary bibliography; to 1939). Manuscript in IBL PAN. Card indexes.

Biographical and Bio-Bibliographical Compendiums

Almanach i leksykon Żydostwa polskiego (Almanac and lexicon of Polish Jewry). Vols. 1–3. Lvov, 1937.

Almanach żydowski wydany przez Hermana Stachla zawierający szereg artykułów wybitnych literatów i publicystów oraz życiorysy czołowych postaci Małopolski Wschodniej (Jewish almanac published by Herman Stachel containing a number of articles by eminent men of letters and journalists as well as biographies of leading figures of eastern Małopolska). Lvov, 1937.

Leksikon fun der najer jidiszer literatur: Arojsgegeben fun alweltlichen jidiszn kultur-farband (Lexicon of the new Yiddish literature: Published by the world Yiddish cultural society). Vols. 1–8. New York, 1956–81.

Łoza, St. *Czy wiesz kto to jest?* (Do you know who this is?). Warsaw, 1938.

Olszewicz, B. *Lista strat kultury polskiej* (List of losses of Polish culture). Warsaw, 1947.

Rawicz, M. *Majn leksikon: Jidische dichter, dercejler, dramaturgn in Pojln cwiszn di cwej grojse weltmilchomes* (My lexicon: Yiddish poets, storytellers, and dramatists in Poland between the two World Wars). Vols. 1–2. Montreal, 1945–47.

Rutowska, M., and Serwański, E. *Straty wśród pisarzy polskich (literatów, publicystów, dziennikarzy i redaktorów) w czasie II wojny światowej i okupacji hitlerowskiej, 1939–1945* (Losses among Polish writers (men of letters, journalists, and editors) during World War II and the Nazi occupation, 1939–1945). Warsaw, 1980.

Who's Who in World Jewry: A Biographical Dictionary of Outstanding Jews. Edited by H. Schneiderman and I. I. Carmin. New York, 1955.

Who's Who in Israel and in the Work for Israel Abroad. Edited by I. Ben (Benditer). Tel-Aviv, 1972.

Literary Anthologies

Borwicz, M. *Pieśń ujdzie cało . . . : Antologia wierszy o Żydach pod okupacją niemiecką* (The song will survive . . . : An anthology of poems about Jews under the German occupation). Warsaw, 1947.

Heller, B. *Lid dos iz geblibn: Lider fun jidisze dichter in Pojln umgekumene bejs der hitleriszer okupacje: Antologie* (The song has survived: Poems by Jewish poets in Poland who perished during the Nazi occupation: An anthology). Warsaw, 1951.

Matuszewski, R., and Pollak, S., eds. *Poezja polska, 1914–1919* (Polish poetry, 1914–1919). Vols. 1–2. Warsaw, 1984.

Słucki, A., and Łastik, S., eds. *Antologia poezji żydowskiej* (An anthology of Jewish poetry). Warsaw, 1983.

Szeps, Z., ed. *Antologia poezji żydowskiej* (An anthology of Jewish poetry). London, 1980.

Recollections

Borwicz, M. *Literatura w obozie* (Literature in the camp). Cracow, 1946.

———. *Uniwersytet zbirów* (University of thugs). Cracow, 1946.

Brzoza, *Moje przygody literackie* (My literary adventures). Katowice, 1967.

Czerniaków, A. *Dziennik getta warszawskiego* (Diary of the Warsaw ghetto). Edited by M. Fuks. Warsaw, 1983.

Dąbrowska, M. *Dzienniki* (Diaries). Selected and with an introduction and notes by T. Drewnowski. Vols. 1–2. Warsaw, 1988.

Frantz, W. *Odłamki wspomnień przez przetak pamięci przesianych* (Fragments of recollections put through the sieve of memory). Cracow, 1972.

Friedman, F. *Zagłada Żydów lwowskich* (The destruction of the Lvov Jews). Lodz, 1945.

Gross, N. *Kim pan jest, panie Grymek?* (Who are you, Mr. Grymek?). Cracow, 1991.

Jastrun, M. *Smuga światła* (A streak of light). Warsaw, 1982.

Kessler, A. *Nie chcę nocy: Wspomnienia, 1939–1945* (I don't want the night: Recollections, 1939–1945). Poznań, 1962.

Księga wspomnień, 1919–1939 (Book of recollections, 1919–1939). Warsaw, 1960.

Nałkowska, Z. *Dzienniki* (Diaries). Edited and with an introduction and commentary by H. Kirchner. Vol. 2 (1903–17), Warsaw, 1976; vol. 3 (1918–29), Warsaw, 1980; vol. 4 (1930–39), Warsaw, 1988.

Safrin, H. *Ucieszne i osbliwe historie mojego życia* (Amusing and curious stories from my life). Lodz, 1970.

Śpiewak, J. *Przyjaźnie i animozje* (Friendships and animosities). Warsaw, 1965.

Vogler, H. *Autoportret z pamięci* (Self-portrait from memory). Vols. 1–3. Cracow, 1978.

Wittlin, J. *Mój Lwów* (My Lvov). London, 1975.

Letters

Schulz, B. *Księga listów* (Book of letters). Collected, edited, and with an introduction, notes, and an appendix by J. Ficowski. Cracow, 1975.

Notes

Introduction

1. A. Hertz, *Żydzi w kulturze polskiej,* Paris 1961, p. 243.

2. Ibid.

3. M. Borwicz, introduction to *Pieśń ujdzie cało: Antologia wierszy o Żydach pod okupacją niemiecką,* Warsaw 1947, p. 30.

4. A. Sandauer, *O sytuacji pisarza polskiego pochodzenia żydowskiego w XXw: Rzecz, którą nie ja powinienem był napisać. . .,* Warsaw 1982, p. 21.

5. W. Panas, "Literatura polsko-żydowska: Pismo i rana," *Akcent* 1987, no. 3. See also W. Panas, "Ja—polski poeta, hebrajski niemowa: Literatura polsko-żydowska i żydowsko-polska (1918–1939)," *Tygodnik Literacki* 1991, no. 16.

6. A. Jawicz, "Udział Żydów w polskiej literaturze międzywojennej," *Nasza Myśl,* Tel-Aviv-Jerusalem 1952; R. Loew, "Poezja polsko-żydowska," typescript, n.p. 1957, "Powrót do wierszy," *Od Nowa* 29 March 1960, "Maurycy Szymel," *Od Nowa* 10 May 1960, "Przypomnienie Karola Dresdnera," *Nowiny-Kurier* 1975, no. 85, and " 'Biblia' w literaturze polskiej: Rzecz o Wilhelmie Falleku," *Nowiny-Kurier* 1975, no. 140; A. Słucki, "Przypomnienie Maurycego Szymla," *Nowiny-Kurier,* 24 Oct. 1969; F. Istner, "Miasto poetów," *Nowiny-Kurier* 1974, no. 34; N. Gross, "Spóźnione spotkanie z Szymlem," *Nowiny-Kurier,* 28 Feb. 1986, "Chaim Löw i Leon Przemski," typescript, n.p., n.d., "Bernard Zimmermann," typescript, n.p., n.d. I owe all typescripts and excerpts from the Israeli press to the kindness of Natan Gross and Ryszard Loew.

7. K. Czachowski, *Obraz współczesnej literatury polskiej 1884–1993,* vol. 3, *Ekspresjonizm i neorealizm,* Warsaw-Lvov 1936, pp. 316–320; I. Fik, *Dwadzieścia lat literarury polskiej (1918–1938),* Cracow 1949, pp. 31–34.

8. Ch. Löw, *Smok w słowiczym gnieździe: Żydzi w poezji Odrodzonej Polski,* Warsaw 1934.

9. See P. Glikson, *Preliminary Inventory of the Jewish Daily and Periodical Press Published in the Polish Language 1823–1982,* Jerusalem 1983; M. Fuks, *Prasa żydowska w Warszawie 1823–1839,* Warsaw 1979; Ch. Shmeruk, "Hebrew-Yiddish-Polish: A Trilingual Jewish Culture" in *The Jews of Poland Between Two World Wars,* edited by Y. Gutman, E. Mendelsohn, and Ch. Shmeruk, Hanover [N.H.] 1989, pp. 304–309; M. C. Steinlauf, "The Polish-Jewish Daily Press," *Polin* 1987, vol. 2, pp. 219–246.

10. M. Levine, "Polish Literature and the Holocaust," *Holocaust Studies Annual,* vol. 3, 1985, p. 190.

11. Ibid., pp. 191–192.

12. Panas, "Literatura," p. 18.

1. The Jewish Aspect

1. A. J. Cohn, "Nasz dorobek literacki," *Izraelita* 1901, no. 10.

2. A. J. Cohn, "Kilka słów wstępnych tłumacza" (A few introductory remarks by the translator), in *Zbawca: Powieść (z drugiej połowy XIV stulecia) z podań ludu pragskiego ghetta spisał S. K.,* translated by A. J. Cohn, Warsaw 1862, p. xi.

3. Cohn, "Nasz dorobek."

4. See M. Brzezina, *Polszczyzna Żydów,* Warsaw 1986, pp. 83–89.

5. I am familiar with a typewritten version of an essay by Aleksander Zyga that deals with the question of the use of the terms "Jew" and "Israelite" in the nineteenth century by circles with different ideological orientations: "Wymienne nazwy 'Żyda' w publicystyce i literaturze polskiej XIX w. na tle głównych orientacji ideowych uregulowania stosunków między Żydami i Polakami." See especially pp. 8, 9, 13, 17, 20–21.

6. L. Rosner wrote about the influence of German terminology on the term Polish-Jewish culture in the article " 'Kultura polsko-żydowska?' Na marginesie dyskusji w sprawie poezji polsko-żydowskiej," *Opinia,* 1933, no. 34. It is interesting that the term "jüdisch-polnische Dichter" was used in German with reference to all authors of Jewish origin who wrote in Polish; see *Menorah: Jüdisches Familienblatt für Wissenschaft, Kunst und Literatur,* 1930, no. 9–10, p. 491.

7. Cohn, "Nasz dorobek."

8. M. B. (Maks Bienenstock?). "Z. Bromberg-Bytkowski, 'Pieśń nad Pieśniami,' " *Nowe Życie* 1924, no. 4, p. 157.

9. R. Brandstaetter, "Zygmunt Bromberg-Bytkowski: W dziesiątą rocznicę zgonu," *Opinia* 1933, no. 11.

10. M. Szymel, "Piętra żydowskiej Warszawy," *Opinia* 1933, no. 8. This phenomenon was described before Szymel and Brandstaetter by Samuel Hirszhorn in "Typy żydowskie w literaturze polskiej," *Nasz Przegląd* 1929, no. 55.

11. H. Heschel [pen name Trejtwart], "Pieśń obczyzny," *Nasz Przegląd* 1923, no. 232.

12. Gutman, Mendelsohn, and Shmeruk's collection of essays includes M. C. Steinlauf's essay "Mark Arnshteyn and the Polish-Jewish theater" (pp. 399–411), which describes the activities of the Polish-Jewish theater, its conception, and the debate about the idea of Polish-Jewish art. See also E. Igel [pen name i. g.], "Sztuki żydowskie na scenie polskiej: Wywiad z Andrzejem Markiem," *Chwila* 1930, no. 3889; M. Friszlender, "Czy potrzebny jest teatr polsko-żydowski," *Nasz Przegląd* 1929, no. 254; J. Podskocz, "Czy potrzebny jest teatr polsko-żydowski: Artykuł dyskusyjny," *Nasz Przegląd* 1929, no. 256.

13. M. Pomeranz, "Poezja polsko-żydowska: M. Szymel," *Nowy Dziennik* 1932, no. 330.

14. S. Pomer, "Żydzi w literaturze polskiej," [part 2,] *Nasz Przegląd* 1933, no. 71.

15. Natan Füllenbaum, member of the Polish-Jewish artistic group Wzlot, wrote in "Wiersze," *Słowo* 1936, no. 5: "Polish speech—of snows and pines—cannot supply the appropriate arsenal for expressing our triply Jewish thoughts. Here we must bow to an irrevocable necessity. It is not the least of our tragedies that Jews must address Jews about Jewish matters in Polish. But as long as the 'must' just stated is applicable, our work is justified. And [so are] those of our poems, written in Polish, which will turn out to be worthy of the honor of being included in Jewish, rather than Polish, literature, much like [Anonim] Gall's chronicle, which belongs to Polish literature in spite of the fact that it is written in Latin."

16. See, for example, N. Sokołów, "Czym jest i czym powinna być tzw. 'powieść żydowska?' "

Izraelita 1892, no. 18; T. Jeske-Choinski, *Żyd w powieści,* Warsaw 1914, pp. 62, 69; S. Pomer, "Egzotyka żydowska: I. Singer, *Josie Kałb,*" *Nasz Przegląd* 1934, no. 99.

17. I. Butkiewiczówna, *PowieśŃci i nowele żydowskie Elizy Orzeszkowej,* Lublin 1937, pp. 20–21.

18. R. Brandstaetter, "As prozy polemicznej," *Opinia* 1934, no. 42.

19. P. Appenszlak, "Smutny poeta: M. Szymel," *Nasz Przegląd* 1935, no. 112.

20. The author of this formula was Anda Eker: "O trzecim tomie wierszy rasowego liryka," *Chwila* 1935, no. 5755.

21. M. Kanfer, "Dwa debiuty," *Nowy Dziennik* 1928, no. 146. The terms "Polish-Jewish literature" and "Polish-Jewish writers" appear in, for example, S. Hirszhorn, "Kongres Penklubów a pisarze żydowscy," *Nasz Przegląd* 1930, no. 159; P. Appenszlak; I. Berman [pen name I. B.], "Debiut poetycki D. Ihra," *Miesięcznik Żydowski* 1934, no. 3, pp. 287–288; I. Berman, "Poeci polsko-żydowscy w parodii," *Nasza Opinia* 1936, no. 32; I. Berman, "Dyskusje literackie," *Nasza Opinia* 1937, no. 92; M. Braun, "Pisarze polscy: Czy 'pisarze żydowscy piszący po polsku,' albo 'pisarze polsko-żydowscy,' " *Ster* 1937, no. 16; Löw, *Smok,* pp. 69–78.

22. S. Pomer, "Żydzi w literaturze polskiej," [part 1,] *Nasz Przegląd* 1933, no. 64.

23. An outline of the history of the literary contributions in Polish by Jewish authors is found in W. Fallek, "Twórczość Żydów na polu literatury polskiej do roku 1918," in *Żydzi w Polsce Odrodzonej,* vol. 2, Warsaw 1933, pp. 74–90.

24. Cohn, "Kilka," p. xi.

25. Z. Librowicz, "Żydzi i beletrystyka," in *Z wrażeń kapociarza,* Warsaw 1878, pp. 20–21.

26. Ibid.

27. R., "Rocznik Żydowski," *Izraelita* 1903, no. 13.

28. See P. Wróbel, "Między nadzieją a zwątpieniem: 'Der Jude' Martina Bubera wobec rewolucji i nowego ładu w świecie po I wojnie światowej," *Więź* 1986, nos. 7–8, p. 71.

29. See M. Kanfer, "W pięciolecie śmierci Szołem Alejchema," *Nowy Dziennik* 1931, no. 134.

30. See E. Mendelsohn, *Zionism in Poland: The Formative Years, 1916–1926,* New Haven [Conn.] 1981, pp. 338–344.

31. L. Reich, "Przed ćwierćwieczem a dziś," *Chwila* 1924, no. 1733.

32. A. Cała, "Kwestia asymilacji Żydów w Królestwie Polskim (1864–1897): Refleksje i dygresje," *Znak* 1986, nos. 377–379, p. 77.

33. See Clara Pomeranz-Carmely, *Das Identitätsproblem jüdischer Autoren im deutschen Sprachraum: Von der Jahrhundertwende bis zu Hitler,* Königstein 1981.

34. A. Stand, "Moderna żydowska w Galicji," in *Safrus,* edited by J. Kirszrot, Warsaw 1905, p. 32.

35. Ibid.

36. Shmeruk, *Hebrew–Yiddish,* p. 307.

37. Sandauer, *O sytuacji,* p. 21.

38. Steinlauf, "Polish-Jewish," pp. 228, 231.

39. M. Bałaban, " 'Miesięcznik Żydowski': Na marginesie dwóch roczników," *Nasz Przegląd* 1933, no. 158.

40. W. Berkelhammer, "Pierwszy tom *Miesięcznika Żydowskiego,*" *Nowy Dziennik* 1931, no. 158.

41. "Nasza 'Opinia': Cele i zadania," *Nasza Opinia* 1933, no. 1.

42. W. Berkelhammer, *Przepiękna książka:* A most beautiful book, *Chwila* 1924, no. 2005.

43. Benedykt Rosenzweig treated the novel of Józef Hartblaj *Jehoszua: Powieść osnuta na tle życia "chaluców"* (1928) as a curiosum: *Chwila* 1928, no. 3338. I was also able to locate the following reviews of early Polish-Jewish publications: a review by J. Warszawiak of Hartblaj's novel, "Nowa

książka polska o Palestynie," *Nowy Dziennik* 1928, no. 141; a review by S. Pomer of B. Zimmermann's *Tirsa,* "Trzy ciekawe książki," *Chwila* 1930, no. 4154; a review by Lector of R. Feldszuh's *Noce palestyńskie* "Palestyna w zwierciadle poezji," *Nasz Przegląd* 1929, no. 55; a review of H. Adler's *Ariela i Jubal: Palestyńskie opowieści romantyczne* titled "Książka z życia palestyńskiego," *Chwila* 1931, no. 4286; a review by W. Barbasz of K. Dresdner's little volume of poetry *Heine i nieznajoma,* "Wśród młodych poetów: *Heine i nieznajoma,*" *Chwila* 1928, no. 3367.

44. Hirszhorn, "Typy."

45. Pomer, "Żydzi," [part 2].

46. *Nowy Dziennik* 1924, no. 102.

47. For example, *Safrus* published Szołem Alejchem's *Notatki komiwojażera,* Szalom Asz's *Motke Ganew,* Józef Opatoszu's *Romans koniokrada,* Zusman Segałowicz's *Cylka z lasu,* I. L. Perec's *Z nieznanego świata: Opowieści chasydzkie i ludowe,* and an anthology of short stories *Płomienie i zgliszcza* (I. L. Ojnochi, I. M. Weissenberg, Z. Segałowicz, J. Rosenfeld, J. Mastbojm, D. Friszman, I. L. Perec, E. Kaganowski, H. D. Nomberg, S. Asz, and L. Szapiro).

48. Alina Cała mentions the assimilationist complexes of the first generation of Zionists in "Kwestia," pp. 79–80.

49. M. Bienenstock, "Wspomnienia," *Chwila* 1920, no. 619.

50. M. Kanfer, "Pamięci Wilhelma Feldmana," *Chwila* 1922, nos. 1094–1095. See also M. Kanfer, "Buczacz i Jerozolima," *Chwila* 1930, nos. 4108–4110.

51. See, for example, the Cracow issue, *Nasza Opinia* 1935, no. 71, and the Stanisławów issue, *Nasza Opinia* 1936, no. 52.

52. J. Korczak, "Cynik," *Chwila* 1926, no. 2557.

53. J. Stryjkowski, "Wielki strach," *Zapis* 1980, no. 14, p. 18.

54. M. Szymel, "Kij w mrowisku: W sprawie artykułów Romana Brandstaettera o poezji polsko-żydowkiej: [Part 3,] Prawda o poezji polsko-żydowkiej," *Opinia* 1933, no. 29.

55. Ibid.

56. Michał Głowinski wrote about the situational specificity of a literary group: "Grupa literacka a model poezji: Przykład Skamandra" in *Z problemów literatury polskiej XX wieku,* vol. 2, Warsaw 1965.

57. A. Lauterbach, "Młodzi poeci Lwowa: Wieczór autorski," *Chwila* 1929, no. 3835.

58. For information about poetry readings by poets associated with *Chwila,* see A. Lauterbach, ibid., "Wieczór młodego Lwowa," *Chwila* 1932, no. 4658, "Godzina z poetą," *Chwila* 1933, no. 5106, and "Przed godziną z poetą: Wobec poniedziałkowego wieczoru poetów lwowskich," *Chwila* 1933, no. 5100; I. Berman, "Wieczór autorski Maurycego Szymla," *Chwila* 1934, no. 5643, and "Trio liryczne," *Chwila* 1935, no. 5671, and Ch. S., "Wieczór autorski M. Szymla, A. Ekerówny, D. Ihra," *Chwila* 1935, no. 5681; W. Fallek, "Poeta nieogarnionej tęsknoty: Liryczny wieczór Maurycego Szymla," *Nowy Dziennik* 1936, no. 315.

59. See Lauterbach, "Godzina."

60. Berman, "Wieczór." Wilhelm Fallek [also] wrote about Szymel's author's evening in Lodz; see Fallek "Poeta."

61. S. Pomer and M. Szymel, "Wiersz napisany wspólnie," *Nowy Dziennik* 1935, no. 5. Szymel dedicated "List jesienny" and "Wieczór w deszczu" to Pomer, and "Woń miodu i mleka" to Eker. Pomer dedicated "Elegia jesienna" to Szymel, and "Pożegnanie młodości" to Daniel Ihr. Dresdner dedicated "Do chaluca" to Daniel Ihr, and Eker dedicated "Jeszcze o śniegu" to Szymel.

62. See Lauterbach, "Wieczór."

63. S. Pomer, "Niepowołane prokuratorstwo: W sprawie żywej poezji młodego Lwowa," *Chwila* 1930, no. 4333.

64. J. Śpiewak, "Przedpiekle wyobraźni," in *Przyjaźnie i animozje,* Warsaw 1965, p. 166.

65. See note by Paul Glikson on the monthly *Wzlot* in Glikson, p. 58. M. Tabak wrote about the publications of this group in "Żydowska literature Stanisławowa," *Nasza Opinia* 1936, no. 52.

66. M. Silberman, "Pięć lat Wzlotu," *Słowo* 1936, no. 81.

67. R. Mahler, "Wzlot w Stanisławowie urządził wieczór litaracki," *Chwila* 1935, no. 5668.

68. Silberman, "Pięć lat."

69. H. Safrin, "Pean o poezji stanisławowskiej," *Słowo* 1938, no. 142.

70. See "Wieczór autorski 'sztegn,' " *Słowo* 1938, no. 142.

71. For a biographical sketch of A. Lutwak, see *Almanach i leksykon Żydowstwa polskiego,* Lvov 1937, vols. 2–3, cols. 326–329.

72. W. Berkelhammer, "Wizja," in *Jewish Almanac,* edited by L. Reich, Lvov 1910, pp. 242–243.

73. See M. Jastrun, *Smuga światła,* Warsaw 1983, p. 243; T. Peiper, *Tędy,* Cracow 1930, pp. 304–305.

74. See *Nowy Dziennik* 1928, no. 61.

75. H. Vogler's recollections about the group of literary associates of *Nowy Dziennik* are found in his *Autoportret z pamięci,* vol. 1, Cracow 1978, pp. 155–156. Some information about the associates of the newspaper in the first decade of its existence is contained in Z. Mozes, "*Nowy Dziennik:* Nieco historii i statystyki," *Nowy Dziennik* 1928, no. 190.

76. Steinlauf, "Polish-Jewish," pp. 221, 223, writes about the genesis of *Nasz Przegląd* and the group of its publishers. See also Fuks, *Prasa,* pp. 259–272.

77. See "Krakowskie grono współpracowników 'Świata Młodych,' " *Opinia* 1934, no. 19.

78. See the announcements in *Nasza Opinia* 1937, nos. 119, 122.

79. M. Strzemski, *Nasze Puławy,* Lublin 1986, p. 333.

80. In his bibliography of the Jewish press in Polish, Glikson makes no reference to any paper published in Puławy.

81. R. Brandstaetter, "Sprawa poezji polsko-żydowskiej: Artykuł dyskusyjny[, part 3,] Kłody pod nogami," *Opinia* 1933, no. 25.

82. M. Szymel, "Kij w mrowisku: W sprawie artykułów Romana Brandstaettera o poezji polsko-żydowskiej[, part 4, Nasze prawa]," *Opinia* 1933, no. 31.

83. Brandstaetter, "Sprawa," part 3.

84. E. Prokop[-Janiec], "Kafka w Polsce międzywojennej," *Pamiętnik Literacki* 1985, no. 4.

85. My sources of information about the reception of Polish-Jewish literature in the Hebrew and Yiddish press are *Nowy Dziennik* 1931, no. 186, about a publication in *Hajnt;* Szymel, "Kij," part 4, about an article in *Tog;* "Głosy i echa literackie," *Nasza Opinia* 1935, no. 12, about publications in *Gazit* 1935, nos. 5–6; a brief note in "Kronika literacka i artystyczna," *Opinia* 1935, no. 25, about publications in *Davar.*

86. R. Brandstaetter, "Sprawa," part 1; part 2, "Społeczeństwo żydowskie a my," *Opinia* 1933, no. 24; part 3.

87. Brandstaetter, "Sprawa," part 1.

88. Brandstaetter, "Sprawa," part 3.

89. Brandstaetter, "Sprawa," part 1.

90. Ibid.

91. Brandstaetter, "Sprawa," part 3.

92. Brandstaetter, "Sprawa," part 1.

93. M. Korzennik, "Skąd i po co ten występ: À propos pewnej sprawy nieosobistej," *Tygodnik Żydowski* 1933, no. 33.

94. M. Szymel, "Kij w mrowisku: W sprawie artykułów Romana Brandstaettera o poezji polsko-żydowskiej, part 1, O tym, który dyskusję rozpoczął. . . ," *Opinia* 1933, no. 27; part 2, "Nasza ojczyzna," *Opinia* 1933, no. 28; "Kij," part 3; "Kij," part 4.

95. R. Brandstaetter, "Neofita," *Opinia* 1933, no. 33.

96. At the very beginning of his literary career, Brandstaetter quarreled with Tuwim; see "Arogant," *Gazeta literacka* 1927, no. 8. He was constantly embroiled in arguments with Antoni Słonimski (see R. Brandstaetter, "Kilka słów o człowieku, który ułatwił sobie życie: Na marginesie Antoniego Słonimskiego 'Wierszy zebranych,' " *Opinia* 1933, no. 17; A. Słonimski, "Kroniki tygodniowe," *Wiadomości Literackie* 1936, nos. 20 and 30 [parts 1 and 2]), as well as with older and younger Polish-Jewish literary figures, namely, Mojżesz Kanfer and Salomon Dykman (see "Miasto w bożnicy czyli jedwabny Żyd," *Opinia* 1934, no. 27; M. Kanfer, "Fałszerz w potrzasku," *Nowy Dziennik* 1934, no. 209; D. Lazer, "Nareszcie tłumacz," *Nowy Dziennik* 1934, no. 244; "Pod skrzydłami ignorancji," *Opinia* 1934, no. 36). Private animosities came through most clearly in Meir Korzennik's open letter, "Wróć to poezji: Do Romana Brandstaettera liścik otwarty," published in the Tarnów *Tygodnik Żydowski* 1933, no. 28, and in the discussion it triggered. In his letter, Korzennik wrote: "I challenge You to a real contest. . . . And not to take up the cudgels for the likes of Boy[-Zeleński] and Słonimski. Others have already done so, I think wrongly. For, to be one of Boy's partisans is to be one of millions in Poland and of a few thousands abroad. And this is not one bit striking or glorious. But to hit out against Boy (regardless of *cui bono*) as You are doing, or to flay Słonimski alive (never mind a few mistakes and setbacks), this takes courage, this is glorious, this is impressive and, by Jove, no one should hold it against You. And they are being unfair when they reproach You with having turned Zionist rather late. . . . Some demand. Some reproach! Better late than never. And especially today, given the favorable circumstances. . . . And so they are not being fair to You. But I know You, you won't break down and, between you and me and the lamppost, you won't hold the bit of hell they raise around You against them." Jeremiasz Feig objected to the nasty tone of the "little letter" in his "Jeszcze *causa* Brandstaetter," *Tygodnik Żydowski* 1933, no. 32. Korzennik replied with the article "Skąd i po co ten występ: À propos pewnej sprawy nieosobistej," *Tygodnik Żydowski* 1933, no. 33, in which he accused Feig of wanting "at all costs to help Brandstaetter, who loves such polemics and claims that in this way he is becoming a 'great' man, to acquire notoriety." In "Psalm ironii i napomnienia na 'ostatni artykuł z cyklu,' " *Tygodnik Żydowski* 1933, no. 31, [Korzennik] called the poet a "homegrown Adolf" (Nowaczynski) and asked: "What do you call it: a Jew, knows little about Jewishness, writes in Polish, and sticks his fingers in the door of national Jewish poetry."

97. S. Samet, "Z Adolfem Nowaczyńskim w Jerozolimie," *Chwila* 1938, no. 6742.

98. Brandstaetter, "Neofita."

99. Szymel, "Kij," part 3.

100. Szymel, "Kij," part 2.

101. Szymel, "Kij," part 3.

102. Szymel, "Kij," part 4.

103. Brandstaetter, "Neofita."

104. Szymel, "Kij," part 3.

105. A. Madler, "O szerszy punkt widzenia," *Opinia* 1933, no. 33.

106. S. Stendig, "Sprawa poezji polsko-żydowskiej: Wobec dyskusji," *Tygodnik Żydowski* 1933, no. 36.

107. R. Brandstaetter, "Plecak jest nam już niepotrzebny," *Bunt młodych* 1936, no. 7. In this article, Brandstaetter stood by his estimate of Polish-Jewish poetry as a transitional phenomenon and declared his unshakable Hebraism: "I have never overestimated the value of Polish-Jewish poetry. Years ago, when I fought for this poetry in the pages of *Opinia* and defended it against the squawks of a certain bald and arid journalistic parrot [most likely a reference to Mojżesz Kanfer], I wrote that I regarded the existence of this poetry as a temporary *malum necessarium,* as the outcome of the actual needs of Polish Jews who don't know Hebrew, as a manifestation that would soon vanish. This is a fatalistic position but it is correct and logical. For I regard Jewish literary productions written in any language other than Hebrew as an abnormal and ephemeral phenomenon that is bound to vanish at any moment, liquidated by a ruthless law of history. Only creations by Jews in Hebrew develop our national culture and shape it in accordance with logical and consistent laws that rule the world." This position did not prevent Brandstaetter in his article "Przeciw myślom w mundurze: W sprawie utworzenia Światowego Związku Pisarzy Żydowskich," *Nowy Głos* 1938, no. 147, from trying to propagate Stefan Zweig's idea of a single association of Jewish writers "regardless of the language they write in. Such an association of Jewish writers who feel a deep and elemental solidarity with the Jewish cultural and historical tradition would represent before the whole world our historical mission." He had written about this idea earlier in the article "Wszechświatowy Związek Literatów Żydowskich," *Opinia* 1935, no. 7.

108. Berman, "Dyskusje literackie."

109. Ch. Löw, "Czy możliwa jest poezja polsko-żydowska," *Opinia* 1933, no. 32.

110. Löw, *Smok,* p. 9.

111. W. Pordes, "O kulturze żydowskiej," in *Żydowski Almanach,* edited by L. Reich, Lvov 1910, p. 134.

112. Ibid., pp. 136–137.

113. Ibid., p. 137.

114. W. Berkelhammer, "O asymilacji," *Chwila* 1921, no. 735.

115. H. A. Strauss, "Akkulturation als Schicksal: Einleitende Bemerkungen zum Verhältnis von Juden und Umwelt," in *Juden und Judentum in der Literatur,* edited by H. A. Strauss and Ch. Hoffmann, Munich 1985, p. 9.

116. See C. Stopnicka Heller, *On the Edge of Destruction: Jews of Poland Between the Two World Wars,* New York 1980, Chap. 7, "Between Tradition and Assimilation".

117. Ibid., p. 214

118. Ibid., pp. 215–216.

119. [The students' novel] began to appear in *Chwila* 1929, no. 1513.

120. For the literary competition of *Opinia* see "Konkurs literacki *Opinii* pod hasłem 'W poszukiwaniu młodych talentów'," *Opinia* 1934, no. 38; "Zamknięcie konkursu literackiego *Opinii,*" *Opinia* 1934, no. 44; "Lista dodatkowa uczestników konkursu literackiego *Opinii,*" *Opinia* 1934, no. 46.

121. Czachowski, p. 316.

122. S. Hirszhorn, "Czy istotnie asymilacja triumfuje," *Nasz Przegląd* 1930, no. 4.

123. A. Rudnicki, *Lato,* Warsaw 1959, p. 116.

124. Ben-Hillel, "O kulturze polsko-żydowskiej słów kilka," *Opinia* 1933, no. 32.

125. Ibid.

126. It is worth noting that the very same explanations of the progress of acculturation in in-

terwar Poland are given by Stopnicka Heller, in *On the Edge,* and by Shmeruk, in *Hebrew–,* pp. 293–294.

127. Galicians were in the majority in the group of Polish-Jewish writers. Thus Szymel, Dresdner, and Eker were born in Lvov, Boruchowicz in Cracow, Brandstaetter, Bienenstock, and Taubenschlag in Tarnów, Löw in Przemyśl, Bertisch, Richter, Silberman, Füllenbaum, and Mayer in Stanisławów, Safrin in Monasterzyski, I. Kanfer and M. Kanfer in Buczacz, and Fenster in Złoczów.

128. E. Mendelsohn, *The Jews of East Central Europe between the World Wars,* Bloomington [Ind.] 1983, pp. 18–19. For school autonomy in Galicia and mandatory schooling for children aged 6–14, see R. Wroczyński, *Dzieje oświaty polskiej 1795–1945,* Warsaw 1987, pp. 215–221.

129. I. Grünbaum, "Asymilacja i polonizacja," *Nasz Przegląd* 1927, no. 80.

130. Steinlauf, "Polish-Jewish," p. 242.

131. There is reason to think that such a name change [from Jewish—to Polish-sounding name] was already popular in the interwar period: the metaphorical name used in the Polish-Jewish press when referring to the assimilated circles was the "Mr. Maurice" milieu: see M. Koren, "Migawki: Goldfaden a Pan Maurycy," *Nowy Dziennik* 1929, no. 132.

132. "Numerus clausus na UJK," *Chwila* 1929, no. 3770.

133. W. Fallek, *Studia i szkice o wpływie "Biblii" na literaturę polską,* Lodz 1931, and "Twórczość Żydów na polu literatury polskiej do roku 1918" in *Żydzi w Polsce Odrodzonej,* Warsaw 1931, vol. 2, pp. 74–90; J. Feldhorn, "Literatura polska w wieku XVI a Żydzi: Szkic bibliograficzny" in *Sprawozdanie Kierownictwa Żydowkiego Gimnazjum Koedukacyjnego Typu Humanistycznego Towarzystwa Żydowskiej Szkoły Ludowej i Średniej w Krakowie za rok szkolny 1928–1929,* Cracow 1929, pp. 3–12, and *"Pomnik strzaskany . . .": Motywy żydowkie w twórczości Cypriana Norwida,* Warsaw 1933; Löw, *Smok* (first [appeared in] *Miesięcznik Żydowski* 1933, nos. 7–8, pp. 27–35 and nos. 9–10, pp. 145–168; 1934, no. 1, pp. 54–67; no. 3, pp. 225–240); Ch. Löw, "Wyspiański a Żydzi," *Miesięcznik Żydowski* 1932, nos. 9–10, pp. 221–237, and "Rodowód Jankiela," *Miesięcznik Żydowski* 1934, no. 5, pp. 385–401; K. Dresdner, "Udział Żydów w poezji polskiej XIX wieku," *Miesięcznik Żydowski* 1932, no. 5, pp. 399–426, "Żydzi w powieściach Korzeniowskiego," *Przegląd Humanistyczny* 1933, no. 3, "Z korespondencji J. I. Kraszewskiego: Listy Armanda Levy," *Przegląd Humanistyczny* 1931, nos. 1–2, and "Krasiński a przechrzci," *Zjednoczenie: Jednodniówka* (Special issue), Lvov 1931; R. Brandstaetter, *Legion żydowski Adama Mickiewicza* (first [appeared in] *Miesięcznik Żydowski* 1932, nos. 1, 3, pp. 20–45, 112–132), and "Tragedia Juliana Klaczki," *Miesięcznik Żydowski* 1932, nos. 11–12, pp. 384–412.

134. See J. Lichten, "Uwagi o asymilacji i akulturacji Żydów w Polsce w latach 1863–1943," *Znak* 1988, nos. 396–397. The author debates the views that diminish the role of identificational assimilation in the interwar period.

135. C. Stopnicka Heller, "Poles of Jewish Background: The Case of Assimilation without Integration in Interwar Poland," in *Studies on Polish Jewry 1919–1939,* edited by Y. Fishman, New York 1974.

136. An investigation of the reception of Hebrew, Yiddish, and Polish literature in [the Polish-Jewish] press would, I think, yield extremely valuable information about the flow of values between the Jewish and Polish cultures. On translations of Yiddish literature in the Polish-Jewish press see E. Prokop[-Janiec], "Recepcja literatury jidysz w Polsce," in *Encyklopedia literatury polskiej XX* (forthcoming).

137. Stendig, "Sprawa."

138. Ben-Hillel.

139. M. Korzennik, "Psalm ironii i napomnienia na 'ostatni artykuł z cyklu,'" *Tygodnik Żydowski* 1933, no. 31.

140. Löw, "Czy możliwa."

141. S. Pomer, "Żydzi," [part 1].

142. S. Pomer, "Historia powojennej litaratury polskiej," *Nasz Przegląd* 1934, no. 149.

143. Hirszhorn, "Kongres."

144. Ben-Hillel.

145. Rosner.

146. See J. Rokicki, "Language as a Social Value in the Relationship between Language and Society," in *Language and Nation: Material from a Symposium Edited by W. Miodunka,* Zeszyty Naukowe Uniwersytetu Jagiellońskiego DCCCX: Prace Polonijne, no. 11, English language editors J. Reed and M. Rzepka, Warsaw 1987, p. 29.

147. On functions of language as a social symbolic value, see ibid., p. 31.

148. Shmeruk, *Hebrew–Yiddish,* p. 309.

149. Steinlauf, "Polish-Jewish," p. 221.

150. Ibid.

151. Brandstaetter, "Sprawa," part 1. The author also wrote: "While it is our dream that the Jewish nation should be reborn only in the glow of the Hebrew language, that it should conjure its cares, sadness, and joys into the sound of Hebrew words, today we are still, unfortunately, far from this ideal. Great numbers of the Jewish intelligentsia in Poland do not know Hebrew. For the time being, we can reach their hearts and Jewish emotions only through the Polish word suffused with the Hebrew spirit." In "Sprawa," part 3, he described the view that "in the future our national literature will be not only Hebrew literature but the literature of Jews in the whole world" as foreign to him.

152. See the article of M. Boruchowicz, "O polsko-żydowską poezję: Na marginesie pewnej dyskusji," *Nowy Dziennik* 1933, no. 263. This article summarized the discussion.

153. A. Rozenman, "Głosy czytelników w sprawie poezji polsko-żydowskiej," *Opinia* 1933, no. 36. It is likely that the author was a specialist in Polish: an outline of the history of the Division of the History of Polish Literature of the Jagiellonian University lists Abraham Rozenman, author of a doctoral dissertation "Dickens w Polsce" (1928); see *Dzieje Katedry Historii Literatury Polskiej w Uniwersytecie Jagiellońskim: Zarys monograficzny,* edited by T. Ulewicz, Cracow 1966, p. 283.

154. See H. Kohn, *Martin Buber: Sein Werk und seine Zeit: Ein Beitrag zur Geistesgeschichte Mitteleuropas 1880–1930,* afterword "1930–1960" by R. Weltsch, Cologne 1961.

155. Pordes.

156. R. Glassner, "Literaci-Żydzi we współczesnym piśmiennictwie polskim," *Rocznik Żydowski* 1904, p. 144. See also W. Pordes, "Żydowska twórczość," *Rocznik Żydowski* 1905.

157. Announcement of Henry Heschel's lecture, *Chwila* 1922, no. 1151.

158. Ibid.

159. Of course, [Szymel] was not the only supporter [of these neoromantic ideas]. They also appear in articles by R. Brandstaetter, for example, "Zygmunt Bromberg-Bytkowski: W dzisiątą rocznicę zgonu," *Opinia* 1933, no. 11, and "Poeta żydowskiej ulicy: M. Szymel, 'Skrzypce przedmieścia'," *Opinia* 1933, no. 21); Jakub Appenszlak, for example, "'Rodzina' A. Słonimskiego," *Nasz Przegląd* 1934, no. 6); and others.

160. Szymel, "Kij," part 3.

161. M. Szymel, "Krajobraz duszy żydowskiej w liryce polskiej," *Opinia* 1935, nos. 9, 10, 14.

162. Löw, *Smok,* p. 6.

163. Szymel, "Krajobraz."

164. See I. Berman, "Żydzi w poezji Odrodzonej Polski," *Chwila* 1935, no. 5678; J. Feldhorn, "Nie smok jest winien a słowiki: Na marginesie książki Chaima Löwa *Smok w słowiczym gnieździe: Żydzi w poezji Odrodzonej Polski," Nowy Dziennik* 1935, no. 63.

165. Ch. Löw, "O 'uświadomionym żydowstwie' i nie uświadomionych Żydach," *Opinia* 1935, no. 18.

166. I. Berman, "O tzw. cechach narodowych w literaturze pięknej," *Nasza Opinia* 1935, nos. 2, 3, 4. The quotation is from no. 4.

167. Szymel, "Kij," part 3.

168. Löw, "Czy możliwa."

169. M. Szymel, "Kim był Józef Elja?" *Opinia* 1935, no. 7.

170. See J. M. Tortosa, *Polityka językowa a języki mniejszości. Od Wieży Babel to Daru języków.* Translated by A. Rurarz. Introduction by J. Perlin, Warsaw 1986.

171. M. Kanfer [pen name M. K.], "Miesiąc książki żydowskiej," *Nowy Dziennik* 1931, no. 275.

172. M. Berkelhammer, "Problem asymilacji," *Nowe Życie* 1924, no. 5, p. 288.

173. Strauss.

174. R. Brandstaetter, "Stwórzmy żydowską samoobronę kulturalną," *Ster* 1937, no. 16.

175. O. Thon, "Znamiona narodowości," *Nowy Dziennik* 1931, no. 324.

176. L. Dawidowicz, "Jewish Identity: A Matter of Fate, A Matter of Choice," in *The Jewish Presence: Essays on Identity and History,* New York 1977.

177. Shmeruk, *Hebrew–Yiddish,* p. 287.

178. Ibid., passim.

2. The Polish Aspect

1. See A. Eisenbach, *Emancypacja Żydów na ziemiach polskich,* Warsaw 1988, p. 43.

2. See Tortosa, *Polityka,* p. 97.

3. See Z. Libera, "Żydzi i sprawa żydowska w literaturze pięknej i pamiętnikach w czasach Stanisława Augusta," in *Kultura, literatura, folklor,* edited by M. Graszewicz and J. Kolbuszewski, Warsaw 1988, pp. 145–146.

4. J. U. Niemcewicz, *Lejbe i Sióra czyli Listy dwóch kochanków: Romans,* Cracow 1931, p. xi.

5. This is the opinion of the priest Gintyłła in 1817. The quotation is taken from Ch. Shmeruk, *The Esterke Story in Yiddish and Polish Literature: A Case Study in the Mutual Relations of Two Cultural Traditions,* Jerusalem 1985, pp. 47–48.

6. Ibid., pp. 48–49.

7. K. Junosza, *Donkiszot żydowski: Szkic z literatury żargonowej żydowskiej,* Warsaw 1899, pp. 4–5.

8. Ibid., p. 245.

9. E. Orzeszkowa, *Meir Ezofowicz,* with an epilogue by J. Krzyżanowski, illustrated by M. Andriolli, Warsaw 1988, pp. 8, 394.

10. K. Cysewski, "Bariera kulturowa i dzieło literackie," *Ruch Literacki* 1984, nos. 1–2, p. 47.

11. Cysewski does this with material that is far less "exotic."

12. M. Meyersonowa, *Z ciasnej sfery,* Warsaw 1878, pp. 2, 10, 12, 15, 16, 18, 20, 22, 37, 38, 43, 69, 87, 94.

13. Cohn, "Kilka," pp. ix, x, xi.

14. Librowicz. There are interpretations of Polish-Israelite literature that see in them only the

wish to substitute Polish for Yiddish. Such interpretations seem unfair. See H. Datner-Śpiewak, "Asymilacja narodu i asymilacja jednostki," *Więź* 1983, no. 4, p. 6.

15. M. Sawicki, *Żydzi, ich dzieje ze względu na stan obecny Polski mieszkańców wyznania mojżeszowego,* Warsaw 1865, pp. 316–317.

16. Ibid., p. 318.

17. Cohn, "Nasz dorobek."

18. See Stopnicka Heller, *On the Edge,* pp. 214–215.

19. P. Kon, "Wi azoj hot Junosza ibergezect Mendeln in Pojlisz?," *Bicher welt* 1928, no. 7, pp. 36–38.

20. It is interesting that in the twenties Jewish topics were seldom treated in Polish literature. The few treatments that did turn up were marked by anti-Semitic bias: for example, A. Gruszecki, *Zawsze ci sami* (1921); J. Weyssenhoff, *Cudno i ziemia cudeńska* (1921), K. H. Rostworowski, *Antychryst* (1925), W. Sieroszewski, *Bolszewicy* (1922).

21. M. Kanfer, "Królestwo Boże," *Chwila* 1922, no. 21.

22. See Steinlauf, "Mark Arnshteyn," pp. 400–401, 409.

23. "Powieści żydowskie w polskim przekładzie," *Chwila* 1925, no. 2138.

24. M. Kanfer, "Literatura i polityka: Na marginesie wydawnictwa Safrus," *Chwila* 1925, no. 2264.

25. "Szalom Asz gościem piśmiennictwa polskiego: Przyjęcie polskiego PEN Clubu ku czci pisarza żydowskiego," *Chwila* 1928, no. 3426.

26. M. Segałowicz, "Niema wiecznych epidemii," *Nasz Głos* 1938, no. 147.

27. B. Lewit, "Żydowska książka po polsku," *Nasz Przegląd* 1937, no. 324.

28. A. Marek, "Płomienie i zgliszcza: Na marginesie znamiennej książki," *Nasz Przegląd* 1929, no. 92.

29. B. Mayer [pen name Arieh], *Pieśni chaluca,* Stanisławów 1934, p. 34.

30. H. A. Fenster, *O tym, co opuszczam,* Warsaw 1932, pp. 14, 15, 17.

31. T. Boy-Żeleński, *Flirt z Melpomeną: Wieczór ósmy,* Warsaw 1929, pp. 211–212.

32. E. Igel [pen name i. g.], "Sztuki"; "Boy-Żeleński heroldem zgodnego współżycia polsko żydowskiego," *Nowy Dziennik* (New Daily) 1928, no. 239; "Boy-Żeleński o teatrze żydowskim," *Nowy Dziennik* 1928, no. 287.

33. Boy-Żeleński, pp. 247–248.

34. H. Galle, "Żydzi w beletrystyce dzisiejszej," *Biblioteka Warszawska* 1 (1905), p. 148.

35. Magdalena Opalski wrote extensively about the position of *Wiadomości Literackie* in relation to Jewish literature and culture: *"Wiadomości Literackie,* 1924–1939: Polemics on the Jewish Question" in Gutman, Mendelsohn, Shmeruk, pp. 438–441.

36. H. Adler, "Żydowska sensacja literackiej Warszawy: Refleksje na marginesie oryginalnego oświadczenia powieściopisarza I. J. Singera," *Chwila* 1925, no. 3280.

37. Szymel, "Piętra."

38. S. Hirszhorn, "Momenty społeczne w *Piętrach:* Na marginesie powieści Appenszlaka," 1933, no. 43.

39. Ch. Löw, "Adam Madler, *Falista linia," Nowy Dziennik* 1934, no. 2.

40. Ibid.

41. S. Pomer, "Żydowskie miasteczko," *Nasz Przegląd,* 1934, no. 150.

42. Löw, *Smok,* p. 79

43. O. Tillemann, "List do autora *Królestwa trzeciej świątyni," Opinia* 1934, no. 14.

44. "Życie literackie," in *Słownik terminów literackich,* edited by M. Głowiński, A. Okopień-Sławińska, and J. Sławiński, Warsaw 1976, p. 513.

45. J. Maciejewski, "Publiczność literacka a instytucje i mechanizmy życia kulturowego," in *Publiczność literacka,* edited by S. Żółkiewski and M. Hopfinger, Wrocław 1982, p. 126.

46. Ibid.

47. See Hertz, *Żydzi,* p. 263.

48. Unfortunately, no publisher is given in some of the publications.

49. See S. Żółkiewski, "Kultura literacka" in *Literatura polska 1918–1932,* edited by A. Brodzka, H. Zaworska, and S. Żółkiewski, Warsaw 1975, p. 17.

50. Shmeruk, *Hebrew–Yiddish,* p. 300.

51. M. Braun, *"Wiadomości Literackie* w ogniu," *Nasz przegląd* 1937, no. 267.

52. This enumeration is certainly not complete: for the most part, Polish-Jewish writers are not listed in any of the existing Polish literary bibliographies. Nor do we yet have a bibliography of the contents of periodicals from the interwar period. The only source of relevant information is the so-called Kartoteka Bara at the Instytut Badań Literackich PAN in Warsaw.

53. M. Szymel, "Chrześcijańskiego Żyda wspomnienia, łzy i myśli," *Opinia* 1934, nos. 44–45. For the editors' comment on this confiscation, see "Konfiskata 44 nru *Opinii," Opinia* 1934, no. 45.

54. "Konfiskata 9 numerów *Opinii* oraz dzieła profesora Klausnera pt. *Jezus z Nazaretu," Opinia* 1933, no. 38.

55. See "Kronika Literacka: *Dwa akordy* Irmy Kanfer po konfiskacie," *Nowy Dziennik* 1936, no. 5. Biblioteka Jagiellońska has a copy of the little volume with the censored part of the text restored by the author.

56. Poets brought up this issue [the Polish-Jewish press's weak response to their works] in their manifestos for Polish-Jewish literature.

57. "Kronika Literacka," *Nowy Dziennik* 1932, no. 166.

58. See *Opinia* 1934, no. 41; *Opinia* 1935, no. 6.

59. T. Kielanowski, "Uchronić od zapomnienia," *Gdańskie zeszyty humanistyczne* 25 (1982), no. 29, p. 191. An evaluation of *Chwila* by Polish circles is found in B. Laskownicki's "W rocznicę *Chwili," Chwila* 1929, no. 3520.

60. Strzemski, p. 286. Strzemski's view undermines, at least partly, Steinlauf's thesis, [as expressed] in Steinlauf, "Polish-Jewish," p. 229: "To put it briefly, the newspaper tried to function as a bridge between the 'darkest Nalewki' and Polish society. However, it is doubtful whether—outside of the occasional instances when politicians or a crowd of journalists eager for polemics reached for it—the paper acquired a significant number of ordinary Polish readers."

61. See Fuks, *Prasa,* p. 261. For the readership of *Mały Przegląd* in Polish circles, see M. Fuks, *"Mały Przegląd* J. Korczaka," *Biuletyn Żydowskiego Instytutu Historycznego w Polsce* 1978, no. 1, p. 7.

62. A. Nowaczyński, *Plewy i perły,* Warsaw 1934, pp. 196, 202, 246. [Nowaczyński] also referred to *Opinia,* as in ibid., p. 214.

63. See, for example, A. Słonimski [pen name A. S.], "Wyczyn seksualny *Naszego Przeglądu," Wiadomości Literackie* 1932, no. 46. See also A. Słonimski, "Kroniki," [part 3], and *Moje walki nad Bzdurą,* Warsaw 1932, p. 162.

64. K. W. Zawodziński, "Lirika" in *Rocznik Literacki za rok 1933,* edited by Z. Szweykowski, Warsaw 1934, p. 44.

65. See T. Sinko [pen name R.], "Wśród nowych książek: S. Pomer, *Elegie podolskie," Kurier Literacko-Naukowy* 1931, no. 36, and "Wśród nowych książek: F. Bertisch, *Kwiaty na ugorze," Kurier Literacko-Naukowy* 1939, no. 19; P. Hula-Laskowski, "Daniel Ihr, *Pożegnanie młodości," Nowa Książka*

1935, no. 5, and "Eker Anda, *Melodia chwili," Nowa Książka* 1939, no. 2, p. 95; W. Jaworski, "Nowości poetyckie: A. Eker, *Na cienkiej strunie," Sygnały* 1937, no. 32.

66. J. Szczawiej, "Na młodym warszawskim Parnasie," *Kurier Literacko-Naukowy* 1934, no. 34; T. Hollender, *"Leopolis Redivivus," Nasza Opinia* 1936, no. 58.

67. Szczawiej, "Na młodym."

68. See J. Birkenmajer, "Przegląd wydawnictw z roku 1931," *Polonista* (Polonist) 1931, no. 4; T. B. Syga, "U poetów, M. Szymel, *Powrót do domu," Gazeta Warszawska* 1932, no. 97; J. J., "Nowe poezje, R. Brandstaetter, *Królestwo trzeciej świątyni," Tygodnik Illustrowany* 1934, no. 8; K. W. Zawodziński, "Poeci Erec Izraela i ghetta," *Wiadomości Literackie* 1936, no. 26, and "Dwie poetki," *Wiadomości Literackie* 1938, no. 29.

69. Panas, "Literatura."

70. Czachowski, p. 317.

71. Ibid., p. 319.

72. Fik, p. 33.

73. Ibid.

74. S. Pieńkowski, "Folklor futuryzmu," "My w zwierciadle żydowskim," "Chałatowa legenda," and "Kłęby Syjonu," in *W ogniu walki: Szkice o sprawie żydowskiej,* Warsaw 1929.

75. Fragment of a review in *ABC* reprinted in *Nowy Dziennik* 1934, no. 91.

76. J. M. Nejman, "Czy góra przyjdzie do Mahometa?" *Nowy Głos* 1938, no. 133.

77. Z. Wasilewski, "Wzór poezji judeo-polskiej," *Myśl Narodowa* 1934, no. 1.

78. *Myśl Narodowa* 1934, no. 1.

79. See "Pieńkowski oskarżony o zniesławienie," *Opinia* 1933, no. 38; "Doktor Brandstaetter contra Pieńkowski," *Opinia* 1934, no. 8; "Reportaż sądowy: A więc kłamali! Roman Brandstaetter contra *Myśl Narodowa," Opinia* 1934, no. 12.

80. The text of Szymel's "Ballada o złotowłosej panience przy klawikordzie" (Ballad about a golden-haired maiden at a clavichord), published in *Nowy Dziennik* 1935, no. 239, is quoted here in its entirety:

The starry wind stands at the open window.
The golden night's sickle troubles the trees—
The grass sleeps ashimmer in dews,
The golden-haired maiden plays the clavichord.
The darkness erases all: elephant and beetle.
What will you play above the darkness that hums in the thickets?
And what are you looking for in your tenderest tones?
And what are you waiting for with lowered eyelashes?

Your clavichord won't play a storm
You won't tear the song from nightingales' mouths.
The starry wind stands at the open window—
The golden night's sickle troubles the trees.

The tones will never bloom with color—
Take off the black, velvet dress,

Throw the crimson painted shawl off your arms,
Oh, go, go away from the clavichord.

Too late. He comes near. Oh, cry, maiden.
You won't escape his dark, cold hands.
He takes your body out of the sweet-smelling garments
And locks it in a coffin, a white coffin.

Who ripped off your crimson painted shawl?
And who tore you away from the clavichord?
The starry wind stands at the open window,
The golden night's sickle troubles the trees.

81. The quotation is taken from "Głupia napaść *Kuriera Lwowskiego* na wiersz Szymla, ogłoszony w *Nowym Dzienniku," Nowy Dziennik* 1935, no. 248.

82. Ibid.

83. I. Berman, "List otwarty do najrozkoszniejszego Imć Pana Zdzisława Kleszczyńskiego alias Sęka," *Nasza Opinia* 1936, no. 91.

84. I. Berman, "Oko w oko z potworami," *Nasza Opinia* 1938, no. 137.

85. B. Schulz, *Księga listów,* collected, edited, and with an introduction, notes, and appendix by J. Ficowski, Cracow 1975, p. 85.

86. J. Nacht, "Skandal literacki we Lwowie," *Nasza Opinia* 1937, no. 75.

87. Wasilewski, "Wzór."

88. "Żydzi w literaturze," *Gazeta Warszawska* 1933, no. 275.

89. Ibid.

90. Wasilewski, "Wzór."

91. S. Pomer, "Żydowskie."

92. L. Belmont, "Obrzydliwy typ hitleryzmu w sosie żydowskim czyli rasista Roman Brandstaetter," *Wolnomyśliciel Polski* 1934, no. 25, and "Klerykalizm we fraku i z cycesem pod narodową kamizelką: Taka sobie maleńka rozprawa z *Opinią," Wolnomyśliciel Polski* 1934, no. 35.

93. Belmont, "Klerykalizm," p. 938.

94. Belmont, "Obrzydliwy," p. 685.

95. Ibid.

96. W. Sebyła, "Nowe poezje: Roman Brandstaetter, *Królestwo trzeciej świątyni," Pion* 1935, no. 25.

97. Ibid.

98. W. Sebyła, "Syjonizm, rasizm czy poezja?" *Kurier Poranny* 1934, no. 136.

99. Sebyła, "Nowe poezje."

100. Sandauer, *O sytuacji,* p. 21.

101. K. Irzykowski, "Udział Żydów w literaturze polskiej," *Kurier Poranny* 1937, no. 224.

102. Contrary to the accepted opinion, Kazimierz Koźniewski claims that this special issue did not come from circles close to *Wiadomości Literackie.* See K. Koźniewski, *Historia co tydzień: Szkice o tygodnikach społeczno-kulturalnych,* vol. 1, Warsaw 1976, pp. 50–51.

103. See M. Opalski, *"Wiadomości."*

104. Ibid., pp. 436, 449.

105. "Prawdziwa i fałszywa asymilacja," *Wiadomości Literackie* 1927, no. 199.

106. L. Piwiński, "Powieść i nowela: H. Adler (Neszer), *Ariela i Jubal: Palestyńskie opowieści romantyczne,*" *Wiadomości Literackie* 1931, no. 395.

107. See ibid.; J. Wittlin [pen name jw], "Wśród książek: K. Dresdner, *Heine i nieznajoma,*" *Wiadomości Literackie* 1928, no. 248; S. Napierski, "Powrót do pseudoklasyków," *Wiadomości Literackie* 1928, no. 235, "M. Szymel, *Powrót do domu,*" *Wiadomości Literackie* 1931, no. 413, "U poetów: J. Lewittes, *Posthumus,*" *Wiadomości Literackie* 1932, no. 453, and "M. Szymel, *Skrzypce przedmieścia,*" *Wiadomości Literackie* 1933, no. 496; Zawodziński, "Poeci," and "Dwie poetki."

108. *Wiadomości Literackie* 1928, no. 248.

109. *Wiadomości Literackie* 1931, no. 413.

110. *Wiadomości Literackie* 1933, no. 496.

111. *Wiadomości Literackie* 1936, no. 26.

112. Napierski; Zawodziński, "Poeci."

113. S. Rogoż, "Patologiczna publicystska," *Wiadomości Literackie* 1936, no. 31.

114. Słonimski, "Kroniki," [part 1].

115. See R. Brandstaetter [pen name R. B.], "Rozmowa z Julianem Tuwimem," *Gazeta Literacka* 1927, no. 6, "Wywiad z Tuwimem," *Wiadomości Literackie* 1927, no. 170, and "Arogant," *Gazeta Literacka* 1927, no. 8.

116. See R. Brandstaetter, "*Pan Tadeusz* po hebrajsku," *Wiadomości Literackie* 1925, no. 100, and "U doskonałego prozaika: Jan Wiktor," *Wiadomości Literackie* 1927, no. 29.

117. R. Brandstaetter, "Plują? Deszcz pada!" *Opinia* 1935, no. 6.

118. Ibid.

119. R. Brandstaetter, "Popas w Mechesówce," *Nasza Opinia* 1935, no. 5.

120. R. Brandstaetter [pen name Apella], "Szadchen na barykadzie," *Opinia* 1935, no. 4.

121. Brandstaetter, "Popas."

122. R. Brandstaetter, "Republika żydowska na Biegunie Północnym," *Nowy Głos* 1938, nos. 44, 51, 58, 65.

123. R. Brandstaetter, "Narodowi hemar-frodyci," *Nasza Opinia* 1935, no. 20.

124. Sandauer, *O sytuacji,* p. 21.

125. See Prokop[-Janiec], "Kafka."

126. D. Herschdörfer, "Pani Zahorska: *Jud Süs,*" *Nowy Dziennik* 1935, no. 123.

127. Shmeruk, *Hebrew–Yiddish,* p. 301.

128. See Opalski, "Wiadomości," p. 442.

129. Pordes, "O kulturze," p. 133.

130. See M. C. Steinlauf, "Jews and the Polish Theater in Nineteenth-Century Warsaw," *Polish Review* 1987, no. 4.

131. Irzykowski.

132. A. Słonimski, *Mętne łby,* n.p., n.d., pp. 112–118, 163–167.

133. R. Brandstaetter, "Dżuma w żydowskiej Grenadzie," *Nowy Głos* 1937, no. 115.

134. See Stopnicka Heller, *On the Edge,* p. 227.

135. See Opalski, "Wiadomości," pp. 441–443.

136. See W. Berkelhammer, "Nekrolog dla panny Racheli," *Nowy Dziennik* 1925, no. 226; M. Kanfer, "Czy *Wiadomości Literackie* są pismem żydowskim?" *Nowy Dziennik* 1932, no. 219; E. Lewinson, "Przez szkła literackie: Z powodu artykułu K. Homolacsa 'Zagadnienie polsko-żydowskie: Artykuł dyskusyjny,' " *Nasz Przegląd* 1933, no. 57; R. Brandstaetter [pen name Apella], "Głosy i echa literackie: W oczach Żyda," *Opinia* 1935, no. 18; J. Appenszlak [pen name Pierrot],

"Między wierszami: 'Maces' P. Mariusza Dawna," *Nasz Przegląd* 1939, no. 167; I. Lubraniecki, "Wpół jest Żydem, wpół Polakiem," *My sami* 1936, no. 2.

137. M. Szymel, *"Cui bono?"* *Nasza Opinia* 1935, no. 2.

138. Kanfer, "Czy *Wiadomości.*"

139. Braun, "Wiadomości."

140. See K. Kożniewski, *Historia co tydzień: Szkice o tygodnikach społeczno-kulturalnych,* vol. 1, Warsaw 1976, pp. 56–57.

141. S. Pomer, " 'U wspólnego stołu': Przyczynek do dziejów mechesowstwa w Polsce," *Nasz Przegląd* 1933, no. 212.

142. S. Pomer, " 'Węzeł gordyjski': Ciekawy przyczynek do kwestii żydowskiej w literaturze polskiej," *Nasz Przegląd* 1933, no. 249.

143. See Dawidowicz.

144. See Opalski, "Wiadomości," p. 436.

145. Löw, *Smok*, p. 8.

146. L. Fryde, "Trzy pokolenia literackie," in *Wybór pism krytycznych,* edited by A. Biernacki, Warsaw 1966.

147. See Witold Dąbrowski's literary biography of Szymel, *Życie Literackie* 1974, no. 35, p. 8.

148. It is easy to find proofs of the special propinquity and popularity of Skamandrite aesthetics and poetics in Polish-Jewish literary criticism. See S. Pomer, "Polski Heine: Julian Tuwim, *Biblia cygańska i inne wiersze,*" *Opinia* 1933, no. 6, and "Czasopisma literackie," *Nasz przegląd* 1935, no. 220; I. Berman, "Półrocze wznowionego *Skamandra,*" *Nasza Opinia* 1935, no. 8, "Poeta gorejący," *Chwila* 1936, no. 6376 and "Satyry Hemara," *Nasza Opinia* 1936, no. 25; M. Kanfer [pen name M. K.], "Skamandryci—klasykami," *Nowy Dziennik* 1935, no. 237; M. Szymel, "Nowy *Skamander,*" *Opinia* 1935, no. 18, "Idę jesienią na ukos! O Tuwimie," *Ster* 1937, no. 41, and "O wierszach niezrozumiałych," *Ster* 1938, no. 8.

149. See Jerzy Kwiatkowski, *Główne nurty w poezji dwudziestolecia,* in *Literatura polska w okresie międzywojennym,* vol. 2, edited by J. Kądziela, J. Kwiatkowski, and I. Wyczańska, Cracow 1979, pp. 13–14.

150. J. Stradecki, *W kręgu Skamandra,* Warsaw 1977, pp. 85–91.

151. Ibid., p. 128.

152. See J. Stradecki, *Julian Tuwim: A Bibliography,* Warsaw 1959.

153. See M. Pytasz, "Przed lekturą 'Kronik tygodniowych,' " in *Skamander,* vol. 2, edited by I. Opacki, Katowice 1982, and "Kwestia żydowska i jej konteksty w 'Kronikach tygodniowych' Antoniego Słonimskiego" in *Studia skamandryckie i inne,* edited by I. Opacki and T. Stępień, Katowice 1985; P. Stasiński, "Międzywojenne felietony Adolfa Nowaczyńskiego: Myśl Narodowa 1921–1934 i Prosto z mostu 1935–1939" in *Poetyka i pragmatyka felietonu,* Warsaw 1982, pp. 57–63.

154. Weyssenhoff, pp. 32, 33.

155. Ibid., pp. 184–185.

156. Ch. Löw [pen name Cha Lef], "Powieść czy pamflet: Panna ze dwora i wampir z Nalewek," *Nowy Dziennik* 1939, no. 57.

157. Pytasz, "Kwestia," p. 44.

158. K. H. Rostworowski, "O uzdrowienie literatury polskiej," *Polonia* 1929, no. 1876.

159. See Stradecki, *W kręgu,* p. 22.

160. See J. J. Lipski, "ONR Falanga a kultura," in *Dwie ojczyzny i inne szkice,* Warsaw 1984.

161. See Opalski, *"Wiadomości,* pp. 447–448.

162. Pomer, "Żydzi," [part 2].

163. R. Brandstaetter, "Legenda siwiejącego poety," *Ster* 1937, no. 4.

164. M. Turkow, *Polacy, Żydzi i mechesy,* Warsaw 1930, p. 9.

165. See Brandstaetter [pen name Apella], "Głosy": "The unpleasant tone and arrogance of *Wiadomości Literackie* just harm the Jews, to whose account the anti-Semites perfidiously debit the methods of a newspaper that has nothing in common with Jewry."

166. R. Brandstaetter, "Palestyna potem i krwią płynąca: Kartki z okrętowego notatnika," *Opinia* 1935, no. 25.

167. Brandstaetter, "Legenda."

168. T. Heller, "*Causa* Tuwim," *Nasz Przegląd* 1938, no. 11. In her diaries, *Dzienniki,* vol. 4, *1930–1939,* part 2 (1935–1939), edited and with an introduction and commentary by H. Kirchner, Warsaw 1988, pp. 279–280, Zofia Nałkowska discloses the behind-the-scenes reasons for the rejection of Tuwim's candidacy, intimately related to the pressure of the anti-Semitic atmosphere: "The rules governing the election of a new member admit no discussion. But at the very beginning of the session, President Sieroszewski turned to us with an apostrophe not to vote for Tuwim because, 'given the currents pervading society' and 'the inappropriate atmosphere' we may expose not only him but also the Academy to unpleasantnesses, insults, and window breaking."

169. Heller, "Causa."

170. Szymel, "Idę."

171. J. K. Weintraub, "Apel," "Ballada o Rzeczypospolitej dywersyey. . . ," "Piosenka prowincjonalna," "Ballada o pewnym plemieniu abisyńskim," "Wiersz o uczonych młodzieńcach," "List liryczny do pana cenzora," "Dzieje polemiki" in *Utwory wybrane,* selected, arranged, and with an introduction by R. Matuszewski; texts prepared on the basis of manuscripts by A. Piorun, Warsaw 1986.

172. "Na pograniczu poezji," *Chwila* 1928, no. 1668.

173. H. Hescheles, "Wieczór poetycki Lechonia, Słonimskiego i Tuwima," *Chwila* 1923, no. 1689. The attitude of the Polish-Jewish press changed radically after Słonimski's publication of the well-known feuilleton "O drażliwości Żydów." See W. Berkelhammer, "P. Antoni Słonimski czyli o drażliwości Żydów," *Chwila* 1924, no. 1971.

174. This discussion was written about by Z. Białek, *Ludwik Fryde jako krytyk literacki,* Cracow 1962, pp. 12–13; W. P. Szymański, "Neosymbolizm—próba zarysu: O awangardowej poezji polskiej w latach trzydziestych" in *Neosymbolizm: O awangardowej poezji polskiej w latach trzydziestych,* Cracow 1973, p. 313; S. Jaworski, *Między awangardą a nadrealizmem: Główne kierunki przemian w poezji polskiej w latach trzydziestych na tle europejskim,* Cracow 1976, p. 213.

175. R. Brandstaetter, "O najmłodszych poetach," *Gazeta Polska* 1931, no. 18.

176. Ibid.

177. Kanfer, "Dwa debiuty."

178. See "List z Palestyny," *Nowy Dziennik* 1928, no. 239; "Żniwiarzom żydowskim odpoczynek po pracy," *Nowy Dziennik* 1929, no. 62.

179. S. Piasecki, "Tajemnica śmierci Mickiewicza," "Sensacja trucicielska," "Ochotnik Levy," in *Prosto z mostu,* Warsaw 1934.

180. I mention just a few of them: "Xawera Deybel i Żydówka Hejnefetter," *Opinia* 1934, no. 43; "Mistrz i uczeń," *Opinia* 1933, no. 4; "Bracia," *Opinia* 1934, no. 16; Szmul Lipiner, "Niemiecki tłumacz *Pana Tadeusza,*" *Opinia* 1934, no. 3; "Żydzi rzymscy w hołdzie Mickiewiczowi," *Chwila* 1938, no. 6695; "Adam Mickiewicz wśród Żydów włoskich," *Chwila* 1938, no. 6692; "Mickiewicz, Żyd i prokurator: Pod szubienicą," *Chwila* 1938, no. 6932; "Od beth-hamidraszu do Mickiewicza," *Chwila* 1938, no. 6946; "Żyd: Zapomniany portrecista Mickiewicza," *Chwila* 1938, no. 7014;

"Adama Mickiewicza myśli wybrane o Żydach i Żydostwie," *Opinia* 1935, no. 22; "Ewolucja poglądów Mickiewicza na kwestię żydowską," *Opinia* 1934, no. 13; "Prorok wśród gawiedzi," *Opinia* 1934, no. 19.

181. Szymel, "Kij," part 1.

182. E. Mendelsohn, "Polish Nationalism and Zionism," in *Zionism,* p. 346.

183. E. Mendelsohn, "From Assimilation to Zionism in Lvov: The Case of Alfred Nossig," *Slavonic and East-European Review* 49 (1971), p. 533.

184. Janusz Maciejewski, author of an extensive essay about the life and work of Braun, was unaware of the feuilletons in *Nasz Przegląd.* See J. Maciejewski, "Wstęp" (Foreword) to M. Braun, *Wybór poezji,* Warsaw 1979.

185. M. Braun, "Moda wiosenna," *Nasz Przegląd* 1938, no. 57.

186. M. Braun, "Syjonizm Adama Mickiewicza," *Nasz Przegląd* 1939, no. 14.

187. M. Braun, "Na straconej pozycji," *Nasz Przegląd* 1939, no. 28.

188. M. Braun, "Samolot Rotszylda," *Nasz Przegląd* 1939, no. 42.

189. M. Braun, "Próba inteligencji," *Nasz Przegląd* 1939, no. 133.

190. Ibid.

191. R. Brandstaetter, "Lista proskrypcyjna," *Opinia* 1933, no. 34.

192. For information about Brandstaetter's lecture, see *Nowy Głos* 1938, no. 90.

193. R. Brandstaetter, "Stwórzmy." [These remarks on Jewish cultural self-defense were] reprinted in "Plaga w żydowskiej Grenadzie," *Nowy Głos* 1937, no. 115.

194. Braun, "Próba inteligencji."

195. See A. Sandauer, "O człowieku który był diabłem," in *Poeci czterech pokoleń,* Cracow 1977; M. Kryński, "Politics and Poetry: The Case of Julian Tuwim," *Polish Review* 1973, no. 4.

196. The hundredth issue of *Nowy Głos,* a jubilee issue (1938, no. 100), is characteristic of the group of authors who published in this newspaper.

197. H. Łazertówna, "Wrogowie," *Nowy Głos* 1938, no. 120; S. Rey, "Spacer," *Nowy Głos* 1938, no. 155. W. Słobodnik joined *Nasz Przegląd,* where he published in 1939 translations as well as original items: "Zamość" (no. 36), "Zagłada" (no. 43), "Heine" (no. 55).

198. A. Prędski, "Serce bez ojczyzny," *Nowy Głos* 1937, no. 1 and subsequent issues.

199. A. Rudnicki, "Lato," in *Sto jeden,* vol. 1, Cracow, 1984, p. 166. Rudnicki also wrote about this return in the article "Przekłute balony," *Polityka,* 9 April 1939.

200. J. Katz, *From Prejudice to Destruction: Anti-Semitism, 1700–1933,* Cambridge [Mass.] 1982; see the chapter "The Scandal of the Jewish Artist: R. Wagner."

201. See J. Bachórz, *Realizm bez chmurnej jazdy: Studia o powieściach Józefa Korzeniowskiego,* Warsaw 1979, pp. 66–67.

202. See A. Jazowski, "Wilhelm Feldman 1868–1919" in *Literatura Młodej Polski,* vol. 4, edited by K. Wyka, A. Hutnikiewicz, M. Puchalska, and J. J. Lipski, Cracow 1977, p. 286.

203. K. Irzykowski, "Brońmy swojego Żyda," in *Czyn i słowo: Glossy sceptyka,* Lvov 1913, p. 220.

204. M. Mutermilch, *Żydzi,* Warsaw 1905, p. 316.

205. A. Kallas, *On i oni wszyscy,* Warsaw 1910, p. 219.

206. S. Pieńkowski, "Pod maską," in *W ogniu walki: Szkice o sprawie żydowskiej,* Warsaw 1929, pp. 20–21.

207. S. Pieńkowski, "Poezja kryptożydowska," *Myśl Narodowa* 1926, no. 41.

208. How intensively the young conducted this "self-defense" on the eve of the war is shown by the bibliographic documentation collected by Marek Pytasz, "Kwestia."

209. Pieńkowski, "Poezja."

210. Rostworowski, "O uzdrowienie."

211. Z. Dębicki, "Ci, którzy idą. . . ," in *Rozmowy o literaturze,* Warsaw 1927, p. 186.

212. Rostworoski, "O uzdrowienie."

213. S. Hirszhorn, "Nędzne cele i liche środki: Popłoch w obozie 'narodowym' z powodu zażydzenia literatury polskiej," *Nasz Przegląd* 1930, no. 40, and "Czy i dlaczego literatura polska jest 'zażydzona,' " *Nasz Przegląd* 1930, no. 30; L. Templer, "Jeszcze o Rostworowskim i Tuwimie," *Nowy Dziennik* 1930, no. 12.

214. S. Imber, "Co nam i tobie Tuwimie. . . ?" in *Asy czystej rasy,* Cracow 1934, p. 39.

215. Imber wrote in ibid., p. 40: "What do we and you have in common Tuwim, what do we and you have in common Słonimski, what do we and all of you who have denied us or have never known us have in common? You have renounced your affiliation to the Jewish nation, you do not know our souls and so treat us frequently like strangers and enemies, your song does not resound with our national language or with the language of our people. They do not praise us because of you, let them not blame us because of you."

216. Brandstaetter, "As prozy."

217. K. Irzykowski, "Żyd to Polak z rezerwą: Do szanownego Pana Stefana Pomera, autora *Elegii podolskich:* Part 2. Udział Żydów w literaturze," *Kurier Poranny* 1937, no. 224.

218. Ch. Löw, "Demaskuję Irzykowskiego!" *Ster* 1937, no. 53; M. Kanfer, "Wstyd że to p. Irzykowski," *Nowy Dziennik* 18 Aug. 1937; M. Braun, "Pan Irzykowski przedstawił się," *Nasza Przegląd* 1937, no. 244.

219. K. I. Gałczyński, "Do przyjaciół z *Prosto z mostu," Prosto z mostu* 1936, no. 21.

220. S. Czernik, "Dwadzieścia lat poezji polskiej, 1918–1939," *Okolica Poetów* 1939, nos. 1–2, p. 34.

221. Ibid., p. 35.

222. Ibid., p. 36.

223. H. Adler, "Pisarze polscy i żydowscy o porozumieniu polsko-żydowskim," *Chwila* 1928, no. 3448.

224. In 1928 Ferdynand Goetel, until then ideologically close to *Wiadomości Literackie* spoke in this spirit: "Pisarze polscy I żydowscy o zbliżeniu polsko-żydowskim: Specjalne wywiady *Chwili* z Ferdynandem Goetelem and Zusmanem Segałowiczem," *Chwila* 1928, no. 3434. See also the pronouncement of Iłłakowiczówna; M. Kanfer, "Żydowscy twórcy neokatolicyzmu," *Nowy Dziennik* 1927, no. 94.

225. See, for example, Stopnicka Heller, *On the Edge,* esp. part I: "The Situation of the Jews."

226. The journalistic texts alone are symptomatic: I. Berman, "Wróg Żydów numer I: Druga przejażdzka po Nowaczyńskim," *Nasza Opinia* 1937, no. 113, "Metody antysemitów," *Nasza Opinia* 1938, no. 147, and "Bolesław Leśmian," *Nasza Opinia* 1937, no. 119; M. Braun, "Próba charakterów," *Nasza Opinia* 1937, no. 94; S. Pomer, "Nieznany antysemita," *Nasz Przegląd* 1934, no. 42, and "Intelektualiści polscy o prześladowaniu Żydów w Niemczech," *Nasz Przegląd* 1933, no. 118; M. Szymel, "Krzywdy," *Ster* 1937, no.46, and "W suterynach umysłu," *Ster* 1938, no. 3.

227. M. Braun, "Jeden dzien Samuela Horsteina," *Opinia* 1934, no. 37; S. Lebenbaum, "Wychrzta," *Ster* 1937, no. 39.

228. R. Brandstaetter, "Gdzie polski Zola? Refleksje na temat polskiej elity umysłowej do kwestii żydowskiej," *Opinia* 1933, no. 3; "Gilotyna i elektryczne krzesło: Dzieje dwóch antysemitów, *Opinia* 1933 no. 38, "Niema kwestii żydowskiej, jest tylko antysemityzm," *My sami* 1936,

no. 7, "Moszkopolis," *Opinia* 1934, no. 9, "Widzenie antysemity," *Opinia* 1935, no. 8, "Do antysemitów," *Opinia* 1934, no. 44, "Ballada o pogromie," *Opinia* 1923, no. 23, and "Nad brzegiem polskiej rzeki," *Nowy Głos* 1938, no. 123.

229. Shmeruk, *Hebrew–Yiddish,* p. 309.

230. This tendency is seen in studies of the history of the Polish Jews. It is discussed by Ezra Mendelsohn, in "Interwar Poland: Good for Jews or Bad for Jews," typescript [n.p., n.d.]

231. This was the position of, say, Rostworowski, who thought that regardless of total assimilation, attachment to Polishness, masterly use of the Polish language, Tuwim was, and would forever be, "a stranger." "We are as different as day and night" said Rostworowski of Poles and Jews, in "O uzdrowienie."

232. Z. Wasilewski, "Na widowni," *Myśl Narodowa* 1934, no. 4.

233. "Leon Wiesenberg—pisarz na indeksie: Kariera pisarska p. Wiesenberga w oświetleniu pisarza antysemity," *Nowy Dziennik* 1938, no. 57.

234. S. Imber, "Rekapitulacja czy kapitulacja. . . ," in *Asy,* p. 54.

235. Berman, "Dyskusje." See also Braun, "Pisarze."

236. Ch. Löw, "Poeci z wypowiedzeniem," *Opinia* 1933, no. 35.

237. Braun, "Próba inteligencji."

3. The Literature of the Cultural Borderland: A Trial Balance

1. Shmeruk, *Hebrew–Yiddish,* p. 331.

2. Ibid., p. 300.

3. Ibid., p. 302.

4. See Maciejewski, pp. 9–32.

5. A. Sandauer, "O Juliuszu Wicie" in J. Wit, *Wiersze wybrane,* Warsaw 1959, p. 6.

6. See Prokop[-Janiec], "Kafka," pp. 131–132.

7. See *Antologia poezji żydowskiej,* selected and annotated by J. Łasik; edited and with an introduction by A. Słucki, Warsaw 1983, p. 319.

8. Braun, "Pisarze."

9. It is worth comparing the two versions of [Wit's] poem "Na skrzypcach grać," [first appearing in] *Nowy Dziennik* 1928, no. 136, [then] reprinted in the volume *Pluski,* Warsaw 1930, p. 11, "Skrzypce." First, the *Nowy Dziennik* version:

Sometimes only Miss Rachel plays the violin in the evening;
The playing makes the office manager very ill,
He can hear no more, can listen no longer,
He slowly opens the window and looks out at the yard.
. . . .
In the meantime Rabbi Shimshon nods over the Talmud,
Exhausted by worry about the perplexed people.
The candle went out long ago, only the moon is shining,
Like a lonely Moses among lonely children.

Now the *Pluski* version:

Sometimes Miss Marysia plays the violin in the evening,
The playing makes the office manager very ill,

He can hear no more, he can listen no longer,
He slowly opens the window and looks out at the yard.
. . . .
In the meantime old Simon nods over the Talmud,
Exhausted by worry about the perplexed people.
The candle went out long ago, only the moon is shining,
Like a lonely Moses blundering through the centuries.

In addition to perfecting the text, the author "Polonizes" some of the figures: "Rachel" is changed to "Marysia" and "Rabbi Shimshon" to "old Simon" . . .

10. Stradecki, *W kręgu,* p. 11.

11. Ibid., p. 116.

12. S. Pomer, "Powieść o pogromach," *Nasz Przegląd* 1934, no. 229.

13. Szymel, "Kij," part 4.

14. I. Howe, "Pisarze amerykańscy pochodzenia żydowskiego" (American writers of Jewish origin), translated from the English by E. Ćwirko-Godycka, *Literatura na Świecie* 1982, no. 12, p. 275.

15. See Stopnicka Heller, *On the Edge,* p. 215.

4. I, a Jew; We, Jews

1. Please see list of abbreviations on p. xix.

2. See Dresdner, "Udział."

3. Moreover, in the works of the writers in question, it took much the same form as in Polish-Jewish literature. Here are some relevant examples:

I, Józef Wittlin, from the tribe of Judah ("Psalm," in *Poezje,* Warsaw 1981, p. 81)

And the blood of king David pulses in my veins,
And I see, when a quiet whisper confides to my ears,
In a sea of stars and sands the outlines of a temple.
(A. Słonimski, "Arka," in *Wiersze zebrane,* Warsaw 1933, p. 76)

Semitic blood flows in me,
Hot blood, passionate blood.
(J. Tuwim, "Pod bodźcem wieków")

The last poem, as quoted in A. Kowalczyk, "Jak Tuwim swój młodzieńczy wizerunek korygował" (How Tuwim modified his youthful image) in *Skamander,* vol. 3, *Studia o poezji Juliana Tuwima,* edited by I. Opacki, Katowice 1982, p. 81, has been preserved in BUW, manuscript no. 237).

4. See M. Czermińska, "Postwa autobiograficzna" in *Studia o narracji,* edited by St. Jaworski and J. Sławiński, Wrocław 1982, pp. 223–235.

5. S. Pomer, "Elegia o moich praojcach," *Nowy Dziennik* 1930, no. 271. An earlier version, titled "Moi ojcowie," was published in *Chwila* 1929, no. 3558.

6. C. Meerson-Becker, "Do mowy żydowskiej," *Nasz Przegląd* 1933, no. 99.

7. J. Lewittes, "Do syna," *Nowy Dziennik* 1933, no. 290.

8. S. Pomer, "Grób mego ojca," *Chwila* 1932, no. 4637.

9. M. Szymel, "Odpowiedź na zarzut," *Nowy Dziennik* 1931, no. 186.

10. N. Füllenbaum, "Asher Yatzar," *Słowo* 1936, no. 75.

11. N. Füllenbaum, "Bore Pri Hagafen," *Słowo* 1936, no. 75.

12. I. Deutscher, "Maasseh bereischit," *Nowy Dziennik* 1925, no. 179.

13. See *Chwila* 1933, no. 1923.

14. Ph. Lejeune, "Pakt autobiograficzny," translated by A. W. Labuda, *Teksty* 1975, no. 5, p. 42.

15. M. Braun, "Rapsod," *Nasza Opinia* 1938, no. 130.

16. W. Szlengel, *"Nihil Novi," Nasz Przegląd* 1937, no. 207.

17. A similar thread appears also in the European tradition; see G. K. Anderson, *The Legend of the Wandering Jew,* Providence [R.I.] 1965, p. 395.

18. H. Safrin, "Ahaswer," *Chwila* 1936, no. 6348. It seems that the presence of the Ahasuerus motif in Polish-Jewish literature reflected its popularity in turn-of-the-century European literature. (See the entry "Ahaswer" in E. Frenzel, *Stoffe der Weltliteratur: Ein Lexikon dichtungsgeschichtlicher Längsschnitten,* Stuttgart 1983, pp. 15–21; H. Filipkowska, "Tułacze i wędrowcy" in *Młodopolski świat wyobraźni,* studies and essays edited by M. Podraza-Kwiatkowska, Cracow 1977. See also Anderson, pp. 293–302. That this motif drew on modernist sources is indicated by its popularity in Zionist poetry of the beginning of the century (a relevant item is Marian Rosenfeld's cycle "Pieśni Ahaswera," published in the *Rocznik Żydowski* in 1904.

19. H. Safrin, "Pieśń o sobie," *Nasza Opinia* 1937, no. 119.

20. H. Safrin, "Judaica," *Nowy Dziennik* 1933, no. 102. This is an earlier version of "Pieśń o sobie."

21. For the historical content of the Jewish holidays see R. Lilientalowa, "Święta żydowskie w przeszłości i teraźniejszości," part 1, *Rozprawy Akademii Umiejętności: Wydział Filologiczny,* ser. 2, vol. 30 (1909), pp. 191–199.

22. M. Silberman, "xxx," *Chwila* 1929, no. 3850.

23. J. Appenszlak, *Mowie polskiej,* Warsaw 1915, p. 1.

24. M. Braun, "Ahaswer," in *Wybór poezji,* selected and with an introduction by J. Maciejewski, Warsaw 1979, p. 153. Braun's "Ahaswer" was first published in *Nasz Przegląd* 1927, no. 139.

25. The image of the Jews as outcasts and wanderers and the problem of the meaning of the Diaspora appeared as early as the middle of the nineteenth century in the works of writers of Jewish origin. These threads were also important in the vision of Israel—"a people that by itself affords a profound lesson"—created by Polish romantic writers.

26. M. Braun, "Fragmenty dziejów," *Nasza Opinia* 1939, no. 209.

27. S. Pomer, "Nad rzekami Babilonu," *Nowy Dziennik* 1933, no. 338.

28. M. Szymel, "Nad rzekami Babilonu," *Nowy Dziennik* 1933, no. 118.

29. Lilientalowa, part 1, p. 200, wrote about the national symbolism of the Pesach holiday.

30. M. Szymel, "Żydzi," *Chwila* 1930, no. 14.

31. W. Szlengel, "Szałasy," *Nasz Przegląd* 1937, no. 268.

32. R. Friedmann, "Opowieść o lasce Mojżesza," *Chwila* 1931, no. 4382.

33. M. Braun, "Assimi: Fragmenty poematu," *Nasza Opinia* 1939, no. 210.

34. M. Szymel, "Od tłumacza," in A. Ptaszkin, *Ani sobie ani muzom,* Warsaw 1936, p. 4.

35. M. Braun, "Fragmenty."

36. D. Ihr, "Brother," *Nasza Opinia* 1935, no. 8.

37. Szymel, "Od tłumacza," p. 4.

38. M. Szymel, "Psalmy nadziei," *Nasz Przegląd* 1934, no. 243.

39. L. Baumberg, "Brzemię niebieskie," *Nasz Przegląd* 1938, no. 136.

40. J.-P. Sartre, *Rozważania o kwestii żydowskiej* (Reflections on the Jewish question), translated from the French by J. Lisowski, Warsaw 1957. Sartre writes: "[L]ike each of us, a Jew has his own character and, in addition, is a Jew. In his case, we are facing something like the doubling of the fundamental relation to another person. He is, so to say, doubly determined."

41. M. Szymel, "Nie chcę być Żydem," *Opinia* 1935, no. 1.

42. I. Kanfer, "Żydowscy aktorzy," in *Dwa akordy,* Cracow 1936, p. 10.

43. S. Richter, "???," in *Wiry,* Stanisławów 1932, p. 3.

44. R. Lilientalowa, part 2, p. 342.

45. H. Safrin, "Unetane tokef. . . ," *Chwila* 1934, no. 5557; S. Dykman, "Netaneh tokef," *Nowy Dziennik* 1936, no. 258.

46. Regina Lilientalowa, p. 366, described Yom Kippur as a kind of All Souls' Day.

47. H. Safrin, "Kol nidrej," *Nowy Dziennik* 1933, no. 268; I. Deutscher, "Kol-Nidre," *Nowy Dziennik* 1925, no. 218.

48. M. Hochberżanka, "Yom Kipur," *Nowy Dziennik* 1933, no. 268. See also A. Eker, "Yom Kipur," *Nowy Dziennik* 1929, no. 281.

49. Similar interpretations are given to Jewish threads in modern literature in English. See D. Daiches, "Some Aspects of Anglo-American Jewish Fiction" in *Jewish Perspectives: 25 Years of Jewish Writing,* London 1980.

50. S. Pomer, "Złota lipa," *Nasz Przegląd* 1933, no. 162.

51. W. Szlengel, "Tobół tułaczy," *Nasz Przegląd* 1938, no. 36.

52. E. Silberstein, "Golusowy sen," *Nowy Dziennik* 1936, no. 44.

53. St. Ossowski, *O ojczyźnie i narodzie,* Warsaw 1984, p. 26.

54. Braun, "Ahaswer."

55. J. Appenszlak, *Piętra: Dom na Bielańskiej,* Warsaw 1933, p. 188.

56. An ironic and provocative variant of [the two fatherlands] motif came up in Słonimski's poem "Dwie ojczyzny":

When you flash, the morning star,
Heaven, earth, and heart are quiet.
You are my snowy Lebanon, darkhaired girl.
I would leave the sad lands of the North and the fertile humus
Like Judean sands and deserts.
I'll give the sea to drown in the depths of your eyes,
For one kiss I'll give two fatherlands.

(A. Słonimski, "Dwie ojczyzny" [Two fatherlands], in *Wiersze zebrane,* Warsaw 1933, p. 70).

57. The first version of [Szymel's] poem, titled "Polsko!" appeared in *Nowy Dziennik* 1928, no. 304.

58. M. Szymel, "Polska," *Lektura* 1934, no. 1.

59. D. Ihr, "Błogosławieństwo," in *Pożegnanie młodości,* Lvov 1934, pp. 24–25.

60. R. Brandstaetter, "Żniwiarzom żydowskim odpoczynek po pracy," *Nowy Dziennik* 1929, no. 62.

61. R. Brandstaetter, "Biblia," *Opinia* 1935, no. 3.

62. The first version [of Brandstaetter's "Elegia"], titled "Wiosna w Warszawie," appeared in *Nowy Dziennik* 1932, no. 193.

63. N. Füllenbaum, "Więdnące korzenie," *Słowo* 1936, no. 46.

64. R. Brandstaetter, "Skarga Srula z Lubartowa," *Opinia* 1935, no. 15.

65. Szymel published "Rozmowa z Panem Mikołajem" in *Ster* 1937, no. 44; "Wspomnienie" in *Chwila* 1937, no. 6642; "Rozmowa o ludziach i drzewach," in *Chwila* 1937, no. 6733; and "Śpiew polskiego Żyda" in *Nasza Opinia* 1938, no. 147.

66. It is interesting to compare the text of "Ojczyzna" with that of "Pieśń nad Pieśniami": 1, 6; 4, 3–4; 7, 5; 8, 11–12.

67. S. Pomer, "Ziemia Święta," *Chwila* 1929, no. 67.

68. L. Jamer, "Czy znasz ten kraj?" *Chwila* 1933, no. 5069.

69. Similar texts, written by children, appeared frequently in Polish-Jewish papers. One such was "Mowo hebrajska," by E. T., which appeared in *Chwila* 1934, no. 355.

70. Appenszlak, *Piętra,* pp. 91–92.

71. Meerson-Becker.

72. D. Ihr, "Do polskiej mowy," *Opinia* 1935, no. 11.

73. D. Ihr, "Do mowy hebrajskiej," *Opinia* 1935, no. 13.

74. D. Ihr, "List," *Nasza Opinia* 1936, no. 25.

75. M. Szymel, "Żydowscy trubadurzy," *Nowy Dziennik* 1929, no. 316.

76. R. Brandstaetter, "Elegia na mowę hebrajską," in *Węzły I miecze* (Knots and swords), Warsaw 1933, p. 20.

77. H. Safrin, "Hymn do pieśni hebrajskiej," *Chwila* 1934, no. 5321.

5. "The Return Home"

1. Saint Augustine writes about the laws of emotional memory in his *Confessions.*

2. F. Bertisch, "Wyprawa po złoto runo," in *Kwiaty na ugorze* (Flowers on the fallow), Stanisławów 1939, p. 19.

3. Please see list of abbreviations on p. 000.

4. Szymel, "Żydowscy."

5. J. Wit, "Okręt Andersena," *Nowy Dziennik* 1926, no. 88.

6. M. Silberman, "W zimowy zmierzch," *Słowo* 1938, no. 143.

7. R. Brandstaetter, "Wspominanie Cezara nad Rodanem," in *Węzły i miecze* (Knots and swords), Warsaw 1933, p. 22.

8. K. Dresdner, "Szechina," *Chwila* 1929, no. 3537.

9. R. Friedmann, "Matka," *Chwila* 1931, no. 4307.

10. J. Wit, "Syn handlarza winem," *Nowy Dziennik* 1926, no. 14.

11. J. Wit, "Wariaci," *Chwila* 1926, no. 35.

12. See J. Cieślikowski, "Okolica dzieciństwa" in *Literatura i podkultura dziecięca,* Wrocław 1975.

13. J. Wit, "Zwycięstwo" in *Lampy,* Warsaw 1936, pp. 10–12.

14. S. Pomer, "Rachela i katarynka," *Chwila* 1929, no. 3579.

15. Pomer, "Złota."

16. M. Szymel, "Na prowincji żydowskiej," *Chwila* 1938, no. 6946.

17. D. Ihr, "Ballada o zaułku," in *Pożegnanie młodości* (A farewell to youth), Warsaw 1933, pp. 21–23.

18. Cz. Endelman-Rosenblatt [pen name Halicz], *Ludzie, którzy jeszcze żyją,* Warsaw 1934, p. 7.

19. H. A. Fenster, "Nasze miasteczko," *Nowy Dziennik* 1930, no. 34.

20. Szymel, "Na prowicji."

21. J. Wit, "Na skrzypcach grać," *Nowy Dziennik* 1928, no. 136.

22. The motifs of Jewish holidays are among the most popular in Polish-Jewish literature. Sabbath: R. Brandstaetter, "Ballada o rabinie z Płocka," *Ktś,* pp. 19–20; K. Dresdner, "Piątek," *Hin,* p. 18; A. Eker, "Bajka o Sobocie," *Odz,* pp. 40–42; "Wiersz o sobocie," *Ncs,* pp. 100–101; H. A. Fenster, "Elegia o sobotnim wieczorze," *Otco,* pp. 17–18; D. Ihr, "Sambation," *Chwila* 1934, no. 5321; S. Pomer, "Moja matka," *Ep,* p. 24; K. Rosenfeld, "Sabbat," *Wcl,* p. 27; H. Safrin, "Lcha Dodi," *Chwila* 1937, no. 6691; M. Silberman, "Opowieść o starym Mendlu," in *W cieniu życia,* Stanisławów 1937, pp. 20–22; M. Szymel, "Gdy w małym miasteczku zapada sobota," Wl 61; "Krawiec z Białegokamienia," *Opinia* 1934, nos. 41–42, "Matka w mroku," *Pdd,* p. 13, "Notatki autobiograficzne," *Pdd,* 9; "O sobocie utraconej," *Sp,* 29, "O staruszku tęskniącym," *Sp,* p. 18, "Sobota," *Chwila* 1926, no. 2475, "Sobota," *Pdd,* p. 10, "Świąteczny wieczór na wsi," *Nowy Dziennik* 1929, no. 302, and "Żydowscy trubadurzy." Hanukkah: A. Eker, "O ośmiu siostrzyczkach," *Odz,* pp. 24–27; "Ballada chanukowa," *Odz,* pp. 28–32, "Co świeczki chanukowe powiedziały Szlomie," *Odz,* pp. 33–37, "W chanukę," *Odz,* pp. 38–39; H. Safrin, "Dzisiaj odzyskacie mowę. . . ," *Chwila* 1938, no. 3490; M. Szymel, "Zapal świeczkę chanukową," *Wl,* p. 69, and "Zima w domu moim," *Wl,* p. 59; J. Werfel, "Chanukowa biel," *Nowy Dziennik* 1933, no. 342. Purim: S. Pomer, "Przyśpiew purymowy," *Nasz Przegląd* 1934, no. 63; W. Szlengel, "Maska Purymowa," *Nasz Przegląd* 1939, no. 64; M. Szymel, "Purymowy wieczór," *Chwila* 1928, no. 3220. Pesach: A. Eker, "Elijahu," *Odz,* pp. 66–68; "Święto Pesach," *Odz,* pp. 64–65; M. Hochberżanka, "Święto," *Nowy Dziennik* 1935, no. 1083; A. Lauterbach, "Hagada," *Chwila* 1924, no. 1837; S. Pomer, "Pesach nędzarzy," *Chwila* 1931, no. 4319; H. Safrin, "Chad gadia," *Chwila* 1936, no. 6125; M. Szymel, "Notatki autobiograficzne," *Pdd,* p. 9; "O proroku który nie przyszedł," *Wl,* p. 60; "Pascha samotnego," *Wl,* p. 75; "Prorok Eli," *Nowy Dziennik* 1929, no. 112; "Przyjdzie Eljasz Prorok," *Pdd,* 16–17; Lag B'omer: M. Szymel, "W lag b'omer," *Chwila* 1926, no. 2557. Simchat Torah: M. Szymel, "Simchat Tora," *Chwila* 1927, no. 3082. Sukkoth: M. Szymel, "Święto szałasów," *Wl,* pp. 72–73; W. Szlengel, "Szałasy," *Nasz Przegląd* 1937, no. 268.

23. A. J. Heschel writes about the metaphorical representation of the the Sabbath in *The Sabbath: Its Meaning for Modern Man,* New York 1984, pp. 53–55, 59–62.

24. I. Manger, "The Poetry of Our Holy Days" in *An Anthology of Modern Yiddish Literature,* compiled and edited by J. Leftwich. Hague 1974, p. 87.

25. J. A. (Appenszlak?), "Wilhelm Wachtel: Z okazji jubileuszowej wystawy artysty," *Chwila* 1925, no. 2187.

26. S. Vincenz, *Barwinkowy wianek,* Warsaw 1983, p. 314.

27. Heschel, *Sabbath;* E. Fromm, *Zapomniany język: Wstęp do rozumienia snów, baśni i mitów* (The forgotten language: An introduction to the interpretation of dreams, fairy tales, and myths), translated from the English by J. Marzęcki, with an introduction by K. T. Toeplitz, Warsaw 1977, pp. 227–234.

28. A. J. Heschel, *The Earth Is the Lord's: The Inner World of the Jew In East Europe,* New York 1950, p. 96.

29. Ch. Löw, "Między poetami," *Miesięcznik Żydowski* 1931, p. 570.

30. Ihr published the following [version of "Do przyjaciół poetow" (To poet friends)] in *Chwila* 1929, no. 3572:

With a smile of sentiment on youthful faces,
Hands shaking with emotion you rummage
In memories. Is the world so still
That to hear life one must repeat the past?

You dream of cramped childhood yards,
Overgrown twisted paths which lead nowhere.
Forked willows over the fathers' inn
Forever entice with a charm all their own.

The old house of worship appears in faint and hazy light,
And gray-haired fathers bow in impotent prayers.
(It is your song got them out of the darkness of the grave,
A song as sad as the clacking of lost cranes.)

The old men can tell you nothing, though they
greet you with outstretched parchment hands—
In this throng of phantoms you will be as alone
As a ray of light lost among blackened stalls.

Leave the cemeteries! Let the shade of a weeping willow
Grieve over the graves and caress them with a mute breath of air.
The strong sun blazes over the wide highway—
Forget the dead when it's time to wake the living.

31. This is how Alina Witkowska interprets romantic idyllism, *Sławianie, my lubim sielanki. . . ,* Warsaw 1972.

6. A New Life

1. See Mendelsohn, *Zionism,* esp. "Conclusion: The Road to Zionism—Mobilization of Support within the Jewish Community," pp. 338–344.

2. M. Kula, "Porozmawiajmy jeszcze raz, na spokojnie, o syjonizmie," *Dzieje najnowsze* 1987, no. 2, pp. 89–124.

3. See W. Berkelhammer, "Wstęp," in Z. F. Finkelstein, *W jarzmie idei: Obrazy z życia Teodora Herzla,* translated by S. Zeisler, Cracow 1935, p. 7; H. Adler, "Czy nie rękami profana? Na marginesie 'powieści-studium' L. Belmonta, *Mojżesz współczesny: Rozdroże Teodora Herzla, Nowy Dziennik* 1931, no. 5.

4. Please see list of abbreviations on p. xix.

5. This is what Jan Błoński called the "worldview of the assimilators," "Autoportret żydowski," in *Kilka myśli co nie nowe,* Cracow 1985, p. 129.

6. J. Appenszlak, *Mowie,* p. 1.

7. B. Mayer, "Do słońca," *Nowy Dziennik* 1932, no. 173.

8. M. Hochberżanka, "Czekaj na mnie. . . ," *Nowy Dziennik* 1933, no. 250.

9. Braun, "Assimi."

10. Braun, "Fragmenty."

11. S. Spund, "Tak bym chętnie," *Chwila* 1931, no. 4466.

12. I. Deutscher, "Modlitwa o deszcz," *Nowy Dziennik* 1925, no. 226.

13. J. Werfel, "Hajfskie wybrzeże," *Nowy Dziennik* 1930, no. 26.

14. M. Silberman, "Kadimah," *Nowy Dziennik* 1930, no. 289.

15. R. Taubenschlag, *"Judea resurrecta:* Pieśń bólu i radości," *Nowy Dziennik* 1921, no. 176.

16. M. Korn, "Modlitwa o deszcz," *Nowy Dziennik* 1928, no. 269.

17. M. Hochberżanka, "Święto."

18. I. Deutscher, "Orka," *Nowy Dziennik* 1925, no. 83.

19. A. Lutwak, "Palestyna," *Nowy Dziennik* 1929, no. 201.

20. R. Brandstaetter, "Elegia cedrowa," *Nowy Dziennik* 1929, no. 250.

21. Z. Schenker, "Nad grobem ofiar palestyńskich," *Nasz Przegląd* 1929, no. 243.

22. Z. Schenker, "W narodową rocznicę," *Nowy Dziennik* 1929, no. 201.

23. A. Marc, "Ziemia," *Nasza Przegląd* 1925, no. 211.

24. H. Adler, "Wstęp" in T. Herzl, *U wrót nowego życia . . . : Powieść-utopia (Altneuland)*, translated by H. Adler, Warsaw 1934, p. 5.

25. Ibid., p. 5.

26. See also N. Füllenbaum, *"Hachsharah," Słowo* 1936, no. 57. A highly evocative description of a hora is also found in [Bernard Zimmermann's] *Tirsa:* "Arms rested on the shoulders of one's neighbor, wings grew from legs, the circle closed and swayed, once to the left and once to the right. . . . First slow and gentle, then ever faster and livelier. The chain tightened, the arms straightened out, the weightless bodies became suspended in space and threw themselves into the whirl of a furious hora. Now silently, quietly, noiselessly, like shadows, now loudly, rumblingly, rhythmically, as if someone were chopping wood, or as if guns were crossing a bridge.

When the rhythm faltered and the steps got mixed up, a song like a hurricane immediately burst from the young chests: 'Mi yivne hagalil, hagalila hagalil . . . ' Every now and then someone moved out of the circle, drenched with sweat, staggered, turned pale, dropped on a bench, and new links stepped in to join the momentarily broken chain even more securely." *(T,* pp. 98–99)

27. J. Kleinberg, "Chalucim," *Okienko na świat* 1938, no. 8.

28. L. Krasucki, *Poezje zebrane,* Włocławek 1923, p. 40.

29. F. Bertisch, "Chwała," *Nasza Opinia* 1936, no. 46.

30. Taubenschlag, *"Judea."*

31. F. T. Aszkenazy, "Hasmonea," Chwila 1933, no. 4948.

32. E. Mendelsohn, *Zionism,* p. 54.

33. Schenker, "Nad grobem."

34. D. Ihr, "List," *Nasza Opinia* 1936, no. 25.

35. H. Fenster, "Ballada o młodych synach starej ziemi," *Chwila* 1931, no. 4255.

36. J. Hartblaj, *Jehoszua: Powieść osnuta na tle życia "chaluców,"* Warsaw 1928, p. 27.

37. See, for example, Natan Füllenbaum's poem "Polemika," *Słowo* 1937, no. 137:

Me, too! I can write
à la Mayakovski
about Eretz too—one can write
much as one does about your Russia.
A rhapsody written with sickles
hewn in the rock with hammers
plowed into the field with tractors
brotherly songs and corpses
trowel and sword—
me too!

For you it is Dnieprostroj, for me it is Tel-Or,
for you he is a burgher, for me a "gibor,"
for you a fascist on a bourgeois's string,
for me tefillin for a hammer swapped,
for you rot, cant, and scoundrel,
for me hamlets torn out of muck with claws.
At the starting line for tomorrow a gear
dynamite in the fingers, the swing, the soul,
thoughts hardened to gnarled sticks,
we'll crush the world of wrongs.
From tiny plots to thinking on enormous scale,
from mudhuts to hundredfold houses,
acres, machines, workshops, cars,
expression of radio-run drilling towers—
Me, too!

And if someone will want to rob
you like a bourgeois, and sell me
at a discount, the anti-state way,
toil and hunger—
know
that on your heads we'll cut with a dagger,
in Hebrew, G.P.U.
The rogue against the wall, fire—and it's over
Me, too!
Well—come to think—perhaps—who knows—
this one thing—I—no.

. . . .
You say, bourgeois fatherland sentiments,
how can a thing—earth or dust—be holy?

In Moscow factories ring
in the center of Moscow—a corpse!
a mummy on Red Square
red eternal flames burn
Lenin's tomb.

My dead are underground—skeletons
and the living above ground—with plows
from top to bottom—on both sides
hold on to the land—with the teeth.

38. Herzl, p. 190.
39. R. Brandstaetter, *Jerozolima światła i mroku,* Warsaw 1935, p. 8.

40. On exoticism, see M. Bachtin, "Formy czasu i czasoprzestrzeni w powieści," in *Problemy literatury i estetyki,* translated by W. Grajewski, Warsaw 1982, pp. 289–299.

41. *Czerwone dusze* was advertised in the *Ilustrowany Almanach Żydowski Wydawnictwa Nowe Życie,* edited by J. Zineman, Warsaw 1933, p. 146, as follows: Read the first book on the life of postwar Palestine, a book of struggles, toil, work, blood, love. R. Benshem, Red souls, 244 pages, large format. The first edition is sold out. A second edition is being printed. The book has been translated into Yiddish and Hebrew and dramatized. The reviews of Red souls have been extremely favorable.

7. The Jewish Self-Portrait: A Trial Balance

1. See M. Szymel, "Ballada o głupcach z Chełma"; S. Pomer, "Miłość wieczna"; D. Ihr, "Hindele i Mendele: Sielanka."

2. Chełm was a kind of East European Jewish Abdera [which, despite being the birthplace of Democritus, Protagoras, and Anaxarchus, was notorious for the stupidity of its inhabitants—Trans.], and the stories about its inhabitants belonged to the classics of Jewish folk humor.

3. For example, "Jom-Kipur Baalszema: Z legend chasydzkich," *Chwila* 1934, no. 5575; "Pieśń o Baal Szemie," *Chwila* 1933, no. 5114; "Fraszka o Herszlu z Ostropola," *Chwila* 1937, no. 6499.

4. See "Złota róża," *Chwila* 1926, no. 2750.

5. See M. Szymel, "Mesjasz," "Lament o Mesjasza syna Dawidowego," "Przyjdzie Eljasz prorok," "O proroku który nie przyszedł"; H. Safrin, "Golem," *Nowy Dziennik* 1933, no. 132, and "Pieśń o golemie z Pragi," *Chwila* 1936, no. 6299.; A. Lauterbach, "Golem," *Nasz Przegląd* 1925, no. 81.

6. See R. Brandstaetter, "Kasrylówka," "Ballada o Dybuku," *Opinia* 1933, no. 48; A. Lauterbach, "Na ostatniej kartce egzemplarza Dybuka," *Chwila* 1924, no. 1733; H. Safrin, "Ballada o pustej karczmie," *Chwila* 1934, no. 5596, and "Ballada o 'Nocy na starym rynku,' " *Chwila* 1935, no. 5788; M. Szymel, "Zielone pola: Z powodu wystawienia sztuki Pereca Hirszbajna pt. *Zielone pola,*" *Nasz Przegląd* 1932, no. 134.

7. [Zionist and pioneer] songs were among the writings of Karol Rosenfeld, Minka Silberman, and Lucjan Krasucki.

8. Ch. Shmeruk, "Jews and Poles in Yiddish Literature in Poland between the Two World Wars: Background Remarks," *Polin* vol. 1 (1986), p. 185.

9. It is very instructive to compare the prose writing of Adler and Feldszuh with that of Józef Aricha in his novel *Chleb i objawienie,* translated by M. Litwinow, Warsaw 1934, representing the literature of the third aliyah. See also W. Glicksman, "The Halutz Ideology and Experience as Reflected in the Yiddish Novel in Poland 1919–1939," *Yivo Annual of Jewish Social Science* (New York), vol. 14 (1969).

10. A. Eker, "Wstęp," in *Melodia chwili,* Lvov 1937, p. 5.

11. Szymel, "Nowy *Skamander.*"

12. The most recent work of this kind is Shmeruk, *Esterke.*

13. See M. Opalski, *The Jewish Tavern-Keeper and His Tavern in Nineteenth-Century Polish Literature,* Jerusalem 1986.

14. E. Prokop[-Janiec], "Szabat—sobota: O międzywojennej literaturze polsko-żydowskiej," *Ruch literacki* 1987, nos. 4–5, and "Shtetl," *Polin* vol. 4 (1989).

15. [That, in their treatment of the Sabbath motif, the languages of Polish-Jewish and Jewish

literature converged] was pointed out by historians of the Jewish literatures during the discussion that followed my lecture "The Sabbath Motif in Interwar Polish-Jewish Literature" at a conference at Brandeis University in April 1986.

16. M. Szymel, "Lato ubogich," *Nasz Przegląd* 1939, no. 197.

Selected Bibliography

Adler, H. [pen name Neszer]. *Ariela i Jubal: Palestyńskie opowieści romantyczne*. Warsaw, 1931.

Almanach i leksykon Żydowstwa polskiego. Vols. 1–3. Lvov, 1937.

Almanach żydowski wydany przez H. Stachla zawierający szereg artykułów wybitnych literatów i publicystów oraz życiorysy czołowych postaci Małopolski Wschodniej. Lvov, 1937.

Anderson, G. K. *The Legend of the Wandering Jew*. Providence [R.I.], 1965.

Appenszlak, J. [pen name Pierrot] *Mowie polskiej: Poemat*. Warsaw, 1915.

———. *Piętra: Dom na Bielańskiej*. Warsaw, 1933.

Appenszlak, P. [Appenszlakowa]. "Smutny poeta: M. Szymel." *Nasz Przegląd* 1935, no. 42.

Aricha, J. *Chleb i objawienie*. Translated by M. Litwinówna. Warsaw, 1934.

Bachórz, J. *Realizm bez "chmurnej jazdy": Studia o powieściach Józefa Korzeniowskiego*. Warsaw, 1979.

Bachtin, M. "Formy czasu i czasoprzestrzeni w powieści." In *Problemy literatury i estetyki*, translated by W. Grajewski. Warsaw, 1982.

Bałaban [Balaban], M. "*Miesięcznik Żydowski:* Na marginesie dwóch roczników." *Nasz Przegląd* 1933, no. 158.

Bartoszewicz, K. *Wojna żydowska w roku 1859: początki asymilacji i antysemityzmu*. Warsaw, 1913.

Belmont [Blumental], L. "Klerykalizm we fraku i z cycesem pod narodową kamizelką: Taka sobie maleńka rozprawa z *Opinią*." *Wolnomyśliciel Polski* 1934, no. 35.

———. *Mojżesz współczesny: Powieść-studium*. Warsaw, 1931.

———. "Obrzydliwy typ hitleryzmu w sosie żydowskim czyli rasista Roman Brandstaetter." *Wolnomyśliciel Polski* 1934, no. 25.

Ben-Hillel, "O kulturze polsko-żydowskiej." *Opinia* 1933, no. 32.

Berkelhammer, W. *My i narody świata*. Cracow, 1922.

———. "O asymilacji." *Chwila* 1921, no. 735.

———. "Pierwszy tom *Miesięcznika Żydowkiego*." *Nowy Dziennik* 1931, no. 158.

———. "Problem asymilacji." *Nowe Życie* 1924, no. 5.

Berman, I. "Dyskusje literackie." *Nasza Opinia* 1937, no. 92.

———. "O tzw. cechach narodowych w literaturze pięknej." *Nasza Opinia* 1935, nos. 2–4.

———. "Poeci polsko-żydowscy w parodii." *Nasza Opinia* 1936, no. 32.

Bertisch, F. *Kwiaty na ugorze*. Stanisławów, 1939.

Białek, [J.] Z. *Ludwik Fryde jako krytyk literacki*. Cracow, 1962.

Błoński, J. "Autoprtret żydowski." In *Kilka myśli co nie nowe*. Cracow, 1985.

Borwicz [Boruchowicz], M. *Literatura w obozie*. Cracow, 1946.

———. "O polsko-żydowską poezję." Na marginesie pewnej dyskusji. *Nowy Dziennik* 1933, no. 263.

———. *Pieśń ujdzie cało: Antologia wierszy o Żydach polskich pod okupacją niemiecką*, Warsaw, 1947.

———. *Uniwersytet zbirów*. Cracow, 1946.

Boy-Żeleński, T. *Flirt z Melpomeną: Wieczór ósmy*. Warsaw, 1929.

Brandstaetter, R. "Arogant," *Gazeta Literacka* 1927, no. 8.

———. *Droga pod górę*. Warsaw, 1931.

———. "Dżuma w żydowskiej Grenadzie." *Nowy Głos* 1937, no. 115.

———. "Elegia cedrowa." *Nowy Dziennik* 1929, no. 250.

———. "Ewolucja poglądów Mickiewicza na kwestję żydowską." *Opinia* 1934, no. 13.

———. "Gdzie polski Zola? Refleksje na temat polskiej elity umysłowej do kwestii żydowskiej." *Opinia* 1933, no. 3.

———. "Głosy i echa literackie," *Opinia* 1935, no. 18.

———. *Jarzma*. Warsaw, 1928.

———. *Jerozolima światła i mroku*. Warsaw, 1935.

———. *Królestwo trzeciej świątyni*. Warsaw, 1934.

———. "Legenda siwiejącego poety." *Ster* 1937, no. 4.

———. *Legion żydowski Adama Mickiewicza*. Warsaw, 1932.

———. "Lista proskrypcyjna." *Opinia* 1933, no. 34.

———. "Narodowi hemar-frodyci." *Nasza Opinia* 1935, no. 20.

———. "Neofita." *Opinia* 1933, no. 33.

———. "Plecak jest nam już niepotrzebny." *Bunt młodych* 1936, no. 7.

———. "Plują? Deszcz pada!" *Opinia* 1935, no. 6.

———. "Popas w Mechesówce." *Nasza Opinia* 1935, no. 4.

———. "Przeciw myślom w mundurze: W sprawie utworzenia Światowego Związku Pisarzy Żydowskich." *Nowy Głos* 1938, no. 147.

———. "Republika żydowska na Biegunie Północnym." *Nowy Głos* 1938, no. 44, 51, 58, 65.

———. "Sprawa poezji polsko-żydowskiej: Artykuł dyskusyjny." Part 1, "Poeci polsko żydowscy." *Opinia* 1933, no. 23. Part 2, "Społeczeństwo żydowskie a my." *Opinia* 1933, no. 24. Part 3, "Kłody pod nogami," *Opinia* 1933, no. 25.

———. "Stwórzmy żydowską samoobronę kulturalną." *Ster* 1937, no. 16.

———. "Tragedia Juliana Klaczki." *Miesięcznik Żydowski* 1932, nos. 11–12.

———. *Węzły i miecze*. Warsaw, 1933.

———. "Wszechświatowy Związek Literatów Żydowskich." *Opinia* 1935, no. 7.

———. *Zmowa eunuchów*. Warsaw, 1936.

———. "Żniwiarzom żydowskim odpoczynek po pracy." *Nowy Dziennik* 1929, no. 62.

———. "Zygmunt Bromberg-Bytowski: W dziesiątą rocznicę zgonu." *Opinia* 1933, no. 11.

Braun [Braunstein], M. "Assimi: Fragmenty poematu." *Nasza Opinia* 1939, no. 210.

———. "Fragmenty dziejów." *Nasza Opinia* 1939, no. 209.

———. "Pisarze polscy: Czy pisarze żydowscy piszący po polsku albo pisarze polsko-żydowscy." *Ster* 1937, no. 16.

———. "Próba inteligencji." *Nasz Przegląd* 1939, no. 133.

———. "Rapsod." *Nasza Opinia* 1938, no. 130.

———. "Syjonizm Adama Mickiewicza." *Nasz Przegląd* 1939, no. 14.

———. "*Wiadomości Literackie* w ogniu." *Nasz Przegląd* 1937, no. 267.

———. *Wybór poezji.* Edited and with an introduction by J. Maciejewski. Warsaw, 1979.

Brod, M. *Heinrich Heine.* Amsterdam, 1934.

Brzezina, M. *Polszczyzna Żydów.* Warsaw, 1986.

Brzoza, J. *Moje przygody literackie.* Katowice, 1967.

Butkiewiczówna, I. *Powieści i nowele żydowskie Elizy Orzeszkowej,* Lublin, 1937.

Cała, A. *Asymilacja Żydów w Królestwie Polskim (1864–1897).* Warsaw, 1989.

———. "Kwestia asymilacji Żydów w Królestwie Polskim (1864–1897): Refleksje i dygresje." *Znak* 1986, nos. 377–379.

———. *Wizerunek Żyda w kulturze ludowej.* Warsaw, 1987.

Cieślikowski, J. "Okolica dzieciństwa." In *Literatura i podkultura dziecięca,* Wrocław, 1975.

Cohn, A. J. "Nasz dorobek literacki." *Izraelita* 1901, no. 10.

———. "Kilka słów wstępnych tłumacza." In *Zbawca: Powieść (z drugiej połowy XIV stulecia) z podań ludu pragskiego ghetta spisał S. K.,* translated and with an introduction by A. J. Cohn. Warsaw, 1862.

———. *"Nasz dorobek literacki."* Izraelita 1901, no. 10.

Cysewski, K. "Bariera kulturowa i dzieło literackie." *Ruch Literacki* 1984, nos. 1–2.

Czachowski, K. *Obraz współczesnej literatury polskiej 1884–1993.* Vol. 3, *Ekspresjonizm i neorealizm.* Warsaw, 1936.

Czermińska, M. "Postawa autobiograficzna." In *Studia o narracji,* edited by J. Błoński, St. Jaworski and J. Sławiński. Wrocław, 1982.

Czerniaków [Chernikov], A. *Dziennik getta warszawskiego.* Edited by M. Fuks. Warsaw, 1983.

Czernik, St. "Dwadzieścia lat poezji polskiej, 1918–1939." *Okolica Poetów* 1939, nos. 1–2.

Daiches, D. "Some Aspects of Anglo-American Jewish Fiction." In *Jewish Perspectives: 25 Years of Jewish Writing.* London, 1980.

Datner-Śpiewak, H. "Asymilacja narodu i asymilacja jednostki." *Więź* 1983, no. 4.

Dawidowicz, L. "Jewish Identity: A Matter of Fate, A Matter of Choice." In *The Jewish Presence: Essays on Identity and History.* New York, 1977.

Dąbrowska, M. *Dzienniki.* Vols. 1–2. Edited by T. Drewnowski. Warsaw, 1988.

Deutscher [Krakowski], I. "Orka." *Nowy Dziennik* 1925, no. 83.

Dębicki, Z. *Rozmowy o literaturze.* Warsaw, 1927.

Dresdner, K. "Brat Gerszon: Jan Andrzej Ram." *Pamiętnik Literacki* 1928, no. 2.

———. *Heine i nieznajoma.* Lvov, 1928.

———. "Krasiński a przechrzci." In *Zjednoczenie Jednodniówka.* Lvov, 1931.

———. "Listy Matiasa Bersohna do Augusta Bielowskiego." *Miesięcznik Żydowski* 1935, no. 1.

———. "Szechina." *Chwila* 1929, no. 3537.

———. "Udział Żydów w poezji polskiej XIX wieku." *Miesięcznik Żydowski* 1932, no. 5.

———. "Z korespondencji J. I. Kraszewskiego: Listy Armanda Levy." *Przegląd Humanistyczny* 1931, nos. 1–2.

———. "Żydzi w powieściach Korzeniowskiego." *Przegląd Humanistyczny* 1933, no. 3.

Dresdner, K., and Goldstein, M. *Kultura i sztuka ludu żydowskiego na ziemiach polskich.* Lvov, 1935.

Eisenbach, A. *Emancypacja Żydów na ziemiach polskich.* Warsaw, 1988.

Eker [Ekerówna], A. *Mama śpiewa kołysankę: Bajki ilustrowane dla milusińskich.* Lvov, 1937.

———. *Melodia chwili.* Lvov, 1937.

———. *Na cienkiej strunie.* Lvov, 1937.

———. "O świerszczyku muzykancie." In *Bajki ilustrowane dla milusińskich.* Lvov, 1937.

———. *Ojców dzieje.* Lvov, 1937.

Endelmanowa-Rosenblatowa [pen name Halicz], Cz. "Żydówka we współczesnej beletrystyce polskiej." *Izraelita* 1902, no. 8.

———. *Ludzie, którzy jeszcze żyją.* Warsaw, 1934.

Fallek, W. *Studia i szkice o wpływie "Biblii" na literaturę polska.* Lodz, 1931.

———. "Twórczość Żydów na polu literatury polskiej do roku 1918." In *Żydzi w Polsce Odrodzonej: Działalność społeczna, gospodarcza, oświatowa i kulturalna,* vol. 2, edited by I. Schipper, and A. Hafftka. Warsaw, 1933.

Feig, J. "Jeszcze *causa* Brandstaetter." *Tygodnik Żydowski* 1933, no. 32.

Feldhorn, J. "Literatura polska w wieku XVI a Żydzi: Szkic bibliograficzny." In *Sprawozdanie Kierownictwa Żydowkiego Gimnazjum Koedukacyjnego Typu Humanistycznego Towarzystwa Żydowskiej Szkoły Ludowej i Średniej w Krakowie za rok szkolny, 1928–1929.* Cracow, 1929

———. " ' . . . Pomnik strzaskany . . . ': Motywy żydowskie w twórczości Cypriana Norwida." *Miesięcznik Żydowski* 1933, no. 2.

Feldszuh [pen name Ben Szem], *Czerwone dusze.* Warsaw, 1932.

———. *Noce palestyńskie.* Warsaw, 1928.

Fenster, H. A. "Ballada o młodych synach starej ziem." *Chwila* 1931, no. 4255.

———. *Di lewone gejt unter: Lider.* Warsaw, 1938.

———. *O tym, co opuszczam.* Warsaw, 1932.

Fik, I. *Dwadzieścia lat literarury polskiej: 1918–1938.* Cracow, 1939.

Filipkowska, H. "Tułacze i wędrowcy." In *Młodopolski świat wyobraźni,* edited by M. Podraza-Kwiatkowska. Cracow, 1977.

Finkelstein, Z. F. *W jarzmie idei: Obrazy z życia Teodora Herzla.* Translated S. Zeisler. Cracow, 1935.

Frenzel, E. *Stoffe der Weltliteratur: Ein Lexikon dichtungsgeschichtlicher Längsschnitten.* Stuttgart, 1983.

Friedman, R. "Matka." *Chwila* 1931, no. 4307.

Friszlender, M. "Czy potrzebny jest teatr polsko-żydowski." *Nasz Przegląd* 1929, no. 251.

Fromm, E. *Zapomniany język. Wstęp do rozumienia snów, baśni i mitów* (The forgotten language: An introduction to the interpretation of dreams, fairy tales, and myths). Translated from the English by J. Marzęcki. Introduction by K. T. Toeplitz. Warsaw, 1977.

Fryde, L. "Trzy pokolenia literackie." In *Wybór pism krytycznych,* edited by A. Biernacki. Warsaw, 1966.

Fuks, M. *"Mały Przegląd* J. Korczaka." *Biuletyn Żydowskiego Instytutu Historycznego w Polsce* 1978, no. 1.

Füllenbaum, N. "Polemika." *Słowo* 1937, no. 137.

———. "Więdnące korzenie." *Słowo* 1936, no. 46.

———. "Wiersze." *Słowo* 1936, no. 51.

Gałczyński, K. I. "Do przyjaciół z *Prosto z mostu." Prosto z mostu 1936, no. 21.*

Glassner, R. "Literaci-Żydzi we współczesnym piśmiennictwie polskim." Rocznik Żydowski 1904.

Glicksman, W. "The *Halutz* Ideology and Experience as Reflected in the Yiddish Novel in Poland, 1919–1939." *YIVO Annual of Jewish Social Science* (New York) 14 (1969).

Glikson, P. *Preliminary Inventory of the Jewish Daily and Periodical Press Published in the Polish Language, 1823–1982.* Jerusalem, 1983.

Głowiński, M. "Grupa literacka a model poezji: Przykład Skamandra." In *Z problemów literatury polskiej XX wieku,* vol. 2. Warsaw, 1965.

Gross, N. *Kim pan jest, panie Grymek?* Cracow, 1991.

Gruszecki, A. *Zawsze ci sami.* Cracow, 1921.

Grünbaum, I. "Asymilacja i polonizacja." *Nasz Przegląd* 1927, no. 80.

Gutman, V., Mendelsohn E., and Shmeruk, Ch., eds. *The Jews of Poland Between Two World Wars.* Hanover [N.H.], 1989.

Hartblaj, J. *Jehoszua: Powieść osnuta na tle życia "chaluców."* Warsaw, 1928.

Heller, T. *"Causa* Tuwim." *Nasz Przegląd* 1938, no. 11.

Hertz, A. *Wyznania starego człowieka.* London, 1979.

———. *Żydzi w kulturze polskiej.* Paris, 1961.

Herzl, T. *U wrót nowego życia: Powieść-utopia (Altneuland).* Translated by H. Adler. Warsaw, 1934.

Heschel, A. J. *The Earth Is the Lord's: The Inner World of the Jew in East Europe.* New York, 1950.

———. *The Sabbath: Its Meaning for Modern Man.* New York, 1984.

Hirszhorn, S. "Czy i dlaczego literatura polska jest 'zażydzona.' " *Nasz Przegląd* 1930, no. 30.

———. "Czy istotnie asymilacja triumfuje." *Nasz Przegląd* 1930, no. 4.

———. "Kongres Penklubów a pisarze żydowscy." *Nasz Przegląd* 1930, no. 159.

———. "Nędzne cele i liche środki. Popłoch w obozie 'narodowym' z powodu zażydzenia literatury polskiej." *Nasz Przegląd* 1930, no. 40.

———. "Typy żydowskie w literaturze polskiej." *Nasz Przegląd* 1929, no. 55.

Hochberżanka [Hochberg-Mariańska], M. "Czekaj na mnie . . ." *Nowy Dziennik* 1933, no. 250.

———. "Święto." *Nowy Dziennik* 1935, no. 1083.

———. "Yom Kipur." *Nowy Dziennik* 1933, no. 268.

Howe, I. "Pisarze amerykańscy pochodzenia żydowskiego" (American writers of Jewish origin), translated from the English by E. Ćwirko-Godycka. *Literatura na świecie* 1982, no. 12.

Igel, E. [pen name i. g.] "Sztuki żydowskie na scenie polskiej: Wywiad z Andrzejem Markiem." *Chwila* 1930, no. 3889.

Ihr, D. "Do mowy hebrajskiej." *Opinia* 1935, no. 13

———. "Do przyjaciół poetów." *Chwila* 1929, no. 3572.

———. "List." *Nasza Opinia* 1936, no. 25.

———. *Pożegnanie młodości.* Lvov, 1934.

———. "Sambation." *Chwila* 1934, no. 5321.

Irzykowski, K. "Brońmy swojego Żyda." In *Czyn i słowo. Glossy sceptyka.* Lvov, 1913.

———. "Udział Żydów w literaturze polskiej." *Kurjer Poranny* 1937, no. 224.

Jamer, L. "Czy znasz ten kraj?" *Chwila* 1933, no. 5069.

Jastrun, M. *Smuga światła.* Warsaw, 1982.

Jawicz, A. "Udział Żydów w polskiej literaturze międzywojennej." *Nasza Myśl* 1952.

Jaworski, St. *Między awangardą a nadrealizmem: Główne kierunki przemian w poezji polskiej w latach trzydziestych na tle europejskim.* Cracow, 1976.

Jazowski, A. "Wilhelm Feldman, 1868–1919." In *Literatura Młodej Polski,* vol. 4, edited by K. Wyka, A. Hutnikiewicz, M. Puchalska, and J. J. Lipski. Cracow, 1977.

Jeske-Choinski, T. *Żyd w powieści.* Warsaw, 1914.

Kallas, A. *On i oni wszyscy.* Warsaw, 1910.

Kanfer, I. *Dwa akordy.* Cracow, 1936.

———. *W mleczną drogę.* Cracow, 1937.

———. "Czy *Wiadomości Literackie* są pismem żydowskim?" *Nowy Dziennik* 1932, no. 219.

———. "Literatura i polityka: Na marginesie wydawnictwa Safrus." *Chwila* 1925, no. 2264.

———. "Pamięci Wilhelma Feldmana." *Chwila* 1922, nos. 1094–1095.

Katz, J. *From Prejudice to Destruction: Anti-Semitism, 1700–1933.* Cambridge, [Mass.] 1982.

Kielanowski, T. "Uchronić od zapomnienia." *Gdańskie zeszyty humanistyczne* 29 (1982).

Kleinberg, J. "Chalucim." *Okienko na świat* 1938, no. 8.

Kohn, H. *Martin Buber: Sein Werk und seine Zeit: Ein Beitrag zur Geistesgeschichte Mitteleuropas, 1880–1930.* Afterword, "1930–1960," by R. Weltsch. Cologne, 1961.

Korzennik, M. "Psalm ironii i napomnienia na 'ostatni artykuł z cyklu.' " *Tygodnik Żydowski* 1933, no. 31.

———. "Skąd i po co ten występ: À propos pewnej sprawy nieosobistej." *Tygodnik Żydowski* 1933, no. 33.

———. "Wróć to poezji: Do Romana Brandstaettera liścik otwarty." *Tygodnik Żydowski* 1933, no. 28.

Kowalczykowa, A. "Jak Tuwim swój młodzieńczy wizerunek korygował." In *Skamander*. Vol. 3, *Studia o poezji Juliana Tuwima,* edited by I. Opacki. Katowice, 1982.

———. *Historia co tydzień: Szkice o tygodnikach społeczno-kulturalnych*. Vols. 1–2. Warsaw, 1976.

Krasucki, L. *Wiersze wybrane: Z teki pośmiertnej*. Włocławek, 1923.

Kryński, M. "Politics and poetry: The Case of Julian Tuwim." *Polish Review* 1973, no. 4.

Kula, M. "Porozmawiajmy jeszcze raz, na spokojnie, o syjonizmie." *Dzieje najnowsze* 1987, no. 2.

Kwiatkowski, J. "Główne nurty w poezji dwudziestolecia." In *Literatura polska w okresie międzywojennym,* vol. 2, edited by J. Kądziela, J. Kwiatkowski, and I. Wyczańska. Cracow, 1979.

Kwiatkowski, J. *Literatura Dwudziestolecia*. Warsaw, 1990.

Lauterbach, A. "Godzina z poeta." *Chwilą* 1933, no. 5106.

———. "Młodzi poeci Lwowa: Wieczór autorski." *Chwila* 1929, no. 3835.

———. "Wieczór młodego Lwowa." *Chwila* 1932, no. 4658.

Lejeune, Ph. "Pakt autobiograficzny." Translated by A. W. Labuda. *Teksty* 1975, no. 5.

Levine, M. "Polish Literature and the Holocaust." *Holocaust Studies Annual,* 3 (1985).

Lewittes, J. "Do syna." *Nowy Dziennik* 1933, no. 290.

———. *Posthumus*. Warsaw, 1930.

Lewittówna, R. "Żydowska książka po polsku." *Nasz Przegląd* 1937, no. 324.

Libera, Z. "Żydzi i sprawa żydowska w literaturze pięknej i pamiętnikach w czasach Stanisława Augusta." In *Kultura, literatura, folklor,* edited by M. Graszewicz and J. Kolbuszewski. Warsaw, 1988.

Librowicz, Z. "Żydzi I beletrystyka." In *Z wrażeń kapociarza*. Warsaw, 1878.

Lichten, J. "Uwagi o asymilacji i akulturacji Żydów w Polsce w latach 1863–1943." *Znak* 1988, nos. 396–397.

Lilientalowa, R. "Święta żydowskie w przeszłości i teraźniejszości." Part I, *Rozprawy Akademii Umiejętności: Wydział Filologiczny,* ser. 2, vol. 30 (1909). Part 2, *Rozprawy Akademii Umiejętności: Wydział Filologiczny,* ser. 2, vol. 7 (1913).

Lipski, J. J. "ONR Falanga a kultura." In *Dwie ojczyzny i inne szkice*. Warsaw, 1984.

Loew, R. "Poezja polsko-żydowska." Typescript. N.p., 1957.

Löw, Ch. "Adam Madler, *Falista linia." Nowy Dziennik* 1934, no. 2.

———. "Czy możliwa jest poezja polsko-żydowska." *Opinia* 1933, no. 32.

———. "Między poetami." *Miesięcznik Żydowski* 1931, p. 570.

———. "O 'uświadomionym żydowstwie' i nie uświadomionych Żydach." *Opinia* 1935, no. 18.

———. "Poeci z wypowiedzeniem." *Opinia* 1933, no. 35.

———. "Rodowód Jankiela." *Miesięcznik Żydowski* 1934, no. 5.

———. *Smok w słowiczym gnieździe: Żydzi w poezji Odrodzonej Polski.* Warsaw, 1934.

———. "Wyspiański a Żydzi," *Miesięcznik Żydowski* 1932, nos. 9–10.

———. "Żydzi w literaturze polskiej." In *Udział Żydów w kulturze,* vol 1. Cracow, 1938.

Łoza, St. *Czy wiesz kto to jest?* Warsaw, 1938.

Maciejewski, J. "Publiczność literacka a instytucje i mechanizmy życia kulturowego." In *Publiczność literacka,* edited by S. Żółkiewski and M. Hopfinger. Wrocław, 1982.

———. "Wstęp" (Foreword). To M. Braun, *Wybór poezji.* Warsaw, 1979.

Madler, A. [Bauman, M.] *Falista linia.* Warsaw, 1932.

———. "O szerszy punkt widzenia." *Opinia* 1933, no. 33.

Mahler, R. "Wzlot w Stanisławowie urządził wieczór litaracki." *Chwila* 1935, no. 5668.

Manger, I. "The Poetry of Our Holy Days." In *An Anthology of Modern Yiddish Literature.* Compiled and edited by J. Leftwich. Hague, 1971.

Marek, A. "Płomienie i zgliszcza: Na marginesie znamiennej książki." *Nasz Przegląd* 1929, no. 92.

Matuszewski, R., and Pollak, S. *Poezja polska 1914–1939: Antologia.* Vols. 1–2. Warsaw, 1984.

Mayer B. [pen name Arieh]. *Pieśni chaluca.* Stanisławów, 1934.

———. *Pieśń Wertera.* Stanisławów, 1932.

Mendelsohn, E. "From Assimilation to Zionism in Lvov: The Case of Alfred Nossig." *Slavonic and East-European Review* 49 (1971).

———. "Interwar Poland: Good for the Jews or Bad for the Jews?" In *The Jews in Poland.* edited by Ch. Abramsky, M. Jachimczyk, and A. Polonsky. Oxford, 1986.

———. *The Jews of East Central Europe between the World Wars.* Bloomington [Ind.], 1983.

———. *Zionism in Poland. The Formative Years, 1915–1926.* New Haven [Conn.], 1981.

Meerson-Becker [Meersonówa], C. "Do mowy żydowskiej." *Nasz Przegląd* 1933, no. 99.

Meyersonowa, M. *Z ciasnej sfery.* Warsaw, 1878.

Nałkowska, Z. *Dzienniki.* Vol. 3, *1918–1929.* Edited by H. Kirchner. Warsaw, 1980.

Nałkowska, Z. *Dzienniki.* Vol. 4, *1930–1939.* Parts 1–2. Edited by H. Kirchner. Warsaw, 1988.

Napierski, S. [Eiger, M.]. "Powrót do pseudoklasyków." *Wiadomości Literackie* 1928, no. 235.

Niemcewicz, J. U. *Lejbe i Sióra czyli Listy dwóch kochanków: Romans.* Cracow, 1931.

Olszewicz, B. *Lista strat kultury polskiej.* Warsaw, 1917.

Opalski [Opalska], M. *The Jewish Tavern-Keeper and His Tavern in Nineteenth-Century Polish Literature.* Jerusalem, 1986.

———. "*Wiadomości Literackie,* 1924–1939: Polemics on the Jewish Question." In *The Jews of Poland Between Two World Wars,* edited by Y. Gutman, E. Mendelsohn, and Ch. Shmeruk. Hanover [N.H.], 1989.

Orzeszkowa, E. *Meir Ezofowicz.* Warsaw, 1988.

Ossowski, St. *O ojczyźnie i narodzie.* Warsaw, 1984.

Panas, W. "Ja—polski poeta, hebrajski niemowa: Literatura polsko-żydowska i żydowsko-polska, 1918–1939." *Tygodnik Literacki* 1991, no. 16.

Panas, W. "Literatura polsko-żydowska: Pismo i rana." *Akcent* 3 (1987).

Peiper, T. *Tędy.* Cracow, 1930.

Piasecki, St. *Prosto z mostu.* Warsaw, 1934.

Pieńkowski, S. "Poezja kryptożydowska." *Myśla Narodowa* 1926, no. 41.

———. *W ogniu walki: Szkice o sprawie żydowskiej.* Warsaw, 1929.

Podskocz, J. "Czy potrzebny jest teatr polsko-żydowski: Artykuł dyskusyjny." *Nasz Przegląd* 1929, no. 256.

Pomer, S. *Elegie podolskie.* Warsaw, 1931.

———. "Historia powojennej literatury polskiej." *Nasz Przegląd* 1934, no. 149.

———. "Nad rzekami Babilonu." *Nowy Dziennik* 1933, no. 338.

———. "Pesach nędzarzy." *Chwila* 1931, no. 4319.

———. "Powieść o pogromach." *Nasz Przegląd* 1934, no. 229.

———. "Przyśpiew purymowy." *Nasz Przegląd* 1934, no. 63.

———. "Rachela i katarynka." *Chwila* 1929, no. 3579.

———. " 'U wspólnego stołu': Przyczynek do dziejów mechesowstwa w Polsce." *Nasz Przegląd* 1933, no. 212.

———. " 'Węzeł gordyjski': Ciekawy przyczynek do kwestii żydowskiej w literaturze polskiej." *Nasz Przegląd* 1933, no. 249.

———. "Złota lipa." *Nasz Przegląd* 1933, no. 162.

———. "Żydowskie miasteczko." *Nasz Przegląd* 1934, no. 150.

———. "Żydzi w literaturze polskiej." [Part 1,] *Nasz Przegląd* 1933, no. 64. [Part 2,] *Nasz Przegląd* 1933, no. 71.

Pomeranz, M. "Poezja polsko-żydowska: M. Szymel." *Nowy Dziennik* 1932, no. 330.

Pomeranz-Carmely, K. *Das Identitätsproblem jüdischer Autoren im deutschen Sprachraum: Von der Jahrhundertwende bis zu Hitler.* Königstein, 1981.

Pordes, W. "O kulturze żydowkiej." In *Almanach Żydowski,* edited by L. Reich. Lvov, 1910.

Pordes, W. "Żydowska twórczość." *Rocznik Żydowski* 1905.

Prokop-Janiec [Prokopówna], E. "In Quest of Cultural Identity: Polish-Jewish Literature in the Interwar Period." *Polish Review* 1987, no. 4.

———. "Kafka w Polsce międzywojennej." *Pamiętnik Literacki* 1985, no. 4.

———. "The Image of the Shtetl in Polish Literature." *Polin* 4 (1989).

———. "The Sabbath Motif in Interwar Polish-Jewish Literature." In *The Jews of Poland Between Two World Wars,* edited by Y. Gutman, E. Mendelsohn, and Ch. Shmeruk. Hanover [N.H.], 1989.

Pytasz, M. "Kwestia żydowska i jej konteksty w 'Kronikach tygodniowych' Antoniego Słonimskiego." In *Studia skamandryckie i inne.* edited by I. Opacki and T. Stępień. Katowice, 1985.

Richter, S. *Wiry.* Stanisławów, 1932.

Rokicki, J. "Language as a Social Value in the Relationship between Language and Society." In *Zeszyty Naukowe Uniwersytetu Jagiellońskiego DCCCX: Prace Polonijne.* Vol. 11, *Language and Nation: Materials from a Symposium.* edited by W. Miodunka. Warsaw, 1987.

Rosenfeld, K. "Pożar krwi." In *Poezje z okopów wielkiej wojny.* Cracow, 1919.

———. *W ciszy łez: Poezje golusu.* Cracow [ca. 1920].

Rosner, L. " 'Kultura polsko-żydowska?' Na marginesie dyskusji w sprawie poezji polsko-żydowskiej." *Opinia* 1933, no. 34.

Rostworowski, K. H. *Antychryst.* Lvov, 1925.

Rostworowski, K. H. "O uzdrowienie literatury polskiej." *Polonia* 1929, no. 1876.

Rozenman, A. "Głosy czytelników w sprawie poezji polsko-żydowskiej." *Opinia* 1933, no. 36.

Rudnicki, A. *Lato.* Warsaw, 1959.

Rudnicki, A. *Rogaty warszawiak.* Cracow, 1981.

Safrin, H. "Ahaswer." *Chwila* 1936, no. 6348.

———. "Judaica." *Nowy Dziennik* 1933, no. 102.

———. "Lcha Dodi." *Chwila* 1937, no. 6691.

———. "Pieśń o sobie." *Nasza Opinia* 1937, no. 119.

———. *Ucieszne I osobliwe historie mojego życia.* Lodz, 1970.

Sandauer, A. "O człowieku który był diabłem." In *Poeci czterech pokoleń.* Cracow, 1977.

———. *O sytuacji pisarza polskiego pochodzenia żydowskiego w XXw: Rzecz, którą nie ja powinienem był napisać . . .* Warsaw, 1982.

Sartre, J.-P. *Rozważania o kwestii żydowskiej* (Reflections on the Jewish Question). Translated from the French by J. Lisowski. Warsaw, 1957.

Sawicki, M. *Żydzi, ich dzieje ze względu na stan obecny Polski mieszkańców wyznania mojżeszowego.* Warsaw, 1865.

Schenker, Z. "Nad grobem ofiar palestyńskich." *Nasz Przegląd* 1929, no. 243.

———. "W narodową rocznicę." *Nowy Dziennik* 1929, no. 201.

Schulz, B. *Księga listów.* Edited by J. Ficowski. Cracow, 1975.

Sebyła, W. "Nowe poezje: Roman Brandstaetter, *Królestwo trzeciej świątyni.*" *Pion* 1935, no. 25.

———. "Syjonizm, rasizm czy poezja?" *Kurier Poranny* 1934, no. 136.

Shmeruk, Ch. *The Esterke Story in Yiddish and Polish Literature: A Case Study in the Mutual Relations of Two Cultural Traditions.* Jerusalem, 1985.

———. "Hebrew—Yiddish—Polish: A Trilingual Jewish Culture." In *The Jews of Poland Between Two World Wars,* edited by Y. Gutman, E. Mendelsohn, and Ch. Shmeruk. Hanover [N.H.], 1989.

———. "Jews and Poles in Yiddish Literature in Poland between the Two World Wars: Background Remarks." *Polin* 1 (1986).

Sieroszewski, W. *Bolszewicy.* Warsaw, 1922.

Silberman, M. *Dzień matki.* Stanisławów, 1938.

———. "Kadimah." *Nowy Dziennik* 1930, no. 289.

———. "Pięć lat Wzlotu." *Słowo* 1936, no. 81.

———. W cieniu życia. Stanisławów, 1937.

Słonimski, A. "Kroniki tygodriowe." [Part 1,] *Wiadomości Literackie* 1936, no. 20. [Part 2,] *Wiadomości Literackie* 1936, no. 30. [Part 3,] *Wiadomości Literackie* 1938, no. 47.

———. *Mętne łby.* N.p., n.d.

———. *Moje walki nad Bzdurą.* Warsaw, 1932.

———. *Wiersze zebrane.* Warsaw, 1933.

Słucki, A., and Łasik, S. *Antologia poezji żydowskiej.* Warsaw, 1983.

Sokołów [Sokolow], N. "Czym jest i czym powinna być tzw. 'powieść żydowska'?" *Izraelita* 1892, no. 18.

Spund, S. "Tak bym chętnie." *Chwila* 1931, no. 4466.

Stand, A. "Moderna żydowska w Galicji." In *Safrus,* J. Kirszrot. Warsaw, 1905.

Stasiński, P. "Międzywojenne felietony Adolfa Nowaczyńskiego: *Myśl Narodowa,* 1921–1934 i *Prosto z mostu,* 1935–1939." In *Poetyka i pragmatyka felietonu.* Warsaw, 1982.

Steinlauf, M. C. "Jews and the Polish Theater in Nineteenth-Century Warsaw." *Polish Review* 1987, no. 4.

———. "Mark Arnshteyn and Polish-Jewish Theater." In *The Jews of Poland Between Two World Wars,* edited by Y. Gutman, E. Mendelsohn, and Ch. Shmeruk. Hanover [N.H.], 1989.

———. "Polish-Jewish Theater: The Case of Mark Arnshteyn: A Study of the Interplay among Yiddish, Polish and Polish-Language Jewish Culture in the Modern Period." Ph.D. Diss., Brandeis Univ., 1988.

———. "The Polish-Jewish Daily Press." *Polin* 2 (1987).

Stendig, S. "Sprawa poezji polsko-żydowskiej: Wobec dyskusji." *Tygodnik Żydowski* 1933, nos. 36–37.

Stopnicka-Heller, C. *On the Edge of Destruction: Jews of Poland Between the Two World Wars.* New York, 1980.

———. "Poles of Jewish Background: The Case of Assimilation Without Integration in Interwar Poland." In *Studies on Polish Jewry, 1919–1939,* edited by Y. Fishman. New York, 1974.

Stradecki, J. *Julian Tuwim: Bibliografia.* Warsaw, 1959.

———. *W kręgu Skamandra.* Warsaw, 1977.

Strauss, H. A. "Akkulturation als Schicksal: Einleitende Bemerkungen zum Verhältnis von Juden und Umwelt." In *Juden und Judentum in der Literatur,* edited by H. A. Strauss and Ch. Hoffmann. Munich, 1985.

Stryjkowski, J. [Stark, P.]. *Ocalony na Wshodzie: Z Julianem Stryjkowskim rozmawia Piotr Szewc.* Montricher, 1991.

———. "Wielki strach." *Zapis* 1980, no. 14.

Strzemski, M. *Nasze Puławy.* Lublin, 1986.

Szaniawski [Junosza], K. *Donkiszot żydowski: Szkic z literatury żargonowej żydowskiej.* Warsaw, 1899.

Szczawiej, J. "Na młodym warszawskim Parnasie." *Kurier Literacka-Naukow* 1934, no. 34.

Szeps, Z. *Antologia poezji żydowskiej.* London, 1980.

Szlanger, M. *Idę . . .* Cracow, 1936.

Szlengel, W. *Co czytałem umarłym: Wiersze getta warszawskiego,* edited by I. Maciejewska. Warsaw, 1977.

———. "Szałasy." *Nasz Przegląd* 1937, no. 268.

Szymański, W. P. *Neosymbolizm: O awangardowej poezji polskiej w latach trzydziestych.* Cracow, 1973.

Szymel, M. "Ballada o złotowłosej panience przy klawikordzie." *Nowy Dziennik* 1935, no. 239.

———. "Gdzie jesteś Ewo?" *Nowy Głos* 1938, nos. 44–76.

———. "Idę jesienią na ukos! O Tuwimie." *Ster* 1937, no. 41.

———. "Kij w mrowisku. W sprawie artykułów Romana Brandstaettera o poezji polsko-żydowkiej." Part 1, "O tym, który dyskusję rozpoczął . . ." *Opinia* 1933, no. 27. Part 2, "Nasza ojczyzna." *Opinia* 1933, no. 28. Part 3, "Prawda o poezji polsko-żydowkiej." *Opinia* 1933, no. 29. Part 4, "Nasze prawa," *Opinia* 1933, no. 31.

———. "Kim był Józef Elja?" *Opinia* 1935, no. 7.

———. "Krajobraz duszy żydowskiej w liryce polskiej." *Opinia* 1935, nos. 9, 10, 14.

———. "Lato ubogich." *Nasz Przegląd* 1939, no. 197.

———. *Mir iz umetik.* Warsaw, 1936.

———. "Na prowincji żydowskiej." *Chwila* 1938, no. 6946.

———. "Nie chcę być Żydem." *Opinia* 1935, no. 1.

———. "Nowy *Skamander,*" *Opinia* 1935, no. 18.

———. "Od tłumacza." In A. Ptaszkin, *Ani sobie ani muzom.* Warsaw, 1936.

———. *Powrót do domu.* Warsaw, 1931.

———. "Psalmy nadziei." *Nasz Przegląd* 1934, no. 243.

———. *Skrzypce przedmieścia.* Warsaw, 1932.

———. "Śpiew polskiego Żyda." *Nasza Opinia* 1938, no. 147.

———. "Świąteczny wieczór na wsi." *Nowy Dziennik* 1929, no. 302.

———. *Wieczór liryczny.* Warsaw, 1935.

———. "Wspomnienie." *Chwila* 1937, no. 6642.

———. "Żydowscy trubadurzy." *Nowy Dziennik* 1929, no. 316.

Śpiewak, J. "Przedpiekle wyobrażni." In *Przyjaźnie i animozje.* Warsaw, 1965.

———. *Przyjaźnie i animozje.* Warsaw, 1965.

Tabak, M. "Żydowska literature Stanisławowa." *Nasza Opinia* 1936, no. 52.

Taubenschlag, R. "*Judea resurrecta:* Pieśń bólu i radości." *Nowy Dziennik* 1921, no. 176.

Tenenbaum, E. *Na początku było kłamstwo.* Lvov, 1932.

———. *Tła: Powieść.* Lvov, 1935.

Thon, O. "Znamiona narodowości." *Nowy Dziennik* 1931, no. 324.

Tillemann, O. "List do autora *Królestwa trzeciej świątyni.*" *Opinia* 1934, no. 14.

Tortosa, J. M. *Polityka językowa a języki mniejszości: Od wieży Babel do daru języków.* Translated by A. Rurarz. Warsaw, 1986.

Turkow, M. *Polacy, Żydzi i mechesy.* Warsaw, 1930.

Vincenz, S. *Na wysokiej połoninie: Barwinkowy wianek.* Warsaw, 1983.

Vogler, H. *Autoportret z pamięci.* Vols. 1–3. Cracow, 1978.

Wasilewski, Z. "Na widowni." *Myśl Narodowa* 1934, no. 4.

———. "Wzór poezji judeo-polskiej." *Myśl Narodowa* 1934, no. 1.

Weintraub, J. K. *Utwory wybrane.* Edited by R. Matuszewski and A. Piorunowa. Warsaw, 1986.

Werfel, J. "Chanukowa biel." *Nowy Dziennik* 1933, no. 342.

Weyssenhoff, J. *Cudno i ziemia Cudeńska.* Warsaw, 1921.

Wit [Witkower], J. *Lampy.* Warsaw, 1936.

———. "Na skrzypcach grać." *Nowy Dziennik* 1928, no. 136.

———. *Pluski.* Warsaw, 1930.

———. "Syn handlarza winem." *Nowy Dziennik* 1926, no. 14.

———. "Wariaci." *Chwila* 1926, no. 35.

———. *Wiersze wybrane.* Edited by A. Sandauer. Warsaw, 1959.

Witkowska, A. *Sławianie, my lubim sielanki.* Warsaw, 1972.

Wittlin, J. *Poezje.* Warsaw, 1981.

———. *Mój Lwów.* London, 1975.

Wroczyński, T. *Dzieje oświaty polskiej, 1795–1945.* Warsaw, 1987.

Wróbel, P. "Między nadzieją a zwątpieniem. 'Der Jude' Martina Bubera wobec rewolucji i nowego ładu w świecie po I wojnie światowej." *Więź* 1986, nos. 7–8.

Zawodziński, K. W. "Dwie poetki." *Wiadomości Literackie* 1938, no. 29.

———. "Poeci Erec Izraela i ghetta." *Wiadomości Literackie* 1936, no. 26.

Zimmermann, B. *Tirsa: Powieść z życia współczesnej Palestyny.* Cracow, 1930.

Zyga, A. "Wymienne nazwy 'Żyda' w piśmiennictwie polskim w latach 1794–1863 na tle głównych orientacji społeczno-politycznych i wyznaniowych Żydostwa polskiego: Rekonesans." In *Literackie portrety Żydów,* edited by E. Łoch. Lublin, 1996.

———. "Wymiennie nazwy 'Żyda' w publicystyce i literaturze polskiej XIX w. na tle głównych orientacji ideowych uregulowania stosunków między Żydami i Polokami." Typescript. N.p., n.d.

Żółkiewski, S. "Kultura literacka." In *Literatura polska, 1918–1932,* edited by A. Brodzka, H. Zaworska, and S. Żółkiewski. Warsaw, 1975.

Index of Names

The abbreviation *r. n.* refers to the writer's actual or real name; *l. n.* to a later name used by that writer.